THE VIGILANT EYE

THE VIGILANT EYE

POLICING CANADA FROM 1867 TO 9/11

GREG MARQUIS

FERNWOOD PUBLISHING
HALIFAX & WINNIPEG

Editing: Marianne Ward
Cover design: John van der Woude
Printed and bound in Canada

Published by Fernwood Publishing
32 Oceanvista Lane, Black Point, Nova Scotia, B0J 1B0
and 748 Broadway Avenue, Winnipeg, Manitoba, R3G 0X3

www.fernwoodpublishing.ca

Fernwood Publishing Company Limited gratefully acknowledges the financial support of
the Government of Canada through the Canada Book Fund, the Manitoba Department
of Culture, Heritage and Tourism under the Manitoba Publishers Marketing Assistance
Program and the Province of Manitoba, through the Book Publishing Tax Credit, for
our publishing program. We are pleased to work in partnership with the Province of
Nova Scotia to develop and promote our creative industries for the benefit of all Nova
Scotians. We acknowledge the support of the Canada Council for the Arts, which last
year invested $153 million to bring the arts to Canadians throughout the country.

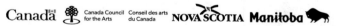

Library and Archives Canada Cataloguing in Publication

Marquis, Greg, author
The vigilant eye : policing Canada from 1867 to 9/11 / Greg Marquis.

Includes bibliographical references and index.
Issued in print and electronic formats.
ISBN 978-1-55266-820-7 (paperback).--ISBN 978-1-55266-860-3 (epub).--
ISBN 978-1-55266-861-0 (kindle)

1. Police--Canada--History. I. Title.

HV8157.M3785 2016   363.20971   C2015-908390-7
                            C2015-908391-5

CONTENTS

This is dedicated to Joe.

ACKNOWLEDGEMENTS

The author wishes to thank his wife Donna for her support and understanding and to acknowledge the support of his colleagues at the University of New Brunswick Saint John and the assistance of the staff at the Hans W. Klohn Commons at UNB Saint John. Finally, he acknowledges the influence of his future colleague Dr. Peter Toner who in 1977 sent him to a local archives to conduct research on Victorian crime and policing for an undergraduate social history seminar. Thanks to editor Marianne Ward and the staff at Fernwood.

INTRODUCTION

This book adopts the symbol of the vigilant eye as a metaphor for the adoption and evolution of the "new" police in Canada. Policing, which emerged as a crucial expression of state authority, has never been uncontested, particularly in the last third of the twentieth century. For many centuries and in many cultures, the eye has served as an important symbol with both positive and negative meanings. In Greek mythology, the giant Argus who guarded the heifer Io had one hundred eyes. In ancient Egypt the all-seeing eye was associated with the sky god Horus. The Eye of Providence was a familiar image in Christian culture that was adopted into Freemasonry and the Great Seal of the United States. In the nineteenth century, the Pinkerton National Detective Agency, commonly viewed as America's premiere crime fighting organization, used the image of the vigilant eye with the motto "we never sleep."

In recent years the all-seeing eye has become a metaphor for the surveillance society. A number of writers have suggested that the real power of the police as an institution in modern society is not their ability to arrest and charge citizens with criminal offences but in their creation and control of information (Ericson and Haggerty 2008). The potential or real use of force by police on behalf of the state is an ongoing source of concern. But the real threat to civil liberties might not be heavily armed tactical squads. In recent decades traditional aggressive tactics against political radicals, for example, have been replaced by subtler methods that may be even greater threats to democracy (Johnson 2003). On the security and intelligence side, intrusive "anti-terror" legislation, such as Bill C-51 passed in 2015, and, on the "regular" law enforcement side, intelligence-led policing, appear to justify these fears.

The role of police in democratic societies tends to be taken for granted until there is a crisis or controversy such as the use of deadly force, violent suppression of a peaceful demonstration or revelations of intrusive surveillance of citizens. Surveys suggest that public confidence in Canadian police, by the standard of other democracies, is high, surpassing that of the United States, Great Britain and France (Expert Panel 2014: 66). Yet few citizens actually come in contact with the police or call on their services. This physical isolation is the product of both social and economic changes in the second half of the twentieth century and a deliberate police strategy. In Canada the extreme example is the Royal Canadian Mounted Police, whose traditional military-style recruit training stressed isolation from society and an inward looking esprit de corps. The police themselves supposedly maintain a "blue wall" or "code of silence" that is rarely broken, even in published memoirs (Stroud 1984). Because most Canadians base their knowledge of policing and other criminal justice services on media and popular culture, they have little understanding of what police actually do. Most of the time of uniformed officers, the bulk of any police service, is not spent on controlling crime, but it can be argued the police by their very existence fulfil a number of important roles (Brodeur 2010: 353).

Police services in Canada have enjoyed relative legitimacy since their inception in the nineteenth century, but historical and criminological research reveals that police attitudes and practices have been contested. That policing abuses rarely reach the status of a national problem is largely explained by the decentralized nature of law enforcement in Canada and, according to some critics, the complicity of political elites and the media. For decades the dominant narrative in Canada was that its justice system, including its police, was tough but fair. Some historians and political scientists argue that the police have enjoyed relative popularity in Canada because the dominant political culture has tended to pay homage to state authority. Both conservative and left nationalists have celebrated Canada's predilection for "peace, order and good government." We are one of the few nations where a police organization, an institution that is feared in most nations, emerged as a key national symbol, at least for English Canadians. The national and international reputation of the North West Mounted Police (NWMP), which in 1920 was reorganized as the Royal Canadian Mounted Police (RCMP), was the product of the conjuncture of skilful public relations, popular culture and an element of objective reality. As Walden (1982) has argued, the Mounted Police was a "symbol of order" for Canadians, and even in the wake of revelations of RCMP "dirty tricks" and illegal activities in the 1970s, the force enjoyed considerable public support. Yet both the historical record and contemporary evidence suggests that the Mounties are not infallible and that public opinion can change (British Columbia Civil Liberties Association 2011: 14–5). In 2012, for example, a national poll suggested that confidence in the RCMP had fallen to a historic low, and attitudes toward the municipal police were almost as negative. At this time many Canadians, reflecting a conservative "common sense" antipathy toward the justice system as soft on crime, ranked the courts even lower. Most criticism was directed not at the RCMP rank and file so much as the force's leadership and a number of specific scandals, such as a controversial serial killer investigation in British Columbia and allegations that management had failed to protect female officers from harassment (O'Neil 2012).

Who are the police and what is policing? The modern term *police* derives from the Greek *politeia,* which described the administration and general wellbeing of the state (*polis*). Greek city states and ancient Rome relied on private policing; wronged parties carried offenders before magistrates, then inflicted the appropriate punishments of slavery, banishment or death. Medieval scholars wrote of the prince's duty to police his domains. By the 1600s the term, although not popular in English usage, was increasingly linked to the rising nation state. The most common association was with "the governance of cities" (Brodeur 2010: 18). It has been associated exclusively with crime prevention only since the nineteenth century (Bayley 1985: 24–38; Conley 1991: 15; Mawby 1999: 2). Emsley (1991: 1) defines police as "the bureaucratic and hierarchical bodies employed by the state to maintain order and to prevent and detect crime." The police, furthermore, are authorized by the state to use physical force in carrying out their mandate (Bayley 1985). The modern state confers legal legitimacy on the police. This is not necessarily the same as moral legitimacy. The police in totalitarian states or dictatorships have legal authority but engage in "morally outrageous" activities (Klockars 1985: 11). Even within democracies, police can lack legitimacy with certain groups or social classes: one thinks of the reputation of the Royal Ulster Constabulary among many Catholics in Northern Ireland starting in the 1920s or the relationship between minorities and police services that have been dominated by white, Canadian-born males (Mosher 1998; Tanovich 2006).

This study is concerned with the evolution of Canada's public police at the municipal, regional, provincial and federal levels. The project was undertaken because, two centuries after the first stirrings of police reform and 140 years after the organization the NWMP, we lack a basic overview of the development of Canadian law enforcement. Given that police services are rooted in past practices and attitudes, it is fundamental that any analysis of the present state and future of policing in Canada begins with an understanding of the past. This book focuses on the evolution of the new body of full-time, uniformed and salaried public servants that appeared in the middle of the nineteenth century, initially to preserve order and enforce criminal law and bylaws in cities. In addition to keeping the peace and responding to citizen calls for assistance, the police became key gatekeepers in the criminal justice system, taking over much of the business of criminal prosecution from private citizens. In Canada a uniformed criminal police service, originally formed to secure the western frontier, was in charge of federal government security and intelligence matters for more than seven decades. Two chapters discuss the policing of class conflict and political dissent, but the bulk of the book deals with operational policing, which despite its importance to the justice system and its impact on Canadians and their communities has been strangely neglected (Marquis 1995a). The role of private security, which has expanded noticeably since the 1960s, will not be discussed in much detail.

Many visitors to Canada believe that we are policed exclusively by the RCMP, whose image has been much romanticized since its inception in the 1870s. In reality most law enforcement is carried out by provincial and municipal police agencies. In addition, by the late twentieth century a wide range of individuals and institutions, from government employees to security guards to nightclub bouncers, performed policing duties. Powers of arrest are granted to customs and immigration officials and fisheries and wildlife protection officers. Private security guards and investigators, although usually lacking the right to carry weapons and make arrests, outnumbered the public police in Canada by the early 1970s, and the growth of this sector has continued. Traditionally private police served not the interests of "society" but their employers, and their main goal was to protect private property. In recent decades the privatization of policing and the blurring of public and private policing made these distinctions less apparent. This trend, which is likely to continue in the future, has been complicated by the possible expansion of "tiered policing" models and animosity by the police rank and file toward private security in patrol roles. Nevertheless, the public police remain a key component of the justice system. Official crime statistics, for example, are based in part on incidents reported to police services (Marquis 2000a, 2000b).

THEORETICAL APPROACHES

Why police? There are two main competing interpretations of causation. The traditional Whig or consensus version, found in most institutional and official accounts of policing, argues that the new police were a rational, humanitarian response to genuine social problems. Mainstream historical accounts of policing in Western Europe, Britain and North America place the institution alongside the broader reforms of the nineteenth century that included schools, penitentiaries and public health measures. The Whig view (history as the history of progress) depicts the police as disinterested state servants who fight crime and preserve order. The media, politicians and general public subscribe to this generally pro-police interpretation. Ideally, police in liberal democracies, historically a small proportion of the world's nations, operate through consent and are guided by and uphold the rule of law (an autonomous legal tradition based on equality before the courts and safeguards on the rights of the accused). According to liberal theory, criminals are a deviant subgroup (liberal theories can disagree about the causes of individual deviance) from whom the public must be protected. Hence the development of the police was both inevitable and necessary (Reiner 1984; Emsley 1991: 2). According to the liberal or consensus view, the police serve not the government, economic elites or themselves, but "the public." Yet liberal interpretations exist on a continuum and can criticize specific police services, leaders and policies for not serving the public interest, for example when they lack sufficient public complaints mechanisms. In terms of political science or public policy understandings of police in democratic societies, a common explanatory framework is the social contract, by which the citizenry entrusts police agencies with a degree of coercive power in return for upholding the law in a neutral fashion (Marquis 2000a; Eng 2005).

The more critical school of thought, which is Marxist or Marxist-inspired, poses the question of who benefits from the police. It links the rise of the police to the commercial and industrial revolutions of the eighteenth and nineteenth centuries and is situated within a more critical understanding of history and society. The transformation from an economy of scarcity to one of surplus resulted in changes to the criminal justice system. The police and courts, according to this perspective, reinforce social and economic inequalities and ultimately benefit the bourgeoisie or elites. Law in this body of academic literature is something that is "done to" the subordinate classes. Various class-conflict interpretations of criminology and social history since the 1960s have stressed the role of police in reproducing class relations. These scholars suggest that the main function of police, courts and prisons is to discipline the working class and marginal elements such as immigrants, racial minorities and youth (Storch 1975, 1976; Harring 1983). The title of one of the most critical recent studies of American policing, which stresses its record of racial oppression, violence, class justice and militarization, is *Our Enemies in Blue* (Williams 2007). The role of local and state police in the pre- civil rights South is an obvious example, yet the history of police-minority relations in the northern states is rife with examples of discrimination and abuse. In recent decades the category of gender, and the law's role in reinforcing gender relations, has been added to the analysis. Boudreau's study of criminal justice in early twentieth-century Halifax, for example, describes the police as part of a system that entrenched the city's "class, gender and racial inequalities" (2012a: ix). The study of what Brodeur (1983, 2010) has termed "high" policing, the monitoring of ideas, individuals and organizations deemed dangerous to the status quo, also challenges liberal interpretations of police history. And a number of scholars have employed class conflict perspectives to analyze the role of policing and the justice system, in concert with "opportunistic politicians," in promoting a law and order agenda as part of neo-liberal restructuring (Gordon 2006: 122–3).

Nuanced approaches to the class-conflict interpretation of state power were inspired by the writings of the Italian neo-Marxist theorist Antonio Gramsci who suggested that the police and other social institutions depend on not only coercion but also the ability to win consent from the masses. In his analysis, the hegemony of the dominant classes was guaranteed through "ruling alliances" orchestrated by the bourgeoisie. Belief in the rule of law is the underpinning of the capitalist state, and the fear of crime is used to co-opt the masses. The writings of the French theorist Foucault, with their insights on surveillance institutions, have further enlightened studies of state formation, crime and policing. Capitalist social relations depend on economic exploitation but also an appearance of equality before the law (Bayley 1985: 14). In 1981 Monkkonen's study of urban law enforcement in the United States concluded that in the era 1860 to 1920, policing switched from an emphasis on "class control," measured by initiative arrests, to "crime control," evidenced by reactive arrests based on citizen complaints. The same period also saw the urban police deemphasize welfare services.

A related analytical concept in disciplines such as history and sociology is the recognition of "intra-class crime" and the pragmatic use of the police and courts by the working class (McMullan 1987: 256). Fyson's (2006) study of criminal justice in Quebec from the 1760s to the 1830s questions the utility of both consensus and conflict interpretations of history. Many criminal prosecutions in the Montreal district between 1790 and 1830 were "intra-class." Although not negating critical arguments about society's exploitative social relations, this approach does suggest a more complex historical role for the police other than coercion of the masses (Marquis 1986a, 1986b). A related theme is how the police became involved with functions or duties that were not anticipated by the original police reformers starting in the 1820s and 1830s. Canadian historian John Weaver (1990) has described this process as "community entanglement."

Police agencies have long been aware of this function and struggled with how it relates to their understanding of professionalism. At various points in the cycle of policing history the service and social welfare roles have been either promoted or attacked, depending on the circumstances. In recent decades critics have suspected that the trend toward community policing is little more than a publicity exercise designed to strengthen police legitimacy. One of the more dramatic examples of the blend of "hard" and "soft" policing is the rise in the United States of "counter-insurgency cops," where tactics employed by the Army and Marines in pacifying cities in Afghanistan are tested in American neighbourhoods. Equipped with detailed intelligence, heavily armed rapid deployment squads not only attempt to rid "failed areas" of guns, gangs and drugs, they also try to win over the locals with various community improvement initiatives. The goal is to detach the "insurgents" from their base of support. For many scholars, civil liberties organizations and community activists this approach is a frightening glimpse of the future of policing in the era of neo liberalism (CBS 2013).

ANTECEDENTS: THE BRITISH ISLES

Canada's criminal justice system was influenced by centuries of developments in England, where the local magistrate was the backbone of England's legal order, both in the criminal and civil spheres. The justice of the peace (JP) has a lineage of over eight hundred years. As part of a bargain with the Crown, the local gentry participated in a decentralized law enforcement system. Originally JPs were petty nobles commissioned by Richard I to maintain the peace. The *Justice of the Peace Act* of 1361 formalized the role of magistracy, which often headed courts leet (manorial courts) by virtue of being lords or stewards of manors (feudal estates) (Emsley 1991: 9). Individual JPs were clothed with a wide range of powers. They were part judge, part prosecutor, part notary and part policemen. Acting in pairs, magistrates exercised even greater authority, such as taking bail, issuing tavern licences and investigating riots. JPs acting alone or in "petty sessions" had the power to summarily try a variety of minor offences and handled the bulk of criminal business in a parish. They also were important in the investigation and prosecution of more serious crimes. Magistrates apprehended suspects, recorded preliminary evidence, remanded prisoners to custody for further investigation, bound them over for trial by jury and secured witnesses and prosecutors (Sharpe 1984: 28–9).

The magistracy, appointed from the upper levels of rural society, was part of the gentry's web of patronage and influence. Its powers peaked only in the nineteenth century. Most held the post for status reasons and rarely attended court or exercised their powers. As the court of quarter sessions, a periodic meeting of county magistrates to conduct administrative and judicial duties, the magistracy tried misdemeanours and felonies (chiefly theft and assault) and acted as local government by administering county buildings, roads, officials and taxes and regulating wages, prices and the poor (Baker 1977: 115–48). One historian concludes that "neither the central government, nor Parliament told them what to do, closely supervised their activity, or even insured that they acted at all…. They did what they did because they wanted to do it and thought that they should do it" (Landau 1984: 2).

Like the constables who functioned as their assistants, JPs varied in diligence and ability. Shakespeare's Justice Shallow and Silence represented the less desirable qualities in magistrates. If many individuals on the commission of the peace were inactive, others energetically pursued criminals, acting more like detectives of a later age. JPs did not enforce all laws blindly but exercised considerable discretion, much like modern police (Klockars 1985: chapter 5). In London and other centres some became too active as "trading justices," supporting themselves full-time through fees (and possibly bribes). Fielding's Justice Thrasher was a stereotypical literary representation of the venal magistrate of the eighteenth century. The appointment of stipendiary magistrates, trained in law, eventually brought a new degree of bureaucratic justice to urban England, but as late as the 1880s half the population lived under the jurisdiction of the part-time, lay magistracy (Conley 1991: 42).

Magistrates' junior partners, constables, were neither detectives nor preventive officers. Nineteenth-century writers depicted these part-time peace officials as infirm, corrupt, inactive or cowardly. Ordinarily they pursued lawbreakers only after a magistrate's order, but their own powers gave them a degree of discretion. They also served warrants and transported offenders between court and jail. As constables could be called away from their farms and workshops, fees and mileage were paid to make up for lost time and business (Emsley 1987: 172–3). The duties of constables increased during the Reformation era when economic and social changes were producing a large class of landless labourers. When "masterless men" or vagrants were a source of concern in towns and rural districts, tenant farmers and other small employers served as constables in order to control labour. Their duties included the enforcement of laws regulating masters and servants. Constables tended to be respectable members of the village or parish, the same yeoman and artisan class that acted as churchwardens and overseers of the poor. Many constables themselves had been in conflict with the law over minor infractions. In some jurisdictions, semi-permanent constables, for a small fee, took the place of other men of the community (Kent 1986: chapter 1).

Although constables were community residents, the execution of their duties was not always uncontested. Partly because of sensitivity to local opinions, they often encouraged alternative dispute resolution, refused to act or delayed in executing warrants. Joan Kent has argued that the constable of the Tudor-Stuart era functioned much like the village headman of non-Western societies dealing with a distant, imperial power. Later criticisms of the constabulary failed to appreciate that they operated between "two concepts of order," the state's on the one hand and the local community's on the other (Kent 1986; Sharpe 1984: 34). When justice revolved around mutual neighbourhood or community supervision, constables turned a blind eye to minor offences except when committed by transients or vagrants. Constables depended on not only local goodwill but also assistance in carrying out their duties. Studies indicate that villagers helped with arrests, the transportation of prisoners, the whipping of vagrants and the collection of taxes. Discretion was exercised by reporting that the parish was free of drunkards or tolerating extra-legal punishment of individuals by the community. When constables attempted to collect taxes, serve warrants, search premises, warn offenders or place them in the stocks, retaliation came in the form of insults, ostracism and physical attack (Kent 1986: chapter 7).

The urban nightwatch was mocked by Shakespeare (the bumbling Dogberry and Verges in *Much Ado About Nothing*) and denounced by police reformers and Whig police historians. According to its critics the watch consisted of the aged, decrepit, cowardly and inefficient or former soldiers addicted to drink. In popular culture the "Charlie" was depicted as an amusing, meddlesome official worthy of torment by street urchins. Yet in recent years the watch, much like the constabulary, has been re-evaluated. London parishes had effective night watches by the 1700s if not earlier. And their role was not simply that of passive patrol but pro-active intervention. Newspaper and court depositions indicate that they stopped and arrested suspicious persons, discovered stolen property and generally anticipated many functions of the "new police" (Palmer 1988). London's involuntary watch gave way to a permanent body paid by public funds, an important step toward professionalism. Yet each watch was concerned primarily with what took place within the boundaries of the parish (Emsley 1987: 174). The watch often was supervised by the beadle (Dickens's Mr. Bumble), a multipurpose officer who combined Poor Law and constabulary obligations with church duties.

THE NEW POLICE

The creation of the "new police" in England, a reform of an ancient law enforcement system, was part of a reshaping of criminal justice thinking and institutions that took a century to implement. The traditional face-to-face paternalist social controls of "semi-autonomous local areas" gave way to greater uniformity, rationality and bureaucracy in methods of arrest, prosecution and punishment. Justices of the peace, houses of correction, constables and watchmen were replaced by stipendiary (salaried) magistrates, penitentiaries and police (McLynn 1989: 31). The police gradually assumed the investigatory role of magistrates, whose duty well into the nineteenth century was to "take the initiative in the detection of crime" (Tobias 1979: 27). England's eighteenth-century gentry, which feared government centralization and executive power, refused to create a police. The very word conjured up images of European despotism and spies meddling in the lives of honest British subjects. Instead Parliament relied on the deterrent of the Bloody Code, an increasingly harsh criminal law, to counter crimes against property. The death penalty also remained on the statute books through a "lack of secondary punishments" (Hay 1975: 24) and for ideological reasons. From 1688 to 1820, the number of capital statutes expanded from roughly 50 to over 220 (ibid.). People could be sent to the gallows for stealing a sheep, picking pockets or cutting down a tree in an orchard or garden. The use of Australia as a penal colony for felons took some pressure off the system. The addition of new capital crimes against property reflected the weakness of policing and a concern to "protect new forms of wealth" (McLynn 1989: xi). The Bloody Code was exemplary, balancing the terror of the law with low conviction rates and displays of mercy by the judiciary (Hay 1975).

The void created by the lack of a permanent police and by overlapping jurisdiction in the metropolitan London region was partly filled by thief-takers who pursued felons purely for commercial gain. Individuals who profited from thief catching and the return of stolen property were active until the advent of the London Metropolitan Police (LMP) and modern insurance in the nineteenth century (Klockars 1985: 34–6; Monkkonen 1981: 35). Thief-catchers, often former constables and bailiffs, usually ran alehouses and relied on informers, bribery, blackmail, protection rackets and violence. Justice was often venal, with most public offices being purchased by their occupants. Victims of theft would pay fees for the return of stolen property or seek a warrant from a magistrate if they knew the identity of the suspected thief. Victims would seek the assistance of not only constables but also friends and family members in making an arrest, conducting searches and seizing stolen property. According to Howson (1987: 286), thief-taking was an inherently corrupt practice that supported "the urban underworld for three centuries." The most notorious, who at his apex functioned both as de facto chief of police and head of London's organized crime, was Jonathan Wild, "The Thief Taker General," who sent many to the gallows and who was himself hanged in 1725. These private sector initiatives, which took advantage of gaps in the justice system, highlighted the weaknesses of coordinating the policing of London's 152 parishes. Other responses to eighteenth-century crime were private associations for the prosecution of felons, which were found in London and beyond. These organizations, dominated by artisans and tradesmen, numbered two thousand by the end of the eighteenth century (McMullan 1995).

The shift to the new police was gradual. Small reforms were undertaken in London by Henry and John Fielding, magistrates in Bow Street, who began to coordinate the pursuit of thieves and other felons in the middle of the eighteenth century. The Bow Street magistrates, in addition to salaried "runners," began to deploy patrols on the main roads. Most police reformers in this period envisioned an expanded force of constables working with full-time salaried magistrates, who in turn would sit in judgement of the prisoners. The City of London's marshal (the City, the area comprising the financial district, was an independent municipality) supervised a small uniformed patrol by the 1790s. Reform voices were raised during the late eighteenth century when the English elite was haunted by the twin spectres of revolution in France and unrest at home. Industrialization and urban growth were breaking down the traditional stabilizing order of the parish. An increasingly stratified society produced greater differences in not only wealth but also culture. Evangelical Protestantism demanded stricter standards of personal and public behaviour from both workers and aristocrats. A series of poor harvests, plebeian violence such as the 1780 Gordon Riots (where three hundred rioters died) and press-inspired fears of crime caused the ruling class to reconsider its hostility to police (Emsley 1991: 14–5). The issue was not crime but public order. The *Riot*

Act of 1714 made it a capital offence for more than a dozen people to assemble and not disperse after a JP read a proclamation. Magistrates could call on the military for assistance in enforcing the act, but this was objectionable on constitutional grounds and also because of the potential of troops to overreact (McLynn 1989: chapter 12). The alternative was an expansion of the civil police. Yet a proposed police force for London and Westminster was rejected by Parliament in 1785 as too radical (Vogler 1991: chapters 1–3). A metropolitan magistrate and "social investigator," Patrick Colquhoun, published *A Treatise on the Police of the Metropolis* in 1796 that summarized a number of reform arguments. By now the term *police* was beginning to lose its broader, regulatory connotations and take on its more familiar crime-fighting meaning, connoting not a series of activities but an institution. Yet Parliament preferred to move slowly. The 1792 *Middlesex Justices Act* was a compromise response to the failure of the earlier Police Bill. The law set up seven police offices, outside the limits of the City of London, each staffed with three stipendiary magistrates and six constables paid by public funds (Palmer 1988: 117–8).

Historians have not adequately examined the connections between penal reform and the rise of the new police. Reform of criminal law, the introduction of professional magistrates in the lower courts, the demise of corporal and capital punishment and an emphasis on incarceration for serious offences (which culminated with the appearance of the penitentiary), in short the modernization of the criminal justice system, coincided with the advent of the police. The Continental thinker Cesare Beccaria is best remembered for his opposition to the death penalty and theory that punishment must fit the crime and be swift and certain. But he also envisioned for European states a large, efficient police that would track down lawbreakers. Jeremy Bentham, the English utilitarian theorist, was of a similar view. The modernized justice apparatus predicted by these writers would be at the same time less harsh but more active, intrusive and effective (Conley 1991: 45; McLynn 1989: chapter 11). Modern critical criminologists call this "widening the net." Branding convicted felons was outlawed and there was a noticeable fall in public floggings and use of the pillory, which were eventually ended by law. If punishment was becoming less severe (90 percent of prisoners found guilty of capital offences in London were not executed) the justice system's tentacles were being extended. Between 1805 and 1842, prosecutions rose by 70 percent. The elite, meanwhile, continued to fear not only crime, but also social upheaval (Sharpe 1984: 186).

Parliamentary committees that examined the police question from 1812 to 1828 continued to encounter patriotic, libertarian resistance against establishing a corps of government "spies." In the short term, support for Home Secretary Robert Peel's *Metropolitan Police Act* was fuelled by fears of rising crime. The new police, contrary to earlier histories of the subject, did not arrive suddenly in 1829. A year prior to the creation of the Metropolitan Police the capital was protected by a horse patrol, a dismounted patrol and night and day foot patrols totalling almost three hundred men. In addition, the Thames River Police, established in 1798 as a private agency to protect vessels, lighters (small craft used to transfer cargo from ships to shore) and wharves dedicated to the West Indies trade from pilfering, was soon taken over as public service by the national government. One of its chief duties was controlling waterfront labour (Emsley 1991: 19–21).

In Peel's age, both a constable and a private citizen, on evidence of a felony, could make an arrest, but the courts expanded the powers of constables beginning in the late eighteenth century. In 1827 this authority was further clarified; unlike the private individual, the constable could "arrest where there were reasonable grounds that a felony had been committed" (Monkkonen 1981: 192n36). Early Victorian police reform also introduced, gradually, another important constitutional principle that would influence Canada, the separation of police and judicial powers. JPs, and the urban police magistrates of the 1790s, not only directed constables and police, they also conducted investigations and ruled on the legality of police actions. The idea that common offenders deserved all the benefits of due process of law would have puzzled late eighteenth-century magistrates and politicians. Social conservative Henry Fielding, for example, wrote on the necessity of class-specific laws. Increasingly, police were removed from the direct control of magistrates and justices of the peace in quarter sessions, and the lower criminal courts, at least in the urban areas, were consigned to stipendiary magistrates (Zirker 1988).

If the one thousand uniformed men and officers that began to patrol Metropolitan London in 1829 did not revolutionize policing, they were an important model and influence. During the 1830s and 1840s, for example, squads from "the Met" were sent to various parts of England and Wales as mobile riot police. The key elements of Peel's innovation, which was inspired by his Irish experience, were centralized command, the beat system, crime prevention and the uniform. Walking the beat, whether in London under the supervision of appointed commissioners or in smaller cities under elected watch committees, was an exercise in net widening. It inevitably produced greater numbers of petty arrests as patrolmen actively engaged suspicious and disorderly persons on the street. Police on the beat, whether in London, New York or Montreal, engaged in "categorical suspicion" based on class, age, ethnicity, gender and other factors (Ericson and Haggerty 2008: 15). As surveillance was extended, rates of public order prosecutions rose significantly. The myth of the friendly and efficient British bobby (the nickname refers to Robert Peel) was a late Victorian creation. The new police were equipped with cutlasses when they encountered sustained resistance in contested neighbourhoods. They also were dismissed in droves, for drunkenness, inefficiency, corruption and brutality (Klockars 1985; Emsley 1991: chapter 3).

By the middle of the nineteenth century, although England escaped the creation of a national constabulary, police reform had affected both rural and urban society, and the national government was playing an important role. In 1835 Parliament passed the *Municipal Corporation Act,* which encouraged the establishment of provincial borough forces. One hundred were in operation by 1838. In industrial centres such as Birmingham, Bolton and Manchester, police were under commissioners, not elected authorities. Starting in 1839 the *Rural Police Act* permitted magistrates of counties or divisions of counties to organize police under chief constables. By 1841, twenty-one counties maintained police services. In 1856 came England's and Wales' first mandatory police legislation, the *County and Borough Police Act,* which forced all local and county jurisdiction to create forces (Emsley 1987). The law was a compromise between local autonomy and centralization. Counties and boroughs maintained their own constabularies and received financial support from the national government. The Home Office, which appointed the commissioners of the Metropolitan Police, also provided three inspectors of constabulary to certify and suggest improvements to the county forces. By the mid Victorian era, England and Wales had a police system that balanced localism and centralization. Watch committees kept borough forces close to the community by limiting their size and subjecting them to political control (Conley 1991: 28–9).

COLONIAL POLICING IN IRELAND

"John Bull's other Island," Ireland, was an important theatre for administrative innovation in the eighteenth and nineteenth centuries. Police reform in Ireland, although linked to broader changes in the criminal justice system, was more avowedly political and considerably less liberal. A paramilitary police, armed, living in barracks and beyond the political control of the majority of the population, played a colonial role. It was never accepted by the bulk of the population as anything other than a force of occupation, even when it employed large numbers of Catholics (Bridgeman 1994). The first modern urban police in the British Isles was organized in Dublin in the 1780s. Rural police reform also arrived in Ireland decades before England. Both innovations had little to do with run-of-the-mill crime. Ireland was a conquered dependency ruled by the English and a Protestant minority. Unlike England it maintained a large standing army whose raison d'être was public security. The most pressing problem for the English overlords was agrarian-related violence, but Dublin, the headquarters of foreign rule, presented its own challenges. In 1786 its police was armed, organized in military fashion and supervised by the central government. During the 1780s, despite the presence of constables and magistrates in the baronies (subdivisions of counties), entire districts were taken over by agrarian rebels. The 1787 *County Police Act* enabled the government to send rural police to disaffected counties, but the major forces of repression continued to be the British army, the militia and the Protestant yeomanry. The principles of 1787 were extended in 1814 with the creation of the Peace Preservation Force (PPF), an emergency paramilitary police armed with muskets and bayonets. Controlled from Dublin Castle and working closely with special magistrates, the PPF or "Peelers" (named after their architect, Robert Peel) patrolled sixteen counties by 1822. That year Chief Secretary Goulburn appointed additional stipendiary magistrates and deployed a new armed constabulary in the rural districts. The conviction rate for most crimes grew at an impressive rate from 1805 to 1834, with the exception of "agrarian outrages," most of which went unpunished (Palmer 1988: 368–75).

Political frustration on the part of Catholic nationalists and an increasingly militant Protestant Orange movement made public order a key issue in the 1830s. Although Catholics had been recruited to the baronial police, PPF and constabulary, Protestants dominated the ranks of the police, stipendiary magistrates and crown prosecutors. In 1836 Under-Secretary Drummond unified the Irish police, the Dublin force excepted, by merging the PPF with the constabulary. The new Irish Constabulary, headed by an inspector general, was tightly controlled by Dublin Castle. The cadet school at Phoenix Park, Dublin, was the first police academy in the British Isles. Named the Royal Irish Constabulary (RIC) in 1867 in recognition for quelling an abortive Fenian rising, the force would exert considerable influence on Britain's colonies, including Canada and Newfoundland (Palmer 1988; Marquis 1997, 2005a).

The uncertain political situation in Ireland excluded the possibility of a locally-controlled police. Public security, the protection of the landlord class and British interests in general, dictated a more professional and less popular justice system. Local justices of the peace were deemed too biased and ineffectual. The Irish police, in contrast to their English counterparts, replaced local civil authority. By the 1850s the twelve thousand men of the Irish Constabulary, posted in over 1,600 stations, served as the eyes and ears of the British rulers, and the force had many of the characteristics of a European *gendarmerie*. Much of our understanding of the RIC had been clouded by the nationalism of Irish historians, for whom Catholics on the force were collaborators. Case studies have concluded that its relations with the Irish population improved by the late nineteenth century, but the members of the constabulary, which by the 1910s considered itself to be an Irish institution, were targeted for assassination during the Anglo-Irish War in the early 1920s. That independence struggle resulted in the partition of Ireland and the birth of the Irish Free State. The RIC was disbanded (Brewer 1990; Marquis 1997).

After the war of independence, Ulster (Northern Ireland) remained part of Great Britain and was policed by the Protestant-dominated Royal Ulster Constabulary (RUC), which was assisted by a controversial part-time auxiliary force, the B Specials. Starting in the late 1960s, sectarian violence involving Catholic and

Protestant paramilitary organizations, the British army and the RUC would take roughly 3,500 lives, half of them civilians and many of these children. By the last third of the twentieth century the styles of policing in Belfast and London could hardly be more different. Most Londoners did not regard contacting the police with complaints or giving evidence as "informing." London's police stations did not resemble fortified bases, and its police vehicles were far less intimidating than the armoured Land Rovers of the RUC. Off-duty bobbies did not worry about being blown up in their cars or gunned down on the street or in their homes. Similarly, residents of London did not worry about being shot by the police, the army or sectarian paramilitary units. By the late 1980s most of England's 120,000 police officers were unarmed. The security establishment in Ulster, in contrast, consisted of several thousand heavily armed police and a greater number of British troops equipped with armoured vehicles and helicopters, all backed up by a sophisticated intelligence operation. Across the border in the Republic of Ireland, the national police, the *Garda Siochana,* was largely unarmed (Palmer 1988: 2–3).

CONCLUSION

The contrast between the evolution of policing in London and Ireland is instructive to this study for two reasons. The first is that both the LMP and RIC models had an impact on law enforcement developments in nineteenth-century British North America. The second is the important reminder that historical context and distinct national development, including politics and culture, are important determinants of policing. The policing situation in Northern Ireland evolved out of the distinct pathway of the nation's troubled history. Starting in the 1990s a peace process encouraged reconciliation, power sharing, disarmament and the creation of a new police entity that would enjoy public legitimacy. One step in the process was stopping the practice of British army escorting police on patrol. Another was removing carbines and submachine guns from police patrol units. The Police Service of Northern Ireland, established in 2001, had ambitious goals to make Catholics 50 percent of total personnel (Independent Commission 1999). This was an extreme example of a police service attempting to reinvent itself to win legitimacy.

Canada's political and legal systems borrowed much from the British world in the nineteenth century, but as this book indicates, American police innovations have also been important. History itself has been important to police identity and public relations, especially in the case of the RCMP, which continues to exploit a romanticized public image that was initially created by British, American and Canadian writers in the late nineteenth century. An examination of critical themes in police history, particularly issues such as the tendency of police leaders and organizations to see themselves as the most authoritative sources of expertise on issues such crime, drugs and national security, can inform current policy debates. As this study reveals, innovations in both criminal and political policing have not always been adopted because of the presence of an objective threat or social problem, despite claims to the contrary. At present one of the major issues under discussion is whether the current model of policing, in an era of falling crime rates, is economically sustainable or whether police organizations should either disengage with "non-criminal" involvements, such as assisting with mental health crises, or actually expand their service role. A second problematic issue is the degree to which police services should adopt "get tough" and militarized approaches (ironically the reverse of the recent process in Northern Ireland). The final critical question surrounds the extent to which short-term concerns about "terrorism" should affect our criminal laws, national security and intelligence efforts and our regular police services. As this study will indicate, debates on the functions of policing, and who is entitled to take part in these deliberations, are as old as Canada itself.

CHAPTER 1

POLICING
EARLY BRITISH NORTH AMERICA

The new police emerged in British North America between the War of 1812 and the adoption of colonial responsible government by the 1850s. In addition to political reform, which included the introduction of municipal institutions, the era was noted for the maturation of commercial capitalism, substantial investment in transportation infrastructure, the advent of free trade within the British Empire and nascent industrialization. It also was a period of institutional reform, much of it shaped by voluntary organizations and religious philanthropists. Actual state formation in the early Victorian period was a piecemeal effort, affected by political deadlock, taxpayer resistance and administrative inefficiency. It was once common to attribute the spread of the new police to the success of Peel's reforms for London in 1829. Police reform supposedly heralded the humanitarian, liberal state. Despite the optimistic pronouncements of the era of utilitarianism, police and other types of reform did not exist outside of class relations. In the words of a Canadian social historian, the modern police were "a visible human embodiment of the sovereign power" (Greer 1992: 17). During the early Victorian era, as the bourgeoisie rose to prominence, social issues such as crime were interpreted increasingly in class terms. A series of institutional responses to social and economic change attempted to control the rate of change. In addition, new standards of behaviour, such as temperance, impinged on pre-industrial social relations. Police reform coincided with reform of penal law, notably the abolition of corporal and shaming punishments and restrictions on the use of capital punishment, all in the name of a more rational and humane legal order. Both state and non-state reformers organized new institutions such as public schools, penitentiaries, asylums and industrial schools. Historians see these strategies as social engineering, but the Victorians spoke of instilling character, thrift and obedience (Fecteau 1994; Storch 1975, 1976).

Canada's evolving police apparatus, decentralized, haphazard and contingent, was a far cry from the more coherent state systems of continental Europe. Canadian policing, in terms of governance, function, style and popular support, was "between Britain and the United States" (Mawby 1990: chapter 5). Both countries inspired police reform in British North America, although in a complex and indirect fashion. Degrees of community input and control in British North America varied among regions and from one town to the next. What was true for Toronto was not applicable for Quebec or Charlottetown. The short-term reasons behind police reform also varied. Neither crime waves nor outbursts of social violence were necessarily the precursors of police institutions.

Most policing innovations in both Canada and the United States took place in urban areas. The rural majority (90 percent of the population in the early 1800s) continued to rely on traditional methods of order maintenance and dispute resolution, subjects which are only beginning to be explored by historians. The early police, like traditional constables and watchmen, in many respects remained a service arm of the magistracy, which in urban centres became more accountable and more middle-class in composition and outlook. Police reform often owed more to changes in local administration than to a perceived crisis in authority. The enforcement of new standards of decorum and control of leisure activities, as will be detailed in this study, often produced clashes with the working class. The visibility and availability of the police led to an evolving process of "community entanglement," with often unanticipated and complex results (Weaver 1990, 1995).

The paternalistic social order of early colonial society depended on the lower orders submitting deferentially to the authority of the elite. The close association of law enforcement with the magistracy did not end, but after the Napoleonic era an important shift toward separation of enforcement from adjudication was evident. The change coincided with the advent of a more representative style of municipal administration. This was no industrialist class exerting itself over a mass of propertyless labourers and their families; municipal government was captured by middle-ranked professionals and merchants and leading artisans and shopkeepers. Although bourgeois women could not vote in local elections until the era of women's enfranchisement, they could influence legislative and enforcement agendas through moral suasion and lobbying. The middle class, for a variety of reasons, also supported stricter standards of public decorum over time (Acheson 1985; Boritch 1988: 144–5). A model for the "white" Empire was Britain's 1835 *Municipal Corporations Act,* which established watch committees to supervise police in boroughs (Emsley 1983: 69–71).

By 1850, although the police had not fully emerged as an independent, professional bureaucracy, the ordering of Canadian towns and cities had begun to change dramatically. The coordinated patrol function brought a dramatic rise in the reporting and prosecution of public order offences, a trend that continued throughout the century. The paternalist system, frontier conditions and the seasonal nature of the economy had tolerated a certain amount of rowdiness, social violence and sexual impropriety. As evangelical Protestantism tightened its grip, paralleled by a puritanical Catholicism among French and Irish Canadians, "respectability" became the key word in early Victorian social discourse. As in nineteenth-century Britain, the new police functioned as "domestic missionaries" (Storch 1976). It is clear that the aim of the police was to change behaviour, particularly that of the poor and working class, but their impact varied from one community to the next.

With popular parties struggling against elites that dominated the courts, legislative and executive councils and militia, the partisanship of the magistracy, arguably the most important centre of traditional law enforcement power, became a major issue. To complicate matters, the rough electioneering tactics of the era made politics a form of gang warfare. Fortified by alcohol and armed with clubs, each candidate's supporters vied for control of the polls, where voters registered their ballot in public. Reformers in Upper Canada charged Tory JPs with partiality in these instances. In 1838 Lord Durham alleged that Conservative magistrates had harassed their Reform and Radical opponents. A decade later, despite the presence of a British garrison, Tories and Reformers fought in the streets of Bytown with stones and guns (Cross 1971).

During the 1820s radical reformers in Upper Canada pushed the elective principle in municipal governance to break the power of local Tory cliques. In 1832 and 1833 the legislature authorized elective police boards for the towns of Brockville and Hamilton. The legislation reflected the older conception of the term police; the boards were prototypical town councils concerned with all manner of urban regulation and "local improvement," including relief of the poor. To lessen the patronage power of the executive, in 1836 a Reform-dominated assembly enacted a *Local Government Act* by which commissioners displaced magistrates from certain administrative duties (Firth 1966; Read 1982: 47, 58–62, 70). As capital of Upper Canada the town of York (incorporated as Toronto in 1834) exerted an influence on police reform in the colony. Its high constable directed a small number of constables in the town and the township. Like their counterparts elsewhere, York's constables wore civilian clothes and did not engage in regular patrols. In 1826 York, like Halifax, appointed a full-time police clerk to work alongside a magistrate at a police office. By the late 1820s the local press was fretting over the town's lack of watchmen and lamps and the corrupt and inefficient nature of its "police," including public sanitation and street bylaws. Radical critics during this decade exposed local administration as an example of Family Compact cronyism and feared that municipal incorporation would merely perpetuate Tory dominance of both local administration and the justice system (Rogers 1984).

The night watch, which had a long history in English towns, proved to be a flexible interim measure for communities without regular police. At various times the watch on both sides of the Atlantic was criticized for its ineffectiveness. Its biggest task was guarding against fire; the second was monitoring strangers and other suspicious characters and servants, apprentices and minors who could not give a satisfactory account of themselves. By the early nineteenth century, seaport cities were moving away from temporary, amateur night protection toward more organized efforts. In 1818 legislation created night watches, supported by tavern licence fees, for Quebec and Montreal. Two years later Quebec established a Police Office with a small force of permanent constables who were issued guns and swords. As in Halifax, these constables augmented the traditional ward constables (Fyson 2006: 164–6). During part of 1814 the governor of Nova Scotia called out the militia to patrol the streets of Halifax. Four years later the legislature enacted a law authorizing a conscript night patrol. Five patrol divisions were supervised by committees appointed by the magistrates. The men of the "patroles," equipped with lanterns and bludgeons, were given the power of constables in order to command public respect. In subsequent years the watch was called out only sporadically. The night patrol was not uniformed until the 1860s prior to its merger with the day police. Hiring regular watchmen was a step toward modernization; it also improved discipline. Conscripted citizens were less likely to put themselves at risk and more likely to break the monotony with carousing. The ratepayers of Saint John, another city that enacted piecemeal reform, supported a permanent watch during the 1830s (Marquis 2003; Acheson 1985). In urban centres the bulk of public order arrests were made by the watch, whether volunteer, conscripted or paid. The watch house, especially if it contained a lockup, was a police station under another name. And salaried watchmen were not always the incompetent or feeble "leatherheads" of legend. In 1820, two men who had robbed an aged farmer in Montreal were arrested owing to detective work by the watch commander. The key in the investigation was a small boy whom the suspects had hired to shadow their victim. Tried in the court of King's Bench, the prisoners were found guilty, sentenced to death and hanged behind the jail before a vast crowd (Marquis 1996).

Nineteenth-century Canadian cities rarely were incorporated simply in order to improve policing or fight crime. Law and order was only a small part of the movement behind York's incorporation in 1834. Radical journalist William Lyon Mackenzie objected to the incorporation bill's sweeping powers in terms of arrest, summary trial and punishment for various offences (Glazebrook 1964: 36–47; Firth 1966). Yet the limited size of the new municipal force (a high bailiff and five constables) and the promise of close supervision by city council allayed radical and reform fears. Indeed the city's first chief magistrate in 1834 was Mackenzie himself, leader of the Upper Canadian rebellion three years later. Tory dominance of city hall, and the police, would be a by-product of the rebellion (Kealey 1984). By the middle of the century Toronto's population, augmented by Irish immigrants, had reached thirty thousand. In 1841 enlightened statist commissioners investigating municipal affairs following an election riot recommended "a well-regulated and efficient police force" appointed and supervised by authorities divorced from local influences. Yet until the 1850s the police would remain a creature of the largely Tory municipal corporation, which reappointed constables yearly. During the 1840s, a routine staffing issue such as the removal of a constable for drunkenness could cause a political uproar. Kealey argues that a general sympathy on the part of constables with Protestant Orange rioters kept the police from enforcing the law in a neutral fashion (Kealey 1984; Rogers 1984).

Quebec's population, commerce and boundaries from 1815 to 1830 expanded, but the city's administrative and law enforcement apparatus remained traditional. Although the number of magistrates grew, they were not responsible to the taxpayers, an increasing proportion of whom were Anglophones. A legislative committee beginning in 1830 studied incorporation, and appropriate bills were framed for Quebec and Montreal two years later. Municipal institutions were introduced with the first civic elections in 1833. As Fyson (2006: 137–8) suggests in a discussion of "policing before the police" in his study of criminal justice in Quebec, magistrates, constables and the watch must have been active and effective given early nineteenth-century incarceration rates. Between 1811 and 1836 the Montreal and Quebec jails admitted 10,000 and 8,500 prisoners respectively, and thousands of others were incarcerated in houses of correction and watch-house lockups. Starting in 1822 the elected officers of the corporation instituted a civic police whose control by politicians, given the ethnic politics of the period, was a subject of no little controversy (Dufresne 2000; Fyson 2006). The new civic corporation of Montreal retained most of the police ordinances of the magistrates who had governed the city since the eighteenth century. The inspector of police, appointed by and supervised by the mayor and common council, was charged with carrying out all bylaws and ordinances, especially those relating to nuisances and streets. The watch committee of council administered a fund derived from roughly three hundred tavern and grocery licences. In emergencies the municipality relied on special constables. The ultimate guarantor of order was the British garrison, which suppressed election rioting in 1832 at the cost of three lives (Marquis 1996; Senior 1981).

To describe mid-nineteenth-century Canadian cities as dominated by political machines goes too far, but political factions and informal cliques did compete for power and patronage. Policing and other services were not immune from these contests. Much to the consternation of Tories, the Montreal city council in the mid-1830s was controlled by Patriote sympathizers. The 1840s Toronto civic corporation, dominated by Tories, extended the politics of patronage to municipal contracts, tavern keepers, carters and cabmen, pedlars and police constables. The opposition party cried foul but once in power, invariably, retained the patronage system. The result was that constables seldom had a job for life. Ward constables often were "elected" on an annual basis by city councils. Journalists and reformers often suspected that the police played favourites with tavern keepers, grocers, carters and other supporters of the municipal corporation as democratic control (by male ratepayers) became the norm in Canada East and the Maritimes. Where police were under direct control of elected officials there was the potential of interference in the laying of charges or in lessening the burdens of fines. A formal or informal appeal to an alderman or chair of the police committee often saved an individual a night in the lockup, an onerous fine or a criminal record.

Halifax is a good example of the gradualism of police reform, and how taxpayer resistance and the jealousy of traditional elites in guarding prerogatives had to be weighed against demands for efficiency and crime control. There was no real panic over rising crime and disorder in the early 1840s when the community, under the rule of appointed magistrates since 1749, adopted elected municipal institutions. The police office, opened in 1815, had made petty justice somewhat more bureaucratic, yet the level of prosecution under the unreformed system seems low by modern standards. Judging from extant returns of committals to the bridewell (or house of correction), from 1820 to 1831 the police office and other magistrates incarcerated less than one hundred persons a year on charges under the 1815 *Police Act* and the colonial vagrancy statute. The police office, in the seven years prior to municipal incorporation in 1841, committed an average of 213 persons to the bridewell and county jail each year (Marquis 2003).

Saint John, in contrast with Halifax where violence was more interpersonal (or confined to periodic *émeutes* by members of the British garrison or Royal Navy on leave), had a genuine public order problem in the years leading to 1850. Particularly during the turbulent 1840s, policing was guided not by a coherent theory of local administration but crisis management. Conflict between Orangemen and Irish Catholic immigrants concentrated in the poorer areas of the city and its neighbour Portland dominated discussions of crime (Marquis 1982). Orange-Green rioting began in 1841. Two years later the magistrates, failing to disperse a large Catholic crowd that had defied Orange celebrations, enrolled 150 Protestant special constables. The city's Protestant majority began to view Orange lodges as an extra-legal but necessary deterrent against Irish Catholic rowdiness. In 1844 the master of an Orange lodge from neighbouring Portland mortally wounded a Catholic at York Point, the major Irish ghetto, and was placed in custody for his own protection. Later that year British troops were called out to quell sectarian street fighting. In 1845 things took a more serious turn, with Orangemen shooting at Catholics on Saint Patrick's Day. With the garrison standing by, the two sides clashed until nightfall. The all-Protestant grand jury refused to indict two Orangemen charged with murder but indicted several Catholics for public order crimes (See 1993: chapter 7).

Social violence in Saint John County revealed the inadequacies of traditional order preservation mechanisms when community consensus was fractured by class, ethnic or religious difference. Appointed ward constables and poorly remunerated watchmen were unable to contain the situation, yet the common council resisted any police legislation that would raise taxation. The fact that most victims in ethno-religious rioting usually were Catholic immigrants made the issue less of a priority. Firearms and other deadly weapons were in use again during 1847, when sixteen thousand famine refugees arrived from Ireland. The lieutenant-governor, following the death of an unarmed watchman, organized the colony's first professional constabulary for the parish of Portland. This small force, placed under a stipendiary magistrate, was given legislative backing in 1848. The Portland police was clearly a Protestant body given the task of supervising a largely Catholic immigrant working class (Acheson 1985; Marquis 1982).

By 1849, the peak year for sectarian violence in New Brunswick, Saint John's law enforcement system was in transition. The day police and night watch had been strengthened, but the aldermen, pointing to increased taxation, resisted a fully integrated force. Thus when Carleton and York county Orangemen arrived in the Loyalist city to celebrate the Glorious Twelfth with their local brothers, the mayor, as chief magistrate, remained responsible for public order. Only one constable escorted him to the flash point. The Orange marchers were well armed with pistols and muskets; when they reached the boundaries of York Point, the two parties clashed. The mayor and Portland's new police magistrate had been unable to persuade the parade leaders to take an alternate route. The small British garrison was deployed, complete with artillery piece, to the south of the rioting to protect the business district; the weak authorities basically waited for the fighting to subside (See 1993). The street combat took at least a dozen lives and wounded many more. The police of Portland and Saint John, in the aftermath, were temporarily armed with militia weapons. Magistrates attempted to be equitable in issuing warrants against individuals in both camps, but juries refused to indict and convict Protestants who represented the dominant culture. It took the riot and its controversial aftermath to bring a professional police force to Saint John. New Brunswick's legislature provided statutory authority for full-time police under the general supervision of a police magistrate (Marquis 1982; Acheson 1985).

St. John's, Newfoundland, was beset by a similar set of class and sectarian tensions. Following protests over food and work shortages in 1817, two hundred respectable citizens mounted an armed patrol. From 1812 to 1824 magistrates in St. John's directed a force of constables that was supported from the license fees of taverns (Baker 1982). Vigilantes preserved the peace again in 1824 when impoverished outport and local labourers and fishers gathered to demand relief. That year the town was protected by one high and six regular constables, all employees of the government. Civic institutions in Newfoundland lagged behind the mainland; St. John's did not obtain a municipal council until the 1880s, and it had no powers over policing, as the Newfoundland Constabulary was a government institution (Marquis 1997).

Urban communities with limited tax bases experimented with a variety of policing types before the 1850s. Hamilton, Upper Canada, is a case in point. Its high bailiff in the 1830s was assisted at various times by volunteer watchmen. During the 1840s the city council hired special constables and salaried sub constables and shared the cost of a mounted patrol with a neighbouring municipality and a railroad company (Weaver 1988). Prescott established a board of police when the town was incorporated in 1843. Its four elected members, selected by the ratepayers, appointed a fifth. Together the board appointed town officers such as bailiff and constable and inherited the quarter session's judicial duties over bylaw infractions (McKenna 1996).

REBELLION AND THE IRISH MODEL

Canada's other model of policing was inspired by Irish practice. In the words of Stanley Palmer, "the harsh nature of Irish society generated harsher forms of social protest, which in turn, coupled with weak and timorous local authorities, required the creation of a police harsh by English standards" (Palmer 1988: xix). Lower Canada in the 1830s, not the Northwest in the 1870s, produced British North America's first *gendarmerie*. When dealing with "problem populations," colonial administrators looked not to London but to Ireland, where police reform had begun in the 1780s (Marquis 1997). This model, which influenced British Columbia, Lower Canada and Newfoundland, eventually produced territorial police organizations such as the Ontario Provincial Police (OPP). But in the pre-Confederation era the best examples were the temporary special constabularies organized in Lower Canada in the late 1830s.

The public order crisis in the colony, a result of the failure of constitutional methods of political redress, was not totally unanticipated. In the district of Montreal in 1837 the state evaporated as insurgent Patriotes strove to establish parish republics. Magistrates and militia officers who had neither resigned nor been dismissed for their political views stepped down or fled to loyal zones. The rebellion was crushed by the British army and loyal militia, but a second uprising followed in 1838. The military governor's November 1838 proclamation declared that "the Courts of justice in the said district have virtually ceased to exist, from the impossibility of executing any legal process or warrant therein" (Report of the State Trials 1839: 2). The lesson of the Lower Canadian rebellions, for state authorities, was that police not accepted as a community institution would have to be introduced from above like an army of occupation, in other words, follow the model of the newly organized Irish Constabulary. Legislative paralysis by 1836 ended the civic charters and fledgling municipal police departments in Quebec City and Montreal. At the time of the first outbreak the cities had no police, yet within a few days of the proclamation of martial law suspicious persons in Montreal and its suburbs had been disarmed. Loyalist militia arrested scores of French Canadians as suspected members of the Fils de Liberté or sympathizers. The militia, whose backbone was the Anglophone commercial class, engaged in nightly patrols until the spring of 1838 (Senior 1988).

In Upper Canada, where the rebellion was localized and less bloody, suspected rebels were arrested by militia and magistrates and examined and tried by the civil authorities, not courts martial. As most JPs, constables and militia officers remained loyal, the colonial authorities saw no need to implement any extraordinary policing measures (Read 1982). Public security policy for Lower Canada was more robust: colonial constabularies in both major cities and the disturbed rural parishes. The commander of the British forces in the colony had asked the governor's special council to establish a mounted police. Quebec, which was denuded of regular troops, was provided with a government constabulary in late 1837. A proposed police ordinance, however, was rejected as too arbitrary, even during a revolutionary crisis. The situation changed between the first and the second rebellion in Lower Canada. The crisis was heightened in 1838 by the existence of the Hunters' Lodges, parties of Canadian refugees and sympathetic Americans who gathered arms and plotted attacks from across the United States border.

Although his mission to Canada was partly conciliatory, Lord Durham, struck by the lack of police and magisterial authority beyond Lower Canada's towns, authorized government constabularies for Montreal and Quebec and a new rural police. This was perfectly in keeping with the enlightened statism and utilitarianism of his famous report. The rural constabulary, lodged in problem areas such as Napierville and Saint Denis, worked with a network of special magistrates. It was not deployed in the district of Montreal until early 1839. Quebec's force of eighty-three was extraordinarily large for its day, suggesting an intended paramilitary capability. Montreal's, which included a mounted patrol, was even larger (Senior 1988; Greer 1992). The *Montreal Transcript* admitted that the rural police was primarily a security organization, "a surer means of obtaining correct information" from disaffected parishes and a barrier to "seditious combinations" (see Marquis

1996). The constabulary, however, promised other "important ends" and operated "for the benefit of every part of the country to which it has yet been extended" (ibid.). The lower incidence of crime proved to supporters (chiefly Anglophone merchants and officials) that the new city forces were superior to "the utterly useless system of watch which prevailed under the general sanction of the magistrates" (ibid.). Greer is correct in stating that the ruling classes imposed "Peel-style police" in Lower Canada; however, the model was not Peel's London precedent but his Napoleonic-era Irish innovation (Greer 1992: 22).

The new urban constabularies employed both Francophones and Anglophones. In early 1839, Montreal Division A consisted of thirty-one Canadiens and twenty-four Irishmen; over a third of Division B was Irish. Eighty percent of the Quebec City force was Irish. Officially Montreal's police used their stations as barracks, but other sources suggest that the men ate and slept in their homes. Thomas Ainslie Young and Pierre-Édouard Leclerc were the urban police superintendents; the mounted police was under Commissioner Augustus Gugy. A French-speaking loyalist, the latter found it difficult to recruit Francophones, who constituted only one fifth of the force (which ranged between two and three hundred). British army veterans were particularly welcome (Greer 1992; Marquis 1996). Not all opposition to the rural police, which was extended to additional parishes such as Saint François, originated with the Patriote movement. A number of English Canadian moderates raised both fiscal and constitutional objections. The *Sherbrooke Courier* doubted that the "Durham extravaganzas" were necessary once the emergency passed. One correspondent argued that Anglo-Saxon tradition necessitated maintaining public vigilance over important institutions like the police and magistracy. The people of Rawdon and Kildare, much like residents of Sherbrooke, protested in 1840 that there was no need to extend the rural police to their loyal and law-abiding township. The *Quebec Chronicle* condemned Durham's ordinance as "the Algerine Bill," a reference to the man-stealing pirates of North Africa. A public meeting at Sherbrooke admitted that the traditional system of voluntarism had poorly served thinly-settled rural districts where bailiffs refused to serve criminal warrants and the twice-yearly sessions often failed to attract a quorum of magistrates. Yet rather than embrace an Irish-style constabulary, the townsfolk proposed modest salaries for magistrates and one or two constables per township (Marquis 1996).

Even in the midst of the revolutionary crisis the Loyalist press of Montreal expected the new police institution to assume responsibility for basic urban regulation. In addition to combatting disloyalty and crime, it could enforce traditional "police" ordinances of the mercantilist city pertaining to markets and roads. Montreal's high constable traditionally received a small salary for enforcing traffic regulations. Rules against engrossing (i.e., hoarding for profit) and short weighting firewood and bread were other important regulatory responsibilities of township officers. By the late 1830s much was made of the need to impound runaway horses and carioles, muzzle stray dogs, fine dangerous drivers and report street nuisances. Arrest statistics suggest that Montreal's new police, its security mandate aside, found other duties to fulfil. In the case of public order and status offences such as vagrancy, the arresting officers in effect became the prosecutor. In one two-month period, public order infractions (drunkenness, disturbing the peace and vagrancy) in Montreal constituted 54 percent of total arrests. The legal response to assault, abusive language, larceny and robbery (36 percent of the total) was generated by citizens who complained to police and magistrates. Defenders of the new system also pointed to its professionalism and alleged nonpartisan character. The combination of police and stipendiary magistrates in the countryside countered the lack of an independent gentry, which in Britain supervised the local courts as a national duty. It was unjust, furthermore, to expect a farmer to quit his plow or a blacksmith his forge in order to escort a culprit to a magistrate or to jail. Both traditional JPs and constables had "local feelings, local affections, local prejudices and local animosities" and "party feeling" often allowed lawbreakers to escape (Marquis 1996). Stipendiary magistrates would be disinterested arbiters and the new police, like the recently reorganized Irish Constabulary, "perfect strangers to their territory," executing warrants without demanding fees or expenses (ibid.).

One innovation that survived the Rebellion era was the Quebec River Police. As Montreal's port expanded it too would receive a government-supported Water Police. Both were modelled on the Thames River Police, originally an anti-pilferage patrol for the West Indies trade. The Quebec force was employed on a seasonal basis; demand was highest in the spring with the opening of navigation and the arrival of dozens of sailing vessels with immigrants, provisions and manufactured items. Although it kept order along the waterfront, the River Police was clearly aimed at controlling the labour market. It rounded up and prosecuted stray sailors who had left vessels in violation of their contract in search of higher wages or less demanding masters. Boarding house and tavern keepers were the crimps or facilitators of this illegal labour recruiting. Controlling the seagoing workforce was also a concern in ports such as Halifax and Saint John, but only in Quebec and Montreal did colonial governments become so heavily involved. In 1846, the Quebec City police made more arrests under the *Seamen's Act* than for assault and battery, threats and insults combined (McCulloch 1990). In 1867 both the Montreal and Quebec harbour police forces came under the jurisdiction of the new Dominion government. A fringe benefit of these constabularies was that they could be used as rapid deployment forces to aid the civic authorities (Fingard 1989; Greer 1992; Marquis 1996).

The 1840s ended with an abortive experiment in government police for the Canada East half of the United Canadas. Lacking confidence in the Montreal municipal police in 1849, Premier L.H. LaFontaine's Reform ministry, which was sponsoring the controversial Rebellion Losses Bill, enrolled friends of the government as special constables. Once Tory opponents heard that the force was to be armed with cutlasses and pistols, the mood on the streets turned ugly and the "specials" had to be protected by the British garrison. From London the colonial secretary, who disapproved of using Imperial troops in a police capacity, endorsed Governor Lord Elgin's support for a government constabulary for the city. Political conflict that year included an armed attack by Anglophones on the government leader's residence (buckshot fired by the defenders killed one of the assailants), rioting and the destruction of the Parliament House. But a fifty-man mounted police organized on the suggestion of police magistrate Charles Wetherall and trained at nearby La Prairie proved too controversial to deploy. Instead the civic authorities swore in two hundred respectable citizens as special constables, and the crisis passed (Senior 1981, 1988; Marquis 1997).

MUNICIPAL RULE AND THE PURSUIT OF ORDER

Municipal self-government was restored to Montreal and Quebec in stages beginning in 1840. The colonial governor reduced the latter's constabulary by 50 percent and ordered its "military distinctions" watered down. As the decade progressed the constabularies played less of a paramilitary role. Quebec regained full control only in 1843 after the city council had protested having to pay the police budget. The mayor, aldermen and councillors were responsible not only for the police, but also the general good order of the city. In the 1840s, property qualifications ensured that civic office in Canada East was restricted to the upper middle class and elite. Aldermen and councillors, according to Montreal's charter, had power to arrest disturbers of the peace, either personally or through militia and peace officers, and could suspend or dismiss any constable for negligence. The charter also banned gaming houses. The police service, under Commissioner Lt.-Col. William Ermatinger, a French Canadian who had served in the British Army, consisted of roughly sixty men. The officers of the constabulary force were obliged to obey the commands of the city council but exercised jurisdiction throughout the entire district of Montreal. Tellingly, the charter also authorized the council "to assess for property destroyed by mobs or during riots," which suggested that social violence was an expected part of urban life at this time. For a number of years the police relied on the British garrison when confronted with large-scale violence; this reliance was manifested with deadly effect in 1853 when Irish Catholics attacked a Protestant church hosting the anti-Catholic lecturer Alessandro Gavazzi.

The new police were expected to be proactive. Montreal's 1840s charter empowered constables to arrest "all loose, disorderly and idle persons" and those "suspected of intention to commit a felony." Prisoners were to be lodged in the watch house and taken before a magistrate at first possible opportunity. If the arrest was made at night, constables, for certain offences, could issue bail (Canada 1845). Year-round, salaried, uniformed police walking a regular beat were a novelty in early Victorian Canada. They did not immediately overawe their opposition, hence the stiff penalties in Montreal's charter for assaults on constables in the exercise of their duties. Inspector Alexandre Comeau suffered personally when he was decoyed from his residence by men disguised as women (a charivari trick) and brutally beaten. On other occasions the mere presence of a magistrate or senior police official was enough to cow the opposition of hostile crowds (Marquis 1996).

Quebec's police during the 1840s was supervised by Captain Robert Henry Russell, formerly of the British Army. One police station was within the city's ancient walls in Haute-Ville; the second, in the more rowdy Basse-Ville, was wrecked by a hostile crowd when used as a cholera hospital in 1849. By the middle of the 1850s there were four stations. Although the city council created a twenty-nine man force in 1843 with the expiration of Lord Sydenham's ordinance, a provincially-appointed inspector and superintendent of police remained as a holdover from the Rebellion era. The civic authorities attempted to continue the barracks rule, but most constables chose to live with their families in private dwellings (McCulloch 1990). The composition of policing in Quebec, a largely Catholic city, contrasted with that of Toronto, Saint John, Halifax or even Montreal, in that Irish Catholics, who did not have to compete with large numbers of Protestants for jobs, became part of the local "power structure" (Grace 2003) early on. By the mid-1850s two thirds of the Quebec police were Irish Catholics, many of them immigrants, and the chief police magistrate was an Irish-born Catholic. In the months when navigation was open the municipal force was complemented by the River Police, which was supported by a tax on shipping. By the middle of the 1850s this seasonal force, whose main task was tracking down deserting merchant sailors, maintained four to five boats, each manned by seven men (McCulloch 1990).

Sectarian animosity, tinged with nativist impulses, led to innumerable public order incidents in the 1830s and 1840s. In 1844, for example, Orangemen in Toronto attacked constables attempting to disperse their procession and assaulted the Tory alderman who had ordered the streets cleared after reading the *Riot Act*. There were at least seven incidents or riots in Toronto involving Orangemen from 1839 to 1849. In 1849, when Lord Elgin visited Toronto, Tory demonstrators were contained by the mayor, constables and a troop of volunteer cavalry. During Montreal's civic elections, Tory paramilitary groups, in an open display of political vigilantism, seized control of a polling station and clashed with the Irish Catholics of Griffintown. The municipal police arrested not armed Tories but the Irish who had defended their turf. Vestiges of the traditional order coexisted with emerging bourgeois culture (Kealey 1984). The brothel riot, for example, a familiar type of vigilante activity in pre-industrial society, was commonplace in early Victorian American cities. Attacks on houses of ill fame by military and naval personnel took place in Halifax in the 1850s and 1860s (Schneider 1980: 26–31; Marquis 2003). At the same time Protestant clergy and women's benevolent associations were organizing city missions and urging magistrates and police to close down disorderly houses tolerated by earlier elites (Fingard 1989).

Municipal control of police reflected majority rule. As with twentieth-century North America, ethnic and racial minorities who were excluded from economic and social privileges and patronage networks risked victimization by the justice system. The higher incidence of arrest amongst immigrant populations was also related to poverty, cultural differences and ecological factors: the poor and newly arrived were more likely to live in neighbourhoods heavily patrolled by the police. In the 1830s and 1840s Irish Catholics were disproportionately represented in pre-Confederation police, prison and poorhouse statistics (Marquis 1986a; Rogers 1984; Kealey 1984). The limited public debates surrounding these patterns anticipated twentieth-century controversies about the overrepresentation of African Americans in terms of arrest, conviction and incarceration. Minority leaders, as they do today, tended to blame police attitudes and practices.

Criminological literature suggests another important if little-studied aspect of nineteenth-century crime and policing: victimization. Offences against persons and property tended to be intra-class, much like most crime in contemporary America is intra-racial. Most victims, like most offenders, were working class or poor (Hagan and Peterson 1995: 14–36). Lawbreakers, according to a study of pre-industrial Detroit, "were victimizing their own neighbours and acquaintances in run-down, lower-class areas; or they were invading and preying upon adjacent 'high-rank' areas, such as commercial districts and upper-class residential enclaves" (Schneider 1980: 132). In Victorian Hamilton it was rare for reported lawbreakers to assault strangers. Most violence was confined to family, friends and acquaintances. Research on Halifax indicates that lower-class individuals were quite prepared to "go to law" against their neighbours, appealing to constables, watchmen and magistrates, although we have no way of knowing the proportion of crimes that were not reported to the authorities (Weaver 1995: 21; Fingard 1989; Marquis 2003).

Most public order charges, unlike traditional private prosecutions for assault, abusive language and larceny, were laid by constables and watchmen. The location of drinking establishments, brothels, dance halls and other forms of plebeian entertainment, together with demographics, local politics and increasing temperance pressures, meant that combatting public drunkenness and disorderly behaviour became the stock in trade of both police and police courts. The trend was evident in the early stages of police reform. Public order offenders were an important part of total prison committals in both Montreal and Quebec prior to the middle of the 1830s (Fecteau 1994: 310–1). Public order arrests constituted at least half of yearly totals in mid-century Toronto and a near proportion in Quebec. Although most of the arrested were male, women were often a sizeable minority of public order offenders. In Montreal in 1854, for example, women were responsible for 1,200 out of 4,200 arrests. The typical offender in Montreal was a male in his twenties or thirties arrested for being drunk or drunk and disorderly in public. In the three years ending in October of 1851 the Halifax police court registered over 1,200 convictions for drunkenness and/or disturbing the peace (Rogers 1984; McCulloch 1990; *Toronto Globe* 1855a; Marquis 2003).

The vigilant eye, judging by the detailed statistics published by city councils, also engaged in a wide variety of regulatory activities, often by default. One mundane but important duty, which in time gave rise to specialized detectives, was the location of stolen and lost property. Merchants, storekeepers and propertied homeowners victimized by burglars, thieves and shoplifters were the most obvious beneficiaries of this practice, but ordinary folk also valued their property and were quite prepared to call for police assistance. In May of 1839, for example, two farmers from Saint Vallière parish visiting Montreal to buy seed lost a tidy sum to card sharps in a tavern. They applied to constables who arrested the swindlers under the police ordinance (Marquis 1996). Stolen articles such as clothing, cloth, tools, dry goods, watches, handkerchiefs and ship fittings were found on suspicious persons or in searches of houses and rooms. Police on patrol also checked the security of locked doors. The "intelligent policeman" who stopped a suspicious woman on Montreal's Notre Dame Street and discovered stolen property justified his intervention on the grounds of her being "a bad character." Pawnbrokers were a constant source of police anxiety and eventually came under police registration and close surveillance. Tavern owners, who also lent money to clients, were suspected of being central to fencing operations. The Montreal inspector of police in 1840 reported that a number of waterfront groggeries, the "rendezvous for soldiers, prostitutes and abandoned characters" dealt in stolen goods. From time to time the police advertised for the public to visit the station houses in order to identify their stolen property (Marquis 1996).

The regulatory authority of the criminal justice system found its most powerful expression in the combination of police and police or municipal courts, which had existed since the 1790s in Montreal and Halifax. Police courts, staffed either by magistrates delegated by the sessions of the peace, mayors and aldermen who were *ex officio* justices of the peace or provincially-appointed stipendiary magistrates, did not provide jury trials but did conduct preliminary examinations in all criminal cases. They also processed summary and bylaw offenders. Canadian legislation in 1849 mandated a stipendiary magistrate and recorder's court for Toronto to replace the police court conducted by the mayor and aldermen (Kealey 1984).

Although viewed as a valuable outlet for popular justice by many urban dwellers, police courts reflected the law's heavy burden on the socially marginal. This was suggested by the ethnic, religious and class composition of those being prosecuted and by biased press accounts that mocked or sentimentalized the plebeian clientele. Officials and journalists also described the use of jails as "houses of refuge" for the poor and idle, and it is clear from Fingard's study of post-Confederation Halifax that many recidivists resorted to the police court and jail as a survival strategy, especially in the winter months. In Montreal in 1854, "the Irish" were the largest ethnic group to be incarcerated, followed by English immigrants, French Canadians and Scottish immigrants. Few "British Canadians," the community's most economically advantaged group, ended up in court and even fewer in jail (Fingard 1989; *Toronto Globe* 1855a).

The modern observer would be struck by the Victorian police court's combination of paternalism and informality, but its regularity and openness was an important stage in the development of bureaucratic justice. By the 1850s and 1860s mayors and aldermen who sat as JPs were replaced by stipendiary (salaried) magistrates. Stipendiaries, whose appointment usually was covered by provincial legislation, had to be trained barristers, a sign that urban petty justice was no longer the preserve of amateurs. Police magistrates, for the press, rivalled and sometimes surpassed chief constables as leading experts on urban crime and social conditions in general. Defence lawyers were a rarity and most defendants were viewed with a mixture of pity and contempt. Either because of pressure from temperance organizations or in response to the growing power of "dry" rhetoric, police and jail reports noted the percentage of prisoners who were "intemperate." In public order and bylaw cases the constable was the prosecutor; the summary proceedings, unless involving assault or theft cases, usually lasted no more than a few minutes. In many cases individuals convicted of petty offences went to jail because they were unable to pay fines (Marquis 1986a; Fingard 1989).

In addition to worries over taxation, early suspicion toward the new police had been based on respect for civil liberties, as they were then understood. Citizens of higher social standing were thought to deserve greater legal protection than the average lower-class person arrested for drunkenness, vagrancy or fighting. The supposed infallibility of the police as prosecutors and witnesses was not immediately nor universally accepted. One Montreal grand jury in 1841, concerned about "malicious prosecution" of individuals by fellow citizens, worried that many had been convicted without any proof of guilt "except that of the policeman who made the arrest" (Marquis 1996). This libertarian comment reflects the persistence of the idea that citizens (or in colonial discourse, "British subjects") needed to watch the police. Occasional criticisms of the actions and intelligence of police constables also issued from magistrates and judges. Yet from the beginning magistrates and grand and petty juries usually sided with police testimony in the courts. The general willingness of magistrates to accept police evidence in summary jurisdiction cases supported a high rate of conviction and put pressure on jails and prisons. The grand jury of the Montreal district opined in 1840 that with the police on the job, crime "was less likely to escape detection and punishment than formerly" (Marquis 1996).

Uniforms, equipment, training and deployment of patrolmen varied from town to town. Toronto's chief Samuel Sherwood in the early 1850s did not enforce strict regulations regarding uniforms and discipline. The result, according to an English observer, was that constables appeared dirty and slovenly. Sherwood's successor, Captain William Prince, introduced "a semi-military style of discipline" and recruited "a superior class, both regards physique and intelligence" (Taylor 1892: 49, 137). Conditions in police stations, which also held overnight lockups, were primitive, but these buildings became a type of crisis centre for families searching for lost children, wives looking for errant husbands and transients seeking shelter form the elements. In this regard station houses reflected the catch-all role of county jails. Although beggars and the homeless were arrested for vagrancy, large numbers of "waifs and strays" were permitted to sleep in police stations. In 1854, for example, the Montreal police arrested only 220 for vagrancy, but sheltered 749 adult men, 574 women and eight boys (Marquis 1986; *Toronto Globe* 1855a).

British North America's police conformed to the English model in several respects: they could be recruited locally, were civilian and generally were not armed with swords or guns. As a Montreal journalist explained in 1849: "English people do not like to see their streets paraded by cutlasses and bayonets" (*Hamilton Spectator* 1849). Montreal and Quebec expected candidates to be bilingual, literate and of good character. During the winter months, Quebec's constables were paid lower wages in keeping with pre-industrial patterns. Outside of these cities, constables did not live in barracks along paramilitary lines, as in Ireland or on the Continent, but among the general populace. In terms of social class, if not ethnicity and religion, they had "more in common with the people on the beat than with the city establishment" (Weaver 1995: 16). This, as much as political accountability, ensured the strong civilian character of Canadian police. Compared to the RIC, there was no officer class, although it was rare until the late nineteenth century for police services to be headed by men who had progressed through the ranks. The early police chiefs were former soldiers, militia officers and men of business. Chief constables preferred to hire young, physically capable men, often from the farm or the ranks of the respectable working class. Aside from physical fitness and proof of moral standing, recruitment was also affected by patronage and personal connections.

RURAL LAW ENFORCEMENT: TRADITION AND INNOVATION

The rural majority (including villagers) remained under the traditional system, which placed considerable responsibilities on the private prosecutor and minimal burdens on the state. Inertia is only one explanation; another is that most rural residents were satisfied by the traditional part-time system. Yet interpersonal disputes and social tensions in the countryside clearly produced violence, theft and vandalism and other crimes (Lewthwaite 1994). Law enforcement and dispute resolution were community based, amateur, part-time and reactive and would remain so in many regions until the twentieth century. Crime was committed not by strangers, but neighbours, employees and relatives. Similarly, for rural Canadians the "law" was embodied not in an impersonal professional, but a neighbour, an employer, political patron or social superior. In Britain, in contrast, the central government provided a push toward modernization with a permissive *Rural Police Act*. By the early 1850s over one-half of the counties of England and Wales had established rural constabularies (Steedman 1984: chapter 1). The possibility of a provincial constabulary was debated in Canada West in the 1850s, but the project was shelved.

Most rural British North Americans remained untouched by such innovations. The lack of a gentry class, which traditionally added to social stability in Britain, placed greater social control duties on the rural middle class. Magistrates were the key players, yet without community support their effectiveness was limited. In Upper Canada's Newcastle district, prosecutions generally began when a colonist made a complaint before a JP, and the victim generally had to act as their own detective in tracking down stolen goods. In terms of summary justice, few members of the colonial elite were involved as complainants or defendants (Lewthwaite 2001: 75–6, 144). In the Gore district, justices of the peace who lived some distance from the jail thought twice about initiating an arrest (Weaver 1988: 28–9). Responses to rural crime and disorder were improvised. Ansom Kemp, JP, of Saint Armand, Lower Canada, called on villagers for assistance when the authorities were tracking down a gang of counterfeiters in 1833. A party of thirty men set out at night, surrounded the suspects while they slept and seized incriminating American banknotes. In 1845, when a tenant farmer shot a neighbour in Tyendinaga Township, Canada West, the sheriff of the Midland district organized a posse in pursuit (Marquis 1996). The situation would not change until provincial forces such as the early OPP began to extend state power into the countryside and northern frontier in the early twentieth century.

One interim measure, prior to provincial government intervention, was to send in outside assistance when local magistrates and constables were unwilling or unable to act. A dramatic example of this was the response to the murder of Protestant farmer Robert Corrigan in Saint Sylvestre, a rural community south of Quebec City, in 1855. Corrigan, a troublesome character, had been embroiled in a feud with local Irish Catholics when he was assaulted by a group of men at an agricultural fair. The feud reflected the relatively high levels of interpersonal violence in agrarian society. Corrigan was able to name his assailants before he died of his injuries. Local magistrates, either out of fear or party feeling, refused to act. A party of three hundred armed Protestants conveyed Corrigan's body to a neighbouring county, to keep the assailants from hampering the coroner's inquest. At first the locals refused to cooperate with external authority, which included a party of constables under the head of the Montreal Water Police and a large force of British soldiers. The fugitives eventually surrendered and seven were indicted for murder. The defendants treated the court proceedings with levity, and there was evidence of both perjury and intimidation of witnesses. The men were acquitted, which gave more fuel to Protestant arguments in the United Canadas that Roman Catholicism was a threat to liberty and public safety. Barlow (1998) concludes that the Corrigan murder epitomized the weakness of the pre-Confederation state.

The rural constable usually was more active in the civil capacity, the key to "going to law" in both pre-industrial and industrial society. Research suggests that the average Canadian did not always differentiate between the civil and criminal sides when attempting to secure justice (Lewthwaite 1994: 363–4). The fact that debtors could be arrested and jailed highlighted this popular confusion. When constables serving legal process encountered resistance, civil matters quickly became criminal. In 1818 James Landergan of Cubit's, on Newfoundland's Conception Bay, had his boat seized for debt by Constable Michael Kelly. He refused, however, to give up his fishing room or shore station. Constable William Keating, after serving a summons calling Landergan to court in Port de Grave, took him into custody on board a Royal Navy vessel for contempt of court. On the basis of Kelly's testimony he was sentenced by the naval surrogate court to thirty-six lashes with the cat-o'-nine-tails. In an appeal to the Newfoundland Supreme Court that tested the constitutionality of corporal punishment as meted out by naval surrogates, the testimony of Keating, who was from Port de Grave, was more sympathetic to the accused (Colonial Office 1825). In this case the property of a fisherman, through intervention by the high constable, ended up in the hands of the mercantile firm to which he was indebted for supplies, a stark reminder of the class nature of justice and the blurred lines between civil and criminal law. In rural society we also see glimpses of the "two concepts of justice," which for centuries had characterized village constables in England. As Storch explains, local magistrates and constables, "rooted in their communities, tied by kinship, friendship, and economic relationships to those they lived among, … often reflected popular or 'folk' conceptions of crime" (Storch 1989: 224).

Because they were part-time amateurs who usually worked alone, rural constables had no corporate identity as policemen. Their relationship with the rural magistrate, about which we know little at present, was crucial. The justice of the peace ruled on the legality of summary arrests and issued warrants and other legal process, which the constable executed. Magistrates sitting alone, in pairs or in sessions of the peace, also were the constables' paymasters. Constables, who were embedded in their communities, were suspected of tempering their responses to breaches of the peace and other legal matters. Another criticism was that constables of limited means were overzealous in order to collect fees and expenses. Turnover, for a variety of reasons, often was high. A judge writing in the middle of the nineteenth century estimated that Canada West's 550 townships and towns contained 2,800 constables. Only a minority were reappointed from one year to the next (Marquis 1993: 17).

In general the state, in terms of ordering rural society, did little more than appoint the part-time officials discussed above. As the temperance issue was to demonstrate, community self-policing remained the key factor. An exception was made for the special conditions brought about by large-scale public works projects. In these cases economic forces, backed by politics, produced administrative and legal change. Prior to Confederation the business and political elites pursued development strategies, based on canals and railways, aided by government financing. During the 1840s up to ten thousand canal labourers were employed at any one time in Canada West. In extreme cases, as when Lachine canal navvies from competing regions of Ireland clashed in 1843, the civil power called on the British military, with often deadly results. If there was no local garrison the less reliable colonial militia was available. Troops also were deployed at a strike by workers on the Beauharnois canal at Sainte-Timothée in 1843 where relations between French Canadian residents and Irish workers had deteriorated. A newly formed canal police did little to assuage social tensions. When a crowd of several hundred protesting labourers ignored the reading of the *Riot Act* and attempted to surround the soldiers, the latter opened fire, killing or fatally wounding six men (Senior 1981). Riot control, rural or urban, remained the responsibility of the magistracy. Their success usually owed more to tact than the threat of force. In 1844 Toronto Orangemen planned to celebrate the Twelfth of July by visiting Niagara by steamer. The embarkation point was Queenstown. On the way the celebrants heard a rumour that up to two thousand hostile Irish canal labourers planned to attack their procession. The Loyal Orange Association leaders called on local justices of the peace to provide protection. The latter negotiated a deal with the "Catholic party": if the Protestant excursionists left their guns behind and played no offensive tunes on their fifes, the authorities pledged their safety. The trip came off without incident. The Queenstown magistrates had skilfully avoided bloodshed, but they had held a body of the Canadian Rifles in readiness to aid the civil power, just in case (*Toronto Globe* 1844).

Like urban disturbances, rural social violence, usually linked to politics or disputes at public works projects, underscored for police reformers the urgency of avoiding the deployment of the military in emergency situations. The *Montreal Gazette*, noting that three parishes in Beauharnois County, Canada East, lacked Francophone JPs, recommended a French-speaking stipendiary magistrate and a police force along the line of the canal. Irish navvies fought amongst themselves that same year along Upper Canada's Welland canal. Violence associated with public works led to special legislation that enhanced the colonial government's involvement in law enforcement. The 1845 *Act for the Better Preservation of the Peace, and the Prevention of Riots and Violent Outrages at and Near Public Works, While in Progress of Construction* introduced the registration of firearms along canal construction lines. This approach would also be employed along the construction route of railways. In "proclaimed" districts all arms, ranging from daggers to muskets, were to be seized, and stipendiary magistrates were to punish those concealing weapons. The law allowed the government, under the Board of Works, to recruit a mounted police force of up to one hundred officers and men. Both the Welland and Williamsburg canal police, largely Protestant in composition, were criticized for aggressive and biased actions. These establishments, despite the backing of the state, were concerned more with protecting strikebreakers and private property than with the fair resolution of disputes. They were assisted by Roman Catholic priests hired to act as police agents. In a nod toward police systems in Ireland or non-white colonies, chief constables and their subordinate officers were given the powers of justices of the peace (Canada 1846; Bleasdale 1981). Pre-Confederation era state constabularies and special rural magistrates were never intended to be permanent. The enlightened statist tradition, stronger in British North America than the United States, would influence the national government in 1873 when it formed a new constabulary for the northwestern frontier. Part-time fee-for-service constables and amateur justices of the peace whose political credentials usually outweighed any lack of legal training were the norm in rural Canada well into the twentieth century. Greer describes the police system of mid-1830s rural Lower Canada as a "ramshackle affair," and in the French parishes indeed it was. But the effectiveness of the traditional English system as it operated among British North America's rural majority should not be underestimated (Greer 1992: 19).

CONCLUSION

At the outset of the nineteenth century in British North America, the vigilant eye was the community itself. By the 1850s, at least in urban centres, it was a group of full-time, uniformed specialists who walked the beat, gathered intelligence on the community, made arrests, initiated prosecutions in the lower courts and maintained records. The term *police* now applied "exclusively to men hired to enforce the law" (Gilje 1987: 267). This was more than a simple change in terminology. The arrival of police services, however rudimentary, meant that the community, or its elites, had delegated authority in preserving order and apprehending malefactors. This was part of a general nineteenth-century trend toward specialization, professionalization and bureaucratization. The justice system was becoming both less cruel in terms of punishment and more intrusive in terms of state surveillance of the populace. As Weaver explains, the reformation of punishment and other branches of the justice system "constituted a narrowing of scope for community participation in matters of local justice and order" (Weaver 1988: 39). Community elites remained willing to tolerate and even exploit occasional violence for political ends, but the very institutions they had created, such as police departments, police courts, penitentiaries and public schools, worked to contain rioting and other forms of social violence. And so did political parties, church congregations, temperance associations and the popular press. The spread of bourgeois culture, as in the northern United States (but not necessarily the South), undermined practices such as vengeance and vigilantism.

Police services appeared during a complex period in the evolution of Canadian society. Three different styles of policing — the traditional, new urban police and state-controlled rural constabularies — were evident in British North America by the 1850s. Liberalism's official message was equality before the law, but enforcement, in practice, reflected the complexities of class and ethnic relations. As paternalism waned, it was replaced with not only the discipline of the market, but also new institutions of social control: asylums, schools, penitentiaries, reformatories and police. Under paternalism and customary law, Canadians had depended on a part-time, user-pay justice, informal community controls and a mixture of cruelty and tolerance. Bureaucratic justice, of which the police were a key component, promised increased surveillance of the population and greater certainty of punishment. Increasingly the chief constable, not the chief magistrate, was at the centre of urban law and order. Magistrates, unless involved in general police administration, would concentrate on purely judicial duties. The combination of beat patrols under centralized command, permanent lockups, new criminal statutes and municipal bylaws governing behaviour and regular police courts would produce a marked rise in recorded offences. It is unlikely that this represented an absolute increase in antisocial behaviour. Police services, by their very "watchfulness," produced greater numbers of minor offenders (Beattie 1995). British North America, in small steps, was on its way to developing the "policeman-state" (Gatrell 1990). Police departments, along with police courts, jails and penitentiaries, also became a source of important social statistics utilized by a wide range of reformers. As both Victorian commentators and modern criminologists attest, the police, despite their official mandate, were not effective at preventing either crime or disorder. The new institution exercised considerable discretion. In the medium term, the approach of the police to working-class populations and their leisure activities was "calculated pragmatism" (Inwood 1990: 141). And if the law of custom was increasingly replaced by the written code of the state, the new order, like the old, depended on citizen initiative in responding to the crimes of assault and theft (Emsley 1983: 163). At least part of the emerging institution of policing was reactive, not proactive.

CHAPTER 2

POLICING
THE NEW DOMINION

In terms of innovation, the post-Confederation era was characterized by two competing styles of policing: municipal and territorial. One model was relatively democratic, the other authoritarian, yet even the latter model enjoyed a degree of legitimacy, partly as the result of a romanticized image popular with people who did not live on the western frontier.

This chapter will focus on the relationship between law enforcement and urbanization and the use of federal policing as a force for white settler consolidation of the West. The North West Territory, acquired in 1870, would be subject to legal experimentation unknown in the rest of Canada, primarily because few of its residents were Canadian citizens (or to use the term of the era, "British subjects"). In addition to NWMP relations with First Nations and settlers, this chapter will explore police interactions with the urban working class, women and ethnic and racial minorities and responses to middle-class and elite reformers who promoted agendas of temperance and social purity. The latter movements made policing, and the justice system in general, highly controversial by the late nineteenth century.

POLICING THE MID-TO-LATE VICTORIAN CITY

As discussed in the previous chapter, the origins of policing were local. Law enforcement was not a priority in the constitutional negotiations, legislative speeches, newspaper editorials and election campaigns that created the Dominion of Canada in 1867. The strongest leader of the Confederation movement from 1864 onwards, and the first prime minister of Canada, John A. Macdonald, envisioned a centralized federalism, where provincial governments had slightly more powers than municipalities. The federal government, under the *British North America Act* of 1867, was responsible for criminal law, but provincial and municipal governments were tasked with its enforcement. As in the United States, in this age of limited government, policing was best kept as a local service, determined by municipal ratepayers and officials. Tax payer resistance and the desire of mayors and town and city councils to be economical was the single biggest restraint on police power in the second half of the nineteenth century. The result was a decentralized system of policing where degrees of civilian control, departmental priorities, deployment, training, remuneration and relations with various elements in the community varied from one urban centre to the next. Despite this, the late Victorian city was both more heavily policed and outwardly more orderly than its pre-Confederation counterpart, and the local police department, although rudimentary by later standards, was a sophisticated urban service bureaucracy. It also tended to have higher rates of arrest, relative to population, than early to mid twentieth-century communities. Canada remained a society of villages and farms; in 1891, Montreal, the nation's largest city, had under 220,000 residents and Toronto, the second largest, less than 190,000. Policing duties tended to be similar whether in small centres such as Charlottetown or large cities such as Montreal, but the nature of each community created special challenges. In Halifax, for example, transient sailors as well as member of the Royal Navy and British garrison often were prominent in offences against public order and patronized brothels as well as legal and illegal drinking establishments. In Quebec City the size of the police department, and of the River Police, fluctuated with the seasonal workforce associated with the shipping sector and the timber trade (Marquis 1980; Fingard 1989).

Despite developing as part of a patchwork system, with regional differences apparent, nineteenth-century Canadian police departments shared common core characteristics. Constables were deployed on regular beats and kept an eye out for suspicious or out of place individuals. Following the night watch tradition, they reported and reacted to fires, defective streetlamps, stray animals and unlocked doors and kept order on the streets. It is unlikely that the average patrolman made more than one arrest a week. The typical arrest was not the result of threats to individuals or property but violations of public order such as drunkenness, disturbing the peace and vagrancy. Police resources were deployed in business districts, waterfront areas and near recreational facilities frequented by the working class, particularly young males. As criminologists have noted, as in the twentieth century the poor bore the brunt of police coercion; they were both over-policed and under-policed as they, and not the middle class, were the typical victims of crime (Stern 2006). Weaver's research on Hamilton reveals that police interventions focused on marginal groups, but that their social control efforts were inconsistent

(Weaver 1995: 115–6). As in other urban environments, the first generation or two of police focused on establishing "minimum standards of order" short of provoking widespread resistance (Inwood 1990: 141). The "pacification" of the nineteenth-century city was gradual and involved institutions, social movements and processes such as evangelicalism, temperance, public education, anti-cruelty movements, public health reform and municipal zoning (Monkkonen 1981).

The official ideology of policing, when it was discussed at all, was that Canada had inherited the "British" approach based on the principles laid down by Robert Peel and his supporters: the police were a civilian, barely or lightly armed organization that was subjected to discipline; was accountable to the rule of law; placed most of its resources into preventative patrol and was somewhat insulated from direct political control in terms of operations. As the chief agency of social control in an era when cities lacked basic welfare and other services, the police adopted a "carrot and stick" approach. Early on, police department records became an important source of social statistics for the Victorian city. The Toronto chief constable's report for 1897, for example, referred to suicides, accidental deaths, ambulance calls, baby farming, stolen bicycles, fortune tellers, cruelty to animals, the licensing of newsboys and bootblacks and the use of distress warrants (*Toronto Globe* 1898). Yet these reports were neither complete nor consistent. In some cities, for example, the police did not record the number of intoxicated individuals they escorted home or the number of disturbances they quelled in private residences. The overall impression is that much of the work of the nineteenth-century police fell under the heading of routine urban regulation.

The class mandate of the police was clearly reflected in arrest statistics that detailed occupational characteristics and through the filter of press coverage of urban police or stipendiary magistrates' courts, the equivalent of the modern provincial court. Measured by volume of prosecution, these courts were literally becoming "police" courts, but they were still valued by the poor and the working class for settling disputes (Marquis 1986a; Fingard 1989: 50). These generalist criminal tribunals handled everything from bylaw infractions such as encumbered sidewalks or unlicensed dogs to preliminary examinations for murder. The statistics for Saint John echoed patterns that were evident prior to Confederation. Between 1863 and 1889, public order arrests averaged 60 percent of the total, followed by arrests for assault at 10 to 15 percent and for property offences at 5 to 10 percent. The latter category included larceny, embezzlement, robbery, burglary, receiving stolen goods, vandalism and counterfeiting. Arrests for crimes against the person and offences such as larceny originated with public complaints; the police themselves were the source of most other complaints. As noted by Marquis, Weaver and others, many property offences were associated with lower-class complainants. Vagrancy arrests fluctuated from less than 1 to 14 percent in this period, and "strangers" or nonresidents were particularly vulnerable (Marquis 1986a, 2003; Weaver 1995: 77). Halifax police reports reflected similar patterns. The emphasis on public order created a statistical effect that suggested that a large minority of the citizenry was hauled into the police lockup on an annual basis (the equivalent of one out of thirteen Toronto residents in 1867) (Marquis 1980; Prince 1868). Where records do survive for late Victorian police courts, they reveal some basic patterns. As Fingard has suggested for Halifax, the "dark side" of the late Victorian city was the embattled existence of "jail bids," a small number of habitual petty offenders who were known to the police as well as to city prison, county jail and Poor House officials. In one ten-year period, one-time offenders were 25 percent of all committals to the city prison, but ninety-two recidivists constituted almost one-third of all committals. For the urban underclass, crime was not deviancy but "a rational strategy for survival" (Fingard 1989: 35, 78). Recidivism was also a factor in Toronto, where in 1885 the police arrested 1,400 people two times or more (*Toronto Globe* 1886).

Although bylaw infractions may have been more representative of the class structure of the community, most people arrested by police services in the Victorian era were plebeian. Between 1866 and 1900, 77 percent of those arrested or summoned to court in Charlottetown were labourers, farmers, tradesmen and mariners (Marquis 1988: 96). The arrest statistics for Toronto for 1872 included a detailed occupational breakdown that included 1,555 labourers, 121 tavern keepers, 120 clerks and 464 prostitutes (Toronto was not the only department to officially recognize the latter occupation). Males outnumbered women (although not as dramatically as in later decades), and Canadians headed the list of nationalities, followed closely by the Irish. Reflective of police practices elsewhere, most offences were misdemeanours (*Toronto Globe* 1873). Once before the magistrate, few offenders were sentenced to jail outright, but in practice many ended up in custody because they could not pay fines.

Another striking feature of the nineteenth-century police court was the large proportion of cases that ended up with discharges or dismissals. This can be explained by a number of possible factors: arrests on the basis of suspicion; use of discretion by station sergeants or inspectors; leniency by magistrates and the failure of private prosecutors to appear in court (*Toronto Globe* 1886). The latter was countered in the late nineteenth century by the appointment of public prosecutors. Ontario, for example, passed legislation in the late 1850s authorizing county crown attorneys. In practice crown attorneys did not intervene in most assault and larceny cases (Weaver 1995: 82–4).

The police themselves were of working class or agrarian origins. In theory (and according to formalized rules) recruits had to be of good moral character and possess basic reading and writing skills. The physical nature of the job was reflected by minimum height and weight requirements. Training was based on the artisanal model of learning the ropes from experienced constables, although various departments experimented with more formal training, including target practice and military drill. Militarization, part of a North American trend, was a deliberate strategy of police chiefs and boards of police commissioners to instill control and discipline. The Toronto department's book of regulations in the 1860s was more than one hundred pages long. In Toronto, police officers could not enter a public house when on duty and could not enter into a debt. In a number of police services (especially the North-West Mounted Police), officers required permission of a senior officer before they could marry. The Toronto patrolman, who was to refrain from smoking, whistling or carrying an umbrella when on patrol, was reminded to be polite to citizens of all social classes and to walk his timed beat at the rate of two and a half miles per hour. Shifts began with military-style inspections of men and equipment. Constables on patrol were instructed to become familiar with all streets, shops, residences and residents on their beat and to make notes of anything out of the ordinary. This militarized and bureaucratic approach to organization and discipline, together with attempts to build esprit de corps, were the seeds of occupational isolation and mistrust of the public that would be manifest by the middle of the twentieth century (Prince 1868; Rogers 1984; Weaver 1995: 98–101).

The relationship of the police to political officials was one of the burning issues in late nineteenth-century law enforcement, and it turned on a question that remains central to modern governance: who controls the police? One of the weaknesses of American urban policing, for late Victorian reformers, was the power of political machines, mayors and councils over municipal services such as policing. This was democratic control in its rawest form. The other extreme, in the British world, was the RIC, which reported to the Chief Secretary of Ireland or the London Metropolitan Police, which in turn was accountable to the national government through the Home Office. As noted in the Introduction, other governance systems in England and Wales were more democratic but still dominated by elites. One American innovation, designed to counter direct political control, was the police commission model. This spread to Canada and was adopted in provinces including Manitoba and Ontario during the late nineteenth century. The Board of Police Commissioners for Toronto consisted of the mayor, a police magistrate and a county court judge. The appointment of judges to a police supervisory body was a conflict of interest, but it was not unknown in other regulatory bodies such as liquor licensing boards. The commissioners set overall policy, acted as a disciplinary and citizens' complaints body and in many levels insulated the police chief and the rest of the department from political pressures (Marquis 1986b: chapter 1). Modern critics have not been convinced of the effectiveness of this governance mechanism (see, for example, Sewell 1985: 166–7).

The responsibility of city councils was to provide funding for annual budgets. Where police commissions did not exist, as in urban Quebec, mayors and municipal councils were in direct control of the police. Another variant was in Saint John, where a colonial government-appointed police magistrate supervised the municipal force from 1849 to 1856. In the latter year control was vested in a chief of police who by statute was appointed not by the municipal government but the provincial cabinet. Although there were variations, based on the few case studies that have been completed it appears that most police chiefs operated their departments with considerable autonomy. At the time this was viewed as a manifestation of Canada's "British" character. And in most towns and cities, one sign of operational autonomy and relative insulation from partisan politics was the relatively long tenure of chief constables (Marquis 1986a, 1993).

Post-Confederation police and press reports detail numerous assaults, brawls and assaults on police, but the large scale rioting of the earlier era was less frequent. In addition to labour-related issues (discussed in Chapter 4), ethnic and sectarian tensions were still capable of producing social violence. In theory the unarmed or lightly armed police would be a less blunt instrument of crowd control than the military. In 1853, for example, the Catholic mayor of Montreal had ordered British regulars to fire on a group of Irish Catholics who were protesting a talk by the visiting Italian anti-clerical lecturer, Alessandro Gavazzi. Ten were killed and fifty wounded (Senior 1981: chapter 7). In 1875 the largely Protestant Toronto police attempted to enforce the law impartially by protecting Catholic processions from attacks by Orangemen. Three years later the force guarded American Fenian speaker O'Donovan Rossa from a hostile Protestant crowd. Another test of police neutrality and discipline were the disturbances in Montreal in 1885 connected to a deadly smallpox epidemic. By the time the disease had run its course, several thousand had been infected and more than 3,200, most of them children, had died. Working-class resistance to quarantines and vaccination combined with French-English tensions exacerbated by news of a death sentence imposed on Louis Riel, leader of the North West Rebellion. Crowds threatened or attacked police stations, the office of the Board of Health, city hall, a newspaper office and the residences of doctors, officials and politicians who supported compulsory vaccination. Although the police battled with rioters on the Champs de Mars, they were criticized for acting too slowly and indecisively. Militia units of infantry, artillery and cavalry, under command of an officer who had helped to quell the North West Rebellion, were deployed to keep the peace (Bliss 1991).

As noted in the previous chapter, the police acquired, often by default, another important function that was only marginally related to crime prevention: delivering a variety of services (Kozminski 2009). The pattern continues to this day, where some estimate that up to 80 percent of police time is taken up with non-crime related duties. As a number of scholars have suggested, the service mission of the police, and the functional role of local police stations within their neighbourhoods or communities, served to legitimate the police institution with the working class, which in the nineteenth century was the source of greatest opposition. These services included returning lost children to their parents and offering overnight shelter to homeless or transient individuals who under other circumstances could have been arrested for vagrancy (Marquis 1986a). In some years the number of persons sheltered surpassed the number of individuals arrested for vagrancy. This service was seasonal and tended to reflect business cycle and labour market trends. In Hamilton in 1878, for example, the police hostel sheltered nearly 1,400 in a three month period. During the 1880s the average was one thousand per late winter season. In many towns the police also provided "waifs and strays" with food (Weaver 1995: 134–6). The use of police stations as emergency shelters reflected the mobile and seasonal nature of the Canadian workforce and the lack of public and private social welfare provision. This role continued in most towns and cities into the twentieth century, when hotels, missions and soup kitchens run by the Salvation Army and other church organizations began to offer basic aid to the less fortunate.

Since their inception, police agencies have never been totally comfortable with their service and social welfare involvements, but these services have played an important pragmatic role. A study of the work of the Toronto police morality bureau for a slightly later period suggests that it was not simply an agent of middle-class moral assault on the working class but was viewed as a source of help, often by default, for working-class people, especially women who had been abused or abandoned by their spouses (Marquis 1986b, 1992). The pacification of the nineteenth century was accomplished by a combination of "hard" and "soft" policing, a strategy that continues to this day. One sign was a gradual drop in resistance to police on the beat, with a corresponding de-escalation of police weaponry. For a number of years following its inception the Saint John police carried pistols and sabres on patrol. These were replaced during the more civilized 1860s with batons, but after a flare up of violence in the early 1870s, patrolmen were armed with pistols. Similarly, in 1883 the board of police commissioners authorized the arming of Hamilton police on night patrol following a series of burglaries. In the 1890s, men on the beat were instructed to sheathe their batons, much like the London bobby (*Toronto Globe* 1883; Marquis 1986a; Weaver 1995). In early twentieth-century Halifax the police chief did not trust his officers to carry revolvers (Boudreau 2012a: 41)

Civil rights and multicultural advocates, as well as legal scholars, have long identified a "racial gap" in terms of public confidence in the police. Like residential segregation, policing is both a cause and effect of ethnic and racial prejudice and discrimination. Although Victorian Canada lacked a sizeable visible minority population in its cities, the twentieth-century racial gap was rooted in the relationships

POLICING THE NEW DOMINION   47

and practices of the late nineteenth-century city. The chief mandate of the urban police was to protect and serve their communities, yet these benefits were not evenly distributed. This was an issue that Canadians prior to the 1960s or 1970s associated with the United States, particularly in the Southern states, but were reluctant to acknowledge in relation to their own society. Although differential treatment by the police and courts of visible minorities was noticeable in cities such as Halifax, and press reports reflected racist attitudes toward Black and other minority lawbreakers, the debate over fair policing, when it was discussed in the press or political sphere, was framed in terms of white ethnic and religious minorities. The most vivid example of differential policing was the arrest and conviction rate of Irish Catholics, particularly those born in Ireland, compared to other "British" residents of cities such as Hamilton, Toronto, Saint John and Halifax. Between the 1850s and 1870s and beyond, this ethnic group was overrepresented in arrest, conviction and incarceration rates (Marquis 1986a; Weaver 1995; Price 1990). The trend applied to men as well as women, such as Irish-born Catherine O'Hern, who was sentenced to jail in Toronto seventy-seven times starting in 1843 (Backhouse 1985: 406). Police services in these late Victorian cities were dominated by Protestants who also controlled the local power structure. The overrepresentation of Irish Catholics anticipated a question that has been raised about the disproportionate presence of African Canadians and First Nations individuals in the modern justice system: was policing reflecting and reinforcing racial and ethnic prejudices, or was it a reflection of urban geography and socio-economic privation?

There is a long history in Canada, from evangelical Protestants in the 1850s to the Reform Party in the 1980s, of blaming crime and other social problems on immigrants (Gordon 2006: chapter 5). Discriminatory immigration policies ensured that the visible minority presence in Canada would be limited. It was almost impossible for Blacks, for example, to enter Canada as permanent residents. The small Black population in Ontario and the Maritimes was descended from Loyalist refugees (some of whom had been slaves), War of 1812 refugees and fugitive slaves and free Blacks who had fled the United States prior to the Civil War. Partly because of their low numbers we know little about how they were treated by the justice system, but based on newspaper coverage of arrests and prosecution, the dominant culture usually looked down on visible minorities, viewing them as untrustworthy, violent, lustful and childlike and not deserving the full protections of "British justice." The visible minority presence in the Victorian city was limited, but evidence from Halifax jail records from the 1860s and 1870s is suggestive. Fingard (1989) has shown that African Canadians were only 3 percent of the population, but that African Canadian women were 40 percent of prostitutes sent to jail (many of them unable to pay their fines). Discriminatory attitudes, and criminal justice involvements, continued into the next century (Boudreau 2012a: 162–8).

Chinese labourers first arrived on the West coast in the 1850s as part of a gold rush. Anti-Asian racism gained force in the 1870s, and starting in 1885 Chinese sojourners or immigrants were forced to pay a head tax. And Chinese immigrants and their children could not hope to become citizens until the 1940s. As the next chapter discusses, during the early twentieth century the Chinese minority would be criminalized in specific ways. There were few Chinese in Canada outside of British Columbia, but in that province their presence created tensions with the white majority. By 1887 many former Chinese construction workers had settled in the Vancouver area. This prompted resentment from organized labour; the Knights of Labour, for example, demanded their expulsion. White workers, some of them unemployed, assaulted the Chinese quarter, setting fire to buildings and plundering property. The provincial government responded by suspending the city charter and imposing a provincial police on the community. The special constables, who were armed with Colt revolvers, were somewhat unpopular with the white majority. In 1888 Vancouver regained control of its police, yet the city would be rocked by anti-Asian riots twenty years later (Stonier-Newman 1991: 53–5). In 1892, a white mob in the frontier town of Calgary, blaming a smallpox outbreak on the small Chinese community, began to attack buildings housing the minority. With the town police unable or unwilling to act, the NWMP intervened to restore order. The issue here was not the protection of a vulnerable minority, but the desire of the police to suppress any major outbreak of vigilante violence (Macleod 1998: 89–90).

Our understanding of the role of police in late Victorian society is derived from three types of primary sources, each one with its limitations: the official reports of police departments, which included statistics on arrests, data on internal organiza-tion and deployment and financial expenditures (internal documentation such as routine correspondence and records relating to personnel, such as disciplinary and service records, did not always survive or end up in archives open to the public); court and other documents relating to investigations and prosecutions involving the police; and contemporary press coverage of policing and crime issues in a given community. Newspaper portrayals of the police, positive and negative, were the single most powerful source of public knowledge, much like the situation in mod-ern society where citizens derive their knowledge on crime and policing not from direct experience but from messages and images disseminated through electronic and print media (Sacco 2005). Although a number of twentieth-century police chiefs and RCMP commissioners penned memoirs, it is rare to find surviving diaries or letters of actual police on the beat or detectives from the nineteenth century. One exception was John Wilson Murray, a late nineteenth-century detective in the employ of the Ontario government, who in 1904 published *Memoirs of a Great Detective* (partially or wholly written by a journalist). Yet Murray's account, however entertaining, was hardly typical of late Victorian policing. And Murray (or his author) made a distinction between policemen and detectives (Phillips and Fortune n.d.).

The relationship between the urban police and the press is a long one. In the United States, the *National Police Gazette*, the so-called "bible of the barbershop," invented tabloid journalism by sensationalizing crime in the 1840s. Featuring grizzly and lurid crimes from the police blotter, the journal branched out to include sports, pictures of attractive women and show business gossip. The target audience of this publication was the working class male. By the late nineteenth century its tough-on-crime approach also condemned or belittled Blacks, immigrants and other minorities as well as elites and corrupt politicians. Although muckraking editors and journalists from time to time criticized police violence, neglect or corruption and sided with specific offenders as underdogs, the press overall was supportive of the larger aims of policing and tended to view police chiefs and other senior officers at the true experts on crime and other urban problems. The police valued their contacts with reporters and the feeling was reciprocated when the latter required information for stories. Boudreau (2012a) sees the early twentieth-century Halifax press as a mechanism of social control. The public avidly consumed local press accounts of police court proceedings and stories of violent or audacious crimes and their investigation, which was the original "true crime" literature. These narratives invariably stressed that crime was the product of selfish or weak individuals, although sympathetic portrayals of offenders were not unknown.

Even today, the public derives most of its knowledge of crime and policing, and reactions such as fear of crime, from media accounts. In 2013, RCMP enforcing a court injunction against shale gas protestors at Rexton, New Brunswick, used aggressive tactics, storming the protestors' camp and arresting several people. Many of the demonstrators were from First Nations communities. Because most residents of the province learned about the events from newspapers, radio and television news programs or online news sources that were heavily influenced by RCMP media releases and interviews, an opinion poll later suggested that a majority of New Brunswickers agreed that the RCMP's actions, which included heavily armed and camouflaged Emergency Response Team officers pointing guns at protestors, had been appropriate (Corporate Research Associates 2014).

LAW AND AUTHORITY IN RURAL SOCIETY

Canada remained a largely rural society in the late nineteenth century, and for the most part rural areas in the central and eastern provinces continued to be served by part-time magistrates and constables. The fact that these individuals were untrained, appointed in many cases for partisan reasons and rooted in their communities, could lead to complications. The gap between rural and urban policing, and the financial hardships imposed on part-time constables, were factors behind an inaugural meeting of the Chief Constables Association of Canada (CCAC) in 1881. In reality this early manifestation of the more permanent CCAC was a meeting of Ontario chiefs and the Montreal chief. One of the proposals discussed was a "government police," meaning a centralized provincial or national constabulary with uniform training and pay rates (*Toronto Globe* 1881). In 1882, the deputy attorney general of Ontario asked judges, sheriffs, Crown attorneys and chief constables whether the province needed full-time salaried detectives or constables in rural areas in order to detect serious crime. Most of the respondents replied in the affirmative, citing a lack of training, financial support and motivation for both JPs and constables. Constables were accused both of being inactive out of fear or impartiality and being too active against personal enemies in the community. The prospect of a centralized, professional approach to rural law enforcement appealed to modernizers, but it was opposed by traditional elites and communities that resented "outside influences" (Sharpe 2011: 23–6).

Historians cannot speak with much authority about levels of crime and the dynamics of law enforcement in rural society. One of the greatest tests for rural constables in the late nineteenth century was the enforcement of provincial liquor licence legislation, or the quasi-prohibitory *Canada Temperance Act*, which permitted townships and counties to ban the retail sale of alcohol. Evidence from prominent criminal cases, usually murders, suggests that in addition to untrained, amateur magistrates and constables, other members of the community helped solve crimes and bring suspects to justice. And prior to the appearance of professional police in rural Canada, coroners played an important investigatory role in murder cases. Both of these patterns were evident following the 1883 murder of farmer Peter Lazier in Ontario's Prince Edward County. In addition, the Lazier case, which resulted in the conviction and execution of two local men, represented the transition to modern policing as it drew in the police chief of the nearby town of Belleville, who took over the investigation and introduced "urban" investigatory methods such as forensic science (however flawed in this particular case) and police deception in dealing with suspects or witnesses (Sharpe 2011).

One of the more dramatic examples of how the part-time, amateur and user-pay approach to law enforcement failed to guarantee neutral "British justice" was the notorious series of events that took place in and around the village of Lucan in Biddulph Township, northwest of London, Ontario, in the 1870s and 1880s. In 1880 feuding among Irish immigrants escalated to the point where a group of vigilantes attacked and killed four members of the Donnelly family, including two women, and set their house on fire. The "vigilance committee" then proceeded to the nearby house of another branch of the family and fatally shot John Donnelly.

These violent assaults were the culmination of a long-standing vendetta that involved threats, arson, vandalism, theft, assaults, animal maiming, brawls, gunfire and lawsuits and countersuits. Many in the community faulted the Donnellys and believed that if their lawlessness could not be eradicated by "British justice," then they deserved to be exterminated (Reaney 2004).

The fifteen people arrested as a result of the investigation included one constable and one JP; the former was a known enemy of the Donnellys and the latter had been a suspect in the unsolved 1857 murder of an English settler. As was typical when serious crimes took place near urban centres, the authorities enlisted the help of the London police, who sent the chief and a detective. The investigation of the Donnelly murders, and the Donnelly story in general, suggests the complex nature of village/rural social relations. The implicated constable, James Carroll, also assumed to be the ringleader of the attack, was tried and acquitted for murder, but subjected to a remarkable admonition by one of the trial judges, who declared that the year he had spent in jail awaiting trial, as well as the very real threat of a revenge attack on his person, was fitting punishment for his serious dereliction of duty. The home of a key witness for the Crown was burned to the ground and two trials failed to convict any of the suspected killers. Despite this, being a member of an infamous family whom many in the community believed to have deserved their fate did not deter William Donnelly from serving as a constable in the 1880s. The Donnelly clan, both before and after the mass murders, had both enemies and allies among the justice officials of Middlesex County (Reaney 2004: 251).

Tentative steps were taken in the late nineteenth century toward the formation of territorial constabularies. Following the establishment of the province of Manitoba in 1870, a Canadian militia officer was authorized to form a twenty-man Mounted Constabulary Force. The name changed to the Provincial Police Force, then the Manitoba Provincial Police. The force delivered policing services in rural Manitoba until it was absorbed by the RCMP in the early 1930s. The British colony of Vancouver Island, which was administered by the Hudson Bay Company, was originally policed by a paramilitary unit of "Voltigeurs." In 1858 the colonial government hired Irishman Augustus Pemberton as stipendiary magistrate and commissioner of police for the town of Victoria. One of his main duties was preserving the peace with the aboriginal peoples of the region, who often camped near the colony's capital. British Columbia, which joined Confederation in 1871, had a small provincial force that dated back to 1858 when the colonial authorities recruited Chartres Brew, an inspector in the Irish Constabulary, as assistant chief gold commissioner and chief inspector of police. That year more than 25,000 prospectors arrived in British Columbia in search of gold. Brew, who also served as a magistrate, appointed constables to preserve order in the gold fields. Both Brew and the commissioner of police at Victoria believed in the use of the Royal

Navy as a deterrent against First Nations violence. In 1864, when members of the Chilcoltin (Tsilqot'in) First Nation killed thirteen white road builders and a ferryman, the authorities mobilized the Royal Navy, the small force of police and special constables in response. Five of the six Natives captured under irregular circumstances were hanged. In 1993 the attorney general of British Columbia apologized for the executions. In 1866 Vancouver Island and British Columbia were united. By the late 1860s British Columbia's constables, many of them in single-officer detachments, were scattered among the colony's mining communities (Stonier-Newman 1991; Marquis 1997).

Following British Columbia's entry into Confederation as a province, the constabulary was tasked with covering a huge expanse of territory where the aboriginal population outnumbered whites. Although Indian administration was a federal government responsibility, the provincial police were heavily involved with the aboriginal population. Starting in the early 1880s the construction of the western section of the Canadian Pacific Railway also occupied the force, as provincial legislation trumped a federal law that banned alcohol sales within twenty miles of the rail line. The expansion of the NWMP and federal customs and excise officers into the province relieved part of the burden on the organization. By 1887 the force, which had expanded to forty-four constables, continued to be tasked with non-criminal duties such as collecting miners' licences and taxes on Chinese workers, settling disputes over water rights and reporting on epidemic disease. In 1895 the force was renamed the British Columbia Provincial Police (BCPP), and all constables were placed under command of the superintendent. The Klondike gold rush to the north brought more BCPP officers into the vast territory between the Skeena River and the Yukon border (Stonier-Newman 1991).

The Ontario Provincial Police (OPP), formally constituted in 1909, was a consolidation of a number of specialized forces and ad hoc arrangements that extended back to the 1860s. Small specialized provincial forces were posted alongside the Niagara and Detroit frontiers, and, with the extension of economic activity north of the Great Lakes, constables were appointed for the Thunder Bay area. In 1875 the government hired a former railway detective, John W. Murray, as a provincial investigator. Murray responded to calls for assistance from local authorities in investigating murders and other serious crimes. In the words of Phillips and Fortune (n.d.), his appointment was a response to localism, which "resulted in patronage, corruption and jurisdictional disputes" impeding the administration of justice. The inadequacies of the traditional village constable in the age of railways and the telegraph were discussed by the newly-formed Ontario Provincial Constables Association in 1895. The expansion of prospecting, mining, forestry and railroads into "New Ontario" after 1900 created a demand for greater surveillance on behalf of the province. In time, mining towns such as Cobalt would organize their own police services. The OPP of 1910, which had fewer than fifty constables scattered in thirty-six detachments, was a skeleton force with a limited impact on the province. In remote areas it enforced fish and game regulations and administered the wolf bounty. On the American border it watched for "undesirables" and seized hand-guns and other weapons. In 1912 the force was deployed to a more controversial operation: keeping the peace between striking miners and strikebreakers and armed private detectives in Timmons. Stationed at Timmons and South Porcupine, the police escorted strikebreakers through picket lines (Higley 1984: chapter 3).

THE NORTH WEST MOUNTED POLICE

The major exception to the localized nature of policing prior to start of the twentieth century was the Dominion government's establishment of a special constabulary for Ottawa's vast colony, the North-West Territories, acquired at little cost or bloodshed from Great Britain and the Hudson's Bay Company in 1870. This huge area, dominated by First Nations people and pockets of Metis and other mixed-race people, would become the provinces of Manitoba, Saskatchewan and Alberta. In the meantime, most of it remained part of a territory whose administration, land and resources was under the control of Ottawa. To help secure this remote region for white settlement, John A. Macdonald, before his government fell because of the Pacific Scandal in 1873, followed up on earlier plans to establish a frontier constabulary under control of the national government. Various influences were evident: the RIC, British cavalry regiments and native constabularies in India. In the wake of the 1869–70 Red River resistance, the force was resolutely white, and unlike the practice elsewhere in the British Empire, "natives" were hired as scouts only. The early North West Mounted Police was closely identified with the Conservatives who were in power from 1879 to 1896 and who viewed the North West as a patronage outlet. Macdonald's National Policy included tariffs to encourage manufacturing, the Canadian Pacific Railway (completed in 1885) and the opening up of the west for white agricultural settlers. When the Liberals, the party of provincial rights, returned to power in the mid 1890s, many expected the NWMP to be radically downsized or even disbanded (Marquis 2005a).

The original force of Mounted Police was organized and recruited in 1873, fol-lowing news of violence against "British" Indians by American hunters and traders in the Cypress Hills area of southern Alberta. A year later roughly three hundred police, with wagons, ox carts, cattle and supplies, embarked on the "Great March" westward from Fort Dufferin, Manitoba. The poorly-planned trek into what is now Alberta was well publicized by an "embedded" illustrator, Henri Julien, whose images appeared in *Canadian Illustrated News*. Having survived near disaster, the police began building posts or barracks, deploying mounted patrols along the international border and interacting with First Nations bands, settlers and ranchers. They had jurisdiction over a huge expanse of land, 300,000 square miles in size (almost a third larger that the entire nation of France). Unlike police services back east, the NWMP was a paramilitary force, equipped with carbines and field guns; in the 1880s the Enfield revolver and Winchester rifle were standard issue.

The role of the NWMP on the Plains was much mythologized at the time and in subsequent decades. Recently, a pollster described the RCMP as Canada's "brand to the world" (Boswell 2013). As Walden (1982: 27) explains: "The nineteenth century desired heroes, and one of those it found and cultivated was the Mounted Policeman." In newspapers, magazines, historical writing and popular fiction in Canada, the United States, Great Britain and beyond, the NWMP, in the face of reality, was depicted as an elite Imperial force based on fair play, honour, physical endurance, the relentless pursuit of duty and minimal use of force. According to Walden (1982: 211), this was part of an international trend in historical works and fiction that valued heroism in an increasingly materialistic, secular and impersonal age: "The Mountie was indisputably a hero. He possessed all the virtues and character traits that distinguished the archetype. He was well bred and often of noble birth, but he was in no sense elitist." Walden concludes that the image of the NWMP (later exploited with some ambivalence by the RCMP) was "a popular fabrication" (ibid.: 3). Within Canada, the force, despite its faults, was associated with great "nation building" projects: the acquisition of the West under relatively peaceful conditions; the completion of the Canadian Pacific Railway; the suppression of the 1885 Rebellion; the establishment of the Yukon Territory; and the extension of Canada's "protection" of the Inuit. In an era when English-Canadian patriotism and British Imperialism were often the same, the Mounties were also viewed as an institution that helped "paint the map red." As Walden and others have noted, French Canadian and First Nations views of the NWMP may not have been as positive (see, for example, Brown and Brown 1973).

Its portrayal as an elite constabulary may have been an exaggeration of journalists, novelists and supportive politicians, but the typical Mountie was recruited from a slightly higher socio-economic bracket than the average urban police constable of the era. One of the attractions in this age of Imperial adventure was that Canada had extremely limited opportunities for young men who sought careers in the military. In 1887 the commissioner of the force wrote that preferred candidates were "short-service" British military veterans or Canadian-born sons of farmers. Young men who were physically fit and capable of travelling and working in all types of weather were supposedly superior to older military veterans. The latter were often assumed to be addicted to drink. The commissioner did acknowledge that young men "of good family and education" also had a role to play within the force (NWMP 1886–87). Between 1873 and 1902, 29 percent of all recruits were skilled workers, 27 percent were farmers, 15 percent were clerks and one in ten had previous police or military experience (Macleod 1976). The force was overwhelmingly Anglo-Celtic and Protestant, but the realities of political patronage meant that French Canadians were recruited as officers and to the subordinate ranks. Despite this, the force never captured the imagination of Quebec's Francophone majority, for whom the West was associated with the suppression of minority rights by an intolerant Anglophone majority. Novelists and journalists stressed that the force embodied all the best qualities of the British, Canadians and American "races" (Walden 1982: 31–2). Publications such as the memoirs of veteran Mountie Sam Steele (1915), who also served in the South African War as commander of Lord Strathcona's Horse and later as an officer in Baden-Powell's South African Constabulary, helped reinforce key elements of the emerging Mounted Police myth: their even-handed and efficient ordering of the West; their benign but paternalistic relations with the First Nations; and their contribution to the building of the British Empire. According to Macleod, the initial emphasis of the NWMP was on preventing violence; morality offences such as gambling, possessing contraband liquor or breaking the Sabbath were of secondary importance (Macleod 1998).

Much like nineteenth-century Ireland, which was a "social laboratory" (Palmer 1988: 25) for Britain, the North-West Territories was a zone for the federal government's legal and administrative innovation based on expediency. One example was the territory's liquor ordinance, which was a form of quasi prohibition that the federal government dare not impose on other regions of Canada. The frontier constabulary had been created for a variety of reasons; one of them was to act as a buffer between the First Nations and railroad construction crews and white settlers. In the 1870s there were up to fifty thousand people on the Plains, most of them First Nations unfamiliar with Canadian laws or institutions. Under Treaties 1 through 7 (negotiated between 1871 and 1877), First Nations leaders were supposed to acknowledge Canadian criminal law and legal institutions in return for the Crown protecting their hunting and other subsistence rights. Treaty 6, for example, enjoined Plains Cree leaders to "maintain peace and good order" and to cooperate with the authorities in helping to bring lawbreakers to justice. The Mounted Police played a role in the treaty-making process by which the crown extinguished aboriginal title to one of the world's most productive agricultural regions. The police tolerated certain Native practices during the early frontier stage, but this was not a formal recognition of customary law.

In the midst of rapid social and economic change, adjusting to a foreign legal system was difficult: in Plains aboriginal societies the act of murder, if punished at all, was handled through blood feud, and what white Canadians deemed horse theft was the honourable custom of horse raiding. According to Hubner (1995) the NWMP, originally somewhat tolerant toward horse theft, became more active in the

1880s when it attempted to curtail horse raiding across the international border. This and other prosecutions for theft were examples of a white settler government criminalizing traditional aboriginal practices. Yet the files of the stipendiary magistrate based at Fort Saskatchewan indicate only seventy-one criminal cases with Indians as defendants in the period 1876–86, and in the Saskatchewan district there is evidence that assaults and pretty thefts in the 1870s and 1880s were ignored (Gavigan 2012: 86; Knafla n.d.).

During the early 1880s the NWMP also became concerned about the sexual exploitation of aboriginal women camping near towns (Smith 2009). Until the early twentieth century, the force adopted a pragmatic response to prostitution as a necessary attribute of frontier life. The police, for example, tended not to investigate houses of prostitution until they had received a complaint. Between 1874 and 1890, the NWMP secured only a dozen convictions against keepers or inmates of bawdy houses. It was more common to proceed against prostitutes under the charge of vagrancy, a misdemeanour that carried a fine or a short jail term. As urban centres such as Calgary, Lethbridge, Medicine Hat and Regina organized municipal police and pushed brothels outside of town limits, the NWMP came under moral reform pressure to act against houses on the outskirts of town. According to Horrall, the Mounties did restrict the movements of prostitutes but continued to regard their services as a necessary evil (Horrall 1998: 175, 178).

Popular culture portrayed the Mounties as the paternalistic protectors of the volatile, childlike aboriginal populations, and for nationalist Canadians the supposed treatment of the First Nations by the police reflected their nation's more civilized frontier policies. In an era when most white Canadians identified western and northern expansion as benign, the NWMP were viewed as agents of progress who ensured a frontier of order. In the long run the Mounties were part of the federal government's assault on tribal independence and Native culture that included the cruel threat, and reality, of malnutrition, starvation and rapid population decline for bands that did not follow government orders. In its first years the NWMP, based on statistics of arrest and convictions, appears to have under-policed the Plains tribes. In the period 1876 to 1886, when they formed the bulk of the population of the Plains, in surviving court files First Nations individuals totalled a third of all defendants (Macleod 1976; Marquis 2005a; Gavigan 2012). There is evidence that First Nations leaders, who supported the ban on alcohol, initially welcomed the police as protectors; after the 1885 Rebellion the situation changed, with the police acting as "ambivalent agents" for the subjugation of the Plains tribes (Daschuk 2013: 127). Gavigan's research indicates that chiefs and headmen in the Treaty 4 and Treaty 6 areas in the early period of Canadian rule made use of the police and criminal courts to protect their people. The authoritarian nature of frontier justice was underscored by two other practices: senior NWMP police officers acted as magistrates in criminal matters, and police posts served as jails. This blurring of legal roles, which had also been instituted in the authoritarian Crown colonies of Vancouver Island and British Columbia, would not have been tolerated in settled "British" communities dominated by whites. Between 1874 and 1898, sixty percent of police court cases in the Saskatchewan district were heard by NWMP officers with the remainder falling to civilian magistrates (Knafla n.d.).

Research has revealed that the members of the first cadre of the NWMP were not unblemished heroes. Many of the original members of this supposedly elite organization were either dismissed for drunkenness or neglect of duty or deserted. Discipline was a problem and relations with Native communities often exploitative. In 1884, for example, one quarter of the force was infected with sexually transmitted diseases and many policemen were involved in the sexual exploitation of First Nations women (Daschuk 2013: 154). The latter were driven to or forced into prostitution by the dire economic conditions facing Plains peoples by the 1880s. The federal government responded to this issue with *Indian Act* amendments in 1880 and 1886 that banned Indian prostitutes from "any premises" and Indians from keeping or frequenting disorderly houses. One reform aimed at improving discipline at NWMP posts was to allow the men to drink beer in their own barracks, so that they would not get into trouble with bootleggers (whom they were tasked with suppressing prior to the 1890s when the territory was under a form of modified prohibition). Among the Yukon detachment during the gold rush years there were problems with abusing alcohol, fraternizing with prostitutes and being absent from barracks without permission; the third most common reported medical problem was gonorrhea (Backhouse 1985: 421; Morrison 1985: chapter 5).

Because of adverse press accounts of the police role in the 1885 rebellion in the District of Saskatchewan, the last major resistance to Canadian rule on the Plains, the reputation of the police suffered. Prior to the outbreak the force had provided intelligence to Ottawa, which was largely ignored, of growing unrest among the Metis, many white settlers and First Nations groups such as the Plains Cree. Years later Sam Steele, who in 1884 had been posted to the Rocky Mountains to oversee security along the final sections of the Pacific railway project, faulted the federal government for not settling the land title grievances of the St. Laurent-Batoche Metis (Steele 1915: 202). There were examples of coercion prior to the resistance. In 1882, for example, the NWMP engaged in a type of ethnic cleansing by removing several hundred First Nations people from the Cypress Hills, along the route of the Canadian Pacific Railway. In 1884 the NWMP was placed under the control of the Department of Indian Affairs as the federal government doubted its willingness to act in a more decisive fashion. Another example of coercion was when the police threatened force when Piapot's Cree band attempted to abandon its reserve in 1884 (Daschuk 2013: 123, 129). The major security challenge for the federal government was the refusal of Big Bear's Plains Cree band to be located on its designated reserve.

Charges that the NWMP "failed" to perform its duty during the North-West Resistance were not totally fair. For one thing, the force was not responsible for the communications problems with the commanders of the Canadian troops sent to the region. At Duck Lake in 1885 a force of fifty-three police and forty-one volunteers attempting to seize supplies clashed with a larger force of Metis acting on behalf of Riel's provisional government. The incident has often been portrayed as an "ambush" by the Metis, but a number of accounts suggest that the "Canadians" fired first, killing two men. Nine volunteers and three Mounties were killed and the force retreated, abandoning Fort Carlton. The police were unable to protect settlers at Frog Lake, where Cree warriors killed nine white men, including two priests, and took a number of hostages. Despite being assisted by the CPR, the Hudson's Bay Company, two steamboat companies, the NWMP and local militia, the five thousand troops (largely Ontario volunteers) sent to crush the rebellion fared little better except at the final battle of Batoche. Three skirmishes or battles with either Metis or First Nations were draws or tactical defeats for the Canadian forces (Macleod and Beale 1984). The subjugation of Riel's Metis fighters and rebellious Plains Cree fell to the military. Yet the Mounted Police had protected five hundred white settlers at Fort Battleford, provided scouts for the military and helped to ensure the neutrality of the potentially powerful Alberta tribes. They also played an important role in the logistics of crushing the twin localized rebellions of 1885 and in the legal aftermath. Nearly one hundred First Nations and Metis men were charged with various offences; Wandering Spirit, whose warriors had attacked Frog Lake, and seven Cree and Assiniboine warriors were hanged in a public mass execution at Fort Battleford. The NWMP assisted in the executions. Riel, convicted of felony treason, was the only Metis to go to the scaffold. He was hanged at the NWMP barracks in Regina. Such are the complex cultural politics of Canada: executed at what until 1920 remained the national headquarters of Canada's most famous police force, Riel became a martyr in Quebec and was recognized as Manitoba's Father of Confederation. Starting in 2007 Louis Riel Day became a statutory holiday in that province.

Following the North-West Resistance, the Mounties became more directly involved with Indian administration. Although the force doubted their legality, the NWMP was tasked with enforcing new pass regulations, an attempt to confine the Plains Cree and other First Nations to their reserves. NWMP Commissioner Irvine believed that the pass system, which was also applied to the Blackfoot of Treaty 7 who had not rebelled, violated treaty rights. In addition to tensions with the Department of Indian Affairs, the police also experienced ambivalent relations with Christian missionaries who operated on various reserves (Smith 2009). Working with Indian agents, the police later became involved in suppressing traditional aboriginal religious practices on reserves. In 1895, amendments to the *Indian Act*, which were supported by Christian churches and missionaries, banned traditional dances "that involved giveaways and wounding or mutilation" (Gavigan 2012: 20). Yet the NWMP appear to have enforced these measures unevenly, ignoring orders to suppress traditional dances, and individual officials, such as stipendiary magistrate James Macleod, a former NWMP commissioner, appear to have treated First Nations in conflict with the law fairly (Gavigan 2012: 21–2, 36–8).

The original premise of the NWMP was that the force would cease to exist once the West had been "civilized" and new towns, counties and presumably provinces were organized. At the very least, once white farmers and ranchers and townsfolk and railways and commercial agriculture dominated the southern Plains, the constabulary would be a smaller body, relegated to the northern frontier of settlement. Not for the last time, short-term events and expediency intervened to ensure the continuity of force. The NWMP, whose numbers were in decline and whose existence was under attack in the early 1890s, survived by moving north. This began in a modest way in 1894 when concerns arose over the impact of the liquor traffic in the Yukon area of the western North-West Territories. The Yukon was attracting growing numbers of gold miners, many of them Americans, prior to the outbreak of its gold rush in 1897, and that industry was under little state regulation. As the rush continued the Canadian government appointed a commissioner or governor for the new territory, expanded the NWMP presence and backed up the police with the Yukon Field Force, a military unit recruited from the Canadian army. As miners filtered inland the police followed and established new posts. Although the gold rush peaked in 1899, the NWMP did not support any diminution in its ranks in the territory, which rose to three hundred in 1903 (Morrison 1985). The majority of the white population in the Yukon, in the words of Steele, were "foreigners" who were given "the protection of the best laws in the world." This included on-the-spot law-making, such as allowing gambling houses (forbidden in the North-West Territories and the more settled areas of Canada) but insisting that they be run honestly (Steele 1915: 327, 329–30).

According to Morrison (1985), the police were the agents of the extension of white, southern culture into the north. Against the backdrop of a boundary dispute with the United States, which was settled in 1902 to the detriment of the Canadian claim to a portion of the Alaska Panhandle, the NWMP also played a strategic role. The NWMP was expected to fulfill Ottawa's wishes, and the Yukon detachment was placed under the direct control not of the commissioner in Regina but the Department of Interior. The commissioner was assisted by an appointed territorial council, which included the commander of the police. Particularly before the advent of civilian bureaucrats in the territory, the Mounted Police were generalist service providers and regulators, often in the absence of statutory authority or extra financial support. They tended to regard the First Nations of the Yukon, who had not been established on reserves, as a "debauched" nuisance and enforced liquor regulations not out of humanitarianism but to lessen disorder. One example of situational authoritarianism was the illegal policy of excluding aboriginals from the towns of Whitehorse and Dawson, a practice that lasted until the 1940s. On the other hand, they distributed relief to starving Indians. In addition to enforcing criminal law and keeping the peace, duties which did not take up much time despite popular culture's depiction of the Yukon as a rowdy, bachelor society, the police collected customs duties, help deliver the mail, monitored navigational safety on rivers, enforced rules pertaining to the minimum amount of supplies and cash required by all newcomers and watched for suspicious characters. Sam Steele, the legendary commander in the Yukon, recalled in his memoirs that the police took care of the sick, buried the dead and helped settle their estates after death. Hefty fines collected by the NWMP helped defray the cost of treating typhoid patients in Dawson (Steele 1915: 312, 322–3). Individuals leaving the territory were searched for contraband gold, and those entering were checked for guns, alcohol and gambling paraphernalia. The police banned liquor in dancehalls, forbade women from drinking in saloons and enforced a quasi-legal medical inspection of prostitutes. According to the standard study of the era, the "most enduring contribution" of the Mounted Police in the Yukon was not crime fighting, but miscellaneous duties including acting as magistrates, serving writs, handling prisoners and lunatics, collecting taxes, serving as land agents and mining recorders, running the postal system and providing veterinary services. According to Morrison (1985), the Mounties solved all murders committed during the gold rush and operated the jails. Rather than the untamed mining frontier of popular culture, the Yukon was a "benign police state" (Morrison 1985: 58).

By the time it was assigned its new duties in the subarctic, the NWMP had become popular with the British, European and American settlers who had filtered in to the Prairie region prior to the immigration boom that started in 1896. A more extensive patrol system and new duties such a fighting prairie fires and enforcing cattle disease quarantines made the police more of a service arm of government. Detachments were expected to report on the agricultural progress and ethnic composition of their districts. NWMP officers were suspicious of American Mormon settlers in the late 1880s because of their reputation for polygamy, but their more relaxed attitude toward the second wave of Mormons reflected the changing priorities of politicians. They also were fairly tolerant toward Russian Doukhobor settlers who arrived in the North-West Territories in 1899, despite a series of protests, including acts of public nudity, by a minority of the pacifist newcomers (Betke 1972, 1980). Relations with white settlers improved with the end of the controversial North-West liquor ordinance, widely evaded, which the police had also resented having to enforce. In the opinion of Methodist minister J.S. Woodsworth (later an ardent critic of RCMP policing of strikes and the political left), the force, like schools, churches, unions and the press, played a vital role in helping immigrants adjust to Canada. Interestingly, he wrote of the patrol maps of the NWMP as resembling a "spider's web" (Woodsworth 1909: 37) covering the rural prairies, a web of surveillance that was benign, not malevolent. Macleod has noted that when the patrol system was cut back starting in 1897 with the redeployment of men to the Yukon, there was an upsurge in reports of cattle and horse stealing in the North-West Territories (Macleod 1998: 92–3).

POLICING IN THE AGE OF SOCIAL REFORM

Although trade unions were active in urban centres and freed from criminal conspiracy charges by the 1870s, Canada failed to develop widespread working-class or socialist political parties on the European model that would subject the legal system and police to systematic class critiques. Disputes between the police and workers (discussed in the next chapter) were localized and episodic and tended to focus on the policing of strikes. Yet during the late Victorian era many police services were subjected to ongoing political and journalistic criticism that reflected a specific social group: middle-class reformers. By the 1870s an international social reform movement attracted large numbers of middle-class and elite men and woman. The many strands of reform were motivated by a complex mixture of humanitarianism and fear of the poor, immigrants and the working class. The Victorian police operated in a cultural context that assumed, and at various levels enforced, separate standards of morality for men and women. Women were expected to be pure, devout, obedient and domesticated. The most radical strain of the social purity movement, championed by early feminists such as many members of the Woman's Christian Temperance Union (WCTU), was the demand for a single standard of morality. The goal here was to raise the drinking, smoking and womanizing male up to the standard of the ideal Christian wife and mother. Much of this was to be accomplished by moral suasion and education, but moral reformers demanded much from lawmakers, the police and courts. Although many historians, criminologists and other social scientists have stressed the class nature of the justice system, for the emerging profession of policing, moral and social reformers were often the enemy, because they were the only group of articulate, middle-class individuals prior to the 1960s that challenged police legitimacy. The movement included high-minded newspapers that supported respectability to the level of not printing advertisements for patent medicines, tobacco or alcohol. Morality enforcement was the Achilles heel of many urban police services and the most likely source of scandal. In the 1870s, for example, Winnipeg's first chief constable was arrested as a "found in" in a house of ill fame. And the NWMP, despite its pragmatic attitudes toward morality offences, was not able to resist the rising tide of social purity in the urban North-West Territories and, starting in 1905, the new provinces of Alberta and Saskatchewan. The late nineteenth-century Winnipeg police, for example, did take action against known prostitutes (Winnipeg Police Service 2014; Horrall 1998: 183–92; Kozminski 2009).

The biggest challenge to the legitimacy of the police in the late nineteenth century was not working-class resistance or protest, or courts or defence lawyers, but a largely middle-class movement aimed at curbing the social costs of alcohol. By the 1870s the movement was having an obvious impact on liquor licensing and enforcement, as provincial and municipal authorities enacted stricter laws and bylaws and the public consumption of alcohol became less respectable. Hotel and saloon owners, who were able to hire lawyers, tended to be the only interest capable of mounting credible legal defences in the lower courts, using powerful arguments defending property rights. Prosecutions for the illegal sale of alcohol, or violation of liquor licenses, often were not successful because of difficulties with evidence and witnesses. Other than serious offences such as murder, liquor cases were one of the rare occasions that police and liquor or temperance inspectors would actually be challenged in the lower courts. As the result of temperance pressure, the number of saloons was cut and saloon hours became shorter and licensing fees higher. Eventually grocery stores in some jurisdictions were prohibited from selling alcohol. The role of alcohol in society inspired the first systematic critiques of the justice system. According to an undercover reporter who posed as a drunk in order to expose abuses in the Toronto central police station and county jail in 1887, the main cause of "vice" was "licensed and protected by law." The sale of alcohol in his view was providing employment for police, jail guards and magistrates. His exposé of the main police lockup stressed its dirty and unsanitary conditions, which included lice and vomit, the lack of segregation of juveniles, the lack of food for prisoners and the incivility and brutality of police. His series of articles revealed that juveniles, persons arrested on suspicion and habitual drunkards were housed with "irreclaimable brutes." The reporter felt that police lockup prisoners were poorly treated because they were socially marginal. Most police officials objected to the exposé, but Mayor William Howland, a noted moral and social reformer, not only agreed with the findings of the *Globe's* investigation, he also suggested that chronic inebriety was a disease that should be treated medically and not punished by the police, courts and jails (*Toronto Globe* 1887a, 1887b, 1887c).

Police in the late nineteenth century, despite their personal views, had to react to stricter liquor control laws that were evolving because of political pressure and changing social custom. For moral and social reformers, police services were often overly cautious or even resistant to enforcement drives. In Halifax in the 1880s, the Society for the Prevention of Cruelty responded to this situation by prosecuting cases of violence and neglect. In most cases the victims were women and children and the offenders were men. The society also functioned as a primitive legal aid bureau for the poor (Fingard 1989: chapter 8). From time to time chief constables warned that stricter laws would give rise to a larger illegal trade that would be harder to prosecute. One political compromise in the face of demands for prohibition (a modified form of which had been attempted briefly in 1850s New Brunswick) was local option, which allowed (male) voters to decide whether saloons, liquor stores, grocery stores selling alcohol could operate within a municipality or county. The 1878 *Canada Temperance Act* (CTA) did result in retail sale being banned in many counties in the Maritime provinces and a few in Ontario, but it was a porous measure in that it did not shut down breweries or distilleries nor outlaw importation for personal use. Enforcement of the act was uneven, which forced temperance activists to employ their own detectives and prosecutors and certain municipalities to hire temperance inspectors when the local police or part-time constables were unwilling or unable to enforce the law. The level of community evasion or resistance suggests that violation of licensing or prohibition laws was viewed as a social crime. What was true of quasi-prohibition laws such as the CTA was true of liquor enforcement in general: the police appear to have exercised considerable discretion. Most police chiefs would agree with temperance activists that drink was the cause of most crime and poverty, but as a group they lacked a uniform response to prohibition (Marquis 2005b).

Moral reform, despite the wishes of most police officials and magistrates, did exert an influence on criminal law in the late Victorian period, a trend that would gather more momentum during the early twentieth century. Reform efforts took the form of temperance tracts, sermons, letters to the editor, public meetings, delegations to city hall and the lobbying of provincial and federal politicians to enact laws to protect girls and women from sexual exploitation. The *Criminal Code* of 1892 and subsequent amendments, for example, contained provisions dealing with keepers and inmates of bawdy houses and disorderly houses. These sections were aimed at houses of prostitution, but the most frequently used police weapon against the sex trade was a charge of vagrancy laid against "common prostitutes or nightwalkers" (McLaren and Lowman 1990). Police crusades against such "victimless crimes" tended to follow press or political exposés of local vice activities. Judging by official statistics, prostitution was not a law enforcement priority. In most cases female prostitutes, not their male clients, were the ones arrested and taken to court. Statistical patterns are imprecise, as criminal law allowed police to arrest intoxicated persons and prostitutes as vagrants. Most sizeable urban communities by the late nineteenth century had one or more neighbourhoods where dancehalls, lower-class drinking establishments and brothels were concentrated. In more diverse cities such as Victoria and Vancouver, these vice zones could be racially exclusive. In some cases vice districts were outside of city limits. Whether the result of formal policies of segregation by police and other municipal authorities or simply a result of the local real estate market, "tenderloin" areas and their residents were well known to the local police. There is evidence that the police acknowledged that many women turned to prostitution out of economic necessity, but given the generally conservative nature of the evolving profession, it is highly likely that police chiefs and their subordinates, like most Canadian magistrates, regarded the sex trade as a necessary evil and were not convinced that prostitutes could be "saved" (McLaren and Lowman 1990). Moral reform was not a uniform threat to police autonomy and professionalism. As would be revealed in the early twentieth century, a more organized police lobby could support specific criminal law amendments put forward by moral and social reformers if they served police interests.

CONCLUSION

By the end of the nineteenth century, Canada was on its way to becoming an urban society, and towns and cities had full-time police departments that fulfilled a variety of duties. However important to the Dominion government in the North-West and Yukon territories and to the popular imagination, the NWMP did not typify Canadian policing. Evidence of working-class resistance to the police remained, but the "respectable" working class, from whose ranks most police officers originated, had favourable views of the institution and of "British justice." Moral reformers criticized detectives and police on the beat for being too close to the more disreputable aspects of plebeian culture such as brothels and unlicensed drinking dens, and "clean government" crusaders would soon denounce policing for politically-linked corruption, as discussed in the next chapter. In the decades after Confederation the combination of permanent police, new criminal laws and municipal bylaws governing public order, demands by municipal and business leaders that the police keep busy and stipendiary magistrates' courts all resulted in new levels of criminalization. Yet by the late 1800s, Canadian towns and cities, which had never experienced serious crimes levels, were relatively more orderly than they had been at mid century. Policing was one part of this long-term taming of the North American city, which also owed much to the spread of middle-class values, temperance, evangelical Protestantism, industrial discipline, public education, mass circulation newspapers, private charity and social welfare and private charity (Monkkonen 1981). Historical evidence also suggests that many short-term crime waves were not a reflection of an objective increase in specific anti-social behaviours but the result of law enforcement crackdowns, as in the 1870s when police escalated sanctions against tramps and the unemployed via vagrancy laws (Harring 1983). Finally, the late nineteenth century foreshadowed the evolving occupational identity of police and their quest for professional status based on controlling crime. The 1881 meeting of chief constables from Montreal, Toronto and ten other Ontario towns and cities, for example, discussed issues such as uniforms, photographic identification of felons, the need to track "foreign criminals," the threat of "ticket of leave" or early release of incarcerated felons, the benefits of police service pensions and a national publication through which police services could exchange information including notices on fugitive criminals (*Toronto Globe* 1881).

CHAPTER 3

POLICING
THE URBAN AGE

The period from 1900 to the end of the Second World War included the begin-ning of police professionalization and lobbying of the provincial and federal governments; early attempts to unionize the rank and file; responses to and adaptations of technology such as fingerprinting, automobiles and radio; and by the 1920s, articulation of a crime-fighting ethos. The latter was only slightly challenged by the employment of small numbers of policewomen starting in the 1910s as partial recognition of a social work role. The modernization and increasing centralization of Canadian policing was epitomized by the creation of the RCMP as potential national constabulary in the wake of the 1919 Winnipeg General Strike, a move that was tied to the elite's fears of radical labour and socialism. Police legitimacy continued to be challenged by morality issues such as "white slavery" and prohibition. Police responses to prostitution and alcohol regulation were highly ambivalent, in contrast to drug enforcement, which coincided perfectly with the masculinized crime-fighting image that was also being promoted in the United States (Potter 1998: 3). The tough-on-crime approach mirrored the larger society's harsh views toward adult offenders and the strong belief than crime was caused by individuals, not society. In rural areas, the demands of alcohol control and automobile regulation furthered provincial policing, a jurisdiction that also involved the RNWMP in Alberta and Saskatchewan from 1905 to 1917, and the RCMP in Saskatchewan starting in 1928. Police agencies, notably the RCMP, were also affected by the Great Depression and the Second World War.

POLICE PROFESSIONALIZATION

During the early twentieth century, Canadian police executives forged their first professional organization, largely as an offshoot of developments in the United States. Police chiefs there had responded to widespread exposés of police corruption by organizing the International Association of Chiefs of Police (IACP). The main goals of the IACP were to protect the image of policing and to raise its standards in terms of recruitment, training, discipline and pay. Greater emphasis was placed on organizing police bureaucracies along military lines, adopting new technology to increase surveillance over both the population and the police rank and file and on the central mission of crime fighting. The latter involved the projection of a threat, in this case a constant reminder that society was imperiled by a class of violent professional criminals. The need to find new threats or challenges was particularly apparent by the end of the nineteenth century in jurisdictions such as Toronto where there was a noted decline in the rate of reported crime (Boritch 1985: 211). For many chief constables, emphasizing the generalist role of police services, which had little to do with serious crime, was not a pathway to professional status.

A related issue was promoting or resisting changes to the criminal law in the interest of crime control, as defined by police leaders. Canadian police chiefs, although sometimes embroiled in departmental scandals over corruption, enjoyed considerable public support but, in a number of cities, were chafing from the attacks of moral reformers. Following the example of the IACP to which a number of them belonged, in 1905 police chiefs, including the influential heads of railway private security organizations, formed the Chief Constables Association of Canada (CCAC). Its aim was to advance policing as a profession and to stress that the profession worked for the good of the nation. Like other national lobby organizations it took advantage of Canada's national *Criminal Code*, which was controlled by Parliament, to push for tougher criminal laws. At times, as in the case of gambling and bawdy and disorderly houses, the CCAC cooperated with the legislative agenda of the Protestant "social gospel" lobby. It also began to speak out on certain social issues and to criticize other aspects of the justice system, such as courts and corrections. In time the CCAC was replicated at the provincial and regional levels. In addition to lobbying governments, these organizations held conventions and issued publications (Marquis 1993).

Central to the quest for professional status was the need to strengthen criminal laws to enhance police power, defend the profession from external critics and defend the reputation of the police as neutral, incorruptible and capable crime fighters. Police chiefs did not always articulate in detail their theories of criminality, but by the 1930s many may have agreed with FBI head J. Edgar Hoover that criminals were violent and selfish "defective people" (Potter 1998: 170). Professionalism involved the adoption of crime-fighting technologies and practices than not only added to police capacity but also bolstered morale and occupational solidarity and leant an aura of "science" to an occupation that traditionally was associated with arresting drunks and vagrants and breaking up fights. Fingerprinting, developed as a more accurate method of identifying convicted criminals than an early biometric system known as the Bertillon method, was given statutory authority in the early 1900s, and a national bureau was begun under the Dominion Police, a small federal police service organized in the late 1860s to enforce federal laws and guard Parliament and other government facilities, with the cooperation of the CCAC. Combined with photographs and other documentation, fingerprint collection grew into a national criminal identification network that helped create important linkages among Canadian police services. The public, influenced by detective stories, mistakenly believed that the typical use of fingerprint records by police was to solve crimes (Marquis 1994).

In larger urban departments, mounted officers patrolled parks and were also effective in crowd control. To lessen the incidence of assaults on officers escorting offenders to the lockup and undercut middle-class outrage over the uncivilized treatment of intoxicated women, departments acquired horse-drawn (later motorized) patrol wagons, colloquially known as Black Marias or paddy wagons. Police departments acquired bicycles, motorcycles and automobiles, telephones and signal systems that allowed headquarters to communicate with constables on the beat. Pioneered in Chicago in 1881, call box and telegraph systems, often shared with fire departments, remained in operation until the 1970s in many cities. Based on combinations of telephones, bells and lights, these expensive systems were also employed to monitor and discipline police workers. Winnipeg installed a Siemens Corporation electric signal system in 1913. Men on the beat checked in on a regular basis and could be summoned in the case of emergency, and keys for the boxes were left with trusted citizens in neighbourhoods. Some systems had special signals for "ambulance," "fire," "riot" and other specific emergencies and were connected, for a fee, to banks and other businesses. The call box system, together with personal visits to police stations, was a primary conduit of citizen complaints to the police until the rise of mass telephone ownership (Winnipeg Police Service 2014).

The CCAC, which accepted only the managerial ranks of municipal, provincial and corporate police (and eventually the RCMP) as members, purported to speak for the entire profession, and on many issues, particularly those relating to crime control, it did. In addition to influencing government, there was recognition of the importance of shaping public opinion, which chief constables traditionally did via contacts with the local press. Yet the rank and file had its own grievances and issues, and many of them were aimed at chief constables and the rest of the police hierarchy, including police commissions. In the lower ranks occupational identity was strong, but its growing militancy overlapped with the expanding labour movement. During the 1910s municipal workers in a number of Canadian towns and cities were attracted to the union movement. As explained in more detail in Chapter 4, the police worker occupied an ambiguous position in the hierarchy of class. A relatively poorly paid employee under quasi-military discipline who was required to work long hours in all types of weather, the typical constable was of working-class origins and not well educated. Yet these same "blue-coated workers" were expected to crack down on the amusements of the lower classes and, from time to time, arrest striking trade unionists, escort non-union workers through picket lines and break up public meetings of socialists and the unemployed.

By the early 1900s the police rank and file tended to emulate the aspirations of the "respectable" working class, which included a "living wage." Although not as well paid as contemporary police officers, the urban police, much like firemen and transit workers, tended to reflect a community's ethnic and sectarian pecking order. In Toronto, the "Belfast of the North," this meant that Canadian-born officers were a minority on the force until after the Second World War, outnumbered by immigrants from Ireland, England and Scotland. Many of these immigrants had been policemen in the "old county." In this period most Toronto police, in a city of working-class home ownership, owned their place of residence. Constables, as they continue to do, also took on outside security work for extra income. Some officers, despite their blue-collar origins, were able to speculate in property, operate small businesses and accumulate capital (Marquis 1986b: 207–9; 217–8).

The official theory that the police had to be neutral in the struggle between labour and capital was raised in the 1910s and 1920s to counter the police union movement. The desire of many members of the rank and file to organize trade unions in cities such as Saint John, Montreal and Toronto echoed a general trend, more noticeable among industrial workers, to form unions in order to engage in collective bargaining. The strong economy of the First World War era gave a boost to union membership, which rose from less than 170,000 in 1914 to almost 400,000 in 1918. On the municipal level, where most police officers were employed, sectors such as outside workers were organizing, and there was some sympathy among the public and politicians for a unionized public sector. Another strong motivation was the rising cost of living because of wartime inflation. More specific to the profession, the assertion of a new rank-and-file sense of cohesion was tied to a defensive reaction to outside critics and management's desire to improve internal disciplinary procedures, which struck many as authoritarian. Union activity emerged in Winnipeg, London, Toronto, Montreal, Quebec and Saint John, among other communities, and for the most part it was opposed by provincial governments, police commissions and chief constables. Municipal politicians, who were dealing with the rise of the "workingman," appeared to be more sympathetic, and specific grievances were often local. The formation of the Toronto police union, for example, was a defensive move by the rank and file pending a police commission inquiry into a recent police riot. Responding to nativist attacks on ethnic businesses in the urban core in 1918, officers had used excessive force and attacked innocent bystanders. Fearing official reprisals, the rank and file took the initiative and engaged in a four-day strike, receiving considerable public sympathy. The Montreal police in 1918 were under attack from the New York Bureau of Municipal Research report, which accused the department of tolerating and profiting from gambling and prostitution. The rank and file also may have been reacting to Montreal's governance framework, which vested power over police appointments with aldermen (CP 1918; Marquis 1989).

New police unions in several cities affiliated with the Trades and Labour Congress of Canada. The CCAC responded by requesting a national law to ban union organizing by police officers, something that not even the repressive Union government of Robert Borden was prepared to invoke. At any rate, with the exception of the RNWMP, police services were under provincial, not federal jurisdiction. In most cases local police unions won minor concessions and were reorganized as police associations. Although lacking union status and collective bargaining rights, and generally maintaining a low profile until the 1960s, police associations worked to safeguard the interests of the lower ranks, enjoyed various degrees of support from the public and municipal officials and exerted some influence on departmental policies and municipal politics in cities such as Vancouver and Saint John. Their influence in municipal politics and on the inner workings of police services would increase in the future. And as the Toronto example suggests, those interests and the public interest were not always compatible, particularly by the late twentieth century (Russwurm 2007; Marquis 1989, 1993: 115–21).

The Winnipeg General Strike of 1919 (discussed in Chapter 4) involved thirty thousand workers, many of whom were not unionized. As part of a general trend among municipal workers, the police rank and file organized a union but promised not to strike. When the police commission refused to negotiate with the union, most of the members also refused to sign an oath of allegiance to the department. More than 250 members, the bulk of the force, were dismissed, as was the chief constable. During the general strike the skeletal force was reinforced by the RNWMP, the military and 1,400 special constables, some of them war veterans. The latter were equipped by arm bands, badges and wooden clubs. When the strike ended, largely because of the heavy hand of the RNWMP and federal government, many of the dismissed men were rehired. The union was outlawed, but the lower ranks were permitted to organize an athletics association that was an antecedent to the later police association. In other cities mutual benefit societies were the seedbed of eventual unionization (Kealey 1992: 308; Winnipeg Police Service 2014).

Another form of unwanted political pressure, for chief constables, was increased lobbying from women's organizations and moral and social reformers for the employment of policewomen and other reforms in the justice system. A number of urban forces employed police matrons, mainly for attending female prisoners in lockup or court. For a number of years groups such as the WCTU had advocated differential treatment and separate facilities, including jails and courts, for women. Many first-wave feminists considered female offenders to be victims of poverty and of male abuse. Their crusade was more about preventing crime than lobbying for equal rights, yet it still presented a challenge to masculine policing (Appier 1998). During the 1910s a number of Canadian police services hired limited numbers of policewomen. They were not armed or deployed on regular beats or as detectives but worked with juveniles and with morality squads. In some cases they patrolled parks, theatres, dancehalls and other leisure spots looking for improper behaviour by courting couples. Winnipeg hired its first two policewomen in 1916 and 1917; both were in their mid forties and worked in morality enforcement. Paid less than male constables, they were the city's only female officers until the late 1930s (Winnipeg Police Service 2014). Based on statements from the Chief Constables Association of Canada, policewomen were thought of as a passing fad by many senior officers, and we know almost nothing about how they were viewed by the rank and file or the general public. During the First World War there was some support for their work in "protecting" young women from soldiers and helping to combat prostitution and venereal disease, which was thought to be a major threat to the war effort. The emphasis of early policewomen on supervising the morality of working-class girls and women revealed their conflicted position in the justice system; agents of maternal feminism that aimed to protect its weaker "sisters" but also enforcers of middle-class morality (Marquis 1992; Myers 2006).

The most dramatic example of "feminized justice" in the era was the institution of a women's court in Toronto starting in 1913. This followed a period where well-educated female social reformers monitored the local police courts on a regular basis. Reformers in Edmonton obtained a women's court that year, presided over by magistrate and prominent maternal feminist Emily Murphy. Headed up by a well-educated female magistrate starting in 1922, the Toronto court was a major victory for the local Council of Women. Most case studies to date suggest that women who sought help from the police and courts when subjected to domestic violence faced many barriers, including the growing professional social work attitude that abuse was not a criminal act but a symptom of family dysfunction and that the ultimate goal was family reconciliation. Maternal reformers had envisioned the court's clientele to be mainly young, first-time offenders, but in the period 1913 to 1934 the majority of cases reflected traditional arrest categories: drunkenness, vagrancy, prostitution, petty theft and violation of liquor laws (Marquis 1992; Sangster 2001; Glasbeek 2009; Boudreau 2012a: chapter 5).

On the issue of prostitution, moral reformers generally were more successful, at least initially. Urban police had long played a cat and mouse game with the sex trade, which tended to be concentrated in brothels and unlicensed bars in specific neighbourhoods. The traditional weapon of the police was a charge of vagrancy, and there was an almost exclusive focus on female prostitutes, not male clients (Martel 2014: 60). There were periodic crackdowns, but for the most part combatting prostitution was not a top priority of late Victorian police departments, particularly in port cities or in the expanding towns of the west, with their mobile, seasonal male workforces. This began to change with the moral reform assault of the late nineteenth century, which put pressure on local governments and police to close down disorderly houses, and on the federal government to tighten up related *Criminal Code* provisions. Amendments in 1913 and 1914 in theory gave police more power over procurers, pimps and male customers ("found ins"). This was part of the general movement, spearheaded by evangelical Protestant churches, that included legislative initiatives on the provincial level such as prohibition and the federal *Lord's Day Observance Act*. The press and political discussion of the issue was affected by moral reform and feminist claims that Canada, like other developed nations, was scourged by "white slavery," a national or international traffic in women who had been tricked or forced into prostitution. The results of this agitation by the early twentieth century included amendments to the criminal law and criticisms of the police, courts and municipal governments for tolerating and in a sense regulating vice via periodic fines. This was one of the messages of a vice survey conducted by Toronto reformers in the early First World War period (Strange 1995).

In a number of cities the police, begrudgingly, responded with enforcement drives that allegedly broke up existing red-light districts. The national peak in prostitution-related arrests was during the early years of the First World War. According to some critics, vice districts, which had included illegal drinking and gambling spots, simply relocated, and drives against brothels forced sex workers onto the streets or into apartments. Despite the initial expectation of its supporters that the Toronto Women's Court would deal primarily with the "social evil," only one-fifth of women detained in lockup in the period 1913–34 were charged with keeping or being an inmate of a bawdy house (Glasbeek 2009: 72–3). Enforcement patterns varied from one community to the next. In the port and garrison city of Halifax, less than 2 percent of charges laid by the police from 1917 to 1922 were prostitution related (Boudreau 2012a: 134). A case study of Vancouver for the period 1918–35 suggests that vice enforcement, especially concerning prostitution and gambling, was routine, pragmatic and mercenary, with fines and forfeited bail monies from operators, "inmates" and "found ins" feeding the municipal treasury. During the 1920s the Women's Division of the Vancouver police was involved in medical inspections of suspected prostitutes who were brought to court. There is evidence that one of the roles of the police morality squad, formed in 1917, was to remind brothel operators of the informal rules of the game. The preference for handling "immoral women" by summary charges and fines, as opposed to jail time, was reinforced by the provincial authorities. The police, magistrates and city authorities tolerated vice as a necessary evil. And in a highly racialized community, the police, in their own way, tolerated the so-called vices of the generally despised Chinese minority (Marquis 1995b).

The First World War brought new duties and pressures to Canadian police services. Like the RNWMP, many departments had their ranks depleted by voluntary enlistments. Winnipeg lost more than 150 men, twenty-nine of whom died. Only seventy-eight returned to the force after their war experiences, and many of these resigned or were dismissed for being unfit for duty (Winnipeg Police Service 2014). As discussed in Chapter 4, the war enhanced the security and intelligence duties of the Dominion Police and the RNWMP and created a new class of subjects for surveillance: enemy aliens. New federal laws and regulations brought increased responsibilities to police services. Under federal legislation designed to combat venereal disease for the good of the war effort, for example, women taken into police custody could be medically inspected for signs of disease. In 1918 Ontario passed its own law permitting such examinations of women under arrest or committed to jails or reformatories (Sangster 2001: 88). Alberta did the same, and in terms of enforcement "prostitutes and 'loose women' were deliberately singled out" (Cassell 1987: 190).

Police chiefs complained about extra duties and the loss of men to the military, yet in most cases police departments during the war experienced a noticeable decline in complaints and arrests, for two reasons. One was the fact that tens of thousands of young men, the source of most public order crime, were in the military. The other was the onset, or near onset, of provincial prohibition laws during the war that appeared to have dramatic effects on arrest, court and incarceration statistics. In a number of cases the final push for provincial prohibition came from pragmatic win-the-war arguments. Although people could be arrested, fined and jailed for violations of prohibition laws, they were provincial, not federal laws, similar to motor vehicle and fish and game acts, and not always taken seriously by the population. The police, with their historic aversion to aggressive morality enforcement, tended to be critical of prohibition in the long run, yet in the short term it appeared to significantly alter the incidence of alcohol-related disorder such as public drunkenness and disturbing the peace (Marquis 2005b).

Canada's police services took comfort in the public's apparent strong support for the crime control model. Two signs of this were the lack of viable citizen movements to abolish the death penalty or to advocate for the rights of prisoners and ex-prisoners. The one exception was growing reform support for a new approach to treating young offenders. The juvenile delinquency movement was based on a combination of humanitarian desire to protect children and youth from the harsher aspects of the justice system, conservative fear of unruly youth and a progressive belief in efficiency and the role of experts. Represented by volunteer organizations such as the Children's Aid Society, the "child savers" also believed in widening the net of categorization and surveillance over delinquent and dependent children, most of whom were from poor and working-class families. A federal law of 1894 had mandated that children under the age of sixteen had to be confined in separate areas of lockups or police stations, apart from adult offenders. The 1908 *Juvenile Delinquents Act* (JDA) permitted municipalities or counties to create a juvenile court and separate short-term detention facilities. These courts pioneered practices such as probation and the use of social workers and psychologists. In time most provinces also maintained one or more reformatories for neglected and dependent children. Under the JDA, children's names were not released to the press, and the new courts operated in a less adversarial fashion. Penalties were less severe than with adult courts, based on the idea that vulnerable youth deserved compassion and understanding and on the theory that first-time offenders should not be exposed to hardened "jail birds." Juvenile courts pioneered the use of probation and suspended sentences, a troubling development for law and order advocates within police ranks. In addition to these dispositions, magistrates were more likely to reprimand juveniles, release them to the custody of their parents or impose fines or restitution orders than sentence them to reformatories or training schools (Carrigan 1998: 109, 140–2; Myers 2006).

The response of police departments to the new approach to youthful misbehaviour was mixed, and once again the views of the rank and file are difficult to discern. Some chief constables, suspicious of all reform, viewed juvenile courts as encouraging law-breaking and undermining the police. It was true that a sizeable minority of crimes of violence and against property was carried out by minors and that the press in a number of cities reported on a so-called "boy problem," groups or gangs of teenagers who loitered in parks or on street corners, smoked cigarettes, carried revolvers and engaged in burglary and petty theft. Other chief constables supported specialized treatment of juveniles for these very reasons. This was an early endorsement of a crime prevention approach that most police services embrace to this very day, based on the strategy of reaching out to at-risk youth before they become young offenders. Still others privately criticized the JDA but refused to condemn it in pubic when it was endorsed by police commissions, judges, newspaper editors and other members of the local power elite. Few police officials appeared to recognize the "net widening" aspects of the new system, which brought children into court for behaviour such as being "incorrigible" or staying out all night, crimes that did not exist for adults. Many prosecutions under the JDA were initiated by police, but parents, teachers and neighbours were also active as complainants. In other words, poor and working-class parents appealed to the police and juvenile courts in attempts to control their children, particularly wayward daughters. Most delinquents were boys, and their serious offences in the 1920s, 1930s and 1940s were largely property related. Girls, a minority of delinquents, tended to be judged more harshly on the basis of their sexual morality (Sangster 2001; Myers 2005; Glasbeek 2009).

FROM THE RNWMP TO THE RCMP

In 1905 two new provinces, Alberta and Saskatchewan, were created out of the North-West Territories. The Mounties were strongly identified with the Prairie region, and settlers outside of incorporated municipalities had come to value the police for not only their general law enforcement functions but also various services. The result was that the new provincial governments entered into an innovative relationship with the NWMP, who in 1904 were awarded the prefix *Royal* in honour of their service to the Dominion and the Empire. (A number of Mounties had also served in Canadian volunteer units fighting in South Africa for Britain in the period 1899 to 1902.) Starting in 1905, the Royal North West Mounted Police (RNWMP) delivered rural policing in Alberta and Saskatchewan. The terms of the service were covered by contracts that, in theory, made the RNWMP a provincial constabulary. But recruitment, training, organization, pay and conditions of service were determined not by the provincial attorneys general but the Commissioner of the RNWMP. Even with the contracts, the future of the Mounted Police, which in 1910 had only six hundred members, was not secure. Although the initial agreements ended in 1917 because of wartime circumstances, the 1905 contract model would be revisited and have a have a profound impact on the national policing scene.

The Mounted Police typified a supposedly "British" characteristic of Canadian police leadership, relative continuity and insulation from political interference. Although in certain jurisdictions such as Vancouver there was considerable turn-over in police chiefs, most Canadian police managers were relatively insulated from political direction. Between 1886 and 1931 the Mounted Police were headed by three commissioners. Toronto had only three chief constables between 1886 and 1946. Many police chiefs, such as John C. McRae, who headed the Winnipeg force from 1887 to 1911, started out as constables on the beat. Promotion from within the ranks had become the dominant model; unlike the military, RIC or LMP, there

was no specially-trained "officer class." Yet there were chief constables recruited
from the private sector or from the military, such as Brigadier-General Dennis
Draper, who commanded a Canadian infantry brigade during the First World War
then worked as a corporate manager before being appointed to head the Toronto
police in 1928. An outspoken enemy of local Communists and a tough exponent
of crime-fighting professionalism, he retired in 1946. The one glaring exception to
this continuity of senior leadership was Vancouver, where chiefs tended to serve
short terms before falling victim to corruption scandals and other controversies.
More research needs to be done on police governance, but for the most part it
appears that boards of commissioners of police, where they existed, insulated chief
constables from public criticism and treated the former with considerable defer-
ence. Training and discipline for the RNWMP remained more militaristic than for
municipal police services; until the 1970s, for example, married men could not
join the Mounties. Yet by the 1920s even the RCMP tended to favour senior officers
appointed through the ranks (Marquis 1986b and 1993).

Outside of war-related duties (discussed in Chapter 4) and the provincial contracts, the RNWMP was mainly deployed in the Yukon and the Northwest Territories.
The Mounties remained in the Yukon after the gold rush ended, but their next frontiers were the western Arctic and Hudson Bay. This fascinated American authors and
screenwriters who increasingly depicted the force as associated with the northern
wilderness (Walden 1982: 157–8). In 1903 the police established a post on Herschel
Island in the Beaufort Sea to enforce Canadian customs laws among the seasonal
American whalers and in theory to prevent abuse of the local Inuit. Along the way
they set up a base at Fort McPherson near the Mackenzie Delta. This led to the police
attempting to extend their authority over the Western Arctic and involved epic and
sometimes disastrous patrols that contributed to the legend of the force. According
to Morrison (1985: 144–5), the police regarded the First Nations of the area "with
a mixture of paternalism and contempt" and as troublesome people "to be avoided
as much as possible." In these same years the Department of the Interior employed
the Mounted Police to exert Canadian sovereignty in the Hudson Bay area, which
was frequented by Scottish and American whalers. One part of the mission was to
protect the muskox population from overhunting. Mounted Police brass were not
keen on expanding into the central Arctic, but the force's northern exposure in the
wake of the unpopular Alaska boundary dispute settlement found nationalistic
support in southern Canada and added to the reputation of the RNWMP.

During the First World War the RNWMP took on extra duties related to the war.
The force also lost men to the war effort. As discussed in more detail in Chapter
4, by 1917 the RNWMP was responsible for national security in the west, a duty
performed by the Dominion Police in the eastern provinces. The Mounted Police
monitored Austrian and German immigrants as security threats and investigated

complaints (or even rumours) of enemy aliens and seditious activities and utterances, most of which were unproven. As also discussed in Chapter 4, the 1919 Winnipeg General Strike, which despite its radical reputation was basically fought over union recognition and wartime inflation, provided Commissioner Bowen-Perry with an opportunity to present the federal government with an ambitious plan. He suggested that the RNWMP, whose operations had been confined to the West and parts of the North, should become more national in scope. This could be accomplished by assigning the force sole responsibility for security and intelligence, an interim step implemented in 1919. In 1920 the full plan was put into effect and the new organization was called the Royal Canadian Mounted Police. In the automobile age few if any of the force was still mounted, but the term remained for historic and marketing reasons, and equestrian skills and marching in riding boots with spurs remained part of depot training for cadets for decades. In 1904 the RNWMP began its popular "musical ride" mounted drill display at fairs in Manitoba and Saskatchewan. Equitation was part of recruit training until 1966 (Horrall 1980).

According to one veteran of the era (Kemp 1958: 67), the "agitators of 1919" saved the Mounted Police from being disbanded, largely because the commissioner's adept exploitation of a crisis. The RCMP absorbed the Dominion Police, the first of a series of "conquests" of competing agencies, and in 1920 its headquarters moved from Regina to Ottawa. Although few Mounties were stationed in the central and eastern provinces and only a fraction of the force worked in security and intelligence, the RCMP was poised for future expansion. Through the merger, it acquired the national criminal identification record collection (fingerprints, mug shots, modus operandi files) of the Dominion Police and it was tasked with assisting other federal agencies such as the Secretary of State in investigating naturalization applications to ensure that "undesirables" were not granted "British" citizenship (Canadian citizenship technically did not exist until after the Second World War). As Hewitt (2006: 64–74) points out, the RCMP was enthusiastically involved in the deportation of non citizens during the 1920s and 1930s. The most common reasons for deportation were previous criminal records, criminality, vagrancy/ unemployment and political radicalism.

The security and intelligence mandate of the RCMP (discussed in Chapter 4) required few resources in the 1920s, and outside of the Northwest Territories, where the Mounties began to expand their presence, the new organization was still trying to justify its existence. During the 1920s, aided by airplanes and radios, the RCMP began to patrol and build posts in the Arctic, among the Inuit. Initially the police had favourable views of this historically self-reliant culture, to the point of explaining a number of murders in a culturally-sensitive manner. Ottawa used the RCMP as a tool of sovereignty in the North, establishing detachments on Ellesmere Island, in part because it feared Danish and American activity in the eastern Arctic.

As the only state agents in the high Arctic, the police collected customs duties, delivered the mail and supplied "the south" with knowledge about the Inuit. From time to time they provided emergency rations and medical aid to the Inuit. As the indigenous peoples of the Arctic became more acculturated and less independent, the police began to view them as negatively as they did the Indians to the south. The most famous exploit of the RCMP in the North is this period was the successful pursuit, from the Northwest Territories into the Yukon, of Albert Johnson, the so-called "Mad Trapper." Johnson was wanted for killing one Mountie and wounding another. Tracked by bush plane and two-way radio, he died in a hail of bullets in early 1932 (Morrison 1985). The hunt for the Mad Trapper and other Mounted Police exploits in the North added to the growing mythic status of the force, which was reinforced by more than 150 novels dealing with the force published between 1890 and 1940. Together with memoirs, RCMP publications and popular culture manifestations such as radio, motion pictures, comic strips and television, this "highly selective" version of Mounted Police history both reflected and reinforced the force's positive image in English Canada (Dawson 1998: chapter 2, 111).

During the 1920s the four Western provinces operated their own provincial constabularies, which relegated RCMP in these jurisdictions to the enforcement of federal statutes. This was a lean decade for the force. One theory (discussed in Chapter 4) is that security and intelligence duties kept the new federal force busy during the 1920s, yet the number of real or imagined radical threats was limited as were the number of officers assigned to their investigation. In an era of contin- ued uncertainly and strong provincial rights, the new RCMP was partly sustained by a crusade against narcotics, a problem created by Canada's harsh drug laws, which treated addicts not as patients but criminals. The pre-1914 federal statutes (1908, 1911) were aimed at opium smoking by Chinese males, especially in British Columbia, and by the 1920s drug enforcement had developed the tone of a racially-tinged moral crusade. In a sense the criminalization of opium and other drugs was an echo of British Columbia's early twentieth-century quest to make "a white man's country" (Roy 1989: 229). The 1908 anti-opium law passed in the wake of anti-Asian rioting in Vancouver banned only trafficking and possession for purposes of trafficking, not possession for personal use. In 1911, to the satisfaction of police, smoking and possession of opium were criminalized.

Individual police chiefs, the CCAC and especially the RCMP and the new federal Department of Health starting in the 1920s advocated tougher laws and were rewarded with the consolidated statue of 1929. Although most drug offenders in the 1920s (many of whom were deported) were Chinese, the police in the inter- war era, assisted by sensationalist journalism such as Emily Murphy's *The Black Candle*, developed the narrative of the "dope fiend," a violent, sexually-promiscuous individual who "infected" the innocent and the weak with the curse of addiction.

Most Canadian cities lacked identifiable "Chinatowns" on the scale of Vancouver, Toronto or Montreal, but Chinese cafes, laundries and other businesses were common in most Canadian urban centres and were raided for gambling or drug offences. They were also suspected of being locations where young white women were led astray. In most cases the penalty for possession was a fine (Boudreau 2012a: 170–3), and there is strong evidence that in Vancouver fines and forfeited bail deposits levied in drug and other types of morality enforcement were a type of informal licensing that brought revenues to the civic coffers (Marquis 1995b).

Given the social profile of illegal drug users (Chinese or lower-class whites), drug enforcement, compared to other types of morality enforcement, fit the police image of crime-fighting, despite the relatively low numbers of arrests. Addicts increasingly resorted to morphine, heroin and codeine and developed a lifestyle that centred on intravenous injection. Although local police morality squads and detectives arrested addicts, the RCMP in a sense "invaded" urban law enforcement and devoted considerable resources to countering traffickers. As Hewitt notes, the enforcement of federal laws such as the *Opium and Narcotic Drug Act* helped justify the continued existence of the RCMP in provinces such as Alberta and Saskatchewan throughout the 1920s when its future seemed uncertain (Hewitt 2006: 59). In the late 1920s the provincial and municipal police laid most drug charges, but by 1940 the RCMP, with the cooperation of local police, had virtually taken over this area. Given that many known addicts were in jail, in places like Vancouver, where the RCMP maintained a large presence, most addicts, who supported themselves by petty theft, were literally "known to the police" (Carstairs 2006: chapter 4).

Later the Mounties and their police allies dropped much of the moral condemnation of "criminal addicts" but continued to defend their theory that addicts were criminals first, could not be reformed and were burdens on society. This echoed the backward propaganda of the American Federal Bureau of Narcotics, which for decades fought off medicalized approaches to the narcotics realm. Many of the tactics used to disrupt the drug traffic had parallels in RCMP Security Service work: surveillance, raids, the gathering of information on persons with whom addicts were living or socializing and the use of informants and undercover operations. The police sent mug shots of convicted addicts to the Division of Narcotic Control in Ottawa, which attempted to track all known addicts. Until the mid 1950s, the police view of drugs and drug users was the single biggest determinant of state policy on narcotics. Historical research suggests that the police did not invent the various myths that came to distort thinking about drugs, but they certainly exploited these "common sense" beliefs. The RCMP clung to the "contagion" and "criminal addict" theories well after the Second World War, and it would make them unprepared to face the explosion of recreational drug use and competing expert discourses in the 1960s and 1970s (Giffen, Endicott and Lambert 1991; Carstairs 2006: chapter 4).

PROVINCIAL POLICE, ALCOHOL CONTROL AND RCMP EXPANSION

The expansion of provincial government activity in the 1910s and 1920s, which involved first modified prohibition and then, increasingly, a system of provincially-owned liquor stores and in some cases licensed drinking spots, coincided with the expansion then the retraction of provincial policing. Other than liquor enforcement, two other factors explained the popularity of these constabularies: the challenges of highway safety enforcement and increased demands for modern policing services in rural areas. Legislation dealing with provincial policing extended back to 1870 in Manitoba and Quebec and 1896 in Ontario. The 1894 *Mounted Police Act* contained a section that permitted the federal government to negotiate policing contracts with specific provinces. As detailed by Lin (2007) the Laurier government expected the new provinces of Alberta and Saskatchewan in 1905 to take care of their own policing needs, but the provincial governments, conscious of the cost of establishing new services and aware of the popularity of the Mounted Police among the white settler population, had other ideas. This began the system of contract policing under which the federal taxpayer subsidized provincial, and eventually municipal, law enforcement. Mounted Police services for the provinces were financially attractive, plus the cost of training, pensions and medical care were covered by Ottawa. In addition, the provinces secured the services of a highly-disciplined force with an image for efficiency and incorruptibility. The advent of the contracts in 1905 coincided with the force being renamed the Royal North West Mounted Police. RNWMP contract forces legally were under the provincial attorney general but under the overall control of the Commissioner and, ultimately, Ottawa. The result was that 90 percent of the total strength of the force at the advent of the First World War was posted to Alberta and Saskatchewan (Hewitt 2006: 161).

As with the OPP and the Sûreté du Québec (SQ), the BCPP not only survived the wave of RCMP expansion that started in the late 1920s (the provincial police lost its mandate to enforce fish and game regulations during this period) but expanded and modernized. By the 1920s provincial constables were issued uniforms. Following a migration of Doukhobors who lived communally in eastern British Columbia, the BCPP became involved with the newcomers, who had become engaged in factional disputes and protests over provincial education and vital statistics registration policies. The former culminated in the unsolved assassination of Peter Verigin when a bomb detonated on a train in 1924, killing ten people. The latter involved nude parades, schools being burned to the ground and other acts of vandalism (the RCMP investigated "Bolshevik" connections to the sect and monitored conditions among their communities). The province prosecuted members of the sect for failing to send their children to school, which led to the BCPP aided by dozens of deputized road construction workers seizing Doukhobor property at Grand Forks, B.C.

Parading in the nude was made a Criminal Code offence in 1931 in response to Doukhobor civil disobedience. By the late thirties the force maintained divisions covering Vancouver Island, the lower mainland, the southern mainland and the interior, which included the Okanagan and the province's vast northern region, including the Peace River district. Equipped with shortwave radio and several boats, the BCPP delivered rural and "frontier" policing but was also contracted to deliver policing services in a number of municipalities. By the end of the Second World War it was policing forty municipalities (Stonier-Newman 1991; Torrance 1986: 33).

The most controversial area of provincial policing in the 1910s, 1920s and 1930s concern alcohol regulation. In this period political controversies raged not over bank robbers or confidence artists but morality enforcement. Most provinces adopted forms of prohibition during the 1910s; the quest to ban the bar and liquor store prompted divisive responses, so much so that British Columbia and Quebec dismantled their dry laws shortly after the war and introduced systems of government control of alcohol sales. The Prairie provinces followed this trend during the first half of the 1920s, followed by Ontario and New Brunswick in 1927. The four Western provinces moved beyond the sale of alcohol, under strict conditions, in liquor stores, to the sale of beer "by the glass" in beer parlours. The advent of government liquor stores and closely-regulated beer parlours as more orderly alternatives to the private liquor dealer and the saloon did not eradicate the black market in alcohol (Marquis 2005b). When Nova Scotia introduced government liquor stores in 1930, the Prohibition era had ended, outside of the lone holdout, Prince Edward Island. Yet both to reassure temperance organizations and to combat bootleggers who competed with the new government liquor stores, a number of provinces expanded their provincial policing efforts or, in the case of New Brunswick and Nova Scotia, created provincial constabularies. The increasing popularity of the automobile affected the timing of these efforts. Other than enforcing the liquor laws, these forces had little criminal policing work. Increasingly, highway safety laws occupied their time and resources (Marquis 1990).

As noted by Marquis (2005b) and others, the Canadian police, whether provincial or federal, had an ambivalent response to enforcing prohibition laws. Although much of their work involved handling "drunks," and much disorder and crime linked to alcohol was behind most law-breaking, the police were uncomfortable with enforcing unpopular laws, particularly those unpopular with the middle class. This was evident prior to the First World War with the RNWMP response to illegal liquor sales in Alberta and Saskatchewan. Although technically the provincial police in these jurisdictions, the Mounties took little proactive action, responded only episodically to citizen complaints and recorded little anti-bootlegging activity in their reports. In 1916 the Commissioner warned the prime minister that wartime security duties meant that the RNWMP was too thin on the ground and that the provincial contracts would have to be terminated. In 1917 the Mounted Police, which wanted to organize a military unit for overseas service, ended civil policing in the two provinces, forcing Saskatchewan and Alberta to organize their own constabularies. One probable factor influencing the decision was the unpopularity among the Mounties in enforcing provincial prohibition (Lin 2007).

In theory the new Saskatchewan Provincial Police (SPP) and the Alberta Provincial Police (APP), like the RNWMP detachments they replaced, were insulated from politics and community influences, similar to the nineteenth-century RIC. The APP was more successful in maintaining an arm's-length relationship with the United Farmers of Alberta government, but the police in Saskatchewan were entangled with the dominant Liberal party, which interfered with appointments, discipline and operations. One form of political influence in both provinces was pressure to enforce prohibition laws. As Lin (2007) notes, this put the provincial police in conflict with not only European immigrants but also the Canadian-born middle and working classes. In contrast to the early NWMP that had encountered a largely Anglo-Celtic settler population, the provincial police, who also dealt with status and non-status Indians and Metis, faced a more pluralistic society. More than a third of the population in Alberta and Saskatchewan were non-British immigrants, and the police were expected to play a role in their "Canadianization" (Lin 2007).

Until the urbanization of much of Canada's indigenous population, which was more evident following the Second World War, First Nations individuals and communities, if they interacted with white law at all, were more likely to come into contact with the RCMP or the BCPP or other provincial constabularies than municipal police. White Indian agents were the dominant government authority figures on larger reserves, and when they required assistance in enforcing the *Indian Act* they called on the RCMP. One of the most dramatic examples was in 1924 when Six Nations Mohawk refused to adopt the government-mandated system of elected chiefs and band councils. After a federal order-in-council removed the hereditary chief, the RCMP intervened.

The Mounted Police was also involved in rounding up children for the nation's network of Indian residential schools, a church-run system that involved up to 150,000 children before its demise in the 1990s. The goal of the schools was to isolate reserve children from their families and to assimilate them into the dominant Euro-Canadian culture. Most of the schools were in the four Western provinces and the North. The rules were strict and discipline harsh, plus, as revealed in heartbreaking fashion in recent decades, there was widespread psychological, physical and sexual abuse. As late as the early twentieth century, mortality rates among the children were high, and for the first several decades, half of the school day was devoted to manual labour. In 2012 the RCMP issued a report that admitted the force had been involved in the system in a "secondary" capacity by returning absent students and fining uncooperative parents but had been largely unaware of abuses at the schools, most of which were run by the Roman Catholic and Anglican churches. The police had merely followed the requests of Indian agents and school officials "without questioning" the legitimacy of the system. Starting in 1933, RCMP officers were appointed truant officers for the schools, which were supported financially by the Department of Indian Affairs. In 2004, the Commissioner of the RCMP issued a formal apology for the force's role in this controversial chapter of Indian policy, but as a number of residential school survivors testified, the experience had caused generations of aboriginal people to mistrust and fear the police (LeBeuf 2012).

The roots of the justice system's failure of First Nations peoples, namely the over-policing of petty offences such as possession of alcohol or drunkenness and the under-policing of crimes of violence against First Nations people, are rooted in this era. The *Indian Act* had strict provisions governing public drunkenness and possession of alcohol, and it seems that these offences were enforced with less discretion against Native people than whites. Police also developed stereotypical images of First Nations people. As the Royal Commission on Canada's Aboriginal Peoples later concluded, the vulnerable position of indigenous peoples in the justice system was caused by a blend of cultural clash, socio-economic deprivation and the legacy of colonialism (Royal Commission 1993). First Nations women in Ontario prior to the 1960s, whether on or off reserve, tended to be arrested for morality and public order offences, such as vagrancy, prostitution or public drunkenness. In many cases police acted in conjunction with Indian agents who had powers of justices of the peace. Many were jailed for being too poor to be able to pay fines, and most came from backgrounds of extreme social deprivation (Sangster 1999).

Outside of Quebec, where a strong provincial identity and suspicion of the federal government kept provincial policing viable, and Ontario, which had the financial resources to maintain its own constabulary for rural and non-incorporated areas, the real winner in provincial policing prior to the Second World War was the RCMP. In 1928 the force returned to the provincial sphere, signing an agreement with Saskatchewan that would be the basis of an important expansion of the force. After provincial prohibition was repealed in 1924, the reputation of the SPP improved. By 1927 Saskatchewan officials were arguing that there was too much duplication between the SPP and the RCMP, which had maintained members in the province to enforce the *Indian Act*, the *Inland Revenue Act* and other federal laws. The fact the all RCMP recruits continued to be trained at Regina kept the force in the public limelight in the province. Scholars disagree as to exactly why the SPP was disbanded in 1928, but financial arguments were paramount at the time. Hewitt (2006: 26) notes that provincial officials were also impressed by the RCMP's willingness to handle the unemployed. The contract with the RCMP (which continues to this day) not only benefited provincial taxpayers, it also buried past controversies associated with the SPP. Alberta, which rejected the federal offer in 1928, was concerned that the RCMP as a contract force would neglect social and other non-criminal services such as enforcement of provincial hunting regulations. With the onset of the Great Depression, the United Farmers of Alberta government was forced into a pattern of deficit spending. In 1932 the APP was disbanded and the RCMP took over rural policing. Under both contracts the provincial government collected all fines from *Criminal Code* and liquor law convictions. This was the same year that the RCMP absorbed the provincial police in the three Maritime provinces (Lin 2007; Marquis 1993: 265).

Another acquisition was the Customs Preventive Service (CPS), which maintained a fleet of vessels to enforced customs regulations. In 1926, during a period when the federal government was embroiled in scandal surrounding corruption in the Customs department, the commissioner of the RCMP had advised a parliamentary committee that the Preventive Service, for the sake of efficiency, should be transferred to the Mounted Police. Following the revelations of the Customs scandal, the CPS was expanded and modernized with new vessels. In 1930, finally acceding to the requests of the government of the United States, which had been under national prohibition since 1920, the Mackenzie King government agreed to ban the clearance of liquor cargoes from Canada to America. This rerouted the black market in alcohol through the French islands of St. Pierre and Miquelon and created new challenges for the CPS in the Gulf of St. Lawrence. The Customs and Excise department was concerned with manufactured goods and booze smuggled in from other countries without duty being paid: the RCMP focused on alcohol smuggled between Canadian provinces, some of which, prior to 1930, were still dry. In 1932 the now Department of National Revenue CPS, consisting of thirty-two patrol boats and their crews, was transferred to the RCMP Marine Division, which maintained anti-smuggling patrols on the Pacific and Atlantic coasts, the Great Lakes and the St. Lawrence river. Until its duties were absorbed by other federal departments, the Marine Division was also involved in search and rescue duties. The experimental police service established in 1920 now consisted of more than 240 detachments and served as the provincial police in six of Canada's nine provinces (Kemp 1958: 159; McDougall 1995).

CRIME FIGHTING VS. ACTUAL POLICING

The official mantra of the profession was that the police were crime fighters, focusing on professional or career criminals that specialized in bank robbery, burglary, fraud, larceny, picking pockets and dealing with stolen goods. In reality crimes of this nature were a small percentage of overall police business and rarely encountered by officers on patrol. Detectives, as they had in the nineteenth century, were mainly concerned with tracking down stolen property. In official reports and newspaper accounts, police services invariably claimed to be clamping down on illegal booze, prostitution, gambling and prostitution, yet most case studies suggest a selective and episodic enforcement response (Morton 2003: 15). The exact extent of these "victimless" crimes in a given community is difficult to determine. As in the United States, police professionalism, with its emphasis on crime fighting, was compromised by the divisive issue of prohibition, and although individual police leaders supported it, the rank and file, like most urban people, did not. The differing police attitudes to drug and alcohol prohibition were determined largely by the nature of the typical users. Although individuals were prosecuted for buying contraband alcohol during and after prohibition, most viewed this as a relatively harmless social crime, not a threat to Canada's "manhood" or "womanhood." Post-prohibition regimes also placed considerable emphasis on provincial liquor commissions, liquor store managers and staff, liquor inspectors and the proprietors of licensed beer parlours and other premises to produce orderly (largely male) drinkers (Marquis 2005b; Thompson and Genosko 2009; Malleck 2012).

So-called victimless crimes continued to be a source of controversy and sometimes scandal for Canadian police services. Montreal, which enjoyed a North America-wide reputation during American prohibition (1900–1932) as a "wide open" city, was periodically swept by media, reform and political accusations of institutionalized police corruption. In 1918 the New York Bureau of Municipal Research opined that the department was not only tolerating organized prostitution and gambling but also ignoring modern approaches such as crime prevention and social service work. The morality squad of the day estimated that up to three hundred brothels operated in what was one of North America's last recognized red-light districts (CP 1918). Vice conditions and police efficiency were investigated again in the mid 1920s when an inquiry headed by a judge repeated the earlier allegations that the department was ignoring vice and failing to deal with basic detective work such as tracking down stolen property (CP 1925). To varying degrees, all cities were affected by periodic controversies over vice and its alleged toleration by police, prosecutors, judges and politicians.

The statistical realities of arrest, pre-trial detention and magistrates' courts contradict much of the rhetoric of crime fighting. In the period 1917 to 1922, 63 percent of convictions in the Halifax police court were for drunkenness, disturbing the peace, violations of the *Motor Vehicle Act* or common assault (Boudreau 2012a: 35). The "jailbird" phenomenon identified by Fingard (1989) for nineteenth-century Halifax was also evident in early twentieth-century Toronto at least in terms of women placed in or sentenced to short-term custody. These women were poor, lived in lower-class tenement neighbourhoods, were often homeless and many were alcoholics. Police professionalism justified itself with images of professional thieves and criminal masterminds. Yet most of the women charged and detained for property offences in Toronto between 1913 and 1934 were accused of shoplifting and other minor thefts, and when sentenced to custody their custodial terms ranged from four to sixty days. In addition, the conviction rate for these offences was relatively low, and in the case of women convicted for shoplifting, most were one-time offenders (Glasbeek 2009: chapter 3).

The average person arrested by the police between 1900 and 1945 could hardly be classified as belonging to a "criminal class." The focus on minor public disorder was a logical result of police walking the beat; unlike the situation by the late twentieth century, the typical constable had little "uncommitted time" when on duty (Brodeur 2010: 158). Most assaults involved family members or acquaintances involved in personal disputes. People who came into conflict with the police tended to be poor, young and male. Most of them were arrested only once in their adult lives, but the bulk were economically vulnerable and lived in substandard housing. One sign of their marginality was a continued lack of concern over, and investment in, police lockups, which in many cases continued to consist of large or small cells with no bunks or bedding, just a concrete floor. In 1944, the cells in the main Montreal police station, which dated from the late 1830s, were described as "medieval" (CP 1944). As in the previous century, the typical offender committed to county jails had already served several custodial sentences. The human "throughput" of the typical urban police lockup elicited occasional pity but almost no interest in rehabilitation. And the links between alcohol and recidivism, despite more liberal attitudes, did not disappear. In fact the national rate of convictions for public drunkenness in the court system was higher in the 1940s and 1950s than it had been in any post-Confederation decade except the 1870s, and well into the 1960s many provincial jail admissions were for drunkenness (Wallace, Higgins and McGahan 1994: 77; Marquis 2012).

Another sign of the general lack of interest in reforming the typical adult petty offender was the relative lack, by the mid twentieth century, of adult probation services. Canada, in contrast to Great Britain where a strong penal reform movement countered potential war on crime crusades, offered little opposition other than fiscal restraint to the crime fighting approach. Although the federal government appointed a royal commission on the penal system in the late 1930s, few reforms were initiated in adult corrections until well after the Second World War. The CCAC, which during the 1920s had continued to speak out against federal and provincial parole, appeared before the royal commission to denounce early release from prisons, defence lawyers, "do-gooders," interfering politicians, lenient judges, juvenile delinquents and probation (Marquis 1993: 144–5). Adult probation was recognized in the *Criminal Code* only in 1921, yet its use was restricted, usually only to first-time offenders vetted by a Crown prosecutor. Although Ontario passed an enabling act in 1922, thirty years later only four communities had hired adult probation officers. By the immediate post-World War period the justice system in England and Wales placed greater emphasis on probation and parole than on incarceration. Yet in Canada jail and penitentiary populations far outnumbered adults under the supervision of probation and parole officers (Couglan 1988).

Despite a growing professional focus and public perception that modern policing concentrated on fighting serious crime, public order violations continued to form the bulk of arrests, and considerable resources were invested in traffic safety and bylaw regulation. The Toronto police, for example, licensed or otherwise regulated taxi drivers, laundries, peddlars, dance halls, meeting halls, billiard parlours and theatrical performances and motion pictures. Weaver's study of Hamilton reveals that most victims of theft in the first half of the twentieth century were blue collar or petit bourgeois, that the articles stolen generally were not valuable and that only 5 percent of reported incidents resulted in a conviction (Weaver 1995: 245).

The emphasis on misdemeanours was burdensome on the poor, the marginalized and minorities. A study of misdeameanour enforcement for Toronto, Ottawa, London, Windsor, Hamilton and Thunder Bay for the period 1892 to 1930 indicates that African Canadians were more likely than whites to be arrested and once arrested treated more harshly in terms of bail, conviction rates and length of sentence. Black women were especially vulnerable. Police appear to have been at least partially motivated by racial prejudice in dealing with African Canadians, and it is highly likely that members of this community feared or at least distrusted police services as agents of white domination (Mosher 1996). A larger study of public order offences for urban Ontario in the period 1892 to 1961 indicates that two visible minorities with a limited presence in communities, Chinese and African Canadians, were subjected to extra police surveillance in terms of bawdy and disorderly houses offences (Mosher 1998: 162, 170–4). Similarly, although the heaviest burdens of drug enforcement in the period 1908–1930 fell on Chinese Canadians (who were 49 percent of total offenders), the racial characteristics of other offenders were also often noted. The RCMP maintained separate statistics for "coloured" offenders until 1937. Although only 6 percent of persons convicted for drug offences in six representative Ontario cities from 1908 to 1930 were Black, this exceeded their presence in the general population (Mosher 1998: 147–53). Yet in most communities, despite the assertions of police, journalists and politicians, there was no actual "criminal class," and the typical offender was a young, white, working-class male (Boudreau 2012a: chapter 4).

Starting in the late 1890s Canada, largely through immigration, became a more diverse society. Between 1896 and 1914 three million newcomers arrived; one quarter ended up in the cities, but most headed to the land. Although most of these immigrants hailed from Britain, the United States and Western Europe, increased numbers came from central and eastern Europe. One result was that by 1921, 14 percent of the population was classified as non British, non-French European in terms of ethnic origins (Li 2000). Provinces such as Alberta, Saskatchewan and Manitoba became more pluralistic, but this diversity was largely confined to white Europeans. Asians and particularly Blacks found it difficult to enter Canada; the new groups were epitomized by Ukrainians, east European peasants who were valued as hard-working farmers but often stereotyped in media and police reports as violent. Similarly, many press accounts of Italian immigrants, many of them sojourning males who located in cities such as Hamilton, Toronto and Montreal, stressed their violent nature. In Toronto social reformers and police were troubled by St. John's Ward, a neighbourhood that contained thousands of Italian and Jewish immigrants who were associated with bootlegging, gambling and other offences. In Winnipeg in 1907, the police court convicted roughly 3,600 individuals; less than half of them were described as "Canadian" (Woodsworth 1909: 206). "Foreigners" (eastern and southern Europeans) generally were viewed as more likely than Asians, Blacks or Jews to assimilate but still a source of social problems, including political radicalism and an inability to respect "British justice." It would be decades before many ethnic minorities would be represented on Canada's police services.

Later studies and exposés of police culture revealed the gender biases inherent in male dominated authoritarian organizations, and the resistance to the hiring of female officers remained strong well after the Second World War. Following the initial flurry of recruitment of a token number of policewomen in the 1910s, the subject was all but ignored in the publications and conferences of the CCAC, which also rarely discussed women as criminals. Little is known about police views of women offenders and victims, but work by Sangster (2001) and others suggests that the relatively low numbers of women arrested in the 1920s and 1930s should not disguise differential attitudes and treatment based on gender stereotypes. Women and girls, although less likely to be arrested than men, were subjected to greater moral surveillance with charges such as prostitution-related vagrancy, keeping or being an inmate of a bawdy house or liquor offences. Poor and working-class women who were assaulted or not supported by their spouses often resorted to the police and courts out of desperation, but case studies suggest that the authorities, which included family courts, probation officers and social workers, were more interested in family reconciliation and securing support payments than in jailing abusive husbands. And police services appear to have discouraged women from charges against violent or abusive spouses (Weaver 1995: 226–7; Sangster 2001).

During the 1920s and 1930s the rise of mass automobile ownership drew police departments into new areas of urban regulation. In terms of the ratio of cars and trucks to population, Canada was one of the most mobile societies in the world. Although as late as the 1930s much of the working class did not own a personal vehicle, automobiles were transforming the economy, urban planning and social practice (Flink 1990). Social conservatives worried that cars spawned immorality, sexual predation and juvenile delinquency, and the police complained that they were being used by bandits and gangsters. Traffic safety and parking regulations began to consume departmental resources and produce specialized units. In 1930, for example, the OPP took over highway patrol from the Department of Public Highways; a decade later the motorcycle patrol was fully absorbed into the OPP, and the force was emphasizing the need for both patrol and unmarked cars to cover more than seven thousand miles of provincial highway. By the late 1940s, following the installation of an FM radio transmission system for southern Ontario, the OPP communications system linked forty-one police stations with three hundred police cruisers equipped with two-way radio. The system logged 200,000 messages in its first year of operation (Higley 1984: 327–9).

Traffic and other bylaw infractions, based on the example of Toronto, came to dominate police formal interactions with the public, with summonses to court far outnumbering arrests. In a number of municipalities the police service was also responsible for the physical infrastructure of traffic control, including signal lights, lane markings on the roads and parking meters (Marquis 1986b). The rise of traffic regulation in the day-to-day activities of the typical municipal police department is illustrated dramatically by shifting statistics for Toronto between 1910 and 1936. At the outset of this period, drunkenness constituted 47 percent of all offences resulting in an arrest or summons. As early as 1919, traffic offences were 27 percent of the total, and the propotion would be higher in most years. The relative importance of public drunkenness as a cause of police intervention continued to decline until it constituted 5 percent or less each year in the 1930s. In 1936, when fewer than five thousand arrests were made for drunkenness, the Toronto police issued more than 32,000 traffic citations and more than 51,000 summonses for bylaw violations (Marquis 1986b: 94). During the 1930s and 1940s, police vehicles in both rural and urban areas were increasingly equipped with radio sets. The era also began the custom of officer productivity being measured by the number of parking and speeding tickets issued.

Another area of actual police duties that did not always match the crime-fighting image was support of other government bodies such as provincial liquor control commissions and welfare agencies that were involved in monitoring, judging and disciplining citizens. Police services, for example, cooperated with family courts and child welfare agencies such as the Children's Aid Society. And the administration, by social workers, of dependent populations under welfare programs such as mother's allowances was a form of policing of the morals of vulnerable members of society, namely deserted wives and their children or those whose spouses were physically incapacitated. In Ontario unwed mothers were excluded from this minimal entitlement program on moral grounds. Similarly, people on municipal relief (or the mother's allowance) were not supposed to buy liquor permits or liquor and if in violation of this rule could lose their benefits. Starting in 1927, OPP and municipal police developed a close relationship with the Liquor Control Board of Ontario (LCBO), which in 1927 began to sell alcohol in government liquor stores. A few years later the LCBO began to license beer parlours in hotels. Until 1962, people in Ontario required individual permits to buy alcohol and remained under liquor commission moral surveillance until the 1970s. As part of its quest for orderly drinking, the LCBO restricted or cancelled the drinking privileges of suspected individuals, including those who had been reported by spouses or other family members. The names of the interdicted were forwarded to police, and the police and courts reciprocated with information on individuals convicted of *Criminal Code* and *Liquor Control Act* (LCA) offences. Under the LCA police conducted thousands of searches annually for contraband liquor, and the LCBO requested police assistance with its investigations. The commission's system of "alcohol surveillance" was "highly integrated with police operations" (Thomson and Genosko 2009: 139).

The Great Depression was a time of crisis for the Canadian state. The policing of working-class protest and socialist organizations (discussed in the next chapter) in certain cities, Vancouver being a prime example, was often regarded as a "crime" problem. In 1934, for example, the victorious mayoral candidate in Vancouver promised to "clean up" and modernize the police department in order to launch a war on crime. Yet in practice the "war" in Vancouver, backed up by a powerful business lobby eventually called the Non Partisan Association, focused on militant labour and Communists (Russwurm 2007). During the Depression years, newspaper and newsreel accounts of high profile American gangsters and bandits, and the FBI's corresponding war on crime, convinced many north of the border, police chiefs included, that Canada was experiencing its own violent crime wave. Hoover targeted violent, mobile bandits and kidnappers (not organized crime) and a supposed "decay in morals" to convince Congress to enact legislation that enhanced the power and status of his "G-men" (Potter 1998: 59). Official statistics for the period 1929 to 1939 challenge the commonsensical theory that poverty and economic dislocation produced higher rates of crime in Canada. The rate of indictable offence convictions (always a minority of the total) did rise during the decade, and politicians issued fear-provoking statements, often linked to fears of political radicalism. RCMP Commissioner J.H. MacBrien regarded radicals (who in his opinion tended to be "foreigners") as criminals (Hewitt 2006: 48–9). The Bennett government, influenced by press coverage of violent crimes, in 1933 and 1934 passed legislation that increased penalties for carrying unregistered pistols and required the registration of all handguns. The latter had been requested by the CCAC, which viewed handguns as a threat to not only law enforcement but "British" Canada. The RCMP maintained the national registry, another addition to its national policing services (Brown 2012: 148–52). At least one case study (Huzel 1986) suggests that crime increased during this crisis decade. One theory is that with fewer people working, more families on relief and those with jobs earning less pay, there was less property to steal. Another theory, difficult to prove, is that when families had to pull together, young people, who were most likely to offend, were under increased parental supervision (Wilson 2011). Yet as Weaver cautions in the case of Hamilton, "criminal justice data cannot prove the existence of either more or less theft and violence over time" (Weaver 1995: 227).

During the 1930s, judging by the number of individual liquor permits and the volume of spirits, beer and wine purchased by provincial liquor commissions, alcohol consumption appears to have experienced a real decline. In some cases liquor commissions lower the prices of both permits and products in order to encourage business and compete with bootleggers. For decades police departments had reported a link between alcohol consumption and the public order offences that dominated arrest statistics. Vagrancy arrests, which social historians have regarded as a form of repression of the poor, did not rise dramatically during the 1930s crisis. There was a spike in arrests for vagrancy in Toronto from 1930 to 1932, but in subsequent years they differed little from the patterns of the 1910s. And as explained above, the status offence of vagrancy was highly discretionary; in most cases it was reserved for persons with no visible means of support, but it was also applied to prostitutes, people who were intoxicated, suspected professional criminals and political radicals. Pressure on public relief and private charities was unrelenting during the 1930s, and in many jurisdictions police stations continued to provide temporary shelter to "waifs and strays." The Toronto police, for example, granted temporary shelter to more than 17,000 people during the decade, yet this was a decline compared to the previous decade (Marquis 1986b: 197).

THE SECOND WORLD WAR

The pressures of war, which included a massive movement of hundreds of thousands of Canadians to military bases and war industries and a host of new regulations and security concerns, brought new challenges to police departments (the security aspects of the war are discussed in Chapter 4). Roughly 10 percent of the population served in the armed forces, many of them young single men who historically were major targets of police attention, and many more were absorbed into war industries and employment in general. The growth of the armed forces and the economic recovery that resulted from massive government spending brought an economic revival and fears of a possible crime wave. As noted in Chapter 4, enemy aliens were registered and in some cases interned and their firearms confiscated. The RCMP was put in charge of a national registration of rifles and shotguns; the files from this program were destroyed following the war (Brown 2012: 153–61). Provincial and municipal police were required to help enforce gasoline and oil rationing rules. Another source of concern was the behaviour of military personnel when they were off duty. This involved the civilian police working with the military police. The expanded military presence meant extra business for bootlegging, gambling and prostitution.

The recruitment of police matrons and policewomen in the early twentieth century had been the result of political pressure from women's councils and moral reform organizations. During the Second World War, the hiring of policewomen was motivated not by maternal feminism or social reform but was part of the general movement to free up men for the war effort. In addition, they were hired in response to anxieties about the interaction of the military and young women (Keshen 2004: 134). Employing women as auxiliaries during the Second World War was not a response to any perceived crime wave by women, as on the national level men were still responsible for 95 percent of convictions for indictable offences and 85 to 90 percent of summary offences. Yet budgetary pressures and lobbying by social reformers did help revive the arguments of the earlier champions of women in policing. Even Montreal, which had not hired women since 1919, changed its policy. The Hamilton police commission also relented and hired two women in 1944 whose duties were similar to police matrons. Yet as in the past, even the more developed example of the Vancouver Women's Patrol Division, which had fifteen members by 1945, was essentially an auxiliary dedicated to morality and juvenile work. In many centres it was difficult to distinguish between police women and matrons, and the former did not always wear uniforms. Press accounts, as they would into the 1970s, emphasized the personal appearance and femininity of second-generation policewomen (Weaver 1995: 182; Marquis 1993: 204–5). Yet their work, however limited, was far from glamorous. Margaret Gilkes, a veteran of the Canadian Women Army Corps, was one of three women hired by the Calgary police service following the war. Her memoir *Ladies of the Night* (1989) recounts the depressing and often violent world of the city's homeless, prostitutes, drug addicts and petty criminals.

Related to the employment of women was a new emphasis on combating sexually-transmitted diseases in the name of the war effort (Sangster 2001). In British Columbia this concern predated the war and resulted in the establishment of treatment clinics and drives by the Vancouver police against suspected disease carriers and "disorderly houses" (Cassel 1987: 2001). Rates for these diseases rose among both the military and the civilian populations in the early 1940s. Large-scale red-light districts in most cities supposedly had been broken up a generation earlier, but exceptions remained. The best know was Montreal's "Main," centred on the intersection of Boulevard Saint Laurent and Rue Sainte Catherine. The area was known for not only its brothels but also cafes, cabarets, illegal bars and gambling joints. Montreal madams and prostitutes were swooped up in periodic raids and premises often padlocked by order of the courts, yet in most cases the convicted paid fines and returned to the trade. A royal commission investigating the SQ in 1944 reported that the provincial and municipal police in Montreal had made fifty thousand vice arrests between 1900 and 1944 and that the Morality Squad knew of sixty brothels and one thousand prostitutes (CP 1944). Allegations of police toleration and corruption persisted throughout the 1940s and would lead to a civic reform movement in the postwar years that launched the career of future mayor Jean Drapeau. Most of the anti-VD effort emanated from the military, which tended to view women, both prostitutes and casual "pick ups," as the chief transmitters of sexually-transmitted diseases (STDs). In Montreal and Quebec City the military threatened to have sections of the city declared off limits to off-duty servicemen unless the police adopted stronger measures against brothels. In Vancouver, concerns about prostitutes frequenting beer parlours resulted in the establishment of separate sections for "ladies and escorts." Policewomen had a role to play in these efforts, primarily monitoring women suspected of carrying STDs. This took them to venues such as "dance halls, pool halls, taverns, bowling alleys" (Keshen 2004: 140).

Law enforcement was affected by another wartime phenomenon, much of which was invented by the media: a perceived surge in youth gangs and other forms of juvenile delinquency. Between 1922 and 1945, the peak years for total convictions for all juveniles were 1941 and 1942 (in the latter year there were more than eleven thousand convictions) (Carrigan 1998: 111). This was partly attributable to short-term urban population growth. Another factor was that many of the "usual suspects," young adult males, were serving in the armed forces. The media, which featured lurid stories on jitterbugging "zoot suiters," blamed the delinquency problem on the housing shortage and family disruption: fathers were either in the armed forces or working extra shifts in industry, many married women were toiling long hours and adolescents were working instead of attending school. One service club blamed popular culture: "undesireable motion pictures, crime magazines and crime radio shows" for adolescent misbehaviour (Wallace, Higgins and McGahan 1994: 92).

The academic historian cannot help but notice that discourse surrounding this issue was motivated in part by professional and institutional imperatives. Most of the experts cited in media reports were not police but social workers, educators, community welfare activists and juvenile and family court judges (Edwards 1942). Community organizations, social agencies, municipalities and provincial governments responded with various initiatives, many of them coercive. The Province of Quebec raised its age for compulsory school attendance and its age for juvenile delinquents from sixteen to eighteen. Montreal established a curfew for youth under fourteen (with exemptions for those who had jobs) (Myers 2006: 71, 138). Other responses included surveys of juvenile delinquency, the expansion of juvenile and family court services and supervised recreation programs. The Toronto Big Brothers organization sponsored a study of delinquency that was published under the title *Street Gangs in Toronto: A Study of the Forgotten Boy.* Media accounts stressed the risk of "sex delinquency" among adolescent girls. In the end, most charges laid by police during the alleged juvenile crime wave were for minor transgressions such as curfew violations (Keshen 2004: chapter 5).

CONCLUSION

During the period 1900 to 1945, Canadian police leaders promoted a version of professionalism based on a narrowed and misleading definition of policing, that their organizations existed to fight crime. More than half a century later, Canada's police services are struggling to reinvent themselves in the shadow of this powerful narrative. Their own operational statistics indicated that crimes of violence and crimes against property constituted a small proportion of offences reported to and by police services. Initiative arrests, for public drunkenness, disturbing the peace and vagrancy, continued to form the bulk of police business. Starting in the 1920s the automobile radically reshaped cities, Canadian society in general and the organization and culture of policing. The adoption of fingerprinting, signal systems and two-way radio enhanced operational efficiency and helped convince the public that the police were enlisting science in the fight against crime. Canada's police system was not really a system, but a decentralized patchwork of municipal, provincial and federal agencies. The greatest success story was that of the new RCMP, which largely through good fortune was spared being downsized into a generalist frontier constabulary for Canada's north. The RCMP's acquisition of the national criminal records collection of the Dominion Police in 1920 and its mandate over security and intelligence set the stage for its central role in constructing the surveillance state. The growth of the Mounted Police notwithstanding, the future of policing would be urban, and there were definite tensions between big-city police services and the federal force, as revealed in the activities of the CCAC. There were also tensions between police chiefs and boards on the one hand and nascent police associations on the other. Despite local controversies, Canadian police services enjoyed considerable operational autonomy and public support. Aside from the Communist-organized Canadian Labour Defence League, there was virtually no civil liberties organization to challenge police abuses of power prior to the middle of the 1940s (Clément 2001). The tough-on-crime approach was shared by the press, which was the most powerful shaper of public opinion on political and social issues.

CHAPTER 4

POLICING
CLASS CONFLICT AND
POLITICAL DISSENT TO 1970

This chapter examines the policing of class conflict and political dissent from the Confederation era to the end of the 1960s. The overt policing of class conflict revolved principally around strikes and lockouts, where police responses ranged from aggressively acting in the interests of employers to exhibiting degrees of sympathy for workers. The enforcement of the vagrancy law and the continued use of jail as a form of debtors' prison for individuals too poor to pay fines for misdemeanours were low-profile but more pervasive examples of class-based justice. Political policing involved the efforts of federal and to a lesser extent municipal and provincial police in identifying, tracking, harassing and prosecuting individuals and organizations, most of them non-violent and legal, that were deemed threats to national security or the political or social order. Canada was not alone in adopting this approach to perceived internal enemies, but much of this activity was carried out in secret, beyond the knowledge of elected politicians. What Platt and Cooper (1974: 3) described as the "liberal reformist" perspective on the police, based on "the belief that it is possible to create a well-regulated, stable and humanitarian police system," is most starkly challenged by the history of policing dissent.[1]

From the Fenians in the 1860s to the 2011 Occupy movement, there is a long history of monitoring and criminalizing political dissent in Canada, and the police have been central to that process. Yet police and security agencies would not have pursued this agenda without the tacit approval of politicians and the mainstream media. At times the line between monitoring and harassing labour activists and the political left, such as provincial police responses to transient workers and the unemployed in early twentieth-century British Columbia, was blurred. The targeting of dissent would not have happened with the police acting alone; they were encouraged and supported by the courts and other powerful pillars of the status quo. On the other hand, as the policing of modern demonstrations suggests, the police have not always acted on the explicit instruction of political officials but have exercised discretion and operational autonomy. The secret monitoring of legal trade unions, political parties and non-violent social movements was a natural extension of criminal detective work, where information was gathered "just in case." The infiltration, intelligence gathering and disruption tactics deployed against organized crime and illegal drug trafficking are similar to those that developed in political policing. "High policing," which according to Brodeur evolved first in late seventeenth-century France, targeted not the "lumpenproletariat" that preoccupied the criminal police but threatening ideas such as religious dissent. A contemporary French magistrate explained the basic philosophy of the political police officer: "the more he watches ... the less he needs to act" (Brodeur 2010: 57).

As recent events in Canada suggest, the reasons for adopting various national security laws and policies are not necessarily related to actual threats, yet these measures can be damaging to individuals targeted and to civil liberties. The approach was often crude, and much of the information gathered was based on hearsay, speculation and innuendo. There was also a make-work aspect to this data gathering (Hewitt 2006), yet as the documentary *The Un-Canadians* (Scher 1996) indicates, during the early Cold War it was potentially harmful to the careers and personal lives of law-abiding citizens. RCMP security monitoring, such as opening mail and listening to private telephone conversations, was also often illegal in addition to being hidden from politicians, the courts and the public. It was only in the late 1970s that these abuses of process became public knowledge. By this time the Security Service had amassed counter subversion files on 800,000 Canadian citizens (Hewitt 2006: 141).

The monitoring of political dissent by Canadian police agencies has tended to reflect a conservative point of view that targets individuals or organizations on the left deemed threats to the status quo. Groups and individuals on the right, in contrast, generally were spared the intensive surveillance that targeted socialists and the union movement. The spread of the Ku Klux Klan into Saskatchewan in the late 1920s, for example, was barely noted by the RCMP (Kealey and Whitaker 1994; Hewitt 2006: 89, 100–1), which instead collected mountains of trivial information on "revolutionary organizations and agitators" on the left. Surveillance of Canadian citizens, usually based on suspicion of past or current associations with Communism, was not limited to fringe elements; the RCMP's "VIP" program maintained files on political and cultural figures such as prime ministers John

Diefenbaker and Lester Pearson, CCF leader J.S. Woodsworth, NDP leader David Lewis, Parti Québecois premier René Lévesque, literary scholar Northrup Frye, entertainer Rita MacNeil, Ontario NDP leader Bob Rae and even British rock musician John Lennon. The Canadian Security Intelligence Service (CSIS), which inherited the RCMP security files in the 1980s, continues to oppose the release of the entire file on "the greatest Canadian," Tommy Douglas, CCF premier of Saskatchewan from 1944 to 1961 and federal NDP leader from 1961 to 1971. The security file on the "father of Medicare" began in the late 1930s when as a Member of Parliament Douglas spoke to a meeting of unemployed workers and presumably continued up to his death in the 1980s. CSIS has opposed declassification of the entire dossier on the questionable grounds that it would endanger confidential informants and jeopardize national security.

Canada, compared to other nations, has been remarkably free from politically-motivated violence. One is hard pressed to find many serious challenges to national well- being in the decades after 1867, yet the state since its inception has attempted to monitor internal threats to its security. Starting in the 1970s there was a shift away from the covert policing of ideas toward preventing acts of political violence, which had started to flare up a decade earlier. In addition, crowd control tactics, especially dealing with labour disputes, became less aggressive. At times police services carried out this mission without much oversight from elected officials, illustrating the downside of police autonomy in liberal democratic states. Yet the higher levels of government were not kept totally in the dark. The RCMP prepared weekly intelligence reports on labour and other organizations, which were sent to the Minister of Justice and the federal cabinet. For most of the twentieth century the target was the political left, and compared to criminal investigations, which in theory must meet the test of probable cause, the threshold for political surveillance was merely suspicion. The officers collecting and sometimes analyzing the "intelligence" were working-class individuals, with no more than a high school education, who had entered the profession as constables. The authority of the state has also been demonstrated, often in controversial and visible fashion, at mass public demonstrations, a phenomenon of the late twentieth century. As with other areas of policing, the response to protests has drawn on professional trends, training, methods and specialized equipment and weapons adopted in the United States and Great Britain, such as mounted police, tear gas, baton rounds (plastic bullets), disruptive psychological warfare tactics, "snatch squads," and "kettling." Counter subversion approaches to mass protest have employed informants, undercover officers and *agents provocateurs,* conducted photographic, electronic and video surveillance, gathered literature from activist organizations and compiled dossiers on protest leaders and groups. More recently, police monitored social media traffic of individuals involved in the Occupy movement.

POLICING WORKERS AND ORGANIZED LABOUR
DURING "THE BRICK AND TEAR GAS AGE"

The above quotation is taken from the remarks of a progressive Ontario Liberal politician to describe the confrontational era of industrial relations that existed prior to the end of the Second World War. David Croll was reacting to the settlement of the 1945 Oshawa autoworkers strike and the advent of the Rand formula, which authorized the automatic check-off for union dues but recommended financial penalties for wildcat strikes (Moulton 1974: 149). Academic studies of the origins and early development of the police services have stressed their role in protecting the interests of political and economic elites. Both Harring (1983) and Williams (2007) identify an explicit class-control mission (which the latter conflates with racial control) for the American police. Canadian labour historians, by focusing on high-profile strikes and lockouts, have assumed that lawmakers, the police, the courts and various branches of government, in addition to corporate interests and the media, have worked against the interests of the union movement, particularly in the era prior to collective bargaining rights and the modern system of industrial relations. It is clear that conflicts between capital and labour, and the class dynamics of municipal and provincial politics, influenced aspects of police development in specific Canadian communities such as Vancouver (Russwurm 2007).

Labour rights were acquired through struggle, and the forces of the status quo such as the legal system were usually a barrier to progress. Unions became legal in Canada in the 1870s; prior to that time they could be prosecuted as criminal conspiracies. But their new legal status did not guarantee that trade unions would be recognized by employers and collective bargaining and other rights protected, or that their organizers would not be fired, blacklisted or monitored by private detectives and their organizations infiltrated. And neither did it guarantee that picketing during strikes and lockouts would not be countered by charges of unlawful assembly or "watching and besetting." In short, the union movement, which by the early 1980s covered almost two out of five Canadian workers, faced an uphill battle, and the police were often an obstacle to social justice. And for decades the RCMP security branch collected detailed intelligence, ranging from reports of informers and undercover agents to newspaper accounts of meetings and speeches, on the doings of labour leaders and organizations.

Between 1900 and the 1970s, Canada experienced at least three hundred violent strikes or lockouts, with fatalities occurring in less of a dozen of them. Although bloodshed was limited compared to classic labour struggles in the United States from the 1870s onwards, Canada in the industrial age had plenty of examples of the police and the justice system in general acting to protect the status quo. The legal arsenal deployed against labour ranged from civil injunctions to municipal ordinances to criminal law. In extreme cases special constables, provincial police and even the military could be deployed. The tactics adopted against radical labour, sometimes in conjunction with private police, anticipated the approach later employed against political threats such as Communists: surveillance, infiltration, raids to seize evidence and arrests. Even moderate labour leaders and organizations were placed under surveillance. Labour organizers could also be harassed with arrests for vagrancy or illegal assembly or threatened with deportation. Even if most arrests ended up without criminal charges being laid, or most of the arrested being acquitted, the threat was disrupted and possibly neutralized (Torrance 1986: 47).

One of the more dramatic confrontations between labour and capital was the Vancouver Island War of 1912–14, involving coal miners in four island communities. This followed confrontations on the mainland between police and Industrial Workers of the World (IWW) construction workers who went on strike against the Grand Trunk Pacific and Canadian Northern railways. The IWW, which appealed to mobile, unskilled and immigrant seasonal workers, also attempted to organize loggers. In 1909 "Wobblies" and socialists had been arrested in Vancouver during a free speech campaign. In 1912 the IWW and socialists renewed their fight over the right to conduct street meetings with the aim of securing greater assistance for the unemployed. The police responded with an attack on a public meeting and dozens of arrests (Leier 1989). In many British Columbia labour struggles the government also relied on undercover private detectives to gather intelligence on unions (Williams 1998). In 1914 miners in Cumberland were locked out after protesting the firing of a miner who had called on the company to live up to provincial safety regulations. The strike spread and the workers and their families were supported financially by the United Mine Workers of America (UMWA). The importation of strikebreakers led to rioting, looting, explosions and arson attacks in 1913. The less-than-neutral provincial government authorized special police, always an unknown quantity in labour disputes, and one striker was fatally shot. The union promised the premier that it would restore order if the special police was withdrawn; his response was to order one thousand militiamen to Vancouver Island. The troops tried to crush the strike by engaging in highly irregular actions such as the mass arrest of unionists at a Nanaimo hall. More than two hundred were arrested and fifty were sent to jail. The union failed to secure recognition from the company, and the strike was ended when the UMWA was forced to withdraw financial support and the First World War broke out (Kavanagh 1914).

Case studies of individual strikes suggest that municipal police and to a lesser extent provincial police and the RCMP on occasion either sympathized with local trade unionists or strove to be as neutral as possible under the circumstances. The Lethbridge mining strike of 1906 is an example of a RNWMP commander attempting to be somewhat neutral in a bitter industrial dispute. The strike is best known for helping to spawn an early federal labour code, the *Industrial Disputes Investigation Act*. The relationship of the Mounties and the UMWA during the Lethbridge strike can be interpreted in more than one way according to Baker's nuanced 1991 case study. The strike drew the attention of the federal government because it created a shortage of coal on the Prairies. There were also episodes of violence, but little of it directed at the RNWMP, despite the suspicion and hostility of the strikers and their families. Lethbridge had a town police force, but the mine and a working-class residential area were located outside of town limits. During the strike there were two riots, several explosions and a number of minor incidents, yet few were arrested. The union attributed the dynamiting of the houses of two strikebreakers to a private detective working for Alberta Railway and Irrigation Company. The immediate Mounted Police presence, combined with nearby officers held in reserve, was relatively substantial, yet the commanding officer attempted to exercise restraint. Tensions were eased by the fact that the strikebreakers lived in their own compound near the mine and did not have to cross picket lines and that many of the younger, more militant strikers drifted out of town. The police rank and file was suspicious of the workers, many of whom were "foreigners." In the end a settlement was mediated by the federal government. Although the strikers were rehired and gained a small wage increase, their other demands, including union recognition, were not granted (Baker 1991).

Another example of police reactions to a labour dispute that questions the simplistic view of police as oppressors of the workers was the 1914 Saint John street railway strike. In this situation the municipal police tasked with preserving order appeared to have sympathized with the striking streetcar workers and even crowds of non strikers who blocked cars operated by replacement workers and attacked company property. The company, recently acquired by local capitalists, had a poor reputation with customers and less than ideal relations with the municipal and provincial governments. It incited more unrest by firing union members and replacing them with imported non-unionists. Large crowds gathered on the streets to support the workers and clashed with a small squad of cavalry that unwisely charged demonstrators. The police did little but watch as citizens toppled two streetcars, incapacitated a power generation plant and smashed windows in the company's headquarters building. The company's car barns were saved by shotgun-toting Thiel and Pinkerton detectives who fired birdshot at attackers. By the time five hundred militiamen, armed with rifles and bayonets, had been called out, tempers had subsided. The union won most of its demands and the legal response to strike-related violence was fairly lenient (Babcock 1982).

In 1918 one of the greatest threats to civil order in eastern Canada was not labour unrest but the powerful combination of French Canadian nationalism and anti-conscription in the province of Quebec. For a variety of reasons, French Canadians did not responded enthusiastically to the war effort; by the spring of 1917 just over fourteen thousand French-speaking citizens had volunteered for the armed forces. And two-thirds of all draft defaulters were from Quebec. The imposition of the *Military Service Act* by the Borden government in 1917, and its enforcement starting in early 1918, was a dramatic example of the coercive power of the state when the normal guardians of order, the police, were unable or unwilling to act. Resistance to conscription, in the form of individual flight, demonstrations, vandalism and rioting that cost one life, had been building in Montreal prior to passage of the law. The calling up of 400,000 conscripts in early 1918 set off a new wave of protest and resistance, this time centred on Quebec City. The unrest followed the arrest of a civilian by two members of the Dominion Police, who at the time were regarded by many residents of the province as little more than bounty hunters. The municipal police lacked the numbers and equipment to contain the large crowds that roamed the city during Easter week, so the federal government invoked the *War Measures Act* and basically took over policing in the city. Military officials were convinced that the municipal and provincial authorities sympathized with the demonstrators and that the city police and firemen were part of the problem. With rumours of plots of armed resistance, the military deployed infantry armed with rifles, bayonets and machine guns, as well as cavalry. The military seized all guns and ammunition in the community and employed French-speaking private detectives to gather intelligence. Following a confrontation where demonstrators hurled objects and wounded soldiers with gunfire, the army opened fire with machine guns and rifles, killing at least four and wounding dozens. More troops were rushed to the city, and sale of guns was banned for a year. The government then amended the *War Measures Act* to allow military district commanders to declare martial law without waiting for a request by the civilian authorities. The hated Dominion Police was reinforced and temporarily merged with the municipal police. The military, which was employed in sweeps into rural Quebec in search of draft evaders, remained in the city until well after the war ended. The army also posted two thousand troops close to Montreal but not in the city itself, which would have been regarded as an act of provocation (Auger 2008).

Despite passing the *War Measures Act* in 1914, the federal and provincial governments did not adopt harsh measures toward organized labour until 1918. During the war, union membership expanded, and by 1916 the number of recorded strikes and number of workers involved began to climb. By 1917, with mounting inflation and a genuine worker shortage, strikes became more frequent. With pressure mounting for conscription, the Borden government contemplated undertaking a national registration of the workforce but instead opted for a voluntary program. With the outbreak of the Russian revolution in 1917, and the supposed threat of international Bolshevism, governments and the business elite feared that labour would be stirred up by "agitators." A Thiel detective working for Hamilton's Steel Company of Canada shared reports on labour radicals with the local police. The reports were sent on to the OPP and the Dominion Police, an example of collusion between the corporate sector and the police (Kealey 1992: 305). The federal government, as with its wartime prohibition policy, enacted a number of controls that lasted into the early postwar reconstruction period. PC 2525, the so-called "Anti-Idlers' Act," made it an offence for males between sixteen and sixty not to be employed. Many police chiefs wanted this draconian measure continued into peacetime, partly because of its usefulness in dealing with agitators. One month before the cessation of hostilities, the federal cabinet banned all strikes for the duration of the war (Marquis 1993: 108).

The high point of working-class unrest during the 1910s was the "great labour revolt" of 1919. With two hundred strikes this was a record year for worker-days lost to industrial actions and affected communities ranging from Vancouver to Amherst, Nova Scotia. The previous year the shooting of labour leader Ginger Goodwin by a Dominion Police special constable had sparked Canada's first general strike, in Vancouver. Goodwin, a socialist conscientious objector and vice-president of the provincial federation of labour, had been evading the draft. The one-day protest was met with violent opposition by returned war veterans who, unopposed by the police, stormed the offices of the Vancouver Trades and Labour Council. One sign of concern about labour unrest was a large-scale movement by the RNWMP into British Columbia in the months prior to the Winnipeg General Strike of 1919. Given that the BCPP was already on the scene, the buildup of Mounties caused concern for provincial and federal officials, and it led to conflicts over jurisdiction that were partially resolved in 1924 when most RCMP officers in the province were deployed elsewhere (Stonier-Newman 1991: 130–2, 152).

The Winnipeg General Strike began with walkouts over union recognition and wages in two sectors, the building trades and metal working industries, and spread to dozens of other unions and thousands of other workers who were not unionized. A strike committee took over the administration of the city and vowed to keep order, much to the consternation of a "citizens' committee" representing the business sector. In Ottawa and elsewhere, the strike was increasingly portrayed as an imminent revolution stirred up by "enemy aliens." The federal government amended the *Immigration Act* to facilitate the deportation of radicals and introduced Section 98 of the *Criminal Code* to give police more powers over sedition. Using these powers, the federal government ordered the arrest of several members of the strike committee, which included two aldermen and a Protestant minister. The offices of labour organizations were also raided, and similar raids were carried out in Vancouver and Calgary. A large protest that followed turned violent when a mounted troop of the RNWMP, wielding revolvers and clubs, clashed with the crowd. Two strikers died as a result of "Bloody Saturday," but few demonstrators were arrested. In the aftermath of the riot, troops patrolled the streets. Following the arrest of two additional strike leaders and the closing down of the *Western Labour News*, the walkout ended. The leader of the citizens' committee that fought the strike, and that recruited 1,800 special constables after the dismissal of the municipal police force, was appointed special prosecutor of the strike leaders. The arrested strike leaders received jail terms of six months to one year. Section 98 remained on the books and was used to harass socialists throughout the 1920s and early 1930s (Bercuson 1974; Dubro and Rowland 1992: 59).

On the national level during the 1920s the labour movement was in retreat, undermined by company unions and corporate welfare schemes and, in many parts of Canada, an improved economic situation. The major exception to the relative labour peace of the "roaring twenties" was industrial Cape Breton, which experienced a series of strikes in the coal and steel sectors, which were major employers. The 1922 coal strike raised the issues of the criteria for sending federal troops to aid the civil power and who should pay for the costs of these expensive deployments. In 1922 the Liberal government planned to remove the new RCMP from the purview of the Department of Justice and place it under the newly created Department of National Defence, a move that was opposed by both the Conservatives and the Progressives in the House of Commons. The Conservative leader argued that the RCMP would be less controversial than the army in containing industrial violence. The coal miners' strike in Cape Breton was triggered by wage cuts announced by the British Empire Steel and Coal Corporation (BESCO). In this and subsequent struggles, BESCO's industrial police and labour spies shared intelligence with the provincial government. Prime Minister Mackenzie King resisted early calls for regular army troops, and the mayor and police chief of Glace Bay advised that things were under control and that the arrival of any outside forces would provoke violence. On the excuse that it needed to protect government-owned mines from sabotage, the provincial government responded to the requisition of a county court judge and sent militia from Halifax. The authorities were also alarmed by the openly Communist associations of the union leadership. Permanent force troops, including elements of the 22nd Regiment from Quebec, complete with machine guns, followed (Macgillvary 1974).

When the Sydney steelworkers walked out in 1923, the provincial government was already on a "war footing" (Manley 1992: 78). Steelmaking was a significant employer on the island, but the union was not recognized by BESCO. The Nova Scotia government had recruited a special police force for industrial Cape Breton, a sign that it did not trust local municipal police, who sympathized with the striking miners, to preserve the peace and protect company property. The new provincial force was trained by RCMP officers. Many steelworkers did not immediately join the strike, which created conflicts on the picket line. As in 1922, troops patrolled the towns of industrial Cape Breton. Despite the large numbers of workers involved in these confrontations, there were few arrests. During the steel strike the provincial police raided the homes of militant unionists, searching for radical literature that could be used to discredit the strikers. On July 1, mounted provincial police assaulted strikers and other citizens who were returning from a church service, setting off a new wave of protest, including sympathy strikes by coal miners. Hit by injunctions and the arrest of two radical union leaders for seditious liberal, the steelworkers' strike collapsed (Macgillvary 1974; Manley 1992).

The dramatic struggles of the coal miners in 1925 were a response to wage cuts and layoffs by an ailing BESCO that started in 1924. The strike would last for several months, and reports of starving, diseased miners and their families, with food supplies and credit cut off at company stores, provoked a national humanitarian response. The UMWA interpreted company demands as an attempt to smash the union and responded with militant tactics. An ongoing struggle for control of a power plant led to a clash with company police that resulted in the fatal shooting of a miner. The strikers roughed up and captured a number of BESCO police and lodged them in the New Waterford jail to await criminal prosecution. The men were liberated from the cells by other company police, whereupon the town council dismissed several local policemen, and a "workers' militia" was established to police the area. As conditions worsened, company stores were looted and once again the emergency provincial police force and regular troops occupied the towns of the coal fields. During its pacification campaign in Cape Breton, the Canadian army, which sent units from as far west as Manitoba, deployed or unloaded machines guns, field artillery, search lights, barbed wire, field kitchens and fixed bayonets.

One result of the class war in 1920s Nova Scotia was that the federal government acted to restrict the use of troops by the civil power and required provincial governments, not municipalities, to foot the bill (Macgillvary 1974). In 1925, the head of the BESCO police, a former British army intelligence officer, when speaking to the annual convention of the CCAC, equated Communism with criminality and described Cape Breton as "one of the chief centres of subversion in Canada" (Marquis 1993:155–6).

Outside of Cape Breton, most strike duty in the interwar era was routine. The Toronto police service started a system of reserves after 1918 and cancelled leaves in advance of anticipated strikes or demonstrations. The signal system, motor vehicles and radio technology permitted the department to deploy resources more efficiently in the event of public order demands. And like many big-city departments, Toronto retained its mounted unit mainly for crowd control duties. In 1935, for example, the mounted unit logged several hundred eight-hour tours of duty in connection with strikes. In advance of a strike or lockout, the police met with union officials and their lawyers to voice the department's expectations, which included "no accusatory banners," limited numbers of pickets and minimal interaction with strikebreakers. These restrictions were actually less onerous than those of the past. Despite advanced planning, workers sometimes engaged in mass picketing that overwhelmed the limited number of police on duty, and the District Labour Council and unions such as the International Ladies Garment Workers complained of police intimidation and interference. Strikers who ended up in court often encountered less than sympathetic magistrates, another source of contention in labour journalism and rhetoric in the 1920s and 1930s. The situation was worsened by an often hostile press and an intimidating or non-existent police complaints process (Marquis 1986b: 109–17).

One of the more controversial actions involving the RCMP during the Depression was the Estevan Strike of 1931. The public image of Canada's elite police force, in the best British tradition, was that its members rarely used force. In contrast to this popular culture image, the Mounties at Estevan fatally shot three strikers; other strikers and citizens were wounded. In contrast to its reputation as a lightly armed constabulary, the RCMP arsenal at Estevan included machine guns. The gravestone for the three dead strikers at nearby Bienfait still bears the inscription "Murdered by the RCMP." Historians of organized labour and the left have denounced the shootings of the coal miners as a brutal example of the class role of the RCMP, but a study by Hewitt (1997) suggests that the fatalities were more an example of incompetence than deliberate brutality. He also shows that although the RCMP leadership, coal company operators and local politicians took a hard line toward the strikers because of their Communist Party associations, the commander on the spot adopted a more nuanced view. The strike itself was peaceful and the Mountie in charge of the detachment predicted that it would remain so as long as strikebreakers were not imported. As in 1919 at Winnipeg, the RCMP at Estevan initiated the violence in response to a parade by strikers. And senior commanders, who were suspicious of "reds" and "foreigners," engaged in a cover-up that is all too familiar in police history. Hewitt's case study introduces "shades of grey" to a story that is often framed in black and white terms (Hewitt 1997: 177).

Following the clashes in Cape Breton between coal miners and steelworkers and their families on the one hand and BESCO police, provincial police and the army on the other, the federal government amended the *Militia Act* to restrict the power of judges to call in the armed forces in aid of the civil power. As Morton (1974: 88) has noted, by the time of the Great Depression, military aid to the civil power was viewed by many as "a hopeless anachronism," as most provinces had recourse to provincial police or RCMP detachments. Yet district military commanders of Canada's small peacetime army instructed their intelligence officers to monitor militant labour in their area. In the early 1930s, the federal government and the

Ontario authorities cooperated in an attempt to destroy the Communist Party of Canada (cpc), organized in 1921, using the sedition charge. Several party leaders were convicted and incarcerated, but the cpc organized a number of successful front organizations such as the Workers' Unity League (wul).

In 1933 the board of police commissioners of the manufacturing city of Stratford, Ontario, requested troops when it feared picket-line violence at two strikes in the city. Focusing on several furniture plants as well as a poultry process-ing facility, the strikes were organized by the wul and aside from a few picket-line scuffles, the throwing of projectiles and attempts to block a number of vehicles, were relatively peaceful. In this case the mayor and city council took a fairly hard line toward the strikers, largely because of the Communist associations of their leadership. Despite the presence of opp reinforcements, the police made few arrests; in contrast, a protest over municipal relief two years later prompted police to arrest two dozen men. One striker was arrested for unlawful assembly, and a union organ-izer was charged with vagrancy. The Conservative provincial government, much criticized by the Liberal opposition, applied for military assistance, which arrived in the form of units of the Royal Canadian Rifles, complete with battle dress, rifles, Lewis machine guns and four Carden-Loyd tankettes, small tracked vehicles that were the predecessor of the Second World War Bren gun carrier. The national Trades and Labour Congress criticized the wul's role in the strike but declared that Canadian workers had a right to picket without the military being called in. The soldiers, stationed in the local armouries, did not come into direct contact with the strikers. Although the workers did win small wage increases, they were unsuccessful in their goal of the closed shop (cp 1933a, 1933b; Morton 1974).

During the 1920s and especially the 1930s police monitored and sometimes broke up demonstrations and strikes by the unemployed, a segment of society that was targeted for organization by Communists. The ambivalent or even hostile response of mainstream labour to organizations of the unemployed made the latter ripe for Communist organization and police surveillance and intimidation. In 1930 the Hamilton police broke up an unauthorized march by the Hamilton Unemployed Association, described by a Canadian Press reporter as "Reds," and arrested eight participants, ironically, for vagrancy. There were similar conflicts between police and the jobless in Montreal that year (cp 1930). The opp monitored organizations of the unemployed as subversive, and the Toronto police broke up jobless camps in the Don Valley, harassed men cut from relief roles to leave the city and confiscated relief cards from suspected agitators (Marquis 1986b: 138).

The most prominent protest of the unemployed was the 1935 On-to-Ottawa Trek, which originated as a protest by single unemployed men who had been con-signed to military-run work camps in British Columbia. By the time the camps were disbanded in 1936, they had accommodated 170,000 men, for an average stay of nearly one hundred days. Demanding "work and wages," the men, under the influ-ence of left-wing organizers, left the camps for Vancouver, where they engaged in more protests. On May Day 1935 a huge crowd gathered in Stanley Park to support the strikers. Other high-profile events included a rowdy protest at the Hudson's Bay department store and the occupation of a Vancouver museum. Although the relief camp protestors were associated with Communists and denounced by the mayor, they enjoyed a measure of support in the city, and the chief of police adopted a relatively liberal attitude toward them (Russwurm 2007: 109–11; Waite 2012: 213).

The strikers then decided to travel by railway box cars to Ottawa to press their demands before Conservative Prime Minister R.B. Bennett, who together with the premier of Ontario had driven the Communist Party underground and who vowed to crush radicalism with "the iron heel of capitalism." As the one thousand trekkers journeyed eastward they gained public support and members. The federal authorities decided they would be stopped before they reached Winnipeg, gateway to the west and scene of the famous strike of 1919, where the provincial govern-ment was not keen on their presence. Without consulting Premier J.T. Gardiner of Saskatchewan, Bennett's government planned to halt the mobile protest at Regina and force the trekkers into a relief camp. The legal argument used was that they were trespassing on railway property. Gardiner, who feared that an RCMP presence would provoke violence, attempted to negotiate a compromise. His fears proved valid when the RCMP attempted to arrest protest leaders, and the Mounties, city police and railway police clashed with the protestors. Police fired into the crowd during the riot, a trekker and a Regina police officer were killed and the trek was ended. The premier blamed the RCMP and federal government for the violence (Waiser 2003; Waite 2012: 216–20).

That same year the RCMP, the BCPP and the Vancouver police were involved in "the battle of Ballantyne pier," when the members of Vancouver and District Waterfront Workers Association and their families marched to the waterfront to protest the presence of non-union longshoremen working on vessels during a lockout. The climate under which the police operated was shaped by anti-Red hysteria whipped up by a business group known as the Citizens' League. In 1923 the International Longshoremen's Association had lost a confrontation with the employers' association, who had hired more than three hundred armed men. The shipping companies employed private detectives to spy on union activity during this period. In 1935 when strikers and their supporters marched on the waterfront, they were repulsed by a large force of city police, BCPP and RCMP, who attacked the strikers with clubs and tear gas. Sixty people were injured and twenty were arrested, one under Section 98 of the *Criminal Code*. The mayor lashed out at Communists while the strikers denounced "fascist brutality." The Shipping Federation, which successfully resisted the strike, was backed by all three levels of government (McCandless 1974). At this time politicians and business interests feared a Communist-orchestrated general strike. One result of the waterfront strike was the formation of a special Red squad, the "Communist Activities Branch," which began to construct RCMP-style files on local subversives. This intelligence section, headed by an officer on loan from the Mounted Police, was controversial with the rank and file as it also supposedly investigated organized crime and police corruption (Russwurm 2007).

Not all public disorder during the early twentieth century was linked to industrial unrest or the suppression of free speech. A riot that reflected not class conflict and political dissent but ethnic and racial prejudice took place in Toronto in 1933, the year that Hitler came to power in Germany. Interestingly, Toronto, whose Jewish population was largely poor or working-class, staged one of North America's first public protests against Nazism. When a so-called "Swastika Club" threatened to exclude Jewish bathers from the public beaches in the city's east end, a few scuffles broke out. But when an anti-Semitic youth gang unfurled a homemade Nazi flag at a softball game at Willowvale Park near a Jewish Canadian neighbourhood, a major confrontation erupted, with both sides reported as using baseball bats and metal pipes. Estimates of the numbers involved in the xenophobic outburst ranged from hundreds to thousands. The police attempted to break up the fighting, which lasted for a few hours. The issue for the Toronto Police Department was not anti-Semitism, which most police officers would have supported, but the disturbance of the public peace. Newspaper accounts suggested that the authorities believed both sides in the fight to be equally culpable (Levitt and Schaffir 1987).

The Unauthorized History of the RCMP (Brown and Brown, 1973) chronicled the Winnipeg General Strike, Estevan and other misdeeds of Canada's famous police force as the much mythologized RCMP was celebrating its centennial. Yet one of the most famous Depression-era labour confrontations associated with the force was one where it played no active role and where the federal government refused to authorize reinforcements despite the request of the a provincial government. In 1937 General Motors workers in Oshawa, organized by the United Auto Workers, an industrial union, walked out over the issue of union recognition. A number of the organizers were formally associated with the WUL. Liberal premier Mitch Hepburn feared that Ontario's mines, mills and factories would be invaded by a new militant labour movement, the Congress on Industrial Organizations (CIO), which had been gaining ground in the United States. He denounced the strike as the work of "foreign agitators" and recruited special constables under the OPP, dubbed "Hepburn's Hussars" by their critics. Far from enjoying operational autonomy, in this case the OPP was acting under the direct order of the premier, who also had a network of informants reporting on CIO activity in Northern Ontario.

In Oshawa the four thousand strikers and their families had considerable support, and the mayor requested that both the OPP and RCMP stay out of the conflict. The OPP actually had an informer in the ranks of the strikers who had also worked for the Toronto Red Squad. Both the union and the provincial government agreed that all liquor stores and beer parlours should be closed. The diary of Prime Minister Mackenzie King indicates that the issue was discussed by the federal cabinet, where the concern was not so much about the rights of the workers or the possibility that the RCMP would provoke violence on the picket line but that the deployment would hurt the image of the Liberal party and drive moderate unionists into the arms of the Communist party. King's justice minister supported the sending an initial force of RCMP as part of a reserve but instructed them to maintain a low profile. King refused to authorize additional Mounties for Oshawa, and when his government offered to mediate the strike, Hepburn accused it of "treachery" and dismissed the RCMP as unreliable. Although General Motors denied it formal recognition, the union did reach a settlement, and the despite its outward repudiation of the CIO, the outcome marked the start of industrial union-ism in Canada. As the Oshawa police chief later noted, the strike had been carried out without a single striker being arrested (Abella 1974; Hannant 1995: 202; De Lint and Hall 2009: 77).[2]

Organized labour became more of a force during the Second World War as a result of industrial expansion. Once again union membership grew significantly. Although most workers supported the war effort, industrial disputes continued. Unlike during the latter part of the First World War, the Liberal government refused to ban strikes and lockouts, turning initially to compulsory conciliation to settle disputes. In 1941 when four thousand workers engaged in a wildcat strike at the Alcan plant at Arvida, Quebec, the federal government responded with the military on the grounds that aluminum was an essential war commodity. A federal cabinet minister spoke out against sabotage, but a royal commission later determined that actual causes of the strike had been tensions over wages and working conditions. That same year the Hepburn government, at the request of Teck Township in northern Ontario, authorized a force of two hundred OPP officers to intimidate striking gold miners in the Kirkland Lake area. Although the union lost this bitter struggle for recognition, the conflict helped obtain, at least for workers in industries under federal jurisdiction, the rights to collective bargaining, union recognition and protection from labour practices.

In the long run this move to predictability and a bureaucratic certification process undercut the need for workers to picket in order to win recognition for their union. Yet there were still conflicts or potential conflicts with police. In 1945 eleven thousand UAW members went on strike at the Ford plant in Windsor, gain-ing widespread publicity with an effective blockade of the plant using cars, trucks and buses. On the orders of Premier George Drew, whose government blamed the stoppage on radicals, a force of 210 RCMP and OPP planned to reopen the plant. The local police attempted to escort company staff through the picket line, and many members of the city council were in favour of asking for the military to end the walkout. Yet the mayor opposed using outside police, in part because other unionized workers, many of whom joined the picket line out of sympathy, would have seen this as a provocation. The provincial attorney general described the Ford strike as an "open insurrection against the Crown" (Moulton 1974: 145; Higley 1984: 319–21).

During this era many trade unionists and their sympathizers could be forgiven for viewing the OPP primarily as a strike-breaking organization. The 1946 Stelco strike at Hamilton was another example of community hostility to the possible use of imported police but with a new twist: the argument that in postwar Canada the worker deserved a fair share of democracy. The United Steelworkers of America walked out over union recognition, wages, the length of the work week and the unwillingness of the employer to deduct union dues from wages. Their struggle had a larger significance as it was an attempt to normalize both the federal government's recognition of collective bargaining in 1944 and the 1945 Rand formula ruling on automatic union dues deductions. The conflict lasted for almost three months, spread to other industries and divided the community. With twelve thousand workers off the job, this was one of the largest strikes to date in Canadian history. The mayor supported the strikers, but the city council was split. On more than one occasion parades of First and Second World War veterans, with the Union Jack and the Canadian Ensign flags, marched past the picket lines in support. The provincial government ordered in more than one-third of the total strength of the OPP and also secured 225 RCMP reinforcements (Higley 1984: 322). A meeting of veterans denounced the recruitment of several hundred OPP and RCMP officers as a standby riot squad as "a betrayal of everything which Canada fought for and a desecration of the memory of Canada's dead" (O'Leary 1946). The federal government sent troops to Hamilton, but in the end the steelworkers and the company reached a settlement.

The institutionalization of collective bargaining in the years following the Second World War did much to normalize labour relations and lessen the need to send large numbers of police to strikes and lockouts. In 1934 the peaceful picketing provisions were restored to the *Criminal Code*, but exact difference between orderly picketing and disturbing the peace depended on on-the-spot decisions of police supervisors and subsequent decisions of local magistrates (Marquis 1986b: 105–6). During the 1950s and 1960s the labour movement was augmented by the recognition of bargaining rights for public sector workers at the municipal, provincial and federal levels. Yet employers still resorted to the courts to fight organized labour, and the police were still involved in a less than neutral fashion.

One of the more blatant uses of police to quell labour was the deployment of the SQ in 1949 against striking asbestos miners. When several thousand miners in the towns of Asbestos and Thetford walked out, the right-wing Union Nationale government of Maurice Duplessis declared the strike illegal and sent in a large contingent of the SQ. This was against the advice of both the Asbestos police chief and the town council, who warned that the arrival of the provincial police would make matters worse. A number of provincial officers were assaulted as the force guarded replacement workers who crossed picket lines. The force also engaged in a highly questionable proclamation of the *Riot Act* as well illegal arrests, intimidation and acts of brutality. Among the arrested was a young intellectual, Pierre Trudeau, who in 1956 edited and contributed to a critical study of the strike, *La grève de l'aminate.* Despite viewing the policeman's truncheon as a weapon against workers and the SQ as the political tool of a corrupt and authoritarian provincial regime in the 1950s, as prime minister Trudeau would suspend civil liberties during the October Crisis, encourage the RCMP to spy on separatists and threaten to jail labour leaders who opposed wage and price controls (Trudeau 1956).

Another example of the use of state power against workers during the early Cold War era was the battle by the Canadian government, Canadian shipping companies, the RCMP and the Seafarer's International Union (SIU) against the Canadian Seamen's Union (CSU). The CSU was a progressive national union that organized merchant mariners on Canadian-flagged ocean-going freighters on the Great Lakes and at east coast ports at a time when Canada still had one of the largest merchant marines in the world. Despite the fact that an SIU strike in 1946 had tied up Great Lakes shipping, three years later the government and shipping companies encouraged this international union in order to destabilize and hopefully destroy the Canadian union when it was on strike in Canada, Cuba and Britain. The attack on the CSU was orchestrated by an American, Hal Banks, who in the early 1960s was convicted of criminal conspiracy and fled the country.

The disruption of the CSU was accomplished by a combination of Red baiting and aggressive tactics, backed up by the RCMP and local police. One of the worst incidents took place in Halifax where several strikers were injured by gunfire. In New Brunswick the two sides scrapped on the Saint John waterfront and at the railway junction community of McAdam. At one point a force of two hundred RCMP and municipal police, equipped with steel helmets and axe handles, intercepted CSU members en route to a rural airport west of Saint John to confront inbound strikebreakers. By the time the strike ended in Saint John dozens of CSU members had been arrested for unlawful assembly, disturbing the peace and other charges. In New Brunswick and elsewhere, the strike, and the union itself, was broken by police intervention (Kaplan 1987; Vair n.d.). Although the SIU, despite its association with corruption and intimidation, was a more acceptable union for employers and governments in the early years of the Cold War, it was nonetheless involved with labour disputes and the police. The Canadian government at one point accused it of trying to destroy the nation's shipping sector. In 1961 police armed with nightsticks engaged SIU pickets on the Port Welland docks near St. Catherines. The strikers were in violation of an injunction. Most of the sailors escaped, but several were arrested (Simpson 1961).

With Newfoundland's entry into Confederation in 1949, the RCMP was contracted to provide provincial policing services to communities outside of St. John's. As part of the promises of Confederation, the Smallwood government was under intense pressure to attract investment and help provide manufacturing employment. A decade later the International Woodworkers of America (IWA) in Grand Falls, Newfoundland, went on strike against the Anglo-Newfoundland Development Company over wages and living conditions in the pulpwood cutting industry. At Badger, in central Newfoundland, a squad of Newfoundland Constabulary and RCMP faced a larger body of strikers blocking a road leading in to logging camps. When the company tried to move strikebreakers in through the picket lines in automobiles, the police and strikers clashed. Accounts varied as to which side initiated the violence but a Newfoundland Constabulary constable later died of his injuries, which turned public opinion against the strike. Premier Smallwood appealed to the federal government of John Diefenbaker for RCMP reinforcements, which were refused. As with the 1937 Oshawa strike, the issue was discussed at the cabinet level, in part because Smallwood, like Hepburn in the past, had publically taken sides with the employer in an industrial dispute. The Progressive Conservative government, which did not want to appear to be anti-union, believed that extra police would be a provocation. This caused not only hard feelings between the Conservative federal government and Newfoundland's Liberal government but also the unprecedented resignation of RCMP Commissioner L.H. Nicholson over government interference in police operations. The Newfoundland government, which decertified the IWA and replaced it with a less militant union, later sued the government of Canada for breach of its provincial policing contract (Hickey 1959; Leahy 2004; Roach 2007: 29–31).

The golden age of postwar collective bargaining did not last long. As union membership, aided by the growth of the public sector, expanded, a younger generation of more militant workers challenged not only employers but also their own union leaders. The postwar industrial relations framework brought relative labour peace at the cost of independent action. If a union engaged in an illegal or wildcat strike, it could be fined and its leaders jailed. Despite this, a new generation of activists reinvigorated the movement starting in the early 1960s. By the middle of the decade there were 1.7 million union members in Canada. In the period 1965–66, the federal Department of Labour recorded more than one thousand actions, most of them brief, and more than half of theses strikes were illegal. Much of the protest was fuelled by anger over the perceived injustice of *ex parte* injunctions, where company lawyers approached judges for legal remedies without the union side being present. Media coverage of labour violence, such as during the 1965–66 Ontario trucking industry strike, did much to shape public opinion and police responses. A new weapon against labour in the case of federally-regulated industries was back-to-work legislation, employed against a massive railway strike in 1966 (McInnis 2012).

The economic turbulence of the 1970s revived labour militancy, and occasionally there were complaints that police were departing from their supposedly neutral stance in labour actions. As in the past, public opinion was divided over union demands, particularly in a decade when the media emphasized problems such as inflation and unemployment. A 1973 strike at a Toronto-area textile plant became a *cause célèbre*, with city councillors, students, artists and other trade unionists accusing the police of bullying tactics (List 1973). In 1976 workers engaged in a wildcat strike at the Alcan plant in Kitimat, B.C., to protest a wage settlement imposed by the federal Anti-Inflation Board. When picketers blocked supervisors and replacement workers inside the aluminum plant, the provincial attorney general sent in a force of RCMP with riot helmets and batons. Picketers were arrested and charged with contempt of court. In 1980 the Ontario Federation of Labour protested that the OPP had been intimidating and provoking striking or locked out workers and basically acting as strikebreakers by escorting replacement workers through picket lines. The attorney general of Ontario as well as Crown attorneys and magistrates were also censured (List 1980).

Despite a supposed new emphasis on a "liaison" or peace-keeping approach to labour disputes, the old methods did not totally disappear. In 1987 the New Brunswick minister of justice was reported as issuing orders to RCMP to fire tear gas canisters at pulp cutters who were blocking a road leading to the Consolidated-Bathurst pulp and paper mill near Bathurst. The woods workers were not unionized and were protesting wages and working conditions. The police deployed 150 officers and arrested thirty-five workers for defying an injunction. An internal report justified the use of gas on the self-employed woods workers and concluded that "the crowd had to be dispersed." The RCMP had employed tear gas in New Brunswick in 1977, against protestors in Kent County who had objected to the expropriation of land to create Kouchibouguac National Park, where more than one thousand people were displaced (Morris 1987).

De Lint and Hall (2009) have produced an interesting study of the evolution of doctrine and tactics in the policing of labour disputes and large-scale protests. They argue that with the advent of neo-liberal public policies starting in the 1980s if not earlier, the likelihood of labour and other protests in reaction to austerity programs, environmental policies and other issues was high. At the same time more policing and security duties were being assumed by private security. In their analysis, police services responded with "intelligent control," which in the case of strikes and lockouts meant a liaison approach with union leaders. The idea was for specialized police officers to meet with strike organizers in advance in order to target "significant threats" and for police services to exercise restraint when dealing with workers on picket lines (De Lint and Hall 2009: 7). The authors, based on examples from Hamilton, Toronto and Vancouver, note a dual approach. In the case of labour disputes there was a minimization of coercion, yet with other types of protest (usually involving young people or aboriginals) and criminal policing there was an obvious trend toward militarization and "covert intelligence" approaches (ibid.: 12, 32). Elements of the liaison approach, which appeared to meet many of the criteria of community policing, were evident prior to the 1970s.

THE RED SHADOW

Although right-wing organizations have attracted some attention, the policing of dissent since 1867 has concentrated on left-wing individuals and organizations and secondarily on nationalist movements such as those seeking to free Ireland and India from British rule or Quebec from Canadian Confederation. Similar to the policing of dissent in the United States, the story of security and intelligence practices at the national level is largely the story of RCMP surveillance of the Communist Party. Canada's modern security and intelligence approach predates Confederation, beginning as a response in the 1860s to Confederate agents, escaped prisoners of war and Southern sympathizers who threatened to violate the neutrality of the British colonies by attacking the Northern states during the Civil War. Toward the end of the war the newest threat were Irish-American Fenians who plotted to overthrow British rule in Ireland. One wing wanted to attack British North America as part of this crusade. In 1864 a secret police was established in Canada East, where there were large Irish communities in Montreal and Quebec City.

Canada West formed a frontier constabulary headed by Gilbert McMicken who employed undercover agents on both sides of the border. Although it failed to warn of the 1866 Fenian attack on Canada West, the Canadian intelligence effort, aided by the extensive efforts of the British Consul at New York, was fairly effective at infiltrating American Fenianism. Following the Battle of Ridgeway, the Canadian frontier force expanded. In 1866–67 the Canadian government, in response to the Fenian threat, suspended habeas corpus and prosecuted a number of suspects. Following the assassination of federal cabinet minister D'Arcy McGee in 1868 by a suspected Fenian, Prime Minister Macdonald authorized the formation of the Dominion Police and appointed McMicken as its first commissioner. Its role was to guard federal government buildings and installations, enforce federal statutes and supervise the new Dominion's rudimentary security and intelligence capacity. Given the organization's limited size and budget, the second and third part of the mandate involved hiring Pinkerton private detectives to carry out criminal investigations, much like the government of British Columbia contracted the company to keep tabs on socialists and labour agitators (Marquis 1993: 61–2; Williams 1998: chapter 7; Whitaker, Kealey and Parnaby 2012: chapter 1).

In the period 1904–08, 5,200 South Asians, mainly Punjabi Sikhs, arrived in British Columbia. Despite being British subjects they were subjected to the same white backlash that was directed at the Chinese and Japanese. In response, the federal government attempted to restrict further immigration with a dubious "continuous journey" requirement amended to the *Immigration Act*. Because of growing nationalist unrest in India, Ottawa decided to place the small "Hindoo" population under surveillance and hired W.C. Hopkinson, a veteran of the Indian police. As a detective he initially reported to the Department of the Interior. His reports on west coast "agitators" were relayed to Ottawa and to the Governor General who sent them on to London. In 1909 Hopkinson, who was also an interpreter, was cross appointed to the Department of Immigration and the Dominion Police in British Columbia. Using informants, he kept tabs on Indian nationalists and foreign language publications in not only B.C. but also the Pacific Northwest. He also reported on the threat of socialists and the Industrial Workers of the World and in 1913 carried out confidential work on behalf of the British India Office. Many of these issues were highlighted by the *Komagata Maru* incident of 1914, when a steamship carrying more than 370 South Asians reached Vancouver. The authorities refused the migrants landing rights although they were British subjects. Police and immigration officials who attempted to board the steamer were driven off, and in the end the vessel was escorted out of the harbour by a Canadian naval cruiser. Following this, infighting among the Punjabi community led to several deaths, and in October 1914 Hopkinson was murdered by one of his informants (Whitaker, Kealey and Parnaby 2012: chapter 2). The role of the Immigration Department in conjunction with the Dominion Police as an intelligence-gathering force in British Columbia continued into the war years, with informants and agents monitoring not only Hindu and Chinese nationalists, but also organized labour (Horrall, 1980).

According to Kealey (1992: 289), Canada's security and intelligence efforts during the First World War were unfocused and "amateurish," largely because of primary responsibility falling to the Dominion Police. When the war broke out, the RNWMP was mainly confined to provincial policing duties in Alberta and Saskatchewan, and it was here that it began its counter subversion role in cooperation with the Dominion Police. The federal authorities registered 88,000 enemy aliens and ended up interning more than eight thousand, including close to three hundred women and children. A larger number of residents of German and Austrian origins were investigated by police. Most of the detainees were Ukrainians who arrived in Canada with Austro-Hungarian passports. By 1917 many of the prisoners were paroled and working. The suspect immigrants were joined by a number of socialists, including Leon Trotsky who was detained at Halifax when attempting to travel back to Europe to take part in the Russian Revolution. The federal authorities also censored "enemy language" publications and, following the outbreak of the Russian Revolution, suspended freedom of speech and association for a number of socialist organizations, most of them "ethnic" in composition. Kealey notes that while the Dominion Police tended to arrest and charge radicals in the last part of the war, the RNWMP preferred the "implantation" of undercover agents, the tactic it would employ for decades (Kealey 1992: 301).

The end of the war did not necessarily lighten suspicious attitudes towards left-wing publications and organizations, particularly of the ethnic variety. In late 1918 British intelligence warned the Canadian government that the Bolsheviks planned to spread propaganda in North America. The government responded to this threat by authorizing the RNWMP to enforce the security provisions of the *War Measures Act* west of the Great Lakes, leaving eastern Canada to the Dominion Police. (At this point the RNWMP had been reduced to fewer than four hundred, all ranks.) The federal authorities also informed Western provincial governments that the Mounties would be available to suppress civil unrest. The minister in charge of the RNWMP took steps to bring Mounted Police cavalry units back from Europe (many reserve division members organized in 1914 had volunteered for overseas service, and in 1918 others enlisted as cavalry in the Canadian Expeditionary Force) and instructed the comptroller of the force that resources should be dedicated to secret services duties "in the principal centres where I.W.W. or other revolutionary agitators might be at work" (Horrall 1980: 173). Even before the Winnipeg General Strike, the assignment of all security and intelligence duties to the RNWMP and the creation of the RCMP in 1920, the Mounties, according to Horrall (1980), had penetrated the major radical groups in Western Canada, supplying detailed accounts on so-called "revolutionary organizations" and "agitators." Initially conducted through the Criminal Investigation Branch (CIB), it was an approach the force would maintain until the middle of the 1980s. Infiltration was modelled on classic private detective operations, the most famous of which was the Pinkerton National Detective Agency's exposure of the Molly Maguires secret society in the Pennsylvania coal fields in the 1870s, and on police tactics against illegal booze and drug rackets. As discussed in the preceding chapter, Commissioner Bowen-Perry took advantage of concerns among political leaders in Ottawa that the Winnipeg strike was potentially revolutionary, despite the force's own intelligence reports and briefings to the contrary, to transform the RNWMP into a new police service with more of a national mandate (Horrall 1980).

The security efforts of the RCMP, eventually named the Special Branch, were compiled into weekly reports of suspected organizations and "agitators," which were then submitted to headquarters. During the 1920s and 1930s detectives working in the CIB, which conducted both criminal and security investigations, forwarded intelligence to headquarters in Ottawa. In addition the commanding officer of each district received a monthly report on radical and labour activities. During the Great Depression an Intelligence Section was organized at Ottawa; by 1939 it had expanded to nine members (Hewitt 2002: 23). The force also condemned Communism in the pages of *The Quarterly*, an RCMP journal founded in 1933 (Hannant 1995: 76). The RCMP *Security Bulletins*, parts of which have been published by editors Whitaker and Kealey, amount to a police documentary history of Canada's labour and left-wing movements. Most of the information consisted of newspaper clippings and accounts of speeches and meetings, but some reports came from undercover officers such as Frank Zaneth (Franco Zanetti) or volunteer and paid informants. As part of a pattern established during the First World War, RCMP operatives often were part of the inner circle of trade unions and socialist organizations, such as the Communist Party of Canada, founded in 1921. No detail, ranging from the activities of a mandolin orchestra to the dynamics of a strike tying up the Vancouver waterfront, was too small for this intelligence gathering operation. A weekly report on agitators in 1920, for example, noted that Reverend J.S. Woodsworth had spoken to a group of unemployed workers in Vancouver on "The History of the Human Race." The audience for the future MP and leader of the Cooperative Commonwealth Federation consisted of eighteen people (Kealey and Whitaker 1994: 221).

Hysteria over "reds" in 1919 was not confined to concerns over enemy aliens having plotted the Winnipeg strike. In the summer of 1919 more than one hundred Montreal police, acting under federal authority, raided the city's "foreign quarters" and seized large quantities of books, pamphlets, correspondence and telegrams, some of it in Russian and Yiddish, which suggested that local "Bolsheviks" were in communication with socialists in Manitoba and Ontario (CP 1919). Earlier a multilingual Toronto police detective had placed enemy aliens, anti-conscriptionists and ethnic radicals under surveillance. The chief constable was provided with transcripts of socialist meetings, a tactic that continued into the 1920s and 1930s. These investigations resulted in the arrest of the editor of *Canadian Forward* and of dozens of members of the Ukrainian Socialist Party. The Toronto police continued to monitor aliens and radicals, and a Toronto detective forwarded recommendations to the Dominion Police and the federal minister of justice to amend the *Immigration Act* and *Criminal Code* to curb subversion (Marquis 1986b: 122–3).

In the interwar years, the RCMP waged an intelligence war against the Communist Party of Canada, which was headquartered in Toronto and whose membership nationally was dominated by Finns, Ukrainians and Jews. The Toronto police, whose own Red squad monitored and harassed local Communists, played a role in this effort. Chief Constable Denis Draper, a former military man, was an outspoken enemy of the Communist Party, but previous chief constables had taken an equally hard line toward political radicals. Prior to the First World War, for example, the department had clashed with the Independent Labour Party and the Social Democratic Party during a free speech controversy. The battle over the right of the political left in Toronto to assemble in public and hear speeches heated up again in the late 1920s, and neither the police department nor the courts appeared to think that Communists should enjoy the rights of "normal" Canadians. In 1931 the federal and provincial governments launched an offensive against the CPC, raiding its Toronto offices and arresting several of its leaders on the charge of sedition. Based on evidence from "Jack Esselwein" (Mounted Police Sergeant John Leopold, who had infiltrated the party), the leaders were convicted and sent to penitentiary for up to five years (Dubro and Rowland 1992: chapter 11). Aside from publicized actions, the RCMP silently built up its files on suspected radicals and organizations and even began to screen new federal civil servants, by conducting fingerprint and criminal records checks (Hannant 1995: chapter 3).

During this period, the Toronto police service harassed and attempted to control more moderate leftist organizations such as the new Cooperative Commonwealth Federation (CCF) via its control of the licensing of meeting halls. Under Chief Constable General Denis Draper, leftists were monitored by a Red squad, which in 1934 was renamed the Special Branch. Draper, like a number of big city police chiefs in this period, espoused an aggressive war-on-crime philosophy. The populist politics of the Great Depression era sometimes resulted in mainstream political leaders acting as champions of the unemployed or workers, as when new premier Mitch Hepburn (who soon became the outspoken opponent of the CIO) replaced two members of the Toronto board of police commissioners in 1934. The commission, under Draper's recommendation, had refused to permit a parade by the Ontario Hunger Marchers' Association, an unemployed workers' group with connections to the WUL, the CCF and the East York Workers' Association.

In 1938, Draper's Special Branch produced a confidential report, entitled "The Red Shadow," which inflated membership in the CPC in the Toronto area by more than 100 percent compared to the actual figure, in order to demonstrate the police service's effectiveness as a counter-subversion organization (Dubro and Rowland 1992: 228; Marquis 1986b: 132–6, 139–40). The OPP organized its own special branch of undercover officers in 1939, to investigate threats of sabotage and subversive organizations such as the CPC, the Canadian Labour Defence League and fascist groups. For the first two years of the Second World War the CPC and its related organizations opposed Canada's military effort and drew extra attention from the authorities. Although the OPP special branch was scaled down in 1941, its interest in monitoring the CCF for possible Communist links was politically risky at a time when many Ontarians were moving to the left. The unit was disbanded before the end of the war, but the CCF, which had formed the official opposition, accused the government of using "secret police" tactics against social democrats (Higley 1984: 284–7 and 306–7).

As in 1914, the outbreak of war in 1939 brought new or enhanced security duties to the police. By 1942, for example, more than 100,000 aliens had to report regularly to the police, and police services were tasked with helping to enforce the national registration of rifles and shotguns and a new registration of all handguns. During the war, under the Defence of Canada Regulations, police registered, finger-printed and photographed German and Italian "aliens," many of them naturalized Canadians. In 1940 several thousand Italians were arrested and sent, without trial, to four internment camps. For the most part these minorities were not subjected to blanket arrest, and the RCMP tended to discount popular anxieties over a possible "fifth column" that were fuelled by press reports (Whitaker, Kealey and Parnaby 2012: 163). In addition to national security considerations, the federal cabinet had been motivated by possible unrest among the "loyal" population against pos-sible internal enemies who did not deserve the protections of "British justice." The Communist Party was banned under the Defence of Canada Regulations and a number of its leaders interned, and the Ukrainian Labour Farmer Temple Association was disbanded and it assets seized. Following the German invasion of the USSR in 1941, attitudes toward the CPC changed, to the frustration of senior RCMP officers who always viewed anti-fascists as more of a threat to Canada than fascists. Earlier the RCMP had investigated Communist links to the Canadian volunteers who had fought fascism in Spain with a hope to securing convictions under Canada's *Foreign Enlistment Act* (Marquis 1993: 198).

As part of its special wartime duties the RCMP also built up a huge wartime fingerprint collection of all members of the armed forces (a million men and women), workers in strategic industries such as munitions plants and merchant sailors. The industrial side of the program was strongly supported by the powerful Department of Munitions and Supply. As Hannant notes (1995: 84), this effort, despite its lack of statutory authority, ended up collecting personal information on one-fifth of the nation's population. Communists were the main targets of this intrusive exercise, and for the most part the unprecedented surveillance of citizens was supported by mainstream labour organizations in the name of the war effort. Despite this supposed neutrality, intelligence reports frequently editorialized. One RCMP Intelligence Bulletin in 1940 claimed that union demands for higher wages were harmful to that effort. In contrast to the FBI, the RCMP did not plant undercover operatives in munitions and other war industry plants but trusted its screening process and corporate security as well as a new organization of special constables. In the immediate postwar era, security screening also applied to Canadian employees of United Nations agencies and Jewish refugees. The RCMP's "civil" fingerprint collection surpassed its criminal collection, inherited from the Dominion Police in 1920, which by 1947 contained records on more than 700,000 individuals (Hannant 1995: 91, 106, 249).

In 1945, following the federal government's decision to transfer sixteen thousand *National Resources Mobilization Act* home-defence conscripts to over-seas service, the RCMP assisted the military in tracking down several thousand defaulters (Whitaker, Kealey and Parnaby 2012: 164, 169; Kemp 1958: 258). The unpopularity of the RCMP in Quebec was captured in the headlines in 1945 when Mounted Police assisting the army provost corps in searching for draft evaders in Drummondville set off a riot. The local police were slow to react to a conflict that had been exacerbated by the incursion of outsiders. A member of the Union Nationale provincial government denounced the operation as similar to "Gestapo tactics." The controversial Drummondville operation netted only four wanted men (Dubro and Rowland 1992: 253–4). Although not involved in enforcing conscription, municipal and provincial police services supported or spearheaded civilian air raid protection organizations. Municipal and provincial police agencies also expanded counter subversion activities. The OPP, for example, kept tabs on ethnic and radical organizations and even the Jehovah's Witnesses, a group whose anti-conscription views also troubled the RCMP (De Lint and Hall 2009: 80–1).

In the removal of twenty thousand Japanese Canadians, many of them naturalized Canadians, from coastal British Columbia in 1942 the RCMP acted in a relatively progressive fashion compared to the local authorities. Following the Japanese attacks on Pearl Harbour and Hong Kong in late 1941, the RCMP was satisfied by the detention of less than fifty Japanese aliens in British Columbia and the promise that Japanese language schools and newspapers would close in order to prevent white threats and attacks. Japanese aliens were ordered to register with the RCMP and report on a regular basis. Despite the fact that British Columbia had its own provincial police, the federal force took a special interest in the Pacific coast province because of its volatile political and labour scenes. During the 1930s, for example, the RCMP, BCPP and Vancouver police regularly shared information on radicals. Both the commissioner of the RCMP and top military officials in Ottawa did not view the Nisei (the Canadian-born) or the Japanese in general, as disloyal. Yet white racism, economic resentment, rumours of spies and saboteurs and news of the fall of Singapore in early 1942 stirred up public feeling against the minority. The commissioner of the BCPP believed that Japanese Canadians could not be trusted, that their continued freedom would invite rioting and that the RCMP did not have a good handle on the security situation.

Despite the advice of the RCMP, the Department of Defence and other voices in Ottawa, in February the federal government ordered the evacuation of all Japanese Canadians, not just men of military age, from coastal "protected areas." The detainees also had their fishing boats, vehicles and businesses confiscated. The RCMP and BCPP supervised the movement of women and children to detention camps in the interior of British Columbia; the men were housed in separate work camps. The policy, later described as one of worst violations of civil liberties in Canadian history, was wildly popular at the time with white British Columbians. In the end, the RCMP was proven correct: no acts of espionage or sabotage were uncovered. Ironically, the BCPP had more trouble from Canada's allies, specifically American troops and construction workers who built the British Columbia section of the Alaska Highway. Working with American military police, the provincial police responded to a surge in complaints about drinking, prostitution and gambling (Sunhara 1981; Stonier-Newman 1991: 214–22).

FROM THE EARLY COLD WAR TO THE NEW LEFT

From 1945 until the late 1950s, Canada experienced its own Red Scare, a quieter but still dramatic version of the American reaction to the international threat of the USSR and fears about espionage and internal subversion. In late 1945 an employee of the Soviet embassy in Ottawa, Igor Gouzenko, defected with evidence of a spy ring, Canadian citizens passing "atomic secrets" to the Soviets. Although the secrets were of minor importance, the crisis, which broke in 1946, signalled Canada's abrupt entry into the Cold War. The Mackenzie King government investigated the matter under the authority of the *War Measures Act*, appointing a royal commission that pressured suspects into testifying and denied them due process. The RCMP arrested and interrogated sixteen suspects, paying little attention to their legal rights. The detainees, forbidden from seeing their families or speaking to legal counsel, were confined in a military barracks. In the end nine were convicted of various offences and sentenced to terms ranging from two to six years. The federal government formed a Security Panel to oversee security screening.

Until this period the Canadian civil liberties movement, which did not produce a national organization until the early 1960s, was largely driven by Communists and social democrats associated with the CCF. Now liberals began to advocate in favour of civil liberties. The abuses of state power associated with the Gouzenko investigations, combined with concerns over wartime censorship, the deportation of Japanese Canadians and Quebec's notorious Padlock Law, gave a boost to local civil liberties organizations. Together with a push in the provincial level, supported by faith groups and organized labour, for human rights codes to prevent religious and racial discrimination, the civil liberties movement pushed for a Canadian Bill of Rights (Clément 2001).

During the early Cold War the RCMP Intelligence Branch was renamed the Special Branch and expanded its surveillance of Communists, labour organizations and immigrants, especially those from nations with strong leftist movements. The federal government established an interagency Security Panel to coordinate national security initiatives and to investigate the loyalty of civil servants. As MacKenzie (2001) notes, from the late 1940s until the late 1950s, many left-wing individuals and organizations were regarded with suspicion. Canada's Red Scare was less flamboyant than the American version, exemplified by the excesses of McCarthyism, but still insidious as it was "outside the normal channels of public security and debate" (MacKenzie 2001: 24). Within the federal bureaucracy the departments of Defence and External Affairs and the Privy Council Office and Prime Minister's Office were subjected to extra scrutiny.

The unsophisticated approach to security and intelligence of the 1950s, and the tendency of politicians and the media to trust the RCMP to "do its job," would lead to major problems in the 1960s and 1970s. As early as the late 1940s the RCMP drew up plans to arrest up to one thousand "subversives," including their children ("red diaper babies"), and send them to abandoned federal prisons. Mass arrest lists were prepared for both Communists and sympathizers. Showing the continued influence of the FBI on Canada's security establishment, the top secret PROFUNC plan (the name stands for Prominent Functionaries of the Communist Party) was revived in the late 1960s with a continued emphasis on leading Communists. A 1969 document spoke of seizing Communist children from parents and placing them in foster care. The list of individuals to be interned in the late 1960s during "a national emergency" included more than seven hundred names, and the RCMP even developed rules for mail censorship and punishments for violations of internment camp discipline. The anachronistic plan remained on the books until it was removed by the federal minister of justice in 1983 (Beeby 2000).

Although the activities of the RCMP security service have been examined in a number of popular and academic studies and Whitaker and Kealey's RCMP *Security Bulletins* series, less is known about the role of municipal and provincial "red" squads. In 1948 the press reported a cooperative drive in Quebec against Communists and "fellow travellers" (sympathizers). Based on raids and interviews, the Montreal anti-subversive squad reported that the city contained 1,800 party members and two thousand sympathizers. Several dozen ringleaders were supposedly following orders from Moscow. The police were aware of thirty-two so-called front organizations, operating in fifteen languages, and twenty-two labour councils or unions with "red" connections. The head of the anti-subversive squad was confident that the police could easily round up all Communists in the event of a crisis. In the early 1950s the sq conducted raids in the Abitibi region and seized "alleged Communist" literature from Ukrainian and Russian organizations (CP 1948; *Globe and Mail* 1951).

In English Canada, Quebec's best known anti-radical measure was its 1937 *Padlock Act*, passed after the federal government lived up to its earlier pledge to remove Section 98 of the *Criminal Code*. Based on civil penalties in other jurisdictions against suspected bootleggers, the measure permitted sheriffs, under the authority of the provincial government, to padlock any residence, hall or place of business suspected of being use to promote Communism. The statute also criminalized the printing and distribution of literature that promoted "Bolshevism" or Communism, which in Quebec could also include social democratic or even liberal ideas. Critics argued that the Padlock Law allowed the Duplessis government to intimidate political enemies and socially unpopular groups such as the Jehovah's Witnesses religious sect. Harassment of this sect even extended to the municipal level in the 1940s, when a Montreal bylaw made it an offence to distribute or even possess pamphlets without a permit. Toward the end of the Second World War scores of Witnesses were arrested in Montreal for simply carrying literature (Lambertson 2004).

One group that received unwanted attention from RCMP Security Intelligence in the 1950s were Ottawa-area homosexuals. Until the late 1960s, homosexual acts between consenting adults were illegal, and gays and lesbians were subjected to prejudice, discrimination, threats and violence well past the late 1960s. Most homosexuals understandably lived a double life, posing as "straight" persons in public. The RCMP, following FBI practice, began investigating homosexual employees of the federal government on the grounds that they were at risk for being blackmailed by Soviet intelligence agents in the nation's capital, the site of foreign embassies. Homosexuality was also deemed a character defect in itself and a bar to enlistment into the RCMP. By the late 1950s the Security Service had seven officers dedicated to this effort, which eventually expanded to cover homosexuals in the Ottawa area who were not federal civil servants. During the 1960s the RCMP even contracted an academic to develop a "fruit machine" that would allow police to determine the sexual preferences of security targets or criminal suspects. By the late 1960s the service had files on several thousand known and "suspected" homosexuals. This anti-gay intelligence effort continued after the *Criminal Code* reforms of the late 1960s, and as late as 1981 the Security Service still dedicated one officer to the "gay security" file (Kinsman and Gentile 2010; Whitaker, Kealey and Parnaby 2012: 191; CP 1981b).

For the RCMP Security Service and local red squads, the Old Left, mainly the Communist Party and its front organizations, had been a relatively easy target. Things became more complicated in the 1960s for not only security and intelligence policing but also public order policing. In the past, riot squads had been deployed overwhelmingly against Communist demonstrators and striking blue-collar workers. During the early 1960s, whether it was police misconduct in Birmingham and other American cities against peaceful civil rights protestors or the deployment of armed police and National Guard and army units during urban riots or campus anti-war or student power gatherings, Canadians and their police thought of rioting as an American problem. As early as 1964 this began to change, as new political movements, attracting young, educated and middle-class Canadians, began to organize demonstrations over various issues. Many of the children of the baby boom grew up to question authority and reject conformity and the conservative conventions of traditional politics. That put them on a collision course with symbols and agents of the status quo such as the police. Their protests were overwhelmingly peaceful, but on occasion tempers flared and the police were accused of overreacting. And the presence of media, including television camera crews, and a new interest in the right of citizens to peacefully protest complicated the politics of public order (De Lint and Hall 2009: 102).

One early example was the protest in Quebec City in October 1964 against the visit of Queen Elizabeth II in honour of the centennial of the Quebec Conference, which had created the blueprint for Canadian Confederation. Young nationalists who supported Quebec independence and rejected the British monarchy organized a rally and parade under the Rassemblement pour l'indépendance nationale (RIN), a group the RCMP suspected of having links to violent separatists. Earlier in the year one of their demonstrations had been broken up by police. On "truncheon Saturday," RIN marchers, who included children of the province's elite, were attacked by Quebec City police during a peaceful march. The unprovoked and dispropor-tionate nature of the violence, which also victimized reporters and members of the public, shocked many Canadians who viewed television coverage of the event. In 1966 the Ottawa police, reinforced by the RCMP (including plainclothes officers who mingled with the crowd), monitored close to three thousand peace activists protesting American involvement in the Vietnam War. The main job of the police was breaking up scuffles between anti and pro-war demonstrators. In an ominous sign of things to come, the RCMP photographed the demonstrators. Smaller dem-onstrations took place in three other Canadian cities (Globe and Mail 1966a).

The mounting challenge of public order by the late 1960s, and corresponding influences from United States law enforcement, was reflected in the organization and training of police agencies and their acquisition of new equipment. In 1963, a leftist separatist movement, which announced that it was not part of the Community Party, began a series of bombings and armed robberies in Quebec. These crimes prompted police raids and arrests. A year later the RCMP, SQ and Montreal police, in response to separatist violence, formed a combined anti-terrorism squad, and the RCMP began to investigate the separatist leanings of federal bureaucrats in Quebec (Tetley 2006: 57; Whitaker, Kealey and Parnaby 2012: 294).

Following several years of destructive rioting in the United States, the Department of the Army, the National Guard and police services studied how to contain civil disorders while minimizing the loss of life. One tactic was to avoid shooting looters and use violence only as a last resort. Riot control tactics included the use of gas, smoke and water cannon, armoured vehicles and mace spray as alternatives to live ammunition. According to one report, armoured vehicles were valued for their "psychological effect" (Gellner 1968). By the late 1960s Canadian police chiefs, boards of police commissioners and city councils were more interested in acquiring crowd control equipment (Marquis 1993: 304). According to critics, the Law Enforcement Assistance Administration (LEAA) program, established by the American government in 1968, was subverted away from a mixed approach to improving the criminal justice system to a more coercive, militarized response to street crime and political dissent, including not only new crowd control equipment but also helicopters, armoured vehicles and computer systems for amassing criminal and "security" intelligence. At this time, many academics, journalists and activists were prone to see parallels between American domestic policing and counterinsurgency in Vietnam (Wolfe 1974). And journalists, photographers and television camera crews, in the age of mass demonstrations, were no longer on the sidelines. In Montreal and elsewhere they were sometimes physically attacked by riot police; police services also demanded, sometimes without legal authority, copies of photographs, film footage and videotapes from media outlets in order to identify individuals who may have broken the law (Canada 1970: 107–8).

As late as 1970 a journalist reported that most Canadian police departments, although preparing for social unrest, preferred to take a low-profile, non-provocative approach. Large departments had acquired riot helmets and riot batons, and most had stocks of tear gas. Given that the RCMP was deploying plainclothes officers in legal demonstrations and that this was standard practice in the United States, it is highly likely that the OPP, the SQ and municipal police services did the same. In 1970 no municipal departments reported owning special vehicles for crowd control, but Toronto police noted the effectiveness of officers mounted on horses (*Globe and Mail* 1970b).

In 1969, when an estimated 100,000 people took part in roughly one hundred protests, the Montreal riot squad was equipped with shields. Police managers explained, somewhat disingenuously, that the equipment was not designed for offensive purposes but to protect officers. The squad, which was specially trained, was formed in the aftermath of the violent 1968 St. Jean Baptiste Day affair in Montreal. On that provincial holiday, despite the presence of 1,400 police, a crowd sympathetic to Quebec separatism (including members of the RIN) had thrown bottles, stones, firecrackers and light bulbs filled with paint at an official podium containing the mayor, the premier and Prime Minister Pierre Trudeau. The police had paddy wagons on standby and used mounted officers, motorcycles and plain-clothes officers to break up the crowd and make arrests. The press described the melee as a "pitched battle" (CP 1968). Dozens of officers and civilians were injured and close to three hundred protestors arrested. Most were released because of problems with identification, but a number, including RIN leader Pierre Bourgault, who had threatened to block Trudeau's appearance by force, were charged with participating in a riot (ibid.).

A number of police chiefs interviewed by 1970 appeared to be uneasy about the more paramilitary appearance and approach of riot squads, regarding the display of helmets and batons as provocative. Toronto had a one-hundred officer riot squad, but it was not always deployed at demonstrations. Earlier in 1970, for example, when five thousand people protested against American military actions in Southeast Asia, the department arrested ninety-one individuals without deploying the riot squad (Churchill 1970). Another sign of the tentative response by the authorities toward crowd control technology was a decision in 1970 by the Ontario government to ban the use of mace, a chemical spray, by police (Gellner 1968; *Globe and Mail* 1970a).

RCMP monitoring of university campuses, which were fairly exclusive and conservative environments prior to the Second World War, began in the early 1920s. One of the justifications behind this increasingly detailed intelligence-gathering effort was that students were "tomorrow's elite" (Hewitt 2002: 12). Professors, guest speakers, student clubs and even student newspapers were monitored, and in the 1930s and 1940s outspoken faculty members were suspected of being Communists or sympathizers. In the 1930s the 400,000-strong Canadian Youth Congress, suspected of being a Communist front, was deemed a special threat (Axelrod 1989). An active peace movement by the early 1960s, and especially the Combined University Campaign for Nuclear Disarmament, drew more attention from the RCMP Special Branch as it challenged a key premise of the Cold War, nuclear deterrence, and attracted students and professors. In 1963, following negative coverage in the media and criticism from the Canadian Association of University Teachers, which was defending academic freedom, the Pearson government promised that there would be no active recruiting of informants on university campuses. Yet by the late 1960s, with the rise of the New Left, RCMP activity on campuses actually increased. Even student council elections were analyzed. One of the challenges was that the administration of certain universities refused open access to student records. Reflecting a similar attempt by the FBI and CIA to explain student unrest as the product of Soviet intrigue, a 1969 Special Branch report labelled "New Left (Student Power) in Canada," although recognizing the spontaneous and grassroots nature of the movement, erroneously listed the Communist Party as an influence; in fact the New Left was fluid, decentralized and highly fragmented.

The Security Service even monitored high school teachers and students (Sethna 2000) and Quebec's new system of Collèges d'enseignement général et professional (CEGEP), which was suspected of being a nursery for separatism. In Quebec the authorities were worried about the impact of radical separatists such as Pierre Vallières, whose 1968 treatise *Negres blancs d'Amérique* struck a chord with Québecois students, artists and intellectuals (the author at one point was prosecuted for sedition for advocating revolution). Hewitt has detailed the special focus by the RCMP on student activism at Simon Fraser University in 1968 and Sir George Williams University in 1969. Special attention was also paid to Opération McGill Français, a campaign by trade unionists, separatists and students in 1969 to turn Montreal's McGill University into a French-language institution. Police intelligence had predicted violence from a crowd of up to ten thousand marchers. The Montreal police placed one hundred riot police in plain sight, but hidden in reserve were an additional 1,200 municipal and provincial police and two hundred members of the RCMP. During the demonstration, which resulted in forty-six arrests, one hundred Security Intelligence officers blended in with the crowd (Hewitt 2002: 93–7, 103, 107–37, 141–65).

In 1967, D Section (Counter Subversion) identified education as one of three "key sectors" subject to radical infiltration and necessitating further informant recruitment (Hewitt 2002: 136). There were a few mainstream intellectuals who were critics of the RCMP prior to the 1970s, including historian Arthur Lower and journalist Sidney Katz. The force, although protected by its "sacred cow" status, nonetheless was conscious of its image (Dawson 1998). In his 1967 memoirs, Commissioner C.W. Harvison defended the security work of the RCMP on the grounds that paid agents of Moscow had been attempting to weaken Canada since the early 1930s. He also suggested that politicians were able to dodge controversies connected to security and intelligence by shifting the blame to the Mounties. According to Mann and Lee (1979), the "blame game" was also practiced by the RCMP against the government and served to keep Canadians further in the dark as to the activities of the Mounties. A year later Deputy Commissioner W.H. Kelly told a parliamentary committee that university students in British Columbia, Ontario, Quebec and Nova Scotia were being stirred up by American agitators such as members of the Black Panthers. In 1968, a Black writers' conference in Montreal had invited American Black Power leader Stokely Carmichael; by this time the RCMP security service was worried by not only the influence of the Panthers, but also Black writers and activists in Quebec, many of whom were from the Caribbean

(Austin 2013: 155–65). Kelly deemed this alleged situation to be detrimental to "the national interest," although he confessed that his conclusion was based on "a feeling but no particular proof" (CP 1969). Kelly, who represented the hawkish wing of Canadian law enforcement, reflected the older "contagion" theory of the Security Service, based on the belief that Canadians by themselves would never turn to left-wing ideas and organizations. The Canadian Association of Chiefs of Police (CACP) endorsed this view and protested against visits to Canada by American anti-war activists and radical European student leaders. Kelly was also suspicious of growing ties between the labour movement and students. Hence the tendency of the RCMP to reflect the theory of Hoover's FBI that Communists were behind all social protest. In both cases the security "experts" were badly mistaken (Kelly was still pointing to Communist subversion as major threat to Canada in 1976) (Kelly and Kelly 1976: chapter 33).

As in the United States where the FBI, the CIA and the White House exchanged information with other federal agencies in order to uncover, monitor and disrupt individuals and organizations, the Special Branch/Security Service relied on other government departments for information. In the 1960s, for example, it exchanged information on suspected radicals with the Department of External Affairs, military intelligence, Manpower and Immigration and National Revenue (Hewitt 2002: 107). Starting in 1968, the newly formed Parti Québecois, which incorporated the RIN, was investigated by the RCMP for possible foreign influences (Whitaker, Kealey and Parnaby 2012: 295). Given the later practices of CSIS, the RCMP presumably also approached provincial governments for information on citizens. In 1977, documents released as a result of the MacDonald inquiry revealed that the RCMP in the 1970s had provided the Department of Employment and Immigration with a list of more than sixty "Communist controlled organizations" in relation to applications for visas to visit Canada. This included the usual list of cultural and ethnic organizations associated with the USSR and eastern Europe, as well as the student movement on ten university campuses. For good measure, the report added "the Quebec student movement" and "the Canadian student movement" (Martin 1977d).

Canadian student protest in the 1960s and 1970s, for the most part, consisted of brief strikes, sit-ins and demonstrations often over routine university policies such as a move at the University of New Brunswick to make students use library cards or the refusal of the administration at Catholic St. Francis Xavier University in Nova Scotia to allow male students to entertain females in their dormitory rooms. More dramatic, because it was fuelled by allegations of racism, was the Sir George Williams University occupation in Montreal in 1969. The incident began with a sit-in by two hundred students angered by the alleged anti-Black attitude of a professor. With the arrival of the Montreal riot squad the protestors took direct action, with some students barricading parts of the occupied building and setting fire to the university computer centre. Most of the protestors where white, but media attention focused on forty-eight Black students, many of whom were from the Caribbean. In the end ninety-eight protestors were arrested. Remarks from the largely white crowd that gathered outside the occupied building before it was stormed by the police indicated both support for the protestors and racist denunciations and cheers for the police. In theory the controversy should have been restricted to the university administration, campus security and the municipal police, but the RCMP, in the name of national security, took an interest in the disturbances. In fact the Security Intelligence had an informer in the inner circle of the occupation (Hewitt 2002: 151; Martel 2012). Interestingly, a memo prepared by the Security Service opined that the controversial occupation could have been avoided by the university administration (Austin 2013: 154–5).

Academics and activists have viewed racialized security and intelligence surveillance and infiltration as another tactic for preserving the social order. The RCMP was not well prepared to deal with the ideological and social changes of the 1960s and did not have any Black officers who could be used to infiltrate Canada's budding Black Power movement. The FBI, in contrast, employed several thousand informers to spy on the American movement (Hewitt 2010). Despite limited and unreliable intelligence, security reports in 1969 mentioned the Black Panthers and the usual leftists, along with foreign students, as likely security threats in Montreal (Martel 2012). In Nova Scotia the RCMP, fearing the influence of the Black Panthers and assisted by informers within the community, spied on Black community organizers. As revealed by *Access to Information Act* requests in 1994, the confidential reports reflected racial stereotypes toward Blacks in rural Guysborough County and the Halifax area as being thieves and drunks who beat their children and preferred to live on welfare. The RCMP appeared so hard-pressed for undercover operatives among the Black community in the early 1970s that it recruited American citizen Thomas Hart for this purpose, through the U.S. Department of Justice (Sheppard 1980; CP 1994a; Tanovich 2006: 58).

The intensity of political protest in late 1960s Montreal was actually one of the stated causes of a controversial strike in 1969 by the municipal police. In addition to the stress of ongoing crowd control and anti-terrorism duties, the police union cited workload and the need to have wage parity with their counterparts in Toronto. In what was dubbed Montreal's "night of terror," members of the Police Brotherhood, in defiance of their leaders, walked off the job and abandoned police stations. The provincial government sent in units of the SQ to provide emergency services, but a number of their vehicles were commandeered by the strikers. During the sixteen-hour strike several banks were robbed, many stores were vandalized and looted and two people were fatally shot. One was an SQ corporal who was on the scene of a strike by independent taxi drivers at the headquarters of a limousine company in Griffintown. More than one hundred were arrested as a result of the so-called Murray Hill riot. The provincial authorities passed emergency legislation that ordered Montreal police and firefighters back to work, and in a preview of the more dramatic crisis of 1970, units of the Canadian army were deployed in case they were needed to help restore order (CBC 1969; O'Reilly 1978). Late in 1969 the Montreal police, equipped with riot gear, steel crowd control barriers, spotlights and loudspeakers, defended the city hall and police headquarters against demonstrators who protested the Union Nationale government's language policies and demanded the release of two FLQ prisoners. The protestors also denounced the provincial justice minister as a "fascist." Crowds smashed store and office windows and hurled a number of Molotov cocktails (Tetley 2006: 68–9).

As noted in chapter 6, the enforcement of drug laws against youth starting in the late 1960s was the greatest challenge to police legitimacy since the prohibition era. Despite tough talk that argued that marijuana was a gateway to harder drugs and a source of income for organized crime, and despite mounting numbers of "cannabis offenders" before the courts, the police appeared to be using considerable discretion with youth possessing marijuana for personal use. Yet in 1971 the Vancouver police struck at a political manifestation of the counter culture when more than one thousand demonstrators gathered at Stanley Park for a "smoke-in." For a number of years a hawkish police chief had been lashing out at the large number of hippies who flocked to the west coast city, and police had been harassing them with loitering and other charges. One sign of policing challenges associated with the 1960s "generation gap" was a news report of a 1966 concert by the Rolling Stones, where the British rockers "made offensive remarks and rude gestures" to police on duty at the Pacific National Exhibition forum, and a police officer was kicked in the groin, "hysterical" girls were carried out of the venue, an usher suffered a concussion and "a policewoman collapsed from exhaustion" (CP 1966). The 1971 protestors flaunted the federal narcotics law and police authority by openly smoking marijuana in a public park. They were protesting both the continued criminalization of cannabis and the use of undercover "narcs." The police, who had agreed in advance not to arrest people for smoking marijuana, ordered the street cleared and attacked the crowd with mounted police, the riot squad and club-wielding plainclothes officers. Many were injured and three dozen individuals arrested. The officer in command justified causing a riot in order to prevent a possible riot, although until the riot police appeared the crowd had been peaceful and festive. After media coverage suggested that officers had used excessive force and that many youth resented the police, a judicial inquiry was appointed by the provincial government. Justice Thomas Dohn condemned the department's tactics, which he described as a "police riot," but blamed the violence on radical "yippie" organizers who supposedly had taken advantage of gullible youth. The inquiry called for better training for police and for future street demonstrations to be banned. As Boudreau (2012b) points out, according to the B.C. Civil Liberties Association, the event proved that police saw youthful protestors not as citizens with a legitimate right to demonstrate, but as a threat to the status quo. On the other hand, reactions in Vancouver indicate that much of the public, concerned about illegal drug use, supported the police department's aggressive stance toward hippies and youth in general (Boudreau 2012b).

CONCLUSION

Organized labour became more respectable and established within a less confrontational system of industrial relations in the post-1945 era. Yet by the 1970s media-fuelled anxiety over "big labour" was undermining support for unions and even the right to strike; despite labour's gains, the forces of the status quo still held the balance of power in strikes and lockouts, and the police played a key role. As Frank (1983) has pointed out, how police services treated workers on the picket line was largely a result of the internal discipline of strikers and their overall reputation in the community. By 1970 most of the security and intelligence duties of the RCMP were hidden from both politicians and the public. As a result of its criminal investigation abilities, the RCMP enjoyed a reputation as "a generally honest and efficient police service" (Mann and Lee 1979: 14). Yet the force, subjected to limited attacks in the media, was not unassailable. In response to various concerns, in 1966 the Liberal government appointed a royal commission into security matters. There were no public hearings, and most of the testimony came from the RCMP. Released internally to the government in 1968, the MacKenzie Commission report seemed lost in a time warp as it identified international Communism as a major threat and justified continued surveillance of universities, unions and peace organizations in the name of counter subversion. Much to the shock of the RCMP, the commission had recommended the establishment of a civilian national security agency following the British model. The RCMP fought back and retained their mandate. Whitaker, Kealey and Parnaby (2012: 265–7) conclude that the appointment of John Starnes in 1970 as the first civilian director of the renamed Security Service was a compromise between the old regime and the vision of Maxwell MacKenzie, head of the commission. In the near future the RCMP would admit to the federal cabinet that it had been breaking the law for years in the name of national security (Cleroux 1991: 54–5). In 1969 Starnes prepared a report for the cabinet committee on security that identified the Quebec situation as a major challenge to Canadian unity. The specific threats in the province were labour unrest, unemployment, student protest and fading support for the Union Nationale government and growing interest in the PQ (Starnes 1998: 203–4).

Notes

1. This chapter and the next benefit from the work of historical researchers such as Kealey, Whitaker, Parnaby and Hewitt who have employed freedom of information legislation to uncover a long-term pattern of internal surveillance on individuals, organizations and social movements. They are also indebted to De Lint and Hall's 2009 study of twentieth-century crowd control strategies and tactics by Canadian police services.
2. Also, Library and Archives Canada. Diary of William Lyon Mackenzie King, April 8, 13, 14, 15, 1937.

CHAPTER 5

COUNTER SUBVERSION, COUNTER TERRORISM AND THE POLITICS OF PUBLIC ORDER

By the standards of most nations in the Western hemisphere, and even of most liberal democracies, Canada has been relatively free of political or "public" violence such as rebellion, assassination, mutiny or acts of terrorism (Torrance 1986: 45). Until the murder of Pierre Laporte in 1970, the last apparent assassination of a public official, Member of Parliament Thomas D'Arcy McGee, took place in 1868 when the Dominion was one year old. Social violence and violent labour disputes were not unknown, and there concerns about various international threats such as violent anarchists at the turn of the twentieth century, but Canadians thought of "terrorism" as something that took place in repressive European states, where ethnic nationalists or political factions were driven to desperate measures by the secret police and army. Yet as patterns of immigration changed, wars and humanitarian disasters produced large numbers of refugees and the cost of international travel declined, fears developed that Canada was becoming less safe. By the late 1960s, for example, separatist bombings in Quebec were of special concern.[1] Perceived threats to national security in the first half of the twentieth century were more ideological than physical, so on many levels the RCMP, local police, politicians and the population in general were unprepared for a series of terrorist acts that broke out in the early 1960s. Although looked upon by many Canadians as unpatriotic, Communists had rarely been accused of plotting or carrying out acts of violence. Despite the lack of evidence of violent plots with external connections, the RCMP feared Soviet espionage and subversion and used these alleged threats to justify breaking the law, such as illegally opening mail. As Sawatsky (1980: 253) has written, both politicians and the public were prepared to allow the police to violate the legal rights of "fringe elements" such as Communists and organized crime. This chapter examines security intelligence, monitoring of political and social movements on the left and the policing of First Nations protest and mass public demonstrations in the period 1970 to 2000.

COUNTER SUBVERSION

Throughout the 1960s a militant fringe of Quebec separatism, inspired by the global struggle against colonialism, engaged in a sporadic terror campaign against symbols of the federal government and English Canadian economic domination that included bombings and bank robberies. These small loosely-connected paramilitary cells desired an independent, socialist Quebec and viewed the provincial authorities as collaborators (Torrance 1986: 37). The RCMP initially responded to violent terrorism as a criminal problem but soon developed a counter subversion approach that in the 1970s broadened into clandestine counter-insurgency operations carried out against not only Quebec separatists, but also elements of the Canadian left. For the most part, this "high" policing was invisible to not only the public but also the regular police (Brodeur 2010). The massive security operation surrounding the 1976 Olympics in Montreal, which involved international and multi-agency intelligence sharing, an emergency law, enhanced border security, electronic surveillance, a security perimeter and movement controls, undercover police and an overwhelming display of force including the military, was a forerunner of the later militarization of the policing of mass public events (Canada 1981: 171).

One complicating factor for the RCMP, the SQ and other police agencies in Quebec was that by the mid 1960s the mainstream separatist movement was social democratic and non-violent. In 1968 it coalesced around a new provincial party, the Parti Québecois (PQ), which attracted the attention of the RCMP from its inception. By the early 1970s federal officials worried that elements of the civil service, and possibly the armed forces, were sympathetic with the PQ (Mann and Lee 1979: 44). For the RCMP, the SQ and the Montreal police, the FLQ was a major challenge to public order, responsible for dozens of incidents, including five deaths and the bombing of the Montreal Stock Exchange and the home of the mayor. Police began monitoring and arresting suspected violent nationalists as early as 1963, the year that a bomb in a military recruiting depot killed a watchman. A group known as l'Armée Révolutionnaire du Québec attempted to rob a gun store and killed two employees. Five of the attackers were arrested and sent to prison. By 1964 the Security Panel that advised the federal cabinet had authorized the RCMP to gather information on members of non-violent separatist organizations such as the RIN for security clearances. A "threat assessment" of Quebec separatism prepared in 1969 indicated that RCMP Security Intelligence, although it was concerned about possible influences of foreign governments, did not see the movement as part of a Communist conspiracy (Starnes 1998: 143–4; Whitaker, Kealey and Parnaby 2012: chapter 9).

The October Crisis of 1970 was precipitated by the kidnapping by FLQ cells of British diplomat James Cross and Pierre Laporte, a member of the Quebec government, and demands that the government release so-called "political prisoners." The federal and provincial governments adopted a tough stance although there were voices that called for a conciliatory response to the kidnappers, and an attempt was made to negotiate through an intermediary. The Canadian army was deployed to Montreal and Quebec City, initially under a section of the *National Defence Act*, in aid of the civil power. This move, which supposedly relieved the police of public order duties so that they could concentrate in tracking down the kidnappers, was supported by all parties in the Quebec National Assembly. The military presence eventually totalled more than twelve thousand. The troops, who reported to the director of the SQ, were legally an extension of the police, and in addition to guarding public buildings they provided security for politicians and their families in the wake of the kidnappings (Crouch 2010: chapter 3). In his book *The October Crisis, 1970: An Insider's View*, William Tetley, who was a minister in Bourassa's government, describes the army as "peacekeepers" and claims that despite the concerns of political opponents, civil liberties organizations and academics, their presence reassured the public and produced no incidents or official complaints. The troops were not recalled until early 1971 (Tetley 2006: 64).

More controversial was a partial suspension of civil liberties under the *War Measures Act*. This followed a well-publicized pro-FLQ rally in Montreal that featured violent rhetoric. On October 16, at the request of the municipal and provincial authorities, the federal government proclaimed specific regulations under the *War Measures Act*. The New Democratic Party, the PQ and civil libertarians considered this an overreaction. Acting under the *War Measures Act*, police carried out hundreds of raids and arrested nearly five hundred leftists and nationalists, many of them students. Most of them were released without charges, a fact that contributed to the debate over civil liberties. James Cross was freed and his captors given safe passage to Cuba. After Laporte was murdered the police pursued his captors, who were arrested and sentenced to prison. Others were charged with seditious conspiracy, membership in the banned FLQ or contempt of court. A temporary *Public Order Temporary Measures Act*, itself controversial within the Liberal government, outlawed the FLQ and extended police powers over persons suspected of plotting or supporting political violence. Many on the left viewed the governments of Canada and Quebec as cynically exploiting the situation to undermine support for Quebec sovereignty (Crouch 2010: chapter 3; Brodeur 2010: 245).

The proclamation of the *War Measures Act* was popular with Canadians at the time; one poll suggested that the approval rate among French Canadians was nearly 90 percent. Another poll suggested that an overwhelming majority wanted the death penalty for kidnappers of public officials.[2] Tetley, later a law professor, wrote a detailed insider's account of the crisis, justifying the overall response of the Quebec and Canadian governments, claiming that following the enactment of the *War Measures Act*, the situation in Quebec became so calm that not even "a broken window" was reported. In his view the authorities were unprepared for the kidnappings, and violence could have escalated to include assassination. For Tetley the emergency law "calmed the population." But he does point to mistakes, such as needless additions to the original list, created by the RCMP, of names of persons to be detained, cases of mistaken identity and police not allowing prisoners to speak to their families or to lawyers (Tetley 2006: 79, 92, 100–1).

Assessments of the October Crisis as a "failure" in intelligence vary. The McDonald Commission cited a lack of trust and coordination among the three levels of policing; the RCMP, for example, waited four days before informing the SQ of the location of Cross and his kidnappers. Yet the commission did not equate a lack of knowledge about all terror plots as a failure (Canada 1981: 189–93, 203; Starnes 1998). Tetley's account has the police unprepared and operating blind (in November the premier spoke of the police working "with one hand behind their back" (Tetley 2006: 73). The charge of failure is based on the assumption that the authorities, based on knowledge of previous plots, should have been able to predict the kidnapping of Cross and Laporte. In 1980 journalist John Sawatsky claimed that the RCMP had shallow roots in Quebec, relied too much on the SQ and Montreal police and had failed to recruit sufficient numbers of informants. Yet the local police were not exactly inactive and supposedly were keeping watch on more than three hundred organizations. The SQ had a special investigation branch and in 1970 joined the RCMP and Montreal police anti-terrorism squad formed at the outbreak of political violence (Canada 1981: 202). Other criticisms came from within the Liberal government, which complained that an unsophisticated security service was locked into an outdated Cold War mentality. In 1993 academic Reg Whitaker revealed that the leadership of the RCMP in 1970 did not support the proclamation of the *War Measures Act* because there was no evidence of an "apprehended insurrection." The RCMP also feared a political backlash in English Canada that could place restraints on the police. Whitaker, Kealey and Parnaby (2012), in their encyclopedic study of political policing, refute the notion that the RCMP, which maintained three hundred security officers in Montreal, had not provided reasonable intelligence and warnings of possible kidnappings. Echoing Whitaker's earlier research, they argue that Prime Minister Pierre Trudeau's main goal during the October Crisis was to overwhelm his political enemies (Whitaker 1993).

The events of October 1970 were controversial at the time, despite apparent strong support in both French and English Canada for temporarily suspending civil liberties. They would become more controversial by the late 1970s with revelations of their impact on the RCMP Security Service. In 1981 Prime Minister Trudeau criticized the McDonald Commission for its conclusion that he had been unable to differentiate between legal dissent and subversion in the early 1970s. Cabinet records released in 1992 revealed that Trudeau, the advocate of "the Just Society" and architect of the Charter of Rights and Freedoms, in 1969 had discussed possible use of military intelligence to monitor Quebec separatists and the employment by the RCMP of "clandestine" methods for gathering information. A former high-ranking Mountie claimed that Prime Minister Lester Pearson in 1967 had equated separatists with Communists in terms of their threat to Canada. This point is worth mentioning as the then director of RCMP Security Service later maintained that he understood that the Trudeau government had directed the force to engage in dirty tricks to disrupt separatists. Others, such as Justice Minister John Turner, cautioned against equating the PQ, a legal non-violent party, with a handful of militant extremists (Cleroux 1992). As it turned out, Turner and more outspoken critics of the reaction to the October Crisis were partially correct. Despite fears of a violent uprising in 1970, a report later carried out on behalf of the Quebec government concluded that active FLQ members during the crisis had numbered less than forty (Duchaine 1981). An earlier estimate of FLQ strength had suggested up to one hundred active members, two to three hundred active sympathizers and up to three thousand passive supporters (Torrance 1986: 36).

In the aftermath of the October Crisis, and because of ongoing security concerns in 1971, including dynamite thefts, bombings and a bank robbery, the RCMP adopted a more aggressive stance in Quebec. Despite considerable support for its retention, the *Public Order Act* expired later that year, forcing police to rely on "other" means for combatting direct action separatists.[3] The federal government created, within the Solicitor General's department, a Security Planning and Research Group (SPARG), which in theory advised the minister on RCMP intelligence reports. According to Whitaker, Kealey and Parnaby (2012: 302) its effectiveness was limited by police resistance. In 1972 a new Committee on Security and Intelligence was formed; it was advised by a Security Advisory Committee. In 1971 Director-General Starnes approved of plans to recruit more informants and engage in disruptive operations against militant separatists. The Security Service also monitored the PQ, which had won seven seats and nearly one quarter of the total vote in the 1970 provincial election. Three years later the party under René Lévesque won a greater share of the popular vote, and in 1976 it shocked many

Canadians by forming a majority government. In the early 1970s senior RCMP officers feared a common revolutionary front that linked domestic organizations with international extremists. Although the approach caused some concern within the ranks of the force, under Starnes the emphasis was on "containment and neutralization" (Sheppard 1980).

The dirty tricks campaign of the 1970s was a logical culmination of decades of RCMP monitoring of unions and the left, combined with the influence of the FBI's COINTELPRO (Counter Intelligence Program). Launched in the 1950s against America's dwindling Communist Party, COINTELPRO utilized the approach of psychological warfare to not only monitor but also infiltrate, disrupt and discredit a series of social movements, most of them on the left. In the 1970s, using the justification of preventing political violence, the RCMP adopted aspects of the FBI's approach. One example was a false FLQ communiqué, issued by the chief superintendent of the RCMP, endorsing violence to secure Quebec independence. Political policing also depended on a constant search for human and electronic intelligence. The latter, when applied to criminal policing, was a source of concern for academics, journalists, politicians and members of the public convinced that police services were indiscriminately and illegally planting "bugs" and tapping telephones. In the early 1970s, J Section of the Intelligence Service acquired surplus electronic surveillance equipment from the CIA (Sawatsky 1980: 268).

Quebec was not the sole focus of RCMP dirty tricks and illegalities. Praxis, a Toronto research institute established by two professors in the late 1960s, was interested in promoting democracy and fighting poverty through community organizing. Despite being listed on a Solicitor General document as being part of the "Extra Parliamentary Opposition," the organization obtained research grants and a contract with the Central Mortgage and Housing Corporation to study the *National Housing Act*. One of its projects planned for 1971 was a "poor peoples' conference." According to Weinberg (2015), the Department of External Affairs warned the Security Service that Praxis contained "subversive elements." In 1970 Praxis Corporation received publicity when it was involved in the Stop the Spadina Expressway campaign and planned to field progressive candidates for the Toronto Social Planning Board Council. One evening, its office on Spadina Avenue was broken into and several thousand pages of documents were stolen. The burglars then set fire to the building, which also housed the offices of the Metro Tenants' Council, The Just Society and Stop Spadina. Some of the stolen documents ended up in the hands of conservative journalist Peter Worthington who had criticized Praxis (Worthington was one of several prominent conservative Ontario journalists who tended to adopt a resolutely pro-police view on most issues). The RCMP denied any involvement with the case but ended up with the stolen documents, which it returned to Praxis in 1977. They claimed that the attack had been carried out by the "radical right." In 1978 Ontario Attorney General Roy McMurtry accused the RCMP of "impropriety" for holding on to the documents and sent an OPP investigation file to the McDonald Commission investigating Security Service abuses (Mann and Lee 1979: 66). In 1988 Praxis, which had launched a damages suit in the Federal Court against the federal government in 1982, agreed to an out-of-court settlement. In 1987 the RCMP revealed that one of their informants in a right-wing organization had acquired the documents (Moon 1988).

In the early 1970s the Security Service attempted to disrupt a radical organization in Vancouver known as the Partisan Party. Operating on a shoestring budget, the members of the group lived communally and published a monthly newspaper. The RCMP operation involved bugging the office and tapping the phones of the organization, plus plans for Mounties disguised as labourers to assault members of the organization and steal a box of files that they carried home each night. Three officers were brought in from Ontario and instructed to carry no identification in case they were arrested. The campaign against the Partisan Party was aided by an "inside man," an undercover Mountie working as a staff member. According to Sawatsky (1980: chapter 20) the operation was more about intimidating the group than acquiring useful intelligence. The attackers would be picked up in a rented car and a surveillance team would watch for any signs of the city police. The planned assault and robbery was called off when it was revealed that one of the leftists in the group carrying the documents was pregnant.

In 1973 RCMP, in the face of mounting academic and journalistic criticism and internal pressures, celebrated its centennial. Brown and Brown's left-wing polemic of that year denounced the Mounted Police as enemies of Canada's Indians and Metis, workers, immigrants, student and women's organizations and Quebec nationalism (Brown and Brown 1973). The RCMP, with its paramilitary training, organizational and disciplinary structures and culture, seemed to belong to another age. Women were recruited for the first time starting in 1974 (Reilly Schmidt 2013a and 2013b). That same year married men were permitted to apply, and the minimum educational requirement for recruits was raised to completion of grade eleven. Of more than one thousand recruits in 1974–75, fewer than ninety had university degrees and fewer than 180 were Francophones (Mann and Lee 1979: 123–4). RCMP pay was not competitive, and the force's disciplinary procedures were also anachronistic.

In 1974 a spontaneous movement developed among the RCMP's rank and file in British Columbia, Ontario and Quebec to organize in order to press for better pay, working conditions and grievance procedures. The Mounties were paid less than most big-city police and, in the paramilitary tradition of the force, did not receive overtime pay. The officers attending these meetings, which debated the merits of organizing a union versus an association, included members of the Security Service. At a mass meeting in Ottawa those present voted overwhelmingly against the 1918 order-in-council that banned union organization for the RNWMP. The Solicitor General expressed some sympathy for the aspirations of the lower ranks, but the deputy commissioner of the force was hostile to any major reforms. His response was to set up a type of company union, the Division Representative Program, in 1972. Little came from the meetings of this organization until 1974, the year of the informal revolt by the rank and file, when the force was granted a significant pay raise and representatives were permitted to intervene in the cases of individual members. RCMP members were finally able to take part in the benefits of postwar prosperity. The force also expanded by 41 percent between 1971 and 1977. By 1978, one fifth of the total personnel was civilian. Pay raises and overtime notwithstanding, the changes to the disciplinary regime were minor in nature. In 1976 a royal commission on RCMP discipline and grievances concluded that its disciplinary system dated from the late nineteenth century (Mann and Lee 1979: 151–2, 173; Sawatsky 1980: chapter 17).

The 1973 centennial celebrations, which took place under the leadership of Commissioner Len Higgitt, offered a "highly selective" history of the force (Dawson 1998: 111). The official narrative in 1973 avoided emphasis on controversial issues such as national security, strikes, ethnicity or race and promoted an image of a modern, tolerant and efficient police that protected Canadian sovereignty and was friendly towards First Nations. As Dawson (1998: 114–21) explains, advertising, public relations, publications and events stressed 1873, not 1919, as the foundational year, distorted the events of the 1885 Rebellion and ignored the period 1910–1950. The celebrations were followed by one of the RCMP's darkest chapters. In 1975, realizing the inherent political dangers, the Trudeau government directed the force to refrain from treating the PQ as a subversive organization. In 1974, RCMP Constable Robert Sampson, apparently moonlighting for organized crime, was arrested for bombing a Montreal business executive's residence. He was sentenced to seven years in penitentiary. In 1976 John Sawatsky broke the story that in 1972 Samson, as part of G Section of Security Service, had broken into and stolen a half ton of documents from the office of l'Agence de Press Libre de Québec (APLQ), a left-wing nationalist organization. Named "Bricole," the operation had been carried out in amateurish fashion (Sawatsky 1980: 248–50). In 1977 three officers, one from each of the RCMP, Montreal Police and SQ, pleaded guilty to charges of failing to obtain a warrant. The presiding judge responded to the confessed crimes with absolute discharges. Commissioner Maurice Nadon, the first French Canadian to head the RCMP, had been unaware of Bricole. He argued against an external inquiry into the matter, assuring the government that the 1972 operation had been an exception (Sawatsky 1980: 248–50, 279–81).

Further evidence that the APLQ operation had been well planned and also involved the SQ and the Montreal police prompted the new PQ government, elected in 1976, to appoint its own inquiry under Jean Keable. One of the main concerns of the inquiry was the degree to which FLQ activity in the early 1970s was actually controlled by the RCMP, the SQ or the Montreal police. This was one of the more damning conclusions of its 1981 report, which stated that the post-October crisis FLQ was basically an arm of the Montreal police anti-terrorist squad. At one point police even supplied a cell with bomb-making materials. In 1979 an RCMP officer admitted to issuing a false FLQ communiqué denouncing separatist intellectual Pierre Vallières who had renounced violence. Neither the SQ nor the Montreal police had been informed of the deception (Johnson 1980; Sawatsky 1980: 279–81; Cleroux 1991: 51–2; Sheppard 1981). The hearings of the Keable inquiry, much like those of Quebec's controversial inquiry into organized crime, broke new ground as they were televised. The election of the PQ and the revelations of the provincial and federal inquiries appeared to increase hostility within the province to the federal force. In 1978, for example, a provincial task force called for the withdrawal of the RCMP, which numbered more than one thousand, from Quebec, except for enforcement of a limited number of non-criminal federal laws. Counter-terrorism policing, the task force suggested, could be handled by the SQ and municipal police (Johnson 1978). One of the revelations at the Keable inquiry was an allegation that the SQ, in cooperation with the local police and RCMP, had bugged an office of the PQ in Shawinigan allegedly being used by FLQ activists (Cleroux and Strauss 1977).

Facing new revelations of Security Service illegal acts and a damaging Quebec public inquiry that could link the Liberal cabinet to RCMP excesses, the Trudeau government in the summer of 1977 nominated its own royal commission under Judge David C. McDonald. Its mandate was to investigate Security Service actions that were outside the law. That year Canadians learned through the media that the Security Service, for forty years, had been copying address information and in some cases opening private mail, in cooperation with local post office officials. Other revelations of illegality that emerged during this period included suggestions that the RCMP had stolen dynamite in 1971 in a failed attempt to discredit the FLQ and had burned down a barn in 1972 at Sainte-Anne-de-la-Rochelle to prevent a meeting between FLQ members and American Black Panthers (Sawatsky 1980: 280; Canada 1981: 131–5).

One of the most sensitive RCMP covert operations in Quebec was Operation Ham, a break-in at Les Messageries Dynamiques, a Montreal computer business, in 1973. In 1972 a source in the federal government had warned the Security Service that the PQ was being funded by foreign money. The target in Operation Ham was the membership list of the separatist party. Four E Section officers illegally entered the premises of the business, stole a computer tape that contained the membership data, made a copy and replaced the original. The copy was sent to Security Service headquarters in Ottawa, but according to Sawatsky the files were "effectively useless" and were destroyed in 1975. The operation had been authorized by the director of the Security Service but had been hidden from the RCMP commissioner and the solicitor general. Other evidence before the McDonald Commission suggested that RCMP criminal investigations, directed against organized, drug and white-collar crime, also resorted to break-ins without warrants. In 1983, a decade after the event, Alcide Yelle, who had been the acting inspector in charge of E Section, was charged and convicted for his role in the burglary. His penalty was a suspended sentence and a few months of probation. Typical of officers involved in controversial security or public order operations, Yelle was not only not dismissed but was promoted to chief superintendent. One of the four officers who took part in the burglary, who retired with the rank of superintendent, in a 2007 interview expressed bitterness at how the Liberal government had betrayed the Security Service and how the media had portrayed RCMP as incompetent (Canada 1981: 230–2; Starnes 1998: 168; Postmedia Network Inc. 2007).

The Keable inquiry suffered a setback in 1978 when the Supreme Court of Canada limited its powers to investigate federal officials and examine documents in the custody of the federal government. Rather than a "fishing expedition" as desired by the PQ, the commission was limited to investigating specific Security Service acts carried out in Quebec. Yet the provincial inquiry was able to access evidence on the RCMP when it involved the SQ and the Montreal police. The McDonald Commission conducted 169 public and 144 in-camera hearings, accepted written submissions between 1979 and 1981 and issued three reports. At one point the RCMP admitted to carrying out over four hundred warrantless entries of dwellings or places of business since 1970.

The two commissions, a dramatic exposé of police deviance, were Canada's equivalent to the Watergate investigation. Many citizens, who tended to trust government institutions and especially the RCMP, were shocked not only by the revelations of police dirty tricks but also the mindset of police witnesses, who reflected not the rule of law but "the end justifies the means." On the other hand, opinion polls suggested that the Mounties retained the confidence of most Canadians.

The McDonald Commission was damaging to both the RCMP and the Trudeau government, but the latter was protected by the traditions of cabinet confidentiality and police operational autonomy. Mann and Lee (1979: 100) noted at the time that both federal cabinet ministers and senior RCMP officers who testified demonstrated "the need not to know" principle on many issues. They also suggested that federal politicians such as Solicitor General Francis Fox feared provoking the RCMP. In the end, the final report of the McDonald Commission, despite evidence available to the commissioners, shielded the Liberal government, which refused to debate the report in Parliament, from full complicity in the dirty tricks scandals.

Although Trudeau in 1980 defended the overall response to the October Crisis, justified the arrests of suspected separatists and rejected the accusation that politics, not security, had been the real motive behind imposition of the *War Measures Act*, according to a number of commentators the RCMP became the "fall guy" for this troubling period in police-government relations, a situation that created considerable bitterness within the force's ranks (Gray 1980).

As revealed by the McDonald Commission and subsequent disclosures of documents, the RCMP anti-subversion campaign was not confined to separatists but extended to English Canadian leftists, including social democrats, and the emerging Aboriginal rights movement. Attempts by Trotskyites to recruit high school students in British Columbia and Ontario, partly through the Young Socialists, founded in 1967, had the RCMP monitoring the political beliefs and activities of sixteen- and seventeen-year-olds, including their letters to newspapers (Sethna 2000). Reflecting FBI targeting of the American Indian Movement, D Section (Counter Subversion) in the 1970s listed Aboriginal organizations as a "key sector" vulnerable to subversion. Other key sectors included political parties, the media, trade unions, post-secondary education and teachers' federations. Key files associated with these operations were destroyed between 1974 and 1977. The investigation or targeting of individuals within these movements eerily echoed the approach of the CIA in undermining unfriendly regimes in places like Guatemala during the Cold War. In 1979 the National Indian Brotherhood complained that the McDonald Commission had ignored an RCMP's dirty tricks campaign against the Aboriginal movement in British Columbia, the Northwest Territories and Ontario. The organizations claimed to have evidence that the RCMP had infiltrated and attempted to disrupt and discredit Native organizations (Martin 1977d; Moon 1979).

In the period 1971 to 1974 the Security Service's Operation Checkmate engaged in a number of disruptive operations in at least three cities. One of them targeted the Toronto-based League for Socialist Action (LSA), a Trotskyist organization active within the 1970s Ontario NDP. In the 1972 federal election the NDP won 18 percent of the vote and elected eleven MPs in Ontario. It was also a viable force in provincial politics, forming the official opposition from 1975 to 1977. In 1977 the Ontario attorney general revealed that the RCMP had infiltrated the NDP on the grounds that it included "ex-Communists" and that the Mounties had interfered with the LSA because of its violent and subversive goals. The Security Service was especially interested in the Waffle, a militant subgroup of younger NDP activists that was expelled from the party in 1972. Investigations of individuals connected to the Waffle netted an unexpected benefit, information on the strategy, finances and the internal divisions of the provincial party. National NDP leader Ed Broadbent in 1977 stated that someone (possibly the RCMP) had broken into party offices in Ottawa (the "black bag job," a burglary to obtain membership lists or other key documents, was a classic COINTELPRO tactic). The decision to target the NDP had been made at RCMP headquarters in Ottawa, and the justification was that surveillance was directed at individuals, not the party as a whole (Martin 1977b, 1977c).

The RCMP's campaign against Ontario socialists involved the use of forged correspondence, leaks to the press, the disclosure of personal medical records, threatening phone calls and a false tax return (Sheppard 1980). Not surprisingly the operation was successful in destroying the LSA. Ross Dowson of the LSA attempted to sue the RCMP for slander, accusing it of having broken the law. In 1979 the RCMP admitted to an Ontario royal commission on the confidentially of health records that it had forged and circulated false documents in an attempt to disrupt and discredit the LSA and the Young Socialists. That year the Ontario government ordered the OPP to investigate the LSA's allegations against the RCMP. In 1980 the McDonald Commission issued heavily redacted documents that indicated that dirty tricks tactics against the left began in 1969, before the October Crisis (Makin 1985; Sallott 1984). In 1980, defence lawyer Clayton Ruby, who was assisting the LSA in its legal struggles, described the actions of the Security Service as "the suppression of the freedom of thought" (in Dowson 1980: foreword).

One example of how the Security Service used the traditional narcotics or the organized crime investigation tactic of "source development" was the case of Ottawa resident Jack Gold, an employee of Revenue Canada. The issue of security screening adversely affecting someone's career was part of the story, which came to light when Gold, backed by the Public Service Alliance of Canada, sued the federal government in 1984. Gold, a senior Revenue Canada bureaucrat who was on secondment to the Department of Energy, Mines and Resources, came to the attention of the RCMP as a result of his political activities. He had joined Revenue Canada in 1958 and passed routine security clearances that year and in 1978. Two years later he had gravitated to the peace movement and in the early 1980s took part in demonstrations against visits by Henry Kissinger and Ronald Reagan. Gold also visited the USSR in 1979 and planned to go there again in 1981 as part of his job. He was also a member of an Ottawa anti-apartheid group.

The RCMP opened a file on Gold in 1980 and informed his employer that he was a potential security risk. A sergeant from the Security Service interviewed Gold and asked him the standard questions about membership in Communist and other groups, including organizations that promoted friendship with Cuba and the USSR. The conversation became more serious when he was requested to provide the names and addresses of relatives, friends or associates who were members of left-wing organizations. Gold refused to name names or to quit his anti-apartheid activities. The RCMP also appeared to have tried to exploit his limited contacts with the Soviet embassy, which existed because of his forthcoming trip. A security officer described his answers as "evasive." Several days after the interview he was fired from Energy and Mines and Resources, supposedly for non-security reasons, and returned to Revenue Canada, where he was demoted to a less responsible position and had his security classification downgraded on the advice of the RCMP. In 1982 Gold was offered a transfer and a more responsible position in Montreal, but by this point he had already hired a lawyer in order to sue the RCMP, Revenue Canada and Energy, Mines and Resources. The Gold case is interesting as it illustrates that as late as 1980, the Security Service employed pressure tactics to encourage vulnerable individuals to provide them with information on other potential suspects. In this case a well-educated senior civil servant, backed by his union, fought back (Kashmeri 1984).

The major recommendation of the McDonald Commission was that Security Service duties be removed from the RCMP, as recommended by the MacKenzie Commission in the late 1960s, and vested in a civilian agency (the commission had studied national security arrangements in the United States, Great Britain, Australia and New Zealand). In 1984 responsibility for security and intelligence was assigned to a new agency, the Canadian Security and Intelligence Service (CSIS). The initial Bill C-157 drew heavy criticism in 1983, as it appeared to allow contravention of the law in the interest of national security. Despite amendments, criticisms continued and the new agency, according to Cleroux (1991), actually exercised more extensive powers than the RCMP. Wiretaps, electronic surveillance, mail openings and break-ins could be authorized by a warrant from a Federal Court judge and approval of the Solicitor General; no external approval was needed for the implantation of human sources into targeted organizations. CSIS was launched with an image that it was not only civilian, modern and more neutral than the old Security Service but also better educated. In reality most of the staff of the new agency transferred from the RCMP. In the late 1980s CSIS made a decision that seriously damaged the ability of historians and others to research the scale and nature of the "insecurity state" when it reviewed close to half a million files and destroyed the vast majority of them (Cleroux 1991: 68–75).

In the years following the establishment of CSIS, access to information requests revealed further details of past Security Service surveillance and infiltration. In 1992, it was revealed that a key intellectual of the Quiet Revolution and influential PQ strategist, Claude Morin, had acted as "'French Minuet," a paid informant for the RCMP from 1974, two years prior to the party's historic election victory, until 1977. A university professor and key architect of the PQ strategy of sovereignty association, Morin later claimed that he had cooperated with the RCMP as a counter-intelligence tactic, to find out what it knew about the sovereignty movement, and had fed his contacts little important information. As evidenced by the example of the theft of the records of the PQ, the Security Service remained interested in finding evidence of foreign influences on the party, which formed the provincial government in 1976 and organized a sovereignty-association referendum in 1980. In 2002 it was disclosed that the Security Service had infiltrated the federally-sponsored Company of Young Canadians (CYC), created in 1966 as a mechanism for recruiting idealistic young Canadians to act as community organizers. Controversial in media and political circles, the CYC was closely watched by the RCMP. A memo in 1971 described the CYC, which was a training ground for a generation of Canadian politicians, as "a relatively safe haven for subversives, criminals and otherwise undesirable elements" (Valpy 2002).

Declassified (but heavily redacted) security files uncovered by Sethna and Hewitt (2009) reveal another RCMP response to the New Left. In 1969 the Security Service began to spy on "second-wave" feminists, who tended to be young, middle-class and well-educated. Many were attending university where they engaged in campus and community activism and worked for causes such as advancing reproductive rights and combating violence against women. The RCMP was aware that the "women's liberation" agenda was reformist, not revolutionary, but given the culture of the service, suspicion of Communism was always in the background. The Vancouver Women's Caucus (VWC) had close connections with Simon Fraser University. As it had for decades with socialists, trade unionists and academics, the RCMP relied on informants and open source information to collect details on the organization and the young women involved. In 1970 the VWC, inspired by the 1935 On-to-Ottawa Trek, planned an Abortion Caravan to protest the lack of full abortion rights despite a partial decriminalization of the law in 1969. The Mounted Police, who feared that the VWC had been infiltrated by Trotskyists, shadowed members of the caravan in unmarked cars as they drove across Canada. A rally on Parliament Hill was monitored by Security Service members who took photographs of the crowd. Much to the embarrassment of the force, the protestors carried out two security breaches. One was their trespass onto 24 Sussex Drive, the home of the prime minister, and the other was an ingenious act of guerrilla theatre. Dressing as middle-class housewives, twenty-five activists, in the spirit of Edwardian suffragettes, chained themselves to benches in the public gallery of the House of Commons and disrupted the proceedings of Parliament. The women, in a gesture of anti-feminist chivalry, were escorted from the gallery but not arrested.

In 1967 the RCMP organized a "tactical troop" or riot squad to protect the Parliament Buildings from demonstrations, but until 1974 it was not deployed (including on one occasion that year when striking railway workers actually occupied Parliament). In the fall of 1974 a Native People's Caravan, consisting of men, women and children, travelled from British Columbia to Ottawa to present a list of demands to the federal government. Tensions in Aboriginal communities had been growing since the issuing in 1969 of the Trudeau government's statement on Indian policy, which had suggested abolishing the *Indian Act*, the status of "Indian" and the Department of Indian Affairs in order to make Native people "equal" to non-Natives. Frustrated by what they viewed as delays and a lack of understanding by the Department of Indian Affairs, in 1974 armed Ojibwa warriors occupied Anicinabe Park near Kenora, Ontario. This movement was also monitored by an RCMP informant who posed as a friendly Black Power militant with knowledge of weapons and explosives (Canada 1981: 487–9).

In the early 1970s the Security Service had begun to gather information on First Nations militancy, especially its connections with the American Red Power movement. In 1973 Ogala Lakota and American Indian Movement militants seized the town of Wounded Knee, South Dakota, as a protest against both tribal government and the U.S. government. The secret memo "Red Power Canada" of April 1973 expressed fears of sabotage and violent confrontation. Land claims, treaty rights and fears of assimilation were acknowledged as grievances by the Security Service, which feared that tactics such as those adopted by the American Indian Movement would seep into Canada, spread by militants who were increasingly travelling into and across the country. The secret report was forwarded to RCMP divisional commanders who were asked to contribute names to a list of potentially violent activists and contribute photographs to a central registry (Mofina 2002a).

In addition to grievances over housing, pollution, land claims and treaty rights, the leaders of the Native People's Caravan demanded that Aboriginal rights be protected in the Canadian Constitution. The group included a small number of Communists and was joined at Ottawa by other non-Native leftists. They occupied an old mill building, which they named the Native People's Embassy, and demanded to meet representatives of the federal government on the day that Parliament opened. Accounts varied as to who was responsible for the violence on Parliament Hill; the RCMP and Solicitor General claimed that police had repelled two attempts by two hundred protestors to enter the Parliament Building and had resorted to force only after being attacked with rocks and other projectiles. Native protestors insisted that the RCMP had provoked the attack. A number of people were arrested, and the Trudeau government attempted to discredit the caravan by claiming that it did not represent the Aboriginal people of Canada and that the violence had been instigated by Marxist-Leninists. The Native Indian Brotherhood and the Canadian Federation of Civil Liberties and Human Rights Associations called for an inquiry into the incident. For First Nations Canadians, the "battle of Parliament Hill," where protestors had been refused an audience with the government and then forcibly ejected, was a reminder of how the forces of the status quo, including the police, did not serve their interests (Plaitel 1974a, 1974b, 1984; Winsor 1974; CP 1974a, 1974b, 1974c, 1974d).

COUNTER TERRORISM

Although Canada was a relatively peaceful nation in the early 1970s with a low rate of violent crime, media coverage of highjackings and acts of international terrorism such as the killing of Israeli athletes and coaches at the 1972 Olympics in Munich by Palestinian militants raised public anxieties over security. In 1971 a poll indicated widespread support for a citizen identity card that included finger-prints and photographs, but under normal conditions Canadians were sensitive to state intrusions into privacy. In some provinces, for example, driver's licences did not include photographs.[4] Canadian security officials had attended the Munich Olympics and were determined that the 1976 Montreal Olympics would be safe. More than 130 nations took part, sending more than ten thousand athletes, officials and coaches. This was challenging in an open society like Canada, and the security operation that unfolded seemed excessive to many. The RCMP organized an International Terrorist Guerilla Section to ensure the safety of political leaders, foreign dignitaries and foreign and domestic airlines. The Quebec Civil Liberties Association was reminded of the lead-up to Expo 67 when police had supposedly harassed "law-abiding citizens" who objected to or were suspected of objecting to the games or who planned to protest the visit of controversial world leaders. The RCMP's "defusing program" began as early as 1972 and involved physical and electronic surveillance. By 1975 the media reported rumours that the RCMP was focusing primarily on Arab Canadians who sympathized with the Palestinian cause. Long-range planning involved liaison with foreign governments to develop a list of "potential terrorists" and international threats such as Palestinian groups, the Japanese Red Army, Europe's Red Army Faction and the American Weathermen. Aside from Arab Canadians and First Nations activists, security officials appeared to think almost entirely of external threats. In an adept public relations move, the RCMP even distributed thousands of wanted posters for the most famous inter-national terrorist of the 1970s, Ilich Ramirez Sanchez, a.k.a. "Carlos the Jackal," who in 1975 had killed two French intelligence agents and an informant plus attacked OPEC headquarters in Vienna (Martin 1976; CP 1976).

The Olympic Village, the residence of the visiting athletes, was patrolled by armed guards and helicopters and protected by metal detectors and X-ray machines. The Montreal police official who was in charge of operations claimed that a two-year intelligence gathering exercise had prevented terrorist attacks. Security officials had tracked threats based on a computerized database of thousands of "suspected and potential terrorists" (Cleroux 1976). Following the event, although no arrests were made, the security director claimed that police had "dismantled" at least one "terrorist" ring and during the games had kept tabs on more than five hundred potential threats (ibid.). Immigration rules had been amended to allow officials to more easily turn away suspected protestors at the border, and special patrols were mounted along the border between Quebec and New York. Once the games were underway the Royal Canadian Navy supplied five destroyer escorts and a supply vessel in the St. Lawrence, and RCAF fighter jets were on standby. Similar security was provided at Kingston, Ontario, site of sailing competitions. The military deployment was described as bigger than any of Canada's U.N. peacekeeping missions: 8,400 troops in direct security duties and five thousand in support roles. In case this was insufficient there was a contingency plan to bring Canadian troops back from their NATO bases in Europe. Members of the armed forces acted as drivers, and large numbers of plainclothes police, posing as maintenance workers, patrolled the Olympic site (CP 1976; Canada 1981: 329–30).

During the 1970s, 1980s and 1990s Canada experienced little domestic terrorism. As in the past, police services adopted trends that emanated from south of the border, such as special weapons and tactics squads or Emergency Response Teams (ERTs) and bomb squads. In 1973 the RCMP established the Canadian Bomb Data Centre. The main rationale for ERTs was the need for police to respond to situations involving hostage taking, armed robbery and suspects carrying weapons. The Toronto police Emergency Task Force (ETF), whose members were "trained as commandos," was formed in the early 1970s following the murder of four officers. In addition to a special weapons team, the unit consisted of a bomb disposal squad and an emergency response unit. The ETF grew out of a 1960s tactical unit organized in response to industrial violence, vandalism, bombings and anti-war protests. Yet the life of a Toronto ETF member was not always exciting, and during slow moments its members issued traffic tickets. In addition, none of the four armed suspects it killed between 1971 and 1984 were "terrorists." In fact many suspects wounded or killed by ERTs in Canada have been persons suffering from mental illness (Lavigne 1984; Culbert 2015).

One exception to the absence of domestic terrorism after the 1970s was the case of Direct Action (also known as the Squamish Five), a British Columbia anarchist group that detonated a bomb outside of Litton Industries, a Toronto-area defence contractor involved in production of the controversial Cruise missile. Many Canadians opposed the Liberal government allowing the United States military to test unarmed Cruise missiles in Canadian airspace, as they saw it as a violation of Canada's image as a non-nuclear nation that promoted peace and disarmament. In 1982 police arrested a number of protestors at Litton's Rexdale plant who insisted that the company convert to non-military production. That year a protest in Halifax against nuclear weapons drew three thousand, the largest in the city's history. In April 1983, 65,000 supporters of peace marched and rallied in Vancouver, and between ten and fifteen thousand paraded in Toronto where they were addressed by two NDP aldermen. There were no confrontations with police except when Toronto pro-Cruise protestors clashed with the peace activists (Cox 1983; Hansen 2001).

Known in their communiqués as Direct Action, the Squamish Five consisted of three young men and two women who represented the militant fringe of the anti-war, environmental and feminist movements. In 1982 these British Columbia-based "urban guerrillas" vandalized the offices of a mining company and a provincial government agency, collected explosives and firearms and planned other politically-motivated crimes. Their philosophy supposedly limited their violent attacks to property, not individuals. Direct Action subsequently bombed a Vancouver Island electrical substation in protest over a controversial plan by British Columbia Hydro to build transmission lines without holding public hearings. The members were also associated with the firebombing of three outlets of a pornographic video chain in Vancouver, carried out in the name of the Wimmin's Fire Brigade. Their most controversial act was the Litton plant bombing, which took place near midnight. The explosion, despite a warning message phoned in to plant security, detonated prematurely and injured several people, some of them permanently. The five suspects were placed under police surveillance, which included the use of the RCMP Security Service Watcher service and electronic listening devices planted in their New Westminster residence several weeks prior to their arrest. Conversations recorded by a wiretap in a second residence incriminated two members of the group in the B.C. Hydro and Litton bombings and the video store fire bombings. The members of Direct Action were captured by the RCMP in 1983 outside of Squamish on their way to target practice. Police found guns, ammunition and explosives and evidence of plots to rob a Brinks cash delivery vehicle and sabotage the Alberta military base associated with the Cruise missile tests (CBC 1988; Mulgrew and Slotnick 1983; Slotnick 1983; Hansen 2001).

The drama surrounding the Squamish Five overshadowed a broader issue, RCMP monitoring of anti-war protesters and the policing of peace demonstrations during the revived Cold War of the 1980s. The Metro Toronto Police placed the local peace movement under surveillance, supposedly in order to gain leads on the Litton bombing. In a controversial move, police raided the offices of three peace groups several weeks after the bombing; many speculated that the warrants authorizing the raids had been granted on shaky legal grounds and that their real purpose was to intimidate and harass activists. As required by the *Criminal Code*, several Toronto area activists were informed that they were under electronic surveillance. When a joint forces operation involving RCMP and Vancouver police arrested the members of Direct Action in early 1983, it promised that more arrests would follow. None did, but the urban guerrillas, who initially faced more than one hundred charges, received lengthy jail terms of between ten and twenty years. During their trials evidence from the RCMP Security Service had been heavily redacted (Mulgrew and

Slotnick 1983). According to one of the members of Direct Action, in the wake of the bombings police in British Columbia and Ontario used the fear of terrorism to discredit and harass the radical left and peace activists (Hansen 2001: 461–3).

The large crowds who protested the Trudeau government decision to allow the testing of the Cruise missile raised concerns within security circles of "foreign influence" during a tense period in the late Cold War. Despite the controversy over the Litton attack, the Cruise issue helped to revive the Canadian anti-war movement. Many Canadians opposed the arms race because they still identified Canada as a peacekeeping nation that supported disarmament, diplomacy and the United Nations. The Mulroney government, which attempted to increase defence expenditures and promote the expansion of arms exports, drew the ire of peace and church organizations. In 1989 a coalition of organizations protested ARMX, a military trade show in Ottawa promoted by the Departments of Foreign Affairs and National Defence. Back in 1982, fifteen thousand had marched in a rally in Ottawa organized by Operation Dismantle. Activists were concerned that the government was supporting the sale of weapons and other equipment to regimes that violated human rights and sending the wrong message on arms proliferation. Ottawa police arrested dozens of protestors at Lansdowne Park, many of whom were released after they promised to avoid the site in the future. The demonstrators scored one victory: in future years Ottawa's city council refused to permit the use of municipal facilities for arms bazaars (French 1989).

Police and security agencies in Canada experienced periodic concerns about possible attacks on the embassies and diplomats of foreign governments. Between 1966 and 1980, several bombs exploded at the Cuban embassy in Ottawa and the Cuban consulate in Montreal. In a bomb attack on the trade office in Montreal in 1972 a Cuban diplomat was killed. According to Sawatsky (1980: 3–4) although blamed on anti-Castro Cubans, the attack may have been an undertaking of the American CIA and possibly the RCMP, to gather intelligence on Cuban espionage operations. Heavily armed Montreal police removed armed Cuban consular employees as they were attempting to destroy sensitive documents. The Security Service retrieved a number of sensitive documents from the scene, including a code book, which was sent on to CIA headquarters (Sawatsky 1980: 5–6).

Security concerns were heightened following well-publicized international incidents such as the occupation of the Iranian embassy in London in 1980, ended by British Special Air Service commandos. In 1982 a Turkish military attaché was shot dead at a traffic light in Ottawa. The Justice Commandos for Armenian Genocide took credit for the murder, which was never solved. Previously a Turkish diplomat had been seriously injured in an attack in his residence. There were also a number of bombings in Toronto attributed to Armenian nationalists. In 1985 an armed Pinkerton security guard died as the result of an attack on the Turkish embassy in Ottawa. Three assailants blasted their way into the building and took hostages. Claiming to be acting in revenge for the 1915 Armenian genocide, they surrendered to the police. The attack raised the issue of how little security the federal government provided for high-risk embassies. The attackers were charged and convicted of first-degree murder. Following their arrest the Toronto transit system was subjected to a bomb threat attributed to Armenian nationalists. According to a Liberal MP, by early 1985 CSIS considered Armenian terrorism Canada's top security threat. The new agency joined with an Ontario task force consisting of the RCMP, OPP and Metropolitan Toronto police that monitored Armenian groups (CP 1985a, 1985b; Montgomery 1985).

As a result of these incidents the federal government expanded the protection of foreign embassies to include the RCMP and enhanced its counter-terrorism capabilities by establishing a new RCMP unit, the Special Emergency Response Team (SERT). SERT grew out of an effort to create a special hostage rescue unit in an era when local police or ERTs were either not common or not trained or equipped to handle terrorist attacks. Interestingly, placing SERT under the federal police was opposed by the CACP, which argued that the anti-terrorist unit was a better fit for the military. The unit had its own base near Ottawa that included a passenger aircraft for practicing hostage rescues and an operational budget that was shielded from the press. Almost immediately questions rose as to whether a civilian unit would be prepared to use lethal force against Canadian citizens. Canadians were not accustomed to thinking of their police as having to employ deadly force. There is some evidence that well into the 1980s, when the typical service weapon was a .38 calibre revolver, police officers relied on firearms only in extreme emergencies. Carsten Stroud's journalistic account of street cops in 1984, for example, depicted drug officers conducting raids with radios and flashlights in their hands (Stroud 1984: 23). As noted above, big city ERTs were inactive during many days of the average year, and most of their calls did not involve suspects armed with firearms. According to police officials, the real goal of ERTs was to secure an area in a crisis situation and negotiate a peaceful outcome. The Toronto unit responded to 1,400 calls between 1982 and 1989 without firing a single shot (Lavigne 1984). The SERT was never deployed, although the RCMP and other large police services did train and equip ERTs for regular police work. Eventually SERT was replaced by a secretive military counter-terrorism unit, Joint Task Force Two, which would be deployed in Haiti and Afghanistan (Marquis 1993: 390; Sallot 2002).

As Canada was becoming a more multicultural nation as the result of the reforms of its immigration policy, one important issue that evaded public scrutiny was the relationship between the RCMP, various federal departments and the intelligence services of foreign governments. There were also allegations that security services from Cuba, India, China, Libya, Iran and South Africa were operating on Canadian soil, primarily to gather intelligence on student nationals and expatriate communities. When immigrants applied for Canadian citizenship, the RCMP contacted security police services in the countries of origin, some of which had authoritarian governments that systematically violated the human rights of their citizens, for background information. In 1980 sources from revolutionary Iran, which had deposed of the authoritarian rule of the Shah, alleged that the former regime's dreaded secret police, SAVAK, had cooperated with the RCMP, the Department of Immigration and the Department of External Affairs, in monitoring Iranian students. Allegedly, a number of student dissidents had been deported to Iran where they had been tortured (CP 1980b).

Starting in 1984 CSIS was tasked with the security screening of immigration, refugee and visa applicants on behalf of the Department of Citizenship and Immigration. By the early 1990s the volume of these requests was roughly 300,000 a year. The *Immigration Act* listed criteria such as espionage, "subversion against democratic government," acts of terrorism and participation in war crimes or "terrorist governments" as grounds for exclusion. CSIS appears to have adopted established tactics of the RCMP for recruiting informants among refugee groups. As noted in the annual report of the Security Intelligence Review Committee, which was tasked with oversight of CSIS, in the late 1990s the agency was threatening applicants, or promising them special consideration, in an attempt to recruit them as informants (Cleroux 1991: 226; Fine 1998). Questions about the efficiency of CSIS security screening arose in 1994 when it was revealed that the former defence minister in the government of Somali dictator Siad Barre had been admitted to Canada. In 1989 the Somali military had massacred four hundred demonstrators (Ha 1994).

Canada experienced its first test of the new security apparatus in 1985, with tragic consequences, when a bomb planted in airline luggage in Vancouver ended up being carried by Air India flight 182, which exploded in the air near Ireland. All 329 passengers and crew members, many of them Canadian citizens, perished, making the attack the worst mass murder in Canadian history. In addition, a bomb originating from Vancouver exploded at Japan's Narita airport, killing two employees. The RCMP was tasked with investigating the Air India case. Suspicion fell on Sikh extremists who were avenging the violent assault by the Indian army on the Golden Temple in Amritsar in 1984 that killed at least four hundred people. For a number of observers the investigation was hampered by a simmering rivalry between CSIS and the RCMP, the most visible sign of which was the latter's refusal to grant the civilian agency access to the Canadian Police Information Centre (CPIC) system, which contained data on criminal records, drivers' licences and registrations and background information on persons known to the police (Cleroux 1991: 168–9).

The Air India plot was the first major challenge for CSIS, and the new agency did not perform well. Although it had acquired permission from a judge of the Federal Court for wiretap surveillance and had recorded the telephone conversations of possible suspects prior to the bombing, it failed to follow up on human surveillance, including an incident when suspects set off an explosion in the British Columbia forest. The RCMP, which was the conduit for intelligence via the Indian government and the Department of External Affairs, failed to keep CSIS fully informed, and the two agencies generally lacked coordination. There were also delays in translating, transcribing and analyzing intercepted telephone conversations. One serious mistake, which affected the later prosecution of two alleged plotters, was the decision by CSIS to erase wiretap evidence tapes. Only one suspect, Inderjit Singh Reyat, was successfully prosecuted. Arrested in England in 1988, he was extradited and convicted of manslaughter in 1991 for his role in the Narita airport deaths. In 2003 he pleaded guilty to manslaughter in the deaths of the Air India passengers and crew, 268 of whom were Canadians. In 2011 he was convicted of perjury in connection with the trial of two co-conspirators and sentenced to eleven years in penitentiary. In 1998 a key Sikh Canadian witness in the investigation was murdered. In 2005, after a lengthy and expensive trial, two Sikh Canadians who had been charged in 2000 with 329 counts of first-degree murder, and other offences, were acquitted. The trial judge decided that the Crown and police had failed to meet the necessary evidentiary burden and singled out CSIS bungling as a key weakness in the prosecution (Whitaker, Kealey and Parnaby 2012: chapter 11; Kashmeri and McAndrew 2005).

The inability of CSIS and the RCMP to uncover a specific threat against Air India in 1985, despite all the available intelligence, and the subsequent failure of the criminal investigation, was a severe indictment of Canada's post McDonald Commission security and intelligence system. In the middle of the 1980s CSIS, which contained many former members of the RCMP Security Service, remained locked in a Cold War mentality and, like the RCMP, distracted by Armenian terrorist threats. Ironically, the worst act of terror in Canadian history "had nothing to do with Communism" (Whitaker, Kealey and Parnaby 2012: 395) or Quebec separatism. Although there was an initial probe in the early 1990s, the federal government and its agencies stalled any meaningful investigation of the Air India incident until 2006, when the Harper government appointed a commission of inquiry. In 2010, twenty-five years after the bombing, the inquiry issued a final report that cited the "inexcusable" failures of CSIS and the RCMP both before the attack and during subsequent investigations. CSIS surveillance was judged to be ineffective and not timely and the two agencies as failing to cooperate or share information. The report also criticized Transport Canada, Air India, CP Air and Montreal airport security. The Air India Inquiry was equally critical of the attitude and failures of the federal government, CSIS and the RCMP in the post-attack period (Canada 2010).

Throughout the rest of the 1980s CSIS, which was under the supervision of the Security and Intelligence Review Committee (SIRC), continued to exhibit growing pains. Criticized for being heavily white, male and Anglophone, it took steps to diversify recruitment and announced that it would not bar homosexuals from its ranks. By the late 1980s it was becoming more trusted by various ethnic and immigrant communities who worried that conflicts overseas could be imported into Canada. The Air India affair suggested that CSIS had wanted to distance itself from the negative associations of the RCMP Security Service by not amassing large amounts of information on Canadian citizens. The CSIS Act excluded activity against "lawful advocacy and peaceful protest," yet many of the old Security Service methods, including tracking non-violent advocacy groups, continued. In 1987, for example, came revelations that Marc-André Boivin, who was arrested by the SQ, had served as an RCMP informant within the Quebec labour movement since 1973. An organizer in the powerful Conféderation des syndicates nationaux, Boivin continued in this role under CSIS. The winding down of the Cold War in the late 1980s appeared to undercut arguments about foreign agents or money influencing Canadian social movements, and CSIS was damaged by leaks that it was spying on peace groups. For a time the NDP government of Manitoba, like that of Quebec, refused to cooperate with the agency. In 1987, agreeing with SIRC that the CSIS Counter Subversion Branch was tracking largely imaginary threats, Solicitor General James Kelleher dissolved the unit. By this point the agency had thirty thousand files on "subversives," some of which had not been updated since the 1950s. A number of files were transferred to the CSIS Counter Terrorism and Counter Espionage branches (Cleroux 1991: 181, 193; Whittaker, Kealey and Parnaby 2012: 391–3).

During the Air India investigation the RCMP discovered that it did not have a single member who could speak Punjabi at a time when there were roughly half a million Sikhs living in Canada. One of the barriers to recruiting Sikhs into the force was their religious requirement to wear turbans. By 1990 the Solicitor General had approved of permitting Sikh recruits to wear their turbans on duty. The change was in the spirit of community policing and a response to statistics that indicated the poor representation of visible minorities within the ranks of the federal bureaucracy. The first Sikh, recruited in 1990, would be the only one on the force for several years. This symbolic move sparked a backlash amongst RCMP veterans and conservative citizens who argued that it was an assault on the traditions and identity of the Mounted Police. Incorrectly identifying the Stetson hat as a traditional part of the Mountie uniform, they assumed that the force had not changed since its inception. The critics reflected a recurrent theme in the politics of policing, that a police service "belongs" not to the citizens or taxpayers but to the police themselves. Many commentators saw the reaction as an intolerant outburst against multiculturalism. At the same time the uniform for female Mounties was changed from a skirt to breeches. Opponents mounted a court challenge based on the argument that turbaned Mounties were somehow unconstitutional. The case proceeded all the way to the Supreme Court of Canada, which in 1996 upheld the new policy (Singh 2010).

Despite the public perception that the RCMP had "lost" the national security file to a civilian agency, in the late 1980s the force returned to the security sphere with the creation of a new directorate, the National Security Investigation Section (NSIS). Prior to this, the RCMP had quietly established a series of National Security Enforcement Units. CSIS had been given the mandate to collect intelligence on individuals and organizations with links to external threats to Canada; it was not a law enforcement agency. The job of the RCMP was to investigate and lay charges in the case of criminal acts arising out of these activities. The public learned about the formation of NSIS when the RCMP commissioner confirmed its existence before a Parliamentary committee in 1989 (Cleroux 1989).

The ending of the CSIS Counter Subversion branch was a matter of semantics for Arab Canadians, particularly those of Palestinian and Iraqi origin, when in 1991 Canada, breaking with a thirty-eight year tradition, became involved in an offensive war as opposed to acting as a peacekeeper. When Saddam Hussein's Iraqi forces invaded Kuwait in 1990 and threatened American and Saudi Arabian interests in the Persian Gulf, the United Nations ordered Iraq to withdraw and imposed trade sanctions. Hussein remained defiant, and in early 1991 a U.N.-backed coalition, led by the United States, liberated Kuwait and attacked Iraq. Canada contributed naval vessels to enforce the U.N. trade embargo and two squadrons of CF-18 jet fighters that took an active role in combat.

Canada's involvement, despite the approval of the United Nations, was controversial at home, but CSIS seemed more concerned not with general anti-war sentiment but the beliefs of several thousand Iraqi immigrants. Consisting of professionals, students and refugees from Hussein's authoritarian role, the Iraqis were mainly first-generation immigrants. Most of them were not supporters of the Iraqi regime, but they worried that coalition airstrikes would kill or injure larger numbers of innocent civilians and contribute to a humanitarian crisis. Although a number of Islamic states were involved in the campaign against Iraq, many in the Arab world viewed the American-dominated coalition as the Western world attacking Arabs. As documented by Kashmeri (2000), many Arab Canadians, especially Iraqis, were interviewed at their jobs or homes by CSIS agents who posed intimidating questions about their political and religious beliefs. In some cases interviewees were shown photos of other Arab Canadians and asked to identify or disclose details about them. Most of them came from nations where the police, especially the security police, were feared. CSIS director Reid Morden justified the intelligence gathering on the excuse that Iraqi Canadians were being blackmailed by agents of Iraq. The RCMP, which in theory was not permitted to investigate organizations, activated its National Emergency Security Plan. So intimidating was the probe of Arab Canadians that the Canadian Arab Federation issued a pamphlet *When CSIS Calls*.

Another controversy involving the RCMP and CSIS was Operation Sidewinder, an investigation of alleged espionage, bribery of elected officials and the control of Canadian companies by the government of China and Chinese organized crime that began in 1995. A secret interim report was issued in 1997 amidst rumours of money laundering, drug trafficking and the illegal sale of visas. Prompted by the large-scale movement of Chinese capitalists into Canada pending the takeover of Hong Kong, the operation was temporarily suspended by CSIS in 1997 and much of the gathered intelligence destroyed. Work was renewed in 1998, despite disagreements between CSIS and the RCMP, and a final report was issued in 1999. A review by SIRC concluded that the 1997 report had been deeply flawed and that Chinese interests posed no serious threat to Canada's security (Canada 2000; Palango 2008: chapter 22).

CROWD CONTROL AND COUNTER-INSURGENCY

By the 1980s, the policing of public order was becoming more challenging. Activists were reacting to neo-liberalism, specifically cuts in social welfare, education spending and environmental protection, or to high-level political meetings dedicated to advancing the agenda of globalization. And in addition to demonstrations over municipal, provincial and federal government policies there were an increasing number of actions involving Canada's First Nations. As in the past (for example, Expo 67) the tradition of operational independence dictated that political authorities deferred the planning and mounting of security operations to police services (Roach 2007). One of the more dramatic examples of a changed role for the police in this era was in Great Britain, where a coordinated and militarized police response, under the regime of Margaret Thatcher, helped defeat the miners' strike of 1984–85 (Reiner 1998). Section 2c of the Canadian Charter of Rights and Freedoms, effective in 1982, guaranteed the right to peaceful assembly. In addition, because of changing technology, public order policing lost much of its low visibility. The growing presence of television cameras and, by the 1990s, personal video recorders, allowed police accounts of events to be challenged. Most demonstrations and protests, as in the past, remained peaceful, but the police were often on-site or nearby and appeared to be collecting intelligence on "extremists." When demonstrations turned violent there were often accusations that the police had either provoked the crowds or had mishandled the situation and violated individual rights and employed excessive force. In 1981, for example, the Quebec

Police Commission criticized the Montreal police riot squad for a brutal attack on youth protesting the 1980 sovereignty-association referendum, describing the operation as an "ambush." The more militarized "look" of criminal policing, such as the deployment of ERTs, easily spilled over into crowd control and responses to blockades, occupations and demonstrations (CP 1981a).

Most demonstrations in Canada prior to the 1980s were small scale and localized, but during that decade protests began to become larger and better organized. Controversies over provincial economic, environmental and other policies and federal government foreign and domestic policies often provoked reactions from not only labour organizations but also anti-poverty and environmental organizations and middle-class demonstrators who had little experience in dealing with the police. De Lint and Hall (2009: 109–12) discuss how the RCMP and the Vancouver Police Department in the late 1970s and early 1980s adopted aspects of the liaison approach to managing strikes and large scale demonstrations, meeting in advance and maintaining communications with strike and protest organizers, and training officers to minimize confrontations. During the protests of the Solidarity Coalition against the Social Credit provincial government, crowds of up to sixty thousand demonstrated without any reported arrests. The model spread to other jurisdictions in the 1980s and 1990s, such as industrial Ontario, where it became provincial policy in the mid 1990s. During protests by organized labour against the Harris government between 1995 and 1998, the liaison approach, which relied on union organizers to keep order in their ranks, apparently succeeded as there were few arrests, despite large crowds (one event attracted up to a quarter of a million people to Queen's Park). In addition to arguments about the benefits of police neutrality, other issues relating to the de-escalation of public order policing included the argument that police services no longer had the resources to be involved with strikes and that officers disliked picket-line duties. Yet as De Lint and Hall note, not all police leaders agreed with the liaison approach (De Lint and Hall 2009: 116–24; 136–7, 230–2).

Although there were still protests over Canada's foreign and military policies, by the 1980s the future of protest lay with Aboriginal rights, environmental issues and resistance to neo-liberal policies affecting health care, education and other government services. In British Columbia starting in 1980 an ongoing dispute over clear-cutting on Crown lands on the west coast of Vancouver Island pitted First Nations and non-Aboriginal protestors against the forestry giant MacMillan Bloedel, the provincial government and local residents who worked in the forestry sector. Backed by Greenpeace and the Sierra Club, several thousand people defied injunctions and took part in road blockades and protests at Clayoquot Sound in the summer of 1993. In one of the largest police responses to civil disobedience in Canadian history, the RCMP arrested more than nine hundred protestors, and in contrast to most urban protests, most of them were charged and prosecuted in a series of mass trials on charges of criminal contempt for disobeying a court injunction. Strictly speaking the RCMP who arrested peaceful demonstrators for standing or sitting on a logging road were acting on behalf of the courts, not the provincial government or a forestry company, but the mass arrests and prosecutions were highly embarrassing to the NDP government, which two years later implemented a more restrictive forest practices code (soon modified in response to industry demands) (MacIsaac 1995).

Media coverage of the Mounted Police forcibly removing protestors engaged in acts of passive resistance in order to protect old-growth forests reinforced the theory that the police served the interests of the powerful. One sign of a more nuanced approach were the comments of a local RCMP inspector in British Columbia in 1985 in the aftermath of the arrest of dozens of members of the Haida First Nation in a protest over logging on Lyell Island. The bigger issue for the Haida and other Aboriginal groups was the refusal of the Social Credit government to engage in land claims negotiations. The RCMP issued the typical police statement that they were not taking sides, only enforcing the law, but called on the provincial government to find a better way to solve disputes over land and resources. Haida leaders were impressed with the RCMP statement. In New Brunswick in 1980, the RCMP exercised considerable caution in reaction to armed protestors squatting in Kouchibouquac National Park. Despite gunshots and the very real chance of injury or death, the police used restraint in order to not provoke greater levels of violence (Yaffe 1980; CP 1980a).

The liaison approach was not always followed with consistency. One of the more controversial operations, involving the use of tear gas against protestors, was the RCMP response to parents in the Acadian region of northern New Brunswick in 1997 protesting against the possible closure of local schools. The media reported the demonstration as four days of "riots." When the protestors blockaded a road, the police responded with a riot squad, tear gas rounds and police dogs that injured a number of people. In contrast with the 1987 pulp cutters protest where the decision to use tear gas was made by the provincial government, in the case of the Acadian parents the decision to use force appears to have been made by the incident commander, a sergeant. The result was a major crisis of legitimacy for the RCMP with citizens filing two hundred complaints against the force. Many complained that riot squad members had not worn name tags. Premier Frank McKenna, who as opposition leader a decade earlier had denounced aggressive police tactics, now defended them in the name of "the rule of law" and proclaimed that the people of the Acadian peninsula had a history of "rebellion when things don't go their way." The protests, incidentally, worked: the schools were not closed. In 2001 Inspector Kevin Vickers (a key participant in the 1999–2001 Burnt Church policing operation and later the Sergeant-at-Arms of the Canadian Parliament credited with stopping an armed terrorist in 2014) issued a rare formal apology to the communities affected (Morris 1997; MacFarlane 2001).

De Lint and Hall's 2009 study of the evolution of Canadian police crowd control doctrine and tactics details how the less provocative liaison response was challenged by a more militarized approach that stressed intelligence gathering and the use of paramilitary units. Although their use was more restrained than in the United States, heavily armed and specially trained tactical units proliferated in Canada throughout the 1990s and, combined with concepts, practices and language borrowed from the intelligence and military world, they changed the tone of law enforcement. In Toronto, protest organizations were monitored as potential enemies, subject to "risk" or "threat" assessments. The Metropolitan Toronto Police, for example, placed the Ontario Coalition Against Poverty (OCAP) under Cold War style surveillance, which included undercover agents and informers. Its rallies and protests usually produced a heavy police presence that included riot squads and mounted officers who appear to have rejected the claim that OCAP, an admittedly controversial organization, had a legitimate right to protest. In 2000, police arrested demonstrators at and following an OCAP rally to protest major welfare cuts by the Harris government. The police and mainstream media justified the aggressive response because of violent protestors who threw projectiles, but activists blamed the police for igniting the violence (De Lint and Hall 2009: chapter 6; Luciw and Freeze 2000). The OCAP continues to protest police brutality and excessive focus on the poor and homeless, criticizing sweeps by Toronto Anti-Violence Integrated Strategy (TAVIS) officers and the installation of closed-circuit television (CCTV) cameras in poor inner-city neighbourhoods.

The protests in Toronto in 1988 against the meeting of G7 leaders were controversial even in progressive circles as many on the left were not convinced of the wisdom of mass demonstrations. Yet they were a sign of things to come and represented major challenges to police operations as well as legitimacy. For the most part the protest organizations involved at the G7 were progressive church and social activist groups. Demonstrators resented the presence at the summit of controversial world leaders such as Ronald Reagan and Margaret Thatcher. The decision to stage the main summit meetings in downtown Toronto was controversial, as the authorities erected a steel and concrete security fence around the perimeter of the event and deployed snipers and helicopters. More than two hundred people were arrested, and there were complaints of excessive force, denial of the right to legal counsel and the isolation of detainees on buses for long periods. Most of the arrested were released without charge. The cost of the security operation was nearly $30 million. In keeping with the future of policing anti-globalization protests, there was evidence of surveillance and infiltration directed against protestors in advance of the event, which suggested a counter-insurgency approach. Journalist Michael Valpy castigated the "petty, unsophisticated and tyrannical" Toronto police, who had suspended officer discretion whether to handcuff women and juveniles and had employed "pain compliance techniques" against peaceful protestors (Valpy 1990). The controversies surrounding the 1988 Toronto summit contributed to the debate on the public complaints process discussed in the next chapter.

By the 1990s, the field of Canadian police studies had developed a new acronym, O&PS, occupations and protests. The most dramatic symbol of the gulf between First Nations Canada and the police was the Oka crisis of 1990. Residents of Kahnawake, a Mohawk community south of Montreal, had grown increasingly frustrated that the local municipality of Oka was authorizing the expansion of a golf course on disputed land. According to the Mohawk the area contained a sacred burial ground. The protest, and the subsequent response of the armed might of the state, captured considerable attention during an era of increased tensions over Aboriginal land lands and treaty rights. The events at Oka, described as "Canada's Wounded Knee," revealed tense relations with not only the police but also the larger white population. In one incident a convoy of Kahnawake Mohawk, minimally protected by police, was assaulted by rock-throwing whites. An elderly Aboriginal man died of his injuries incurred in this attack. The protest spread to Kanehsatake, a Mohawk reserve west of Montreal, and Akwesasne, a Mohawk community near Cornwall that straddled the borders of Quebec, Ontario and New York.

This was not the first major clash between the SQ and Quebec's indigenous people. The provincial police had intervened at Kahnawake in 1973 following the eviction of non-Native residents and had raided the Mi'kmaq reserve at Restigouche (Listuguj), Quebec, over a dispute over salmon fishing in 1981. The SQ raided Akwesasne in 1987 over gambling regulation, and two years later RCMP ERTs descended on Kahnawake in response to unlicensed tobacco sales. During this controversy Native warriors blocked the Mercier Bridge, a major artery for greater Montreal. By 1989 the provincial government was aware of a growing number of firearms at Kahnawake, and the provincial ministry of Native Affairs warned that tensions were mounting. Earlier in 1990, Mohawk warriors and their opponents had squared off at Akwesasne and two men had been killed. There were rumours that the federal and Quebec governments were somehow mixed up in the struggles there (Séguin 1990).

As their protest escalated in 1990, the people of Kanesatake mounted a barricade to block access to the disputed land, and both sides faulted the other for a failure to negotiate. The SQ, which had dispatched tactical and riot control units to the scene, attempted to enforce a court injunction by seizing and dismantling the barricade. Gunfire erupted and the police used tear gas and concussion grenades. Although he wore a protective vest, Constable Marcel Lemay died when a bullet entered his upper body. The local Mohawk had been and would continue to be reinforced by Native warriors, some of whom had military experience. The SQ set up its own barricades, and Quebec's premier called for intervention by the Canadian army, a move that was condemned by the premiers of British Columbia, Manitoba and Ontario. As the warriors dug trenches and foxholes, the area began to resemble a war zone, with "non-combatants" (women and children) behind the lines and the Red Cross delivering supplies to Kanesatake. The standoff inspired Aboriginals in British Columbia, Alberta and Ontario to set up blockades and engage in other acts of resistance. In August the Canadian armed forces took over from the SQ, launching Operation Salon, the largest peace-time deployment of the army in aid of the civil power since the FLQ crisis. The military secured the area with razor wire, employed night vision technology, fixed bayonets, machine guns, howitzers, armoured personnel carriers and helicopters and even used jet fighters to intimidate the barricaded protestors who had amassed a small arsenal of automatic weapons and rifles. The military also employed psychological warfare tactics to disrupt and divide the resistance. Media releases and a video suggested that any attack on the army would be met by overwhelming force. Negotiations lead to the barricades at Kahnawake being removed several days later, but the last holdouts at Kanesatake stood down on the seventy-eighth day of the siege. Of one group of thirty-nine Mohawks prosecuted, thirty-four were found not guilty and charges were dropped in five cases. Another thirty Mohawk were convicted of various offences. The events of Oka hardly solved the issue of police–First Nations relations, as there were further clashes with the SQ at Kanesatake in 1997 (CP 1990b).

Oka had both a local and a national legacy. Aboriginal resentment toward the SQ increased, and the force hit back against the Anglophone media for what it deemed to be unfair coverage. Opinion polls indicated an ebb in public satisfaction with the SQ and a decline in support for police in general. The death of Lemay was never solved, and in 1991 the head of the SQ faulted not the police raid but "terrorists" who had employed force to "destabilize the government" (Poirier 1991). The provincial human rights commission in contrast criticized the police action at Oka. According to Brodeur (2010: 170) the affected First Nations communities became havens for organized crime, a situation that continues to divide their residents. In 1994 Mohawks warned the provincial police to stay out of Kanesatake, Kahnawake and Akwesasne, but as recently as 2011 police launched a large-scale raid on the illegal drug trade in the communities (CP 1992, 1994b). The crisis brought only marginal improvements to the issue that had precipitated the standoff, delays by government in negotiating specific land claims such as the one at Oka. Two decades later, the minimum average time to conclude specific land claims was several years and for comprehensive claims more than twenty (Atleo 2010).

On the national level the crisis helped lead to the appointment, in 1991, of a

Royal Commission on Aboriginal Peoples. One of the many issues examined by the commission was the role of indigenous Canadians in the justice system. In terms of policing, Oka inspired more sophisticated responses to First Nations blockades and occupations that reflected a combination of carrot-and-stick tactics (CP 1991). These were tested unsuccessfully in 1995 in a controversial OPP operation against First Nations protestors that resulted in the death of an Aboriginal man, Dudley George. The Stoney Point band's land claim to Ipperwash Provincial Park near Sarnia dated back to the 1940s when the area had been taken over by the military. In frustration Native protestors occupied the park, and the OPP, backed by the Conservative government of Mike Harris, responded with an aggressive counter-insurgency approach that involved controlling media access to the area and deploying both the Crowd Management Unit (CMU) and the Tactical Response Unit (TRU). After protestors tried to drive a car and a school bus in the direction of the police, a member of the TRU claimed that he spotted a man with a gun and opened fire, killing George. Two others were wounded, and the police, who had fired at the vehicles, claimed that they had heard gunfire from the demonstrators. Although the protestors had rocks and sticks, no firearms were ever found. The incident not only raised issues about the training and rules of engagement for police snipers, it also suggested a biased if not racist attitude by Premier Harris (Edwards 2003).

A subsequent Liberal government appointed a commission of inquiry into the Ipperwash affair, which reported in 2007. Commissioner Sidney Linden interpreted his mandate as facilitating the healing process for all involved. Arguing that "an aboriginal protest is not a soccer crowd" (Linden 2007: 48), he advised that First Nations people protecting burial sites and other ancestral lands should be treated differently than regular demonstrators and that all mediation and negotiating efforts should be exhausted before the police took overt action. The OPP at Ipperwash had been guilty of taking "precipitous action" during the night, without informing protestors of their intentions. The deployment of the CMU in formation, equipped with helmets, visors, batons, bulletproof vests, guns and police dogs, had intimidated the demonstrators, who had surged forward only after one of their own had been surrounded and clubbed repeatedly by police (receiving twenty-eight serious wounds to his head). Linden found that the CMU had been deployed based on erroneous and unverified intelligence. The acting sergeant who fired the fatal shot was investigated by the Ontario Special Investigations Unit (SIU) and convicted of criminal negligence. Ipperwash Park was returned to the Chippewa of Kettle and Stoney Point, but many continued to be troubled by what the affair revealed about police deception and lack of transparency (Linden 2007; Edwards 2003).

Unlike the events at Ipperwash, which resulted in a political victory for Aboriginals and a public inquiry into police tactics, largely as a result of the sacrifice of Dudley George, a dispute in British Columbia that same year involving the RCMP produced no victory for Native people, no inquiry and no criminal charges against police. In the late 1980s members of the Shuswap Nation began performing the traditional Sun Dance at T'peten, also known as Gustafsen Lake, on land owned by a white rancher. In the view of the Shuswap the land had never been ceded to the Crown and remained part of their ancestral territory. In 1995, after Sun Dance enthusiasts built a fence on his property, the rancher ordered them to be evicted. Protestors, some of them armed, set up camp, and the RCMP responded with its ERT. Although negotiations took place, the police attempted to brand the protest as "an act of terrorism" and militarized their operations by borrowing armoured personnel carriers from the army. Assembly of First Nations Grand Chief Ovide Mercredi, who was involved in negotiations, criticized the RCMP for provoking violence by cutting off radio telephone communications with the camp. The level of local support for the protest camp, many of whose members did not belong to the area's First Nation, was limited; this strengthened the hand of the RCMP, which deployed four hundred officers to the operation (Howard 1997a and 1997b).

The protestors fired warning shots one night at mysterious prowlers, who turned out to be camouflage-clad Mounties on a reconnaissance mission. Two officers wearing protective vests were hit by bullets. At one point the ERT used explosives to destroy a truck being driven by two men and killed a dog belonging to the protest camp. Following the destruction of the truck, several thousand rounds of ammunition were expended during a forty-five-minute firefight that miraculously killed no one. One woman was wounded during the one-month standoff that ended with arrests and charges laid against eighteen protestors. The RCMP spent $5.5 million on the operation. The prosecution of the protestors on sixty charges in a high-security courtroom in Surrey resulted in thirteen being sent to jail. One of the occupation leaders was sentenced to more than four years in penitentiary (Howard 1997a and 1997b; Cernetig 1997).

Optimistic accounts of the post-Gustafsen era in police-Aboriginal relations stressed the fact the RCMP engaged in dialogue with elders, sought to defuse rather than escalate tense situations and eventually issued their own separate apology for the role of the force during the Indian residential school era, which was especially controversial in British Columbia. Yet other accounts suggest that the heavy-handed response to an act of trespass revealed the true colours of the RCMP and its cynical willingness to manipulate the press and engage in "psychological warfare" against protestors (Hall 2000), and more than one journalist and academic has pointed out that the land claims process, despite assurances that non-confrontational tactics are more constructive, continues to be dragged out by federal government stalling tactics (Matas 2010).

The Atlantic region was not immune from protests over Aboriginal policies, but in the case of competition for resources, conflict also raised the problem of non-Native vigilantism. The manner in which the police and other government agencies dealt with the latter did not always reassure First Nations leaders that their communities enjoyed equal protection under the law. In the 1980s the Innu of Labrador were locked in a battle with the Canadian military, the RCMP and the federal and provincial governments over air training by NATO pilots. The two levels of government, during a revival of tensions in the Cold War, hoped to expand the use of CFB Goose Bay, for economic development reasons, for low-level training flights by jet fighters of NATO allies such as Great Britain and West Germany. The Innu complained that the flights disrupted hunting, trapping, fishing and their lifestyle in general, and engaged in protests such as the occupation of runways. The Innu, who like many northern peoples suffered from various social and economic problems, claimed that Canada was illegally intruding on Nitassinan, their ancestral lands. By the fall of 1998 the RCMP had laid more than two hundred charges, and Newfoundland justice authorities displayed considerable insensitivity to the cultural context of the protests. In the late 1980s, as the Cold War was waning, CSIS became involved, seeking evidence that Innu protests were being manipulated by external forces. With the threat of international Communism receding, in 1988 CSIS began to monitor "Native extremism" in Canada (Cleroux 1991: 254). Following concerns raised by the national NDP, SIRC exonerated the role of CSIS in Labrador, explaining that the investigation had been localized, not part of a national operation, and had not involved wiretaps or electronic surveillance. The national study was real and had been ordered following a number of statements of Canadian Aboriginal leaders that predicted violence if various grievances were not addressed (CP 1989, 1990a; Cox 1990).

The last decade of the twentieth century was an unprecedented era for Canada's First Nations and their quests for self government, land claims, enhanced treaty rights, redress for past wrongs such as residential schools and a share of natural resource revenues. These efforts, which involved lobbying and protests, drew attention from CSIS and the RCMP and other police services. In 1999 the Supreme Court of Canada ruled that the Mi'kmaq of the Maritime provinces enjoyed a treaty right to fish "for a moderate livelihood," subject to federal government regulations. Although most Aboriginal bands in the region signed agreements with the Department of Fisheries and Oceans (DFO), the Esjenoopetij First Nation (EFN) on Miramichi Bay refused and prepared to conduct its own lobster fishery. For the next two years tensions were high between Native and non-Native fishers in parts of New Brunswick and Nova Scotia. In 1999 white fishers destroyed large numbers of lobster traps belonging to the EFN. At one point hundreds of white fishers, some of them armed, blockaded the port of Yarmouth, Nova Scotia, in a protest over the recognition of the Native fishery.

In 2000, lobster traps in Miramichi Bay were destroyed and shots were fired in confrontations between Aboriginal and white fishers. That season white fishers were authorized to set 240,000 traps in the bay, but when a Mi'kmaq fisher attempted to position ten traps, DFO intervened. DFO, the Coast Guard and the RCMP deployed resources to the area after the Mi'kmaq erected a blockade. The band received aid from other First Nations in the form of food, boats and lobster traps and volunteer warriors. The police deployed ERT officers on boats when tensions escalated and on one occasion rammed two Mi'kmaq boats, capsizing one of them. The actions of 2000 resulted in 160 charges being laid against EFN members. Yet compared to earlier standoffs, the RCMP did not maintain a large heavily-armed force on the land. Inspector Kevin Vickers explained that this "measured approach" was based on mutual respect and "problem solving," with enforcement as the last option. The RCMP, for example, chose not to provoke Native warriors who carried weapons. The operation was expensive, costing the federal government $3.7 million for policing and $3.2 million for the DFO presence (De Lint and Hall 2009: 228–9; Kern 2009: 307–19).

Despite this softer approach, which included visits by First Nations officers in plain clothes (i.e., not in uniform), it is not clear that most reserve residents trusted the Mounties in light of their support of DFO and their inaction against white fishers. First Nations leaders accused the authorities of not protecting their lobster traps from non-Natives and the community from aggressive protests by non-Native fishing boats. In the summer and fall of 2001 hundreds of trap lines were cut. As depicted in the documentary *Is the Crown at War With Us?* (Obomsawin 2002) Esjenoopetij boats, despite the deployment of unarmed Mi'kmaq "rangers" on the water, were treated aggressively by armed DFO officers who rammed and swamped small Mi'kmaq craft and used pepper spray and batons on Aboriginal men who ended up in the water. The situation was monitored by the Christian Peacekeepers, a group that normally acted as human rights monitors in places such as Israel's West Bank (Kern 2009: 307–19).

Despite the apparent popularity of the liaison approach in the case of industrial disputes, by the 1990s there were signs that police were more likely to employ riot gear, tear gas and pepper spray against certain types of demonstrators. Students and anti-globalization protestors, who in the minds of the authorities often included violent anarchists, in addition to being young were generally not property owners or voters or even local residents. Consequently they were more vulnerable to harassment and intimidation. Their involvement in large, loosely-organized protests also made them more of an unknown and therefore more of a risk, in terms of public order risk assessments. In 1990 when students in Quebec organized against postsecondary tuition increases, police in riot gear faced 1,500 student protestors at the National Assembly, and more than two hundred protestors were arrested in

Montreal. A decade later there were more police than protestors on hand when Windsor, Ontario, hosted a meeting of the general assembly of the Organization of American States (OAS). The event drew a wide range of protestors, including those with grievances against various regimes in Central and South America. The labour, environmental and anti-globalization protestors hoping to delay or close down the conference met an aggressive response from police, including undercover officers and helicopters. The OAS delegates were protected by concrete blocks and a chain-link fence, and police outnumbered demonstrators by nearly two to one. Several hundred American activists were prevented from crossing into Canada, indicating that police had shared information with customs officials. Nearly eighty were arrested, most for breaching the peace, and there was evidence of pre-event surveillance of protestors. Visitors were evicted from housing and prevented from using campgrounds and subjected to intimidation and other police actions of questionable legality (De Lint and Hall 2009: 239–44).

Not all confrontations between police and demonstrators, even those that turned violent, were met with force. In some cases rather than provoke crowds, police adopted a relatively low profile. One example was a series of disturbances in downtown Toronto in 1992 following the fatal shooting by police of a twenty-two-year-old Jamaican immigrant. A protest organized by the Black Action Defence Committee initially focused on the United States Consulate, in reaction to the acquittal of white police officers in California for the beating of African American motorist Rodney King. The demonstrators moved on to city hall where they were blocked by police in riot gear and police horses; as the procession moved up Yonge Street it was joined by others, including people who began to vandalize and loot shops on the street. The city had experienced recent outbursts on the closing night of the Canadian National Exhibition and on New Year's Eve, but this riot had political overtones. Minority advocates and academics spoke of the pent-up frustrations of the city's Black community. Few people were arrested and even fewer charged with offences. One outcome of the 1992 protest was the appointment, by the NDP government, of a task force on race relations headed by Stephen Lewis (*Edmonton Journal* 1992).

The decision to host the Asia-Pacific Economic Council (APEC) summit in Vancouver in 1997 made sense in terms of Canada's growing volume of trade with Asia, but locating it on the campus of the University of British Columbia, in hindsight, was an act of provocation. University students, after all, were often the most vocal defenders of human rights and critics of globalization. One reason the affair (later dubbed "Peppergate") received so much media coverage was the role of the Prime Minister's Office in security planning and even operations, which appeared to violate the tradition of police operational autonomy. The APEC events, which involved police violating the civil liberties of peaceful protestors holding signs or standing on sidewalks, also raised concerns about the role of senior politicians and their unelected advisors in directing police operations. An APEC "threat assessment" group included the RCMP, CSIS, the Vancouver police, the Department of National Defence and the Canadian customs and immigration departments. More than one thousand names, including those of law-abiding peace activists, were added to the list, and intelligence was shared with American intelligence and police agencies. The RCMP established an official protest zone on the UBC campus and attempted to disrupt the APEC-Alert! protest before it could take place. One court document clearly indicated a diffusion strategy of arresting key student leaders in advance. The document also referred to a Vancouver Police Department "Strike Force," which despite its dramatic name was tasked with monitoring peaceful protest. An abiding concern for the federal government was that visiting APEC leaders like President Jiang Zemin of China and President Suharto of Indonesia not be "embarrassed" by the presence of demonstrators. In practice this meant that the legal rights of citizens to demonstrate peacefully would be curtailed.

UBC students still remembered the massacre of Chinese students at Tiananmen Square in 1989. This time, China was being criticized for its Tibetan policies. The authoritarian leader Suharto was particularly odious to human rights supporters as his invasion of East Timor had led to 100,000 deaths. Law student Karen Pearlston was threatened with arrest, under no specific law, when she tried to fasten protest signs to a security fence three days prior to the arrival of the heads of state. Another student was detained for fourteen hours for carrying signs with slogans such as "Democracy." When a security fence was toppled during a demonstration (opinions varied as to why it fell) the RCMP responded with pepper spray, police dogs and arrests. Staff Sergeant Hugh Stewart, photographed soaking peaceful young protestors with a large canister of pepper spray, earned national notoriety as "Sergeant Pepper." In keeping an established pattern, the arrest of more than seventy protestors appears to have been more of an intimidation or incapacitation tactic than a sincere legal move, as only one individual was given a court date and his charge was later dropped (Pearlston 2000; Pue 2000). In a move that harkened back to the classic era of counter subversion, RCMP NSIS officers engaged in infiltration tactics, including a clumsy attempt to hide a six foot, four inch, 240 pound officer within a group of young, festive, Halloween costume-clad protestors (Pugliese and Bronskill 2001e).

Following the APEC summit, an initial hearing process under the RCMP Public Complaints Commission collapsed because of controversies. A subsequent commission of inquiry concluded that the RCMP was guilty of poor planning, incompetence and needless use of pepper spray against protestors engaged in acts of passive resistance. The Mounties were also condemned for violating the Charter rights of student protestors. The Hughes Report faulted the police for allowing more aggressive protestors to reach the security fence and for strip-searching female detainees in public areas (apparently the Commissioner for Public Complaints Against the RCMP had no problem with strip searches of protestors in general). Prime Minister Chrétien refused to cooperate with the inquiry, which was criticized for not examining broader issues connected to the event. In the end Chrétien, who made light of the use of pepper spray on peaceful demonstrators, was untouched by the inquiry, but his staff was criticized. Aside from short-term negative publicity, the impact on the RCMP was minimal. In fact Sergeant Pepper was sent to Quebec to train police in crowd control tactics in advance of a 2001 summit (Pearlston 2000; Pue 2000; Abbate 2001).

In addition to events such as the APEC and OAS meetings, police services were also involved in a series of apolitical outbursts related to sporting and popular music events. Often the people involved were young, male and consuming alcohol. The first major event of this type was a riot in Montreal in 1955 that involved neither socialists nor trade unionists, but hockey fans. Many also interpreted the Rocket Richard riot as an important precursor to Quebec's Quiet Revolution, as it involved mostly Quebecois hockey fans upset with the decision of the Anglophone president of the National Hockey League (NHL) to suspend Maurice "Rocket" Richard of the Montreal Canadiens for violence. To make matters worse the president of the NHL attended the next game at the Montreal Forum, which was interpreted as an act of provocation. Fans rioted along Rue St. Catherine, looting stores and overturning cars. Dozens were arrested and many were injured (Melançon 2009). Certainly compared to the wave of modern sports riots that began in the United States in the 1980s, the 1955 Montreal riot had political overtones.

In subsequent years rock music concerts competed with sports events as sources of apolitical social violence. In 1992, the American rock group Guns N' Roses, performing at Montreal's Olympic Stadium, cut short its set after the opening act, Metallica, did the same thing. A minority of the 53,000 disappointed fans became agitated, and three hundred riot police were deployed to quell the resulting violence (*New York Times* 1992). In the following year, after the Montreal Canadiens defeated the Los Angeles Kings, crowds in Montreal rioted and did $10 million damage, including police cruisers. More than 160 people were injured, including forty-eight officers. A subsequent inquiry by a retired Quebec judge opined that Montreal police should enforce a "zero tolerance" policy toward mass violence and respond aggressively with canine units, water cannon and other crowd control equipment (CP 1993).

Although sports riots, as in the United States, could break out for trivial or unfathomable reasons, they could also be dangerous for participants and police. In 1994 NHL playoff-related violence returned to Vancouver, and the response of the Vancouver police and RCMP to the incident would have an impact on planning and tactics used in police responses to future mass events. In this case the game in question was not even being played in Vancouver. When the Vancouver Canucks lost the last game in their Stanley Cup round in New York, there were fifty to seventy-five thousand fans, including bar patrons, in the downtown core of Vancouver. The police anticipated trouble and had two hundred officers and sixty reserve officers in the downtown core, including RCMP units. Rowdy fans and others vandalized and looted stores, and the police responded by firing tear gas canisters and baton rounds (rubber bullets). Known within police circles as "attenuated energy projectiles" (AEPs), these polyurethane projectiles were first deployed in crowd control situations in the United States in the early 1970s. The official excuse for arming police with baton round launchers was to protect officers from rioters who hurled bricks, bottles and other projectiles. Officers were trained to hit targets below the rib cage, but following a fatality in 1974, American police services ceased using the weapon until the 1980s. Their most controversial use was in Northern Ireland by the British Army and Royal Ulster Constabulary in the 1970s and 1980s where seventeen people, including eight children, were killed and hundreds were injured. Medical professionals and human rights organizations have raised serious concerns about police use of AEPs, but they were adopted by many Canadian police services. During the crisis in Vancouver the Vancouver Crowd Control Unit (subsequently renamed the Public Order Unit) and the RCMP Tactical Troops deployed tear gas, but gave little advance warning to the crowds. The RCMP also had canine units. The Vancouver police ERT was equipped with the Arwen 37 anti-riot gun, originally developed for military use in Northern Ireland. The use of this weapon raised concerns after the riot, but the police service explained that it was deployed not to control riots but to protect officers from specific individuals.

By the end of the violence five hundred police had been deployed and more than two hundred people were injured. One man (described by an independent inquiry as an "agitator") hit by an Arwen 37 baton round was in a coma for a month and suffered brain damage. The injured man sued the City of Vancouver, but his claim that the police had used excessive force was dismissed by the Supreme Court of British Columbia. Despite this finding, a provincial police commission inquiry recommended against the use of AEPs in such scenarios. The Vancouver police service argued that until alternate equipment appeared on the market, tactical units required AEP launchers in order to ensure officer safety (Howard 1994; Furlong and Keefe 2011: 42–3).

CONCLUSION

A month before the September 11, 2001 terrorist attacks on New York and Washington, which produced not only controversial new national security legislation but also increases to the security budget of the RCMP and a more overt interest by the federal government in national security issues, a series of articles by journalists Pugliese and Bronskill suggested that the RCMP, CSIS, federal government departments and the military were already engaged in the "criminalization of dissent" and employing tactics from the Cold War era against peaceful activists and organizations. This included reporting on speeches by NDP leader Ed Broadbent and NDP MP Svend Robinson, "interviews" of activists by the RCMP and CSIS, the sharing of intelligence on the peace movement with the Military National Counter-Intelligence Unit and the carrying out of "threat assessments" of peaceful organizations such as the Raging Grannies, Greenpeace, the Council of Canadians, the Green Party, the United Church of Canada and the Nanoose Conversion Campaign (the latter was directed against the presence of American nuclear weapons at a naval testing area on Vancouver Island) (Pugliese and Bronskill 2001a–f). The common denominator with these individuals and organizations was that they were on the political left.

Although the RCMP in particular attempted to adopt a less aggressive approach to First Nations occupations and blockades by the late 1990s, the policing of mass protests surrounding political conventions and international summits raised serious questions of freedom of speech and assembly, human rights, privacy and police accountability. In response to mass public protests, the RCMP created a Public Order Program, through which the federal force exchanged "security intelligence and information on crowd control techniques" with other police services. Because of the supposed threat of violence, a spokesperson for the RCMP explained, the program also explored "non-lethal or defensive tools" suitable for crowd control (Pugliese and Bronskill 2001a). The Canadian state, in the post Cold War era, appeared to be preparing for war against protestors, the overwhelming majority of whom were attempting to peacefully exercise their constitutionally-protected rights. Future mass security events (such as the 2001 Summit of the Americas in Quebec City, discussed in the epilogue) would involve officers from three levels of policing and from across the country. Justified almost entirely on the threat of violent anarchists, these massive operations were not only displays of force but expensive training operations and exercises in bonding and occupational solidarity. Even if one adheres to a liberal/reformist view of the state, the policing of recent mass events raises disturbing questions. Following the APEC controversy, the Vancouver Police Department, which has a long and troubled history of public order policing, began to bill community organizations for the costs of policing their demonstrations (Pearlston 2000).

The policing of strikes and the political left (especially the RCMP's intelligence gathering operations on peaceful political and social movements) were classic examples of the problem of permitting the police to exercise operational autonomy from elected officials. Yet political leaders tended to defend overall police conduct in these situations, and most of the policies and incidents detailed in this chapter, when actually visible to the public, appear not to have undermined confidence in the police. A wide segment of the public that embraces "common sense" views on law and order tends to also disparage social justice and First Nations and environmental protest. As the epilogue of this study argues, the situation by the early twenty-first century, with its dual emphasis on soft and hard policing, reinforces the argument that Canadian policing, increasingly militarized and intelligence-driven, is in danger of departing from its original civilian principles in favour of a cynical counter-insurgency approach, largely removed from civilian oversight and accountability.

Notes

1. Canadian Institute of Public Opinion, news release, June 4, 1969.
2. Canadian Institute of Public Opinion, news releases, October 19 and December 12, 1970; January 9, 1971.
3. Canadian Institute of Public Opinion, news releases, April 18 and May 1, 1971.
4. Canadian Institute of Public Opinion, news release, February 20, 1971.

CHAPTER 6

THE POLICE AND POST-1945 SOCIETY

In the five decades following the Second World War, policing increasingly reflected the demands of a highly urbanized and pluralistic society. This was the heyday of the efficiency-driven model of policing based on calls for service and mobile patrols. Police services continued to tell the public, and themselves, that their primary mission was to fight crime. The era was also associated with the rise of legal/civil rights challenges to "law-and-order" policing; the expansion of the RCMP; controversies over the policing of minorities and youth; and demands to make police agencies more representative of Canadian society and more accountable to voters and taxpayers. This chapter also examines police responses to legal and social change (debates on capital punishment, homosexual rights, illicit drugs, women's rights) and new trends in dealing with communities and delivering services.

One of the key issues for this period is the impact of the Charter of Rights and Freedoms on police powers starting in the 1980s. Although legal scholars disagree on the Charter's overall significance, especially for youth and minorities (Manikis 2012), the aim of its framers was to make the state, and state agencies such as the police and courts, more accountable to the rule of law. The CACP was apprehensive of the Charter expanding individual rights, hampering the police and giving too much power to the courts, which police considered "unpredictable and unaccountable" (Marquis 1991: 403). Despite unprecedented legal, media and social activist criticisms of Canadian policing, the public remained apathetic on the issue of police governance. In the words of former Toronto mayor and police reformer John Sewell (1985: 14), "just like sex and religion it's a subject that polite conversation avoids."

The decades after the Second World War were a time of prosperity, expansion of government activity and, by the 1960s, rising crime rates. The latter was related to the Baby Boom that resulted in a larger percentage of youth in the society, yet it remains unclear if actual levels of crime were on the rise or if reporting procedures simply improved (Sewell 2010: 17). "One of the best predictors of increasing crime rates," according to Torrance (1986: 227) "is increased numbers of police." Mirroring the expansion of the welfare state and the rise of the expert, corrections were modernized with a greater emphasis on reform and rehabilitation. Municipal police departments expanded with the growth of urban and suburban populations; the latter encouraged the formation of regional forces, most famously with the creation of Metropolitan Toronto in the late 1950s.

The RCMP not only maintained its provincial contract presence, it also expanded into municipal contracts. In 1950 the federal force expanded dramatically when it took over both the Newfoundland Rangers and the British Columbia Provincial Police. According to Horwood (1986: 147), the Smallwood government agreed to "rent" the RCMP because of the financial advantages of the provincial contract. Many of the Newfoundland Rangers were absorbed into the RCMP. The situation in British Columbia was somewhat different. The Liberal coalition provincial government, with no prior warning or consultation with the municipalities, announced that it would save $1.7 million a year by contracting out to the RCMP. The public reaction was negative; many supported the BCPP, which was older than the federal force and a symbol of provincial identity, and others complained that the government had given the public no warning. Stonier-Newman (1991) notes that by the late 1940s the British Columbia government believed that Ottawa was controlling an unfair share of tax revenues and welcomed the contract as a subsidy of an essential provincial service. The BCPP, which had considerable investments in equipment, technology and a crime laboratory, also faced replacement costs and a rank-and-file demand to be paid at the same rate as the RCMP. Added to the mix was a rumour that the provincial government feared unionization of the police, which was forbidden under RCMP regulations. Another theory is that the RCMP wanted to expand its reach in British Columbia out of fear of Communism. Most of the more than five hundred members of the BCPP, who were organized in more than 120 detachments, transferred into the federal force. One of the challenges for the RCMP in British Columbia was renewed violence, including bombings and arson attacks, involving Doukhobor extremists between 1958 and 1962 (Torrance 1986: 31–3).

RAPID RESPONSE AND THE ROAD TO ISOLATION

By the 1950s Canada became one of the most motorized societies in the world, and the police followed suit. Following a trend evident prior to the 1940s, urban departments moved resources away from foot patrol to "prowl" or squad cars. Equipped with two-way radio, patrol cars could cover large areas of a town, city or rural district. Their increasing popularity spelled an end to the street-level telephone box signal systems that had structured beat activities for decades. Citizens were now more likely to telephone police headquarters for assistance. A dispatcher would then deploy one or more patrol cars to the scene. The goal for police managers who supervised this "fire-brigade" style of policing and defended it to the press and politicians was to cut response times. Motorized patrol was important for the OPP, the SQ and RCMP provincial contract forces whose principal duties were enforcing highway safety legislation. Urban police also became more involved in traffic regulation, which according to some studies increased alienation between the police and the policed. In 1959 traffic offence convictions nationally totalled more than two million (Marquis 1993: 246).

The urban beat cop, a fixture for a century, was gradually replaced by a more specialized type of officer who was somewhat removed from the community and focused on responding to citizen calls. Centralized command, the creation of large patrol divisions and the regular rotation of officers were aimed at breaking ties to specific neighbourhoods (Skogan 1992: 86–7). Despite the crime-fighting ethos of the profession, many of these calls dealt with non-criminal matters, which resulted in a considerable percentage of citizen calls being screened out. To cite a recent example, the Ottawa Police Service (OPS) in 2013 reported more than 850,000 calls for service or information; of these, 259,000 or 30 percent resulted in officers being deployed to a scene, and of these incidents, 150,000 were citizen initiated and 109,000 were internally generated. Excluding traffic offences, the OPS reported just over 32,000 *Criminal Code* offences (Ottawa Police Service 2013). Police on patrol performed traffic duty and remained on the lookout for suspicious or "out of place" people, most of whom tended to be young, poor or members of minorities. As the above examples suggest, not all recorded police activity was citizen-initiated. Operational studies such as the Kansas City Preventive Patrol experiment of 1972–73 revealed that the number or pattern of mobile patrols in the city had no impact on rates of property crime or on citizen awareness of the police presence. The trend toward patrol cars continued nonetheless but did not affect all Canadian communities at the same pace. In 1964, for example, the four hundred-person Quebec City police had only forty-two cars and twenty motor-cycles, and many constables remained on foot patrol. Yet citizen emergency calls were turning police services into more of a reactive, rather than a proactive, agency of social control. The Quebec department in 1964 received 49,000 calls for service and made more than 5,000 arrests (*Quebec Chronicle-Telegraph* 1964). Few big city police departments totally disbanded foot patrols, but walking the beat carried neither the prestige nor the promotional prospects of other assignments.

In the 1970s the spread of the 911 emergency dispatch system established the mature fire-brigade model of policing. The new model was characterized by "incident orientation" (responding to an overt act or emergency, not the broader reason behind the call); a "reactive orientation" that did not value prevention; "limited analysis" and "limited response" (Chacko and Nancoo 1993: 6–7). Police services measured efficiency on the basis of average response times and clearance rates but remained highly dependent on citizens to report and in a sense help "solve" crime.[1] The clearance rates for homicide were high, but those for motor vehicle theft and burglary were low. Police on patrol also generated crime statistics by calling for assistance, which meant that a large proportion of calls that required "officers on scene" were internally generated. Claims that the police services prevented crime were not always empirically based. And the rate of reported crimes "solved" was, and remains, relatively low, particularly in the case of property offences. A study of the Peel Regional Police in the 1970s revealed that on a typical eight-hour shift, patrol officers were involved with a single serious "contact" and two minor "contacts." Police services invested considerable resources responding to private alarms, most of which were false (Sewell 2010: 42–3, 119; Ottawa Police Service 2013).

Whether in pairs or in single-officer patrol cars (which were controversial with police associations), the typical Canadian police officer was now summoned by a dispatcher rather than the citizenry. Police-reported incidents formed the basis of the Uniform Crime Reporting (UCR) system used by the Dominion Bureau of Statistics (later Statistics Canada) to measure crime rates. Even before the full flowering of mobile policing, police culture, according to academics, had isolated the occupation from the general public. In 1962 a royal commission into the wrongful arrest of a Toronto rabbi explained that police culture "manifested in the maintenance of a bold front with the public, feats of physical courage, support of fellow officers, direct language and the use of colourful language" (Marquis 1986b: 226). The underlying assumption was that police work involved physical demands and dangerous situations and that the nature of the job made officers suspicious, conservative and cynical (Chan 2009: 2–3, 23, 297). So the real isolation associated with this period may not have been physical, but social and occupational.

Motorized patrol and the fire-brigade response, despite the official emphasis on crime fighting, did not totally cut police off from their broader functions, as only a minority of calls for assistance dealt with crime. And the more serious calls involved the same types of incidents that had preoccupied the traditional beat cop: drunkenness, disorderly conduct and fighting (Normandeau and Leighton

1993: 29). Also, half or more of calls for service in most urban departments usually originated from a small minority, 3 to 5 percent of addresses, individuals and families in crisis. In the United States by the 1980s, according to Skogan (1992: 89), police had lost contact with "ordinary people" and gained more contact with "problem people." The situation in Canada, because of lesser social and economic inequality and lower rates of violent crime, was less dramatic. Certain elements of the community were clearly a problem for the police but also a reason for expanding police budgets. A connection with the public, in the form of a tip or a witness, was also absolutely essential when it came to successfully investigating serious offences (Braiden 1993: 219–20).

The social service aspects of policing have been questioned by scholars (see, for example, Brodeur 2010: 153), but official reports for the second half of the twentieth century suggest a wide range of miscellaneous duties performed by police services. As academics have pointed out, the dominant crime-fighting image was a type of "sales pitch" by which police services justified their budgets. From time to time, the police have identified new enemies or threats to public order and safety and have suggested remedies by which they could be contained, such as new laws, new equipment, specialized units and larger police service budgets (Kashmeri 1982).

SOCIAL CHANGE, LEGAL REFORM AND POLICE RESPONSES

Starting in the 1960s, and gaining pace in the following decade, the Canadian justice system was swept by a wave of liberalization that challenged the traditional crime control rationale of policing. A series of "progressive reforms," usually pushed by lawyers, undermined police authority (Roach 2007: 83). The expansion of individual rights and due process pushed policing toward a more rule-bound environment, although police services were generally successful in fighting off the threat of external civilian review. Canadian society became more fragmented, pluralistic and questioning of authority. A better educated public, according to social scientists, expected more from public institutions. Human rights and privacy concerns were being enshrined in legislation. In addition, the police faced critical commentary from print and electronic media. The expansion of the welfare state and government support of economic development reflected an optimistic view that social and economic problems could be solved by new laws, planning by experts and increased public spending. Provincial governments passed and amended police acts, which encouraged province-wide standards and imposed a degree of regulation. In Ontario and Quebec, provincial governments also promoted the amalgamation of small municipal police services. In the area of morality, the state, often to the consternation of police leaders, became less interventionist, lifting restrictions on alcohol consumption, divorce, birth control and homosexuality. Police were not alone in resisting social and legal change; in the 1970s they were supported by blue-collar voters who generally had more in common with the police than with the middle class (Ontario 1974: 12).

Three of the era's legal reforms had immediate impacts on police operations. In 1972 the *Criminal Code* was amended to abolish the traditional status offence of vagrancy. Jailing people for being poor no longer made sense to the modern welfare state. At roughly the same time the federal government introduced bail reform, a measure designed to streamline the pre-trial process and cut incarceration costs. The measure was adopted by the Liberal government following recommendations of the Canadian Committee on Corrections. The CACP, when presenting to the committee in 1967, had opposed the spirit of the age by not only rejecting law reform but also calling for stricter laws and an expansion of police powers. The police did support one major criminal law change of the era, 1968 amendments to the *Criminal Code*, the product of lobbying by a national safety coalition, that gave police more powers over impaired drivers. The so-called "breathalyzer law" starting in 1969 established a universal minimum blood alcohol content level that defined impairment. Although popular with the public, the new law initially was enforced with considerable variation and discretion and faced a number of court challenges. Within a decade or so the breathalyzer was generally credited with having significantly reduced the rate of highway accidents and fatalities. Impaired driving charges became a leading category for *Criminal Code* charges and convictions in most provinces, almost always the result of proactive policing (Brodeur 2010: 166–7; Marquis 2012).[2]

Speaking to the CACP in 1970 Justice Minister John Turner explained that the Trudeau government viewed aspects of traditional bail procedures as discriminatory toward the poor and planned to empower police to release suspects at the scene of certain incidents and issue them a notice to appear for fingerprinting in the case of indictable offences. In 1970 the government passed legislation that gave the National Parole Board power to grant pardons in certain cases to persons with criminal records. The CACP supported bail reform in principle but expressed concerns over specific aspects. Although the vagrancy, bail and criminal records changes of the early 1970s threatened the crime control model, the police were reassured by the launch, in 1972, of a new computerized criminal records database, house within the Canadian Police Information Centre (CPIC). The plan for CPIC emerged from a 1966 federal-provincial conference on organized crime and was influenced by the FBI's National Crime Information Center (Marquis 1993: 284–5, 327–9). Once police had access to the system through terminals in their patrol cars they had a powerful tool for monitoring individuals and communities.

Another change to operational policing resulted from the amendment of provincial liquor control statutes and the adoption of practices that de-escalated the traditional approach to public drunkenness. Most repeat offenders in urban centres by the middle of the twentieth century were poor, chronic, drunkenness offenders for whom the "drunk tank" was simply a revolving door. By the 1970s relatively fewer people were being arrested for public drunkenness, and police departments, guided by provincial addiction and public health authorities, were attempting to divert many of these individuals to treatment or simply release them to the community (Marquis 2012).

The most dramatic police response to legal reform in the 1960s and 1970s was the profession's response to the capital punishment debate. This was an emotional and highly symbolic issue, and the conservative attitudes of both police chiefs and the rank and file were shared by a large part of the population. In the late 1940s the CCAC (renamed the Canadian Association of Chiefs of Police in the 1950s) reaffirmed its support for the death penalty as a cornerstone of the criminal justice system. Capital punishment for murder supposedly served the goals of specific and general deterrence. The commonsensical interpretation of the causes of crime traded on the concept of bad or defective individuals, and prior to the 1960s there were few law professors, social scientists or other experts to challenge traditional police theories on crime.[3] The issue was highly symbolic for both abolitionists and retentionists because although it concerned only a tiny fraction of convicted offenders, it set the tone for the entire system of corrections. The CACP, advising a parliamentary committee studying *Criminal Code* amendments in 1954, pointed out that most states in the United States retained the death penalty and invoked a fatalistic view of human nature — the Old Testament tale of Cain and Abel — to justify the execution of murderers.

Abolitionist opinion in Canada was muted until the 1960s, but both Liberal and Progressive Conservative governments in the 1940s and 1950s limited the use of the noose, commuting most death sentences to life in prison. In 1961 Parliament created the offences of capital murder (premeditated killing or the killing of a police officer or prison guard when on duty) and non-capital murder (punishable by life in prison). The last two murderers to be hanged were executed in Toronto in 1962 (a year when eleven police officers were killed in the line of duty). In 1967 Parliament voted in favour of a five-year moratorium on executions and limited capital murder to cases involving police and prison guards as victims. Although opinion polls suggested that most Canadians supported capital punishment in principal, the partial moratorium was extended in 1973. Three years later Parliament, by a margin of six votes, abolished the death penalty permanently. As part of the Trudeau government's Peace and Security package, convicted murderers were required to service at least twenty-five years before being eligible for parole (Marquis 1991: 397–400; Comack 1990; Marquis 1993: 265–6, 285–9, 340–5).[4]

Police chiefs, the CACP and the Canadian Police Association (CPA) representing the rank and file, opposed abolition and protested that both the moratorium and the de facto end of hanging after 1962 placed police in greater danger. Between 1961 and 1970, thirty-six officers were murdered; twenty-one suspects were convicted but only one executed. The police also pointed to the supposedly growing threat of organized crime as a reason for retaining the death penalty. The battle highlighted the reality that the police no longer monopolized law and order issues. In a brief to the federal government the CACP contrasted the "practical" criminology of the policing profession with the theoretical and impractical views of academics and warned that abolition would encourage not only more homicides but also more crime in general. In 1975 the OPP Association paid for newspaper advertisements seeking public support for the enforcement of the death penalty for first degree murder. The campaign mentioned growing crime levels and also faulted bail reform and liberal parole for contributing to the crime problem. Solicitor General Warren Allmand, responding to accusations that abolitionists were soft on crime, explained that crime prevention was more efficiently pursued through better trained and equipped police and gun control. Having lost the battle over the death penalty in 1976, the police rank and file began to attend increasingly larger public funerals for officers killed on duty and an annual memorial service on Parliament Hill in Ottawa. The funerals and memorial services added to the "common sense" view of the police as heroes and policing as a dangerous occupation. Journalists and academics viewed these exercises as cynical public relations events; Toronto police reformer and former mayor John Sewell considers them a form of "intimidation" (Marquis 1993: 342–4; *Globe and Mail* 1975; Sewell 2010: 65).

In 1979 the CPA, which adopted a higher public profile in the 1970s, an era of union militancy, spent considerable sums in a pro–death penalty advertising campaign and hoped that Joe Clark's Progressive Conservative government would reopen the issue. The growth of rank-and-file militancy was a mixed blessing for police chiefs and governance bodies. In 1964, for example, members of the CACP criticized police associations as having "divided loyalties" and "gnawing into administration." Yet the rank and file were useful allies in the quest for increased budgets and legislative change and the protection of operational autonomy (Warson 1964). The return of Trudeau's Liberals in 1980 dampened political enthusiasm for revisiting the debate, but starting in 1984 Brian Mulroney's Progressive Conservative government contained a number of "law-and-order" backbenchers. That year the commissioner of the RCMP, in advance of a pro–death penalty march by police on Parliament Hill, criticized the approach as having little place in a democratic society and possibly undermining the support of the public. With media reporting high-profile crimes such as child sex slayings and the murder of police officers, opinion polls were suggesting that a majority of citizens supported the CACP, the CPA and individual police chiefs in advocating the return of the death penalty. The Public Service Alliance of Canada, which represented several thousand prison guards, broke with the mainstream labour movement in supporting capital punishment. In 1987 Prime Minister Mulroney, who personally supported abolition, permitted a free vote on the matter in the House of Commons. The MPs (including seventy-nine Progressive Conservatives), voted down a pro–death penalty resolution by twenty-one votes, proof for criminologists that Canadian police leaders and organizations did not benefit from the same crisis-driven law-and-order politics that affected both Great Britain and the United States during the 1980s (CP 1984; Comack 1990; Taylor 1987).

Despite their defeat on the capital punishment issue, the police lobby did not go away empty-handed during the 1970s and 1980s; the Trudeau government's wiretapping and gun control changes of 1976–77, for example, fit the crime-control model (Marquis 1991: 309). During this period the CACP lobbied for a more restrictive approach to federal corrections, which were being guided by rehabilitative and cost-savings measures such as mandatory supervision, where most penitentiary inmates served the last third of their sentence in the community (more than thirteen thousand were released between 1971 and 1978). The CPA was increasingly vocal on sentencing and correctional policies such as parole, claiming in 2002 that officers risked their lives "every time they put on [their] uniform" because of early release of violent offenders (Mofina 2002a, 1993: 338–42).

Another leading criminal justice reform of the postwar era was the scrapping of the 1908 *Juvenile Delinquents Act* in the interest of providing youth in conflict with the law with the same due process safeguards as adults and removing the paternalistic status offence of delinquency. One characteristic of the enforcement of the *Juvenile Delinquents Act* was a lack of uniformity from one city to the next. The enactment of the Canadian Charter of Rights and Freedoms in 1982 invested the issue of the rights of young offenders with greater urgency. The *Young Offenders Act* (YOA), which was operational by 1984, was the result of more than a decade of negotiations between the federal and provincial governments. The police, notably the CACP, provided input into the new act, which removed the status offence aspects of the 1908 law, including the charge of "contributing to delinquency." Starting in 1984, young offenders (aged twelve to seventeen) could only be charged with offences for which adults could be charged and faced an adversarial court process, with the right to counsel and to cross-examine witnesses. In most cases the maximum penalty was two years (three years when the penalty in an adult court was a life sentence). The rehabilitative core of the original act, which had established differential penalties and protected the identities of the youth involved, remained. A number of police spokespersons feared that the YOA would encourage youthful lawbreaking, a view that was supported by mayors, victim's rights organizations and conservative newspaper columnists. During the 1990s public opinion, affected by media accounts of violent crime, believed that youth crime was rampant and that youth courts were too lenient. This pressure had some impact, as in 1992 the penalty for first degree murder was raised to five years (and in 1995 to ten years) (Carrigan 1998: 149, 253). Despite commonsensical critiques that youth crime was spiralling out of control, most of it involved minor property offences and low-level violence.

Criminologists and children's rights advocates countered that the YOA was overly punitive and that Canada was incarcerating too many youth. The conviction rate for youth courts averaged in the 60 percent range, and most offenders were sentenced to probation and/or community service. Many of the charges laid in a given year were not for new offences but administrative offences such as breach of probation. There was also evidence that "zero tolerance" policies instituted by school boards in the 1990s inflated the number of charges. The *Youth Criminal Justice Act* (YCJA) of 2003 met some police concerns but retained the key goals of diversion and rehabilitation. It also had an impact on police-generated crime statistics, as there was a noticeable fall in the charge rate for youth per 100,000 youth in the population, in large part because of the diversion options in the legislation (Marquis 1993: 362–5; John Howard Society of Alberta 1998; Sanders 2000; Mallea 2011: 75–9). As criminologists have pointed out, the discretionary power of the police under both the YOA and the YCJA, notably the decision whether to lay charges, makes generalizations about the failures or successes of the youth justice system, or trends in youth crime, empirically unreliable (Doob and Ceasoroni 2004: 84).

Another high-profile theme in the politics of law and order with a connection to youth was drugs. Until the 1960s, illegal drugs were not viewed as a major problem by police, and the courts and the moralistic police view of addicts had, with some exceptions, undercut more modern and humane attitudes and policy options. Large cities had a subculture of illegal drug users, usually junkies who used and sold heroin and were involved in larceny and prostitution. Denied treatment or much sympathy from law enforcement or medical officials, these lower-class injection drug users were among "the usual suspects" known to detectives and drug squads. In the words of Carstairs (2006: 113), "Police knew most of the users and arrested them frequently." These so-called "criminal addicts" were located primarily in Vancouver, Toronto and Montreal and lived under the surveillance of the RCMP in cooperation with local drug or morality squads. Local police usually deferred to the RCMP because of the cost of investigating drug offenders and the preference of the federal Division of Narcotic Control that prosecutions be handled by federal prosecutors (Giffen, Endicott and Lambert 1991: 537). One result of this pattern was that by the late 1960s, when illicit drugs became a lively political issue, municipal and provincial police services had little experience in the area (Martel 2006: 50–1).

By the middle of the 1960s recreational drug use was broadening out to a new generation of younger, non-criminal users who favoured the substances of the counterculture, namely marijuana, hashish and LSD. In contrast to the typical "junkie," these consumers were younger, more middle-class and educated, and most did not have prior criminal records. Because of their youth and class background, and divided public opinion over "soft" drugs, they also enjoyed considerable sympathy from journalists, educators, addictions and public health experts, judges and politicians. Responding to medical, activist and media pressure, and attempting to make government relevant for younger citizens, in 1969 the Trudeau government appointed the Le Dain Commission to investigate the non-medical use of drugs. The inquiry convened hearings, commissioned studies, accepted briefs from nearly three hundred organizations and issued four reports, including one on cannabis. In the end the government chose not to legalize cannabis, but it did enact minor changes to prosecuting and punishing drug offences and planned to move cannabis from the *Narcotic Control Act* to the *Food and Drug Act* (Martel 2006).

In testimony to the Le Dain Commission and parliamentary committees, lobbying of politicians and statements to the press, the RCMP led the police counterattack against liberalization. Police chiefs had varied views on the issue, and possibly because of this, the CACP, although expressing opposition more than once to liberalization, was not heavily involved in the debate. By the early 1970s the RCMP had more than 250 officers investigating narcotics, and the emphasis in enforcement was on younger offenders (including controversial undercover work in high schools). Starting in the early 1970s the SQ, OPP and other police services began to expand their own anti-drug operations. By 1975, for example, the SQ had two hundred officers posted to fifteen alcohol and morality squads investigating trafficking and possession, and other officers were being trained to recognize signs of drug use. The RCMP, which submitted highly-selective medical evidence to the Le Dain Commission, argued that cannabis was a gateway drug that encouraged laziness and the hippie lifestyle, was linked to theft and violence and was increasingly under the control of organized crime. Removing penalties for simple possession, the police argued, would undermine general drug enforcement. The RCMP accused supporters of legalization of not being representative of the public or having ulterior motives and reminded the commission that Canada's international treaty obligations blocked decriminalization. The police were not alone in fearing the decriminalization of soft drugs in the early 1970s and were joined by the federal Justice and Solicitor General departments, elements of National Health and Welfare, several provincial governments and a number of influential non-governmental organizations (Cleroux 1975; Martel 2006: 50–4,

121–4, 136–9, 166–9, 190–1, 196–7). The public, at least when prompted by pollsters, also appeared to be alarmed by drug use among the young.[5]

The policy and political debate of the era did result in some changes in policing and prosecution. The RCMP supposedly pulled out of direct investigations of high schools, and in 1969 a legal amendment permitted the imposition of fines for simple possession as opposed to jail. By 1972 only 5 percent of simple possession convictions resulted in incarceration. A further amendment of that year gave judges the discretion to grant absolute discharges, but this practice was not adopted in a meaningful way. Much of the public and many politicians remained convinced that Canada was being swept by a drug epidemic. Other police services expanded anti-drug operations (which were a costly addition in terms of budgeting), and this combined with the increasing popularity of recreational drug use led to more arrests, although police services admitted that enforcement efforts were uneven. Between 1973 and 1978 nearly 100,000 were convicted under the *Narcotics Control Act*, most for simple possession. Prosecutors and judges played an important role in determining outcomes; in Ontario, for example, judges made greater use of discharges in the case of simple possession charges. In contrast to the typical offence, where the police were reactive, most drug charges were laid as a result of a proactive approach, based on surveillance, informants and "buy and bust" tactics, or as spin-offs from other incidents (Martel 2006: 190–3; Marquis 1993: 346).

Despite the claims of police, prosecutors and provincial and federal officials that they were either winning or losing the battle against drugs, drug arrest statistics in no way reflected the actual nature or level of drug consumption in a community. Statistics Canada (Tremblay 1999: 5), for example, has stressed that the "level of drug enforcement by police" is the key determinant of official statistics. Yet epidemiologists and criminologists continued to attempt to measure overall drug use and its impact on society. Suggesting links between alcohol, drugs and crime was a powerful tactic for seeking research or treatment dollars, not just more police and jails. One estimate was that by the late 1990s the black market in illicit drugs was worth $7–10 billion a year. American politicians found it advantageous to launch a draconian "War on Drugs" during the 1980s that posed severe burdens on minority populations and radically expanded the prison population. Canada was affected by the rhetoric of this war, which was fanned by public fears of AIDS and "crack cocaine babies," but when the Mulroney government launched its drug strategy in 1987, the emphasis according to most analysts was on combating substance abuse (which also included alcohol) as a medical, not a criminal problem. Supply reduction was a minor part of the strategy, supposedly targeting the upper levels of domestic and international trafficking, not people selling a few joints in a bar. One of the trade-offs of Canada's Drug Strategy was that the RCMP, a police agency, was given resources for "drug awareness programs" (Tremblay

1999; Pieterson 2004). For the RCMP and other police services, drug enforcement, despite its cost and marginal impact on illegal markets, was worth the effort as it was a key "common sense" crime control program that resonated with the public (Gordon 2006: 134–5).

The official promotion of a harm-reduction approach did not necessarily coincide with a de-escalation by police services against drug users and sellers. In 2007, for example, the rate (per 100,000 population) of police-reported drug offences was the highest in thirty years. Canada's National Drug Strategy had deviated from one of its key stated goals as most arrests were for simple possession. Yet there was a dramatic fall in the rate of reported offences between the late 1970s and the early 1990s, which was possibly related to the introduction of the Canadian Charter of Rights and Freedoms. As the overall police-reported crime rate began to fall in the late 1990s, police activity against drugs, primarily cannabis, began to pick up. Perhaps police were laying drug charges for other reasons or laying extra charges knowing that the acquittal rate was 50 percent or higher. The statistics also revealed that although rates of youth accused of drug offences climbed dramatically after 1991, many were not actually charged but given cautions or diverted to various programs (an approach institutionalized as a result of the 2003 *Youth Criminal Justice Act*). Youth who were convicted usually received probation. Although cannabis offences generally dominated reported drug offences each year, one noticeable increase was the number of cannabis production offences (indoor grow-ops and outdoor fields). British Columbia had the highest rate of police-reported drug offences. In 1997 federal drug control was consolidated under the *Controlled Drugs and Substances Act*, which provided police with more options beyond laying charges. In 2007 heroin, the old standby of pre-1960s narcotics enforcement, was involved in only 1 percent of reported incidents (Dauvergne 2009).

As noted in earlier chapters, historically Canadian police services had enjoyed the support of the middle class and much of the working class, except during the prohibition era of the 1910s and 1920s. The police also benefited from a generally favourable attitude, from most members of the public, toward public institutions in the early Cold War years. A glance at arrests, court and prison statistics in the 1950s or early 1960s indicated little change in the demography of crime. The police tended to arrest young, poor or working-class males, largely for relatively minor offences such as drunkenness, disorderly conduct, vagrancy, petty theft and minor assaults. In most urban centres a small number of repeat offenders, many of whom were alcoholics, inflated arrests statistics. Starting in the late 1960s, the class aspects of Canadian law enforcement, heretofore not controversial with the average middle-class citizen, were openly challenged by that very middle class. Many organizations and individuals who appeared before the Le Dain Commission, for example, complained about police tactics in drug enforcement.

One of the most controversial incidents of the era was a raid by the Niagara Regional Police and RCMP on a Fort Erie bar in 1974. The police, armed with a special general warrant known as a writ of assistance, were attempting to disrupt the drug trade in the area. Although the traffickers appeared to have escaped, more than one hundred patrons were arrested and thirty-five women were subjected to anal and vaginal searches. The operation, condemned as "foolish" and "unnecessary" by a provincial inquiry, netted only several ounces of cannabis, most of which was found on the floor. Although controversial by the standards of the day, the raid was perfectly legal in the pre-Charter era (Borovoy 2007a: 129; Clément 2008: 137–8). Police boards and chiefs, accustomed to decades of complacency, were often shocked by mounting critiques in the media and from politicians and advocacy organizations. The more militant rank and file was often hostile. In 1974 for example, the formerly staid *Globe and Mail* embraced the liberalism of the age by not only investigating public complaints of police violence by groups such as the Jamaican-Canadian Association but also conducting its own lie detector tests on alleged victims (McAuliffe 1974).

Prior to the 1970s, aside from reactions to occasional local scandals or controversies, Canadians, at least judging by opinion polls, appeared to support their local police service, and the RCMP retained prestige as a national institution. As direct contact with the police was limited, much of what citizens knew about policing and the rest of the justice system was shaped by media reports (Gallagher et al. 2001). The more fragmented society of the 1960s and 1970s, with various institutions and traditions under attack, often elicited a conservative police response to critics. Following the lead of American scholars as such as Jerome Skolnick, author of *Justice Without Trial* (1967), academics, activists and journalists theorized that police subculture was a major barrier to fair, democratic and accountable policing. In the 1960s the older generation of police leaders remained under the spell of veteran FBI director J. Edgar Hoover, who continued to explain political and social unrest in terms of a Communist conspiracy. Former RCMP Commissioner Harvison (1967: 265–6) claimed that lawyers, judges, politicians, journalists and the public did not really understand the complexities of law enforcement. He also suggested that the privacy and other legal rights of criminals should be abridged. In 1968 the president of the CACP explained that social unrest was keeping qualified young Canadians from joining the police. Explaining that the Chicago police had acted properly at that year's Democratic National Convention when they attacked demonstrators, E.A. Spearing, head of Canadian National Railways special investigations, blamed radical "agitators" and liberal "do gooders" for worsening relations between the police and public. Yet he called on his profession to launch a concerted education effort to regain public support (Platiel 1968). Stroud's journalistic ethnographic account of early 1980s "street cops" revealed frustrations with or distrust of superior officers, politicians, defence lawyers, lenient judges and the public in general (Stroud 1984).

By the 1970s, media, politicians and academics were noticing the growing power of police associations or unions, not only in negotiating favourable collective benefits but also influencing departmental operations and disciplinary regimes (Jefferson 1981). They also competed with the CACP and regional and provincial police chiefs organizations in speaking out on criminal justice policies and lobbying government. One of the best known and most controversial was the Toronto Police Association, founded in 1944, a few years before the Ontario government authorized collective bargaining for police services. These associations were forbidden from affiliating with the larger trade union movement, strikes were banned and in the case of stalled negotiations, settlements were imposed by compulsory arbitration. In 1957, with the establishment of Metropolitan Toronto, the police association expanded into the Metropolitan Toronto Police Association (MTPA). In time police strikes were permitted in a number of provinces. The first legal strike in Canada took place in Sydney, Nova Scotia, in 1971. When police went on strike in communities such as Chatham and Saint John, New Brunswick, or Dartmouth and Halifax, Nova Scotia, in the 1970s and early 1980s, basic services were provided by supervisors and the RCMP. Disputes were not always about pay and benefits but included staffing and related operational issues. In 1964 the CACP in conference had discussed the looming threat of police unions that were exacting unreasonable concessions such as mandatory overtime and promotion by seniority (Marquis 1993: 368–9; Warson 1964).

Where they were forbidden from striking, as in Ontario and Quebec, police associations employed media relations and job actions such as slow-downs to put pressure on management. In 1976 members of the MTPA stopped wearing their hats when on duty as a protest over benefits. The police commission warned that disobedient constables could be disciplined under the *Police Act*. The association stepped up its pressure tactics, advising members to issue fewer summonses and parking tickets, to set up fewer radar traps, to issue more cautions for first-time offenders as opposed to making arrests, to refrain from high-speed car chases, to be cautious in leaving their own patrol zones, to appear in court for every summons issue or arrest made and to stop working unpaid overtime. In cities such as Toronto, police associations succeeded in opposing the implementation of single officer patrol cars or ensuring that officers patrolled in pairs in higher risk assignments and on late-night shifts. In a bold display of "worker's control," the Montreal Police Brotherhood, strengthened in 1982 by the amalgamation of all police services on the island of Montreal, unilaterally implemented a new shift system (Grant 1976; Marquis 1993: 370). The generosity of collective agreements and the prevalence of militancy in the form of press releases, job actions and strikes was proof, for some observers, that police associations wielded too much influence. For sociologist Denis Forcese, police associations were also successful in furthering the police as "agencies of repressive intervention" (Jefferson 1981).

One of the more aggressive unions was the association representing Canada's fourth largest police service, the SQ, which mainly served rural and small town Quebec. In 1971, dissatisfied with contract negotiations, the service's quasi-militaristic system of discipline and management's refusal to pay overtime for extra duties during the FLQ crisis, the SQ staged a forty-four hour strike. The strikers appeared to enjoy considerable public sympathy. In 1977 the association staged a brief wildcat strike over the issue of one-officer patrol cars following the murder of a constable. The Parti Québecois government compromised by permitting two-officer patrols for evening and early morning shifts. The association's president warned that the members would not enforce laws with which the association did not agree and that wildcat strikes could not be ruled out in the future. In 1990, taking advantage of anticipated public unrest on St-Jean Baptiste day in light of the Meech Lake constitutional accord, the SQ association threatened to boycott the national holiday. No longer permitted to strike, the association, embittered over salary levels and transfer policies, was resorting to job actions (CP 1971; Johnson 1971; CP 1977; Picard 1990, 1995).

GENDER, POLICING AND CRIME

Because of their relative insulation from politics and the public in general, militaristic policies on recruitment and promotion and tendency to be monopolized by dominant ethnic groups, police services tend to be poor mirrors of social change. The failure to reflect the actual society they serve remains one of the greatest failings of Canada's police services (Expert Panel 2014: 29–30). The postwar era produced another important innovation in law enforcement, the recruitment of women not as "policewomen" along the lines of the 1940s but regular officers, integrated into all operations. As late as the late 1950s, the few women in urban departments were valued only for gender-specific duties such as communications, morality or juvenile work. In Montreal in 1947, for example, two policewomen working with the homicide squad posed as expecting unwed mothers in order to entrap abortionists. In the late 1950s the Metro Toronto police instituted a youth bureau, which included policewomen, to not only assist the juvenile court but also amass dossiers on juveniles with whom police came into contact (Amaron 1947; Westall 1959). A suggestion that policewomen could direct traffic, guard prisoners or be assigned to patrol, for the editor of the *Globe and Mail* (1958: 6), was "going too far." In the late 1950s the Toronto police commission allowed married women to join the force but ruled that motherhood was a barrier to employment.

Although the corporate, political, legal and media sectors were still overwhelmingly dominated by men in the 1960s, women, including married women, were working in larger numbers, and their education levels and incomes were rising. Small numbers of policewomen were hired throughout the 1960s, but correcting the gender imbalance in the ranks was not a priority for police managers, and more paramilitary services such as the RCMP and OPP resolutely remained male bastions. Policewomen remained an add-on to regular juvenile, morality and detective work, and their uniforms, complete with skirts and semi-fashionable shoes, resembled airline stewardesses or workers in other "pink collar" occupations that stressed femininity. In some departments female officers carried revolvers and handcuffs in their purses. In terms of security and intelligence, the absence of women within the ranks of the RCMP until the middle of the 1970s meant that a totally male police service had to rely on paid and volunteer informants and open source intelligence for tracking the emerging women's liberation movement, which it began to monitor in the late 1960s.

Following the report of the Royal Commission on the Status of Women in 1970 and the activities of provincial governments in responding to the women's movement, it was increasingly difficult for public organizations such as the police and military to deny women regular employment. Police services did employ increasing numbers of women as civilian employees during the 1970s. Winnipeg began to hire female constables, as opposed to "policewomen," in 1974; the first women started walking the beat four years later. The department was forced to relax its physical requirements: women had to be at least five feet, four inches tall and weigh at least 110 pounds. The Montreal Urban Community Police (MUCP) hired Lison Ostiguy as its first regular female officer in 1979; a decade later the force was still more than 92 percent male. The role for female officers in Montreal in the late 1970s fell under the heading "community relations" and involved working with rape victims and youth. At this time many male officers still resented having to work with women on patrol. By 1997 the majority of women on the MUCP were constables, but there were also non-commissioned officers and officers and women were found in most operational roles (CP 1979; LeBeuf and McLean 1997).

Many police chiefs no doubt regarded the recruitment of women as regular officers as a necessary evil to appease politicians. Much like female corrections officers, the pioneering generation of women officers faced harassment and hostility from their male peers. And although by the 1980s they were being assigned to regular duties, they were especially valued in sexual assault and domestic violence investigations. Ostiguy, appointed inspector in 1993, recalled that the MUCP in the late 1970s was not prepared, psychologically or operationally, for female officers and believed that even in 1997, police management and unions were obstacles to "the complete integration of policewomen" (LeBeuf and McLean 1997: 115). Others argued that women's perspectives augmented the traditionally aggressive, action-oriented approach of policing with non-confrontational, problem-solving skills appropriate to the new emphasis on community policing. The research on these issues remains inconclusive (Expert Panel 2014: 85–6). Whatever the reasons, women finally entered the ranks of "real" policing in the 1970s. Both the OPP and RCMP hired women as regular officers in 1974. The RCMP provided "feminized" uniforms for female recruits, which were not standardized with those of male officers until 1990 (Reilly Schmidt 2013a, 2013b).

Academic studies often suggested that the measure of the success of female officers was the degree to which they embraced the masculine culture of policing. A journalist's detailed account of Canadian policing in the early 1980s depicted women in mobile and foot patrol and undercover work as being on "tentative ground" in terms of their male peers (Stroud 1984: 38). As a former member of the Laval police revealed in 1997, that culture could be misogynistic and resistant to the employment of women in regular operational roles (LeBeuf and McLean 1997: 121–4). According to one account, male veterans dismissed the first female Mounties as "crips," an abbreviation for cripples (Sethna and Hewitt 2009: 477). There were also reports of "chivalrous" attitudes and actions toward female officers, such as when they were threatened or assaulted by members of public. Partly because of problems with burnout and turnover, progress was slow. It took thirteen years for the first woman to become a non-commissioned officer in the Winnipeg department, and twenty-one years for a woman to make inspector. In 1991, when 50 percent of Canadian probation officers and 22 percent of corrections officers were female, women were only 7 percent of "sworn officers" in policing. Few of them were non-commissioned officers (supervisors) or officers (Winnipeg Police Service 2014; Mahony 2011).

One role for the small but expanding number of female officers by the 1980s was undercover work to combat street prostitution. Although prostitution itself remained legal, in 1986 the police were given more power over "communication" between prostitutes and prospective clients. The removal of vagrancy from the *Criminal Code* in 1972 had taken away a traditional tool in the police regulation of the sex trade. In its place was the offence of soliciting in a public place for purposes of prostitution. There were problems with the interpretation of the law that were only partially resolved by an amendment in 1983. Between 1977 and 1983 there were only 10,624 prostitution-related incidents reported "to" (in reality, by) the police nationally, and in some years soliciting incidents were surpassed by bawdy-house offences. The law was changed to "communicating" in 1986 because many downtown residents and business owners regarded street soliciting as a nuisance. An earlier decision by the federal government to allow each municipality to deal with public solicitation on its own terms had led to a Supreme Court decision (Duchesne

1997). One result of the post-1985 law (especially in Vancouver, Toronto and Montreal) was a jump in the percentage of males being charged. A new emphasis in police undercover work was on "johns," or customers (McLaren 1986). The law was also strengthened in the case of persons charged with patronizing or living off the avails of underage prostitutes. Starting in 1986 there was a dramatic rise in the total number of offences reported nationally, sometimes reaching levels that were five or six times higher than in the 1970s and early 1980s. In the middle of the 1990s Regina had the highest reported communicating rate, relative to population, in the nation. Feminists, legal rights advocates and sex trade workers pointed out that the post-1985 law posed a greater burden on prostitutes and made their work less safe by driving it to less visible locales. According to Statistics Canada, sixty-three known prostitutes were found murdered in the period 1991 to 1995 (this did not include the disappeared). Although a greater percentage of those being charged were men, a larger number of women were being targeted, by male undercover officers. The johns were often discharged or given light penalties whereas most sex trade workers, who already had criminal records, faced harsher sentences and probation orders that exiled them from more visible "strolls" to more dangerous areas. So in this case, the involvement of policewomen, according to one line of argument, actually hurt women in the sex trade (Marquis 1993: 366–8; Duchesne 1997).[6] The worst example of a police policy of containment of the street-based sex trade took place in Vancouver in the 1990s and early 2000s, a situation which, according to the 2013 Oppal Report, contributed to the disappearance and murder of dozens of women from the impoverished Downtown Eastside area. Many were victims of Canada's deadliest serial killer, Robert Pickton, who was arrested in 2002 (Missing Women Commission of Inquiry 2012).

In addition to the recruitment of women, police agencies faced demands from legal reformers, feminist organizations, academics and journalists to address issues such as sexual assault and domestic violence where the victims tended to be women. Activists argued that women were discouraged by police from laying assault charges against spouses or intimate partners. Complicating social norms was the anachronistic legal reality that prevented women from charging their spouses with rape. Women involved in the sex trade, most of whom faced violence on a regular basis, were not always taken seriously by police when they made complaints. Similar allegations were made about the treatment of First Nations women. Women continued to be a minority of persons charged with *Criminal Code* offences but were just as likely as men to be victims of violence. Victimization studies in the 1980s and 1990s suggested that neither men nor women were likely to report crimes of violence to the police (Missing Women Commission of Inquiry 2012; Mahony 2011). Lobbying by women's organizations, the changing attitudes of doctors, social workers and psychologists, media coverage of the issues and the responses of politicians put pressure on police organizations, which gradually began to show greater sensitivity to the issue. Traditionally many police officers responding to domestic violence complaints had not encouraged victims to press charges, a situation compounded by the attitudes of Crown prosecutors and judges. Reflecting the rise of domestic violence and sexual assault as prominent public issues, police services became more active and mandatory charge policies were debated and in some cases implemented. Haggerty (2001: 32) notes that from 1983 onwards, police agencies, reflecting changed public attitudes, made greater attempts to record the incidence of violence against women. Despite improved training and greater awareness of the realities of domestic violence, the problem persisted, with Canadian woman still being killed or assaulted by husbands or boyfriends and women and children seeking refuge in women's shelters. And victimization surveys by the early 1990s indicated that few women who were sexually assaulted ever approached the police.

The vulnerability of women to male violence was underscored in tragic fashion by the attack by Marc Lépine on female students at Montreal's École Polytechnique in 1989. In an act of rage against feminists, Lépine fatally shot fourteen women and then himself. The "Montreal Massacre" became a national issue for women's organizations and gun control groups. With the support of many police organizations, the Conservative government in 1990 began to explore how to tighten up gun control. Since 1977 fully automatic weapons had been banned in Canada and gun owners forced to apply for firearms acquisitions certificates. In 1991, as the legislative response to gun control demands was stalled, the CACP, the CPA and the Canadian Criminal Justice Association supported the Coalition for Gun Control in its call for stricter regulations. Hugely controversial with hunting organizations, gun clubs and other advocates for firearms ownership, Bill 68, enacted in 1993 by the Liberal government, required all owners of "non restricted" weapons to register them with the Canadian Firearm Registry, maintained by the RCMP. These were shotguns and rifles, the typical weapon owned by hundreds of thousands of hunters. Women's organizations viewed the long-gun registry as necessary state intervention to protect women; crime control and public health experts saw it as a mechanism for lessening violence. The police viewed it as both an investigatory tool and a way to protect officers responding to domestic violence and similar calls. Between 1961 and 2009, 133 officers were murdered on duty and 90 percent of the fatalities were caused by guns (long guns followed by handguns). Critics responded that "real criminals" did not register their guns, that most gun owners were responsible and that the police did not require such detailed information to do their job. The registry was operational by 1995; long-gun owners initially were given several years to complete the registration process. As the program became associated with cost overruns and other controversies and political resistance mounted, there were reports that many rank-and-file officers did not support the registry, despite the many public safety arguments behind it. At its peak, Canadian police services were checking the firearms registry up to ten thousand times a day (Dunn 2010; Brown 2012).

Another gender issue that intersected with policing was the plight of homosexuals. Long demonized by mainstream society, homosexuality was driven underground by social disapproval and the criminal law. Many now regard the past prosecution of gays for offences such as "gross indecency" as a form of political repression (Kinsman and Gentile 2010). In cities such as Toronto, as part of morality enforcement the police engaged in token prosecutions of men engaging in sex in public places such as parks. Police services were also aware of bars and restaurants in larger cities that were frequented by gays and lesbians. As attitudes became slightly more tolerant of homosexuality in the 1960s, many senior police officials clung to traditional morality. The head of the Toronto morality squad in 1966, for example, lashed out at civil liberties advocates for undermining morality, explaining that "homosexuals are the major carries of venereal disease." The inspector ranked gays with pornographers, illegal gamblers, drug addicts, prostitutes and organized crime as anti-social elements. In 1963 the former head of the morality squad estimated that greater Toronto was home to forty thousand homosexuals, lesbians and "bi-sexual practitioners," "perverts" who engaged in male prostitution and who were involved in "private clubs and bizarre rites"(*Globe and Mail* 1966b; Warson 1963). In 1969 the Trudeau government amended the *Criminal Code* to decriminalize homosexual acts in private between consenting adults. In 1968, with a few chiefs dissenting, the CACP had voted largely on moral grounds against any decriminalization of homosexual acts. One private sector member even claimed that "the search by homosexuals for partners often leads to assault, theft, male prostitution and murder" (Plaitel 1968).

The *Criminal Code* reforms of 1969 did not ease tensions between the police and a growing and more self-conscious gay community in the 1970s and 1980s. In 1973, for example, the Toronto Homophile Society claimed that undercover police were entrapping unsuspecting homosexuals in public parks and charging them with indecent assault. Heterosexual activity in parks, the organization complained, was ignored (*Globe and Mail* 1973). Gays also complained that they were not being protected from homophobic physical attacks on public transit and elsewhere. There were also controversies in downtown Toronto in the late 1970s and early 1980s between the gay community and the police. In 1977 the city was in an uproar following the murder of a twelve-year-old boy in the downtown Yonge Street strip that was associated with massage parlours and adult stores. The result was an intense and highly-politicized campaign to clean up that area of Yonge Street, where the Eaton Centre had just opened. Because of stereotypical associations of homosexuality with child molestation, Toronto's growing gay community suffered a backlash following the murder. In 1981, 150 police simultaneously raided four bath houses and arrested more than three hundred men, most of them as "found ins." The operation, although not unlawful, prompted a large protest march that denounced the action in general and acts of violence and verbal abuse more specifically. The provincial government responded with legislation that established the office of Public Complaints Commissioner for Policing. At the time the police rank and file was involved in political activities countering civilian review of policing and gay rights activism in the city. In a recent municipal election the MTPA had appeared to oppose police critic John Sewell, the incumbent mayor who lost the election. In keeping with Cold War style patterns of infiltration, it was later revealed that four protestors who carried a banner denouncing police brutality were in fact undercover officers. Police Chief Jack Ackroyd explained that the officers were not *agents provocateurs* but had been in the crowd "to keep the peace." The bathhouse raids occurred on the first day of a provincial election campaign where "pro-family" anti-gay organizations were active (Borovoy 2007a: 129; Clément 2008: 152; Beare 2007: 343–6). From the point of view of many homosexuals, the police were the enforcers of an intolerant society. The most tragic example of the use of gross indecency charges to persecute homosexuals, in the eyes of activists, was a controversial operation in St. Catherines, Ontario, in 1984. Using video camera surveillance, the Hamilton-Wentworth Regional Police arrested thirty-two men for indecent acts in a shopping mall washroom. One of the arrested men, possibly out of shame, burned himself to death. Despite this controversy, video surveillance in Ontario washrooms continued, under guidelines prepared by the provincial police commission (*Globe and Mail* 1985).

Related to police treatment of homosexuals in the justice system was the reluctance of police services to hire lesbians and gays. In 1977 the National Gay Rights Coalition complained that the RCMP, by continuing to define homosexuality as a "character weakness," was living in the nineteenth century. The Solicitor General explained that the federal government did not discriminate against potential employees on the basis of sexual orientation but stated that the government could not prevent individual prejudices. This theory, reminiscent of the excuses used to prevent African Canadians from volunteering in the First World War, blamed the absence of homosexuals in police services on the hostility of the rank and file to gays (Martin 1977a). In 1984 the commissioner of the RCMP retracted earlier comments that known homosexuals should not be hired as civilian employees but continued to oppose the recruitment of gay officers, not on the grounds of personal prejudice, but because police officers would oppose the move and that the reputation of the force would suffer. That year the Solicitor General announced that all security files on homosexuals had been destroyed. By 1985 things had changed; the equality provisions of the Charter of Rights and Freedoms had taken effect, and provincial governments were beginning to update their legislation to meet the new rules.

The federal human rights commissioner described as "absurd" the exclusion of homosexuals from the armed forces, the RCMP and CSIS (the military investigated homosexuality as "sexual deviation," an offence worthy of dismissal). In 1986 the Mulroney government promised to enact a more comprehensive equality policy but did little to follow up (Nierobisz, Searl and Théroux 2008). That year the attorney general of Nova Scotia, supported by the Maritime Association of Chiefs of Police, vowed that his government would invoke the "notwithstanding clause" of the Charter of Rights and Freedoms to block any federal law that dictated the hiring of homosexuals by police services. Attorney General Ronald Giffin, who also exploited public fears about AIDS, argued that gay police would be subjected to blackmail and physical abuse (Martin 1986). In 1992 the military dropped its ban on homosexuals as the result of a court challenge. Despite studies, court rulings and promises by politicians, sexual orientation was not added to the *Canadian Human Rights Act* until 1996. Prior to this time the RCMP had removed homosexuality as a supposed "character weakness" for recruits. Openly gay officers began to surface in the RCMP in the early 2000s, but in 2001 it was revealed that recruits were still being asked about sexual orientation. Research on the experience of gay and lesbian officers in this period is limited, but later studies suggest that homosexual, minority and female officers generally report less job satisfaction that the straight, white, male majority (Szeto 2014: 12).

THE ENIGMA OF COMMUNITY POLICING

During the 1970s and 1980s Canadian law enforcement agencies devoted considerable energy to community policing. Ontario's *Police Services Act* (1990), for example, identified community policing as a core principle. The rhetoric and practice of community policing had developed out of "community relations" in the 1960s, which was primarily a public relations exercise, and crime prevention thinking in the early 1970s. Looking back at period publications such as Chacko and Nancoo's book *Community Policing in Canada* (1993), discussions within police and criminology circles of the concept by the end of the 1980s now seem naive. Within police studies literature there is little agreement as to what this movement actually was, why it appeared or what it has accomplished, yet after almost four decades most police forces continue to insist that they are following its principles, and many academics report on it as a genuine innovation. Official reports continue to refer to community policing as an objective reality, but a recent justice inquiry in British Columbia investigating missing and murdered women is less sanguine: "The concept of community policing remains poorly understood and unevenly implemented in many jurisdictions," where the emphasis remains on "catching the 'bad guys,'" not preventing crime (Missing Women Commission of Inquiry 2012: 133).

Other terms associated with the movement were team policing and problem-oriented policing. The latter implied that the community, not the police, would define the "problems." The goal of one wing of this supposedly new approach was to make the community less dependent upon police services whose resources were being taxed by citizen expectations and rising personnel costs. Another was to reduce fear among the population. This was a potentially problematic strategy for police departments in that citizen calls for service were the main source of crime statistics and justification for budgets. A dramatic drop in crime could, in theory, lead to diminished funding for police services. There was also an inherent professional bias against community policing when advocates explained that it was a form of crime prevention and when community organizations expected the police to act like community organizers. The crime-fighting ethos, however mythical, was heavily embedded in rank-and-file culture, and any suggestion that its main focus should not be arresting and prosecuting criminals was bound to provoke resistance. And so were suggestions that community confidence could be built through public complaints mechanisms. To varying degrees police services were facing pressure on this front. In 1981, for example, activists concerned about police abuses in Toronto founded the Citizen's Independent Review of Police Activities (CIRPA). On the other hand there were advocates of expanding the police role in the community (Friedman 1992: chapter 4). In the early 1980s Toronto experimented with an Office of Public Complaints Commission, overseen by a civilian board appointed by the police association, the metropolitan city council and the provincial government. Few of the complaints investigated resulted in disciplinary actions (Sewell 1985: 190–2).

Specific community policing manifestations included community newsletters, liaison committees, community meetings, neighbourhood or "storefront" police stations, outreach programs such as Neighbourhood Watch and Block Parents and a reliance on volunteers and community patrols. Community policing often proposed a limited return to foot patrol in the urban core (Sherman 1998). By 1984, the 320 officers dedicated to foot patrol in Toronto barely outnumbered those in the traffic section and were outnumbered by more than seven to one by those in mobile patrol. Internally, the movement stressed decentralized command and control, a move to generalist policing and supposedly rewarding "soft" approaches. Crime prevention was viewed as a partnership with the community. Within police and expert circles, changes in the 1980s and 1990s were often described as radical, but there is little evidence that the public took notice. And in many large centres it was difficult to define, identify or organize a single "community." As a number of critics have pointed out, most of these initiatives were initiated or controlled by police services, and many of the interactions were with established "pro-police" community organizations. In the United States, minorities, tenants and residents of public housing were less likely to be involved (Sewell 1985: 78–9; Skogan 1992: 169). That community policing was the path to the future, at least for experts, was confirmed in the 1990 federal government position paper *A Vision of the Future in Canadian Policing: Police Challenge 2000* (Canada 1990). One of the goals in that document was for police services to abandon "methods of patrol that isolate them from their primary resource — ordinary citizens." *Police Challenge 2000*, reflecting its social science roots, also stressed "healthy communities," defined by "income equity, social justice, properly fed and housed citizens" and other positive social and economic outcomes (Canada 1990: 1–2).

As various community policing projects were being considered or implemented, police, criminologists and political officials began to react to the "broken windows" theory of urban pathology. This was enunciated in a much-cited article by American authors Kelling and Wilson in 1982. Their theory was that visual cues such as litter, graffiti and vandalism, combined with tolerance for minor infractions such as public drinking and urination, lowered the quality of life in a neighbourhood and encouraged more serious crimes such as drug dealing and gun violence. In this case community policing meant not doing less but doing more, by adopting aggressive patrols and a "zero-tolerance approach" (Skogan 1992: 110, 165–6). It also implied working with planners, architects and builders to design more orderly or "defensible" urban space. This seemingly reasonable case for "quality of life" policing would, in the next decade, help launch major "take back the streets" campaigns in American cities. A radical criminology interpretation views community policing as a calculated strategy to infiltrate communities and bolster police legitimacy with elites and middle-class citizens. Using the analogy of military counter-insurgency, Williams (2007) argues that community policing is not only compatible with more aggressive militarized approaches, but that the two strategies, like any military pacification of hostile territory, are compatible. Comparing police services to the military, he reminds us that standard military counter-insurgency doctrine emphasizes the provision of services to a civilian population. Within the analysis, the strategic planning and community engagement components of community policing, critics have suggested, were the roots of a strategy of enhanced surveillance and cooption, all under the guise of a benevolent image (Friedman 1992: 105–6).

Critics have argued that community policing, with some exceptions, had limited impact on the poor and many immigrants and is really designed to serve and reassure middle-class citizens. One type of police outreach popular with middle-class parents was Drug Abuse Resistance Education (DARE), an anti-drug education program founded by Chief Daryl Gates of the LAPD in the 1980s. DARE, a child of the War on Drugs, aimed at combating illegal drugs, gangs and violence. As a public relations exercise it has been wildly successful, showing that police care for children and families and, despite their lack of medical training, are the real experts on drug abuse. It is an assertion of "common sense" knowledge similar to the police response to the Le Dain Commission from 1969 to 1973. DARE was an expansion of various programs, attempted in the past, to put police officers in schools. In Canada hundreds of specially-trained DARE officers, who usually are assigned to community relations duties, delivered "zero tolerance" messages to tens of thousands of students in hundreds of elementary schools. The effectiveness of the program in meeting its stated objectives of reducing future drug abuse has little scientific backing, but DARE persists in many jurisdictions in Canada and is popular with parents of young students who are urged to abstain from drugs, tobacco and alcohol. For police agencies, the collateral benefits of the program, such as bolstering the police image and furthering the largely symbolic aspects of community policing, are more important than its stated goals (Ennett, Ringwall and Flewelling 1994; Palango 2008: 265; Expert Panel 2014: 123).

The multidimensional aspect of community policing was suggested by the 1991 document *Beyond 2000*, a planning study created for the Metro Toronto police to guide the department into the next century. A basic challenge for a city of Toronto's size and diversity was actually defining "community." The Toronto police service supposedly had been developing community policing initiatives in various districts since the early 1980s. The document had a reformist tone and embraced classic community policing initiatives such as greater civilian involvement, decentralization of command and a more nuanced approach to neighbourhoods. Rather than rely on specialist officers and squads and officers who were rotated through divisions (Toronto's version of precincts), the department of the future would ideally emphasize generalist officers who had knowledge of the community. The goal was to minimize the number of 911 emergency calls and to end the isolation of the department from neighbourhoods. Recognizing that many if not most police resources were dedicated to non-criminal matters, the plan identified a need to change public expectations of police and shift responsibility for certain problems to non-police agencies. Planners also acknowledged that the population of greater Toronto was aging and, as a result of Canadian immigration patterns, contained more visible minorities and non-English speakers. In a nod to "soft" policing strategies, *Beyond 2000* also suggested that the police service could organize community projects such as litter cleanups and encourage youth to stay in school. The plan was endorsed by both the Police Services Board, chaired by Susan Eng, and Chief William McCormick. Reflecting the bureaucratic imperative of big city police departments, McCormick warned that community policing would be expensive, as it would require more uniformed officers. In his view, the new approach would not be a substitution for traditional "law-and-order" policing but an enhancement (Appleby 1991b).

By the 1990s a counter narrative to community policing was emerging in the United States, and like most trends in law enforcement it gained some traction in Canada. Law enforcement "hawks" argued that although community policing was popular with academics, interest groups, the liberal media and certain police chiefs, it was a threat to "street cops." The latter supposedly viewed the 1970s and 1980s as an era when the police lost control of the streets to drugs, gangs and guns. They pointed to the "New York miracle," through which an expanded and more aggressive police force cleaned up the streets through a zero-tolerance approach, stop-and-frisk tactics and a mobile "street crime unit." "Taking back the streets" supposedly began when the Transit Police began to apprehend subway turnstile jumpers and uncovered weapons and persons wanted on outstanding warrants. The leadership of the New York Police Department targeted high crime areas and kept local commanders accountable through a crime analysis known as COMPSTAT. Supporters credited this intelligence and results driven approach with falling rates of violent crime but at the cost of civil liberties and relations with minority communities. Blacks and Hispanics in New York tended to be stopped in disproportionate numbers, and there was evidence of not only growing disrespect and harassment but also violence. Similarly the LAPD during this period appeared intent on creating a dossier "on most young black men" in the city (Repetto 2012: 129; Johnson 2003; Potter 1998: 199).

In the postwar years, the public police grew in number; police service budgets expanded and members were better paid, better trained and better equipped. In 1988 the total cost of policing in Canada was $4.39 billion. The structural problem was that law enforcement was mainly a municipal responsibility, yet towns and cities had limited revenue sources (usually property taxes). Each generation of policing identified new challenges and appeared to require new technology and equipment, and manufacturers and suppliers were prepared to oblige. In short, policing became big business, and protective services were often the single biggest budget item for municipal governments. The police often blamed judicial activism and the expansion of rights for the accused for increasing staffing demands and budgets. The *Stinchcombe* decision of the Supreme Court of Canada (1991), for example, required the Crown to provide full disclosure of police evidence to the defence. Police occasionally grumbled about these obligations, but in reality few criminal prosecutions proceeded to trial. The expanding size of police services from 1960 onwards was a result of not only specialization and bureaucratization, but also civilianization. In the early 1960s the police, on the national level, had outnumbered civilian administrative, support and technical staff by five to one.

Fifty years later the number of civilian employees nearly equalled the total number of sworn officers (Expert Panel 2014: 95).

Cost was certainly a driver in RCMP contracts. In the late 1970s 44 percent of the cost of RCMP contracts for municipalities under fifteen thousand people was borne by Ottawa. By the late 1980s the federal taxpayer covered 34 percent of the costs of provincial and territorial RCMP contracts but only 12 percent for municipalities with more than fifteen thousand residents (Canada 1990: 6). Budgets became major headaches for police chiefs and commissioners who were the go-betweens between the rank and file and the representatives of the taxpayers. In response to rates of crime that stabilized or even fell, police chiefs invariably took an aggressive stance, claiming that budgetary increases were essential to keep citizens safe. By the 1980s demographers and criminologists, reporting that Canada's population would age in the future because of a plummeting birthrate, predicted that crime rates would fall as would the need for police. Yet costs continued to mount, even as the ratio of police to population during the 1990s hit a plateau. By the early twenty-first century the average annual cost of a typical municipal officer (salary, benefits, pension and equipment) was $100,000. In the case of the RCMP the figure was $150,000 (Palango 2008: 268–73; Sewell 2010: 38).

The increasing cost of public policing was one reason behind the expansion of private security in the post-1945 era. By 2001, for example, Canada's 62,000 police officers were outnumbered by an estimated 84,000 security guards and private investigators. Private security guards were poorly paid and less educated than police, and more of them were women and members of visible minorities. Contract security personnel were subject to provincial licensing regulations, but these did not apply to in-house security. Private security guards specialized in patrolling private property such as malls and office complexes or working for local business organizations (Taylor-Butts 2004; Expert Panel 2014: 67–8). For example in Vancouver, Granville Mall and Gastown business interests employed a security patrol, loss prevention officers and a group of "downtown ambassadors" to counter crime, disorder and homeless people in the interest of the retail and tourism sectors. These private security personnel, who exercised the same legal powers as ordinary citizens, monitored and recorded information on panhandlers and photographed convicted shoplifters and shared the photographs with area merchants (Mopas 2005; Huey, Ericson and Haggerty 2008). In some cases, such as public housing projects, private security has been contracted by the public sector. The security guard workforce, which was characterized by considerable turnover, was both younger and older on average than the police labour force. Although lacking arrest powers and often portrayed in community policing literature as partners in the quest for safer communities, private security was often resented by the police rank and file (Marquis 2000a). There was evidence of increased cooperation between public police and private security during the 1990s, a decade when the numbers of public police ceased to grow and municipal and provincial governments attempted to impose fiscal austerity. A study of modern Halifax concludes that the city is policed by a combination of public and private agencies: "public police, private security guards, peace officers, police auxiliaries, private investigators, in-house security personnel, bouncers, special constables, by-law enforcement officers, and extra-duty public police officers" (Murphy and Clarke 2005: 228).

POLICING A MULTICULTURAL POPULATION

Canadian policing remains a profession dominated by white males whose first language in either English or French. Yet in the late twentieth century, as society changed, there were calls to make police services more diverse. At the same time that official reports and policy statements were predicting the positive, transformative potential of community policing, elements within many communities were identifying the police not as a service but a threat. In the 1970s, the new policy of multiculturalism was understood as the right for minorities within Canada to preserve their culture. By the 1990s, according to Li (2000), many associated multiculturalism with expansive goals, not just toleration but the pursuit of social equality in terms of education and jobs. Fair treatment by the justice system was part of this newer understanding. By the 1990s, minority organizations, community activists, academics and journalists were employing a new term, racial profiling, for an older set of beliefs and practices, the disproportionate reaction of police to visible minorities such as Blacks and First Nations. Community policing in theory had attempted to build bridges between the police and minority communities, yet racial profiling, according to critics, was a result of historic law enforcement attitudes as well as the more aggressive street-level policing of the 1990s, which focused on poor and minority neighbourhoods. These attitudes and practices had profound implications for ethnic and race relations. Attempts to address these problems, through minority recruitment and cross-cultural training, were uneven and resulted in resentment within the rank and file (Palango 1998: 241; see also Baker 2006).

Notable examples of this trend were anti-panhandling bylaws enacted in various cities, and media, police and political concerns about "squeegee kids," homeless or street youth who attempted to wash the windows of automobiles for money. The official panic over the homeless by the late 1980s was induced by media reports, the statements of politicians, business and tourism interests and new residents of older neighbourhoods subjected to gentrification. In the United States, the apparently growing population of homeless people, many troubled by mental illness and substance abuse, was not always looked upon favourably by the police (Skogan 1992: 185). The neo-conservative Harris government of Ontario ended up passing the controversial *Safe Streets Act,* which starting in 2000 banned not only "squeegeeing" but also a wide range of vaguely-defined behaviours. According to legal experts and social activists many of the act's provisions were unconstitutional, and the law itself was an attack on the poor and those suffering from addiction and mental illness. Gordon (2008: 75) describes it as a partial return to a vagrancy law, based on associating the "undeserving poor" with criminality. Not for the first time in Canadian history, a punitive approach was adopted on the excuse that the poor were "bad for business." A similar law was adopted in British Columbia and allowed police to ticket individuals for begging, unlicensed street sales and squeegeeing, or to ban them from specific areas (Hermer et al. 2005: 60–1; Parnaby 2003).

Since the inception of the beat system, patrol officers had employed discretion and lore to decide how they would interact with persons on the street. Detectives believed that they had an ability to "read" situations and act on intuition ("hunches"). The 1904 *Memoirs of a Great Detective* (possibly influenced by fictional detectives) had explained that discerning the truth was "largely a matter of intuition" (Phillips and Fortune n.d). As high profile examples like the conviction of teenager Steven Truscott in 1959 for murder indicate, the results of this reliance on intuition as opposed to physical evidence were not always positive for due process, civil liberties or actual justice. But most victims were too powerless to obtain justice, complain or seek redress. The media tended to ignore these issues or, by reporting on racial and ethnic minorities in a biased fashion, reinforce stereotypes and justify discriminatory practices. Police commissions, police chiefs and police unions denied that such practices existed. To do otherwise would have been admitting to systematic discrimination, something that is prohibited by provincial human rights codes and the Canadian Charter of Rights and Freedoms. Yet academic studies, including limited historical research, suggests that prior to the 1960s, systemic racism in the justice system, for example in Ontario, was a real problem and linked to a broader set of attitudes and social relations that also affected employment (Mosher 1998: 197). Recruitment statistics revealed a stark picture. In 1989, when visible minorities were 17 percent of the Metro Toronto population and 12 percent of its workforce, they were only 4 percent of the police service. In contrast, 40 percent of police parking control officers were visible minorities. The situation was worse for the RCMP and the OPP (less than 1 percent each), and for other Ontario forces the figures ranged from zero to less than 4 percent. As the Ontario Task Force on Race Relations was told by experts, the mission of police services was seriously compromised when they did not reflect the communities they served (Appleby 1989a; Task Force on Race Relations 1989).

Anecdotal and statistical evidence suggested that certain minorities were more likely to be stopped and questioned by police, both while walking and driving, and were more likely to be charged, less likely to be released on bail prior to trial and suffered stronger punishments than whites. According to Tator and Henry (2006: 211), racial profiling attributes "certain criminal activities ... to a group in society on the basis of skin colour or ethno-cultural background." A large proportion of the white population of Canada, whose views the police tend to reflect, shared these views. Tensions in cities such as Toronto, which had a growing visible minority population, were evident by the 1970s. Unlike in the United States where the collection and publication of race-based crime statistics is common, by the 1970s the practice in Canada had died out. There was support among police chiefs in the 1980s to add race as a category in a planned reorganization of the Uniform Crime Reporting (UCR) system, but the move was blocked as a result of controversies such as the 1989 claim by Toronto police inspector Julian Fantino that Blacks were more likely to commit crimes than whites (Haggerty 2001: 91–3). Starting in the late 1980s the Toronto Police Services Board prohibited publication of race-based crime statistics because of the political sensitivity of singling out minorities such as African, Chinese and Vietnamese Canadians who felt that they were being victimized by racial profiling in not only the justice system but also education, housing and employment (Lewis 1992). On the other hand, the RCMP, the CACP, individual police services and the Criminal Intelligence Service of Canada (CISC), in reports and statements on organized crime, often identified ethnic or racial gangs involved in drug distribution, extortion, kidnapping, loan sharking, assaults, murders and smuggling (CISC, organized as a cooperative criminal intelligence network under the RCMP in 1970, began publicizing its reports in the 1980s). During the 1980s, for example, police organizations warned of Chinese and Vietnamese gangs preying in immigrant communities.

Racialized policing was part of a historic pattern of inequality, exacerbated by poverty and lack of political influence, that created high rates of incarceration for First Nations people in the decades after the Second World War and tensions between the police and Aboriginals in cities such as Saskatoon. In 1961 only 13 percent of Canada's Aboriginal population was located in towns and cities; by 2011 the figure had risen to 56 percent, and many First Nations citizens reported involvement with the justice system, as victims, offenders or witnesses (Expert Panel 2014: 30). One of the more egregious cases was the 1990 death of young Neil Stonechild, who died of exposure in a field outside the city. It took thirteen years to confirm that the victim, who had been intoxicated, had been abandoned at the site by two police officers. In 2000 three additional Aboriginal men, two of whom had possibly been in the hands of the police, were found frozen to death. A similar case involving the Vancouver Police Department came to light in 1998. Although the officers involved received light punishments (in one case, a one-day suspension), publicity surrounding these tragedies yielded positive results in Saskatchewan, with the appointment of a commission on First Nations and Metis Peoples and

Justice Reform. Similarly, the trial of two men in 1987 for the murder of a young Aboriginal woman, Helen Betty Osborne, at The Pas in 1971 and the fatal shooting of J.J. Harper by a member of the Winnipeg Police Service led to the appointment of the Manitoba Aboriginal Justice Inquiry (Manitoba 1999). Marginalization does not always mean overt acts of harassment and violence; as the British Columbia Missing Women Commission of Inquiry (2012) has argued, it can also translate into the under-policing of disadvantaged populations such as Aboriginal sex workers who have a constitutional right to equal protection under the law.

In 1996 a study indicated that 43 percent of African Canadians in Toronto reported being stopped by police within the past two years. The police and their defenders in the media and political sphere countered that Black and other minority citizens were stopped more often because they were more likely to be carrying drugs or guns or to be wanted on outstanding charges and other criminal justice violations. Drug enforcement in the period 1992 to 2002 was one reason behind the targeting of minorities (Gordon 2008: 137). Complaints against the police by Toronto's Black community were evident as far back as the early 1970s. Police leaders and their supporters attempted to deflect or minimize race-based criticisms by resorting to the classic "bad apple" theory of police misconduct or suggesting that critics were a vocal minority. They were able do so in cities such as Toronto as they had the backing of conservative politicians, journalists and other defenders of white privilege. Often minority activists and supportive academic researchers were accused of being "anti-police" or attempting to impose "political correctness" on law-abiding citizens (Mosher 1998: 198).

The provincial and the federal governments were often more responsive to these issues. For example provincial officials, who in the late 1980s had responded to the 1971 wrongful conviction of Mi'kmaq Donald Marshall for murder with an inquiry into Nova Scotia's justice system, were under pressure to act on these issues in the 1990s. The 1995 report of the Commission on Systemic Racism in the Ontario Criminal Justice System and work by criminologists highlighted the pervasiveness of racial bias in law enforcement, including statistics that indicated that police were more likely to deploy firearms when arresting Blacks for minor offences as compared to whites. There was evidence that controversial American-style drug profiling, which had been promoted by the Drug Enforcement Agency, was imported into Canada in the 1990s, largely by the RCMP, which trained drug squad or street crime officers across Canada (Tator and Henry 2006: 74).

Related to general complaints about racial profiling were controversies surrounding the fatal and non-fatal shooting by police of minority citizens in cities such as Toronto and Montreal. In 1979 Jamaica-born Albert Johnson was fatally shot by Toronto police who thought that he had been brandishing an axe. At the time there were few Blacks on the 5,400 person force, which relied on a small "ethnic squad" to provide a liaison with immigrant communities. In 1987 relations deteriorated between the African Canadian community and the MUCP following the fatal shooting of nineteen-year-old Anthony Griffin, who had been arrested on an outstanding charge. Griffin was shot in the head after he fled from a police cruiser. Activists complained of a long series of police abuses in Little Burgundy and other areas of the city, and for years the MUCP met these accusations with denials that racial bias existed. In 1989 alone police in Quebec killed seven individuals and wounded nine others in more than one hundred recorded use of force incidents (Poirier 1990). Finally a reformist police chief in the early 2000s admitted that profiling was a genuine problem, and the MUCP responded with proactive initiatives. Graduates of the provincial police academy were provided with training on how to avoid racial profiling. In 2001, in *R. v. Golden*, the Supreme Court of Canada acknowledged that racial minorities received excessive attention from police and needed to be protected from "racist stereotyping by individual officers" (Tanovich 2006: 52). Yet as discussed in the epilogue, police services continued to deny that systemic discrimination existed, and conservative politicians such as Ontario Minister of Public Security and Safety Bob Runciman, an exponent of the Harris government's "common sense" approach to crime, accused Black leaders of benefiting from tensions with the police (Wente 2003).

The downside of the increased urbanization of Aboriginal Canadians was revealed most starkly by the arrest and incarceration rate of First Nationa and Metis people, especially in Canada's western provinces. Within Aboriginal culture, the image of the police was not always positive: the term for police in one British Columbia First Nations language was *nayachucknay* ("those who take us away") (Missing Women Commission of Inquiry 2012: 109). In 1997 Aboriginal Canadians were 3 percent of the national population but 12 percent of the federal penitentiary population. Within a few years they would constitute an incredible 24 percent of all federal and provincial inmates. The situation was particularly dire in Manitoba and Saskatchewan. Social deprivation and other risk factors drew many Aboriginal youth in Winnipeg's North End into gangs, creating more tensions with the police (Mallea 2011). The potential for conflict between police and Aboriginals in Western Canadian towns and cities was compounded by the heavily white nature of law enforcement. In 1998, for example, there were only twelve aboriginal officers on the Winnipeg Police Service, whose strength was more than one thousand. Brandon, which also had a poor record of police-minority relations, had only three aboriginal officers. Police officials in both centres complained that despite concerted attempts, they had been unable to recruit greater numbers of Aboriginals. In addition to mistrust based on a century or more of colonialism, the minimum education requirements of many Canadian police forces and the demand for clean criminal records excluded many members of disadvantaged minorities

(Manitoba 1999). One of the many related criminal justice issues was the plight of First Nations women, who according to activists were being assaulted and murdered in disproportionate numbers with little response from the authorities. In 2014 the RCMP released a study that suggested that Native women, 4 percent of the national female population in the period 1980 to 2012, were 12 percent of total women murdered and an equal percentage of women officially reported as missing (RCMP 2014).

Part of the move toward self-government among First Nations communities, paralleling indigenous control of education and social services, was the evolution of policing services. For First Nations leaders the use of RCMP or provincial agencies on reserves was a legacy of colonialism, yet this was how most of these communities were policed. The Department of Indian Affairs and Northern Development started a band constable program in 1969, funded by the department. By the late 1990s, there were roughly two hundred of these constables, many of them located on Manitoba reserves. Manitoba was an important jurisdiction for testing police-Aboriginal relations, because by the 1990s status Indians and non-status Indians and Metis were roughly 12 percent of the population. The original aim of the program had been to provide constables to assist outside police agencies, which often placed the constables in a difficult position. In Manitoba they were not permitted to carry firearms. Another model was tribal policing such as the system operated by several Dakota and Ojibway reserves in Manitoba starting in the late 1970s. The cost of this service was borne by the federal and provincial governments, and its governing body, a police commission, was not autonomous but included non-Aboriginal representatives. In 1973 the RCMP began a special constable program for Indian reserves. In 1989, just before the program ended, there were fewer than two hundred Native special constables across Canada (Manitoba 1999). In the mid 1980s the federal government established a task force on Indian policing. One of its recommendations, established in 1991, was the First Nations Policing Program (FNPP), through which the federal government and the provinces supported the policing of Aboriginal communities. Between 1996 and 2013 the FNPP grew from 244 to 381 communities and from several hundred positions to more than 1,200. The aim of the program was to help Canada's more than five hundred First Nations communities, which have limited financial resources, secure adequate policing services. Recently the Auditor General of Canada, who noted that Ottawa spent $1.7 billion on the program between 1991 and 2013, criticized its lack of transparency and standards and questioned the effectiveness of certain expenditures (CBC 2014b).

Since the 1960s, police reformers have advocated not only cross-cultural training to make police more sensitive to racial and ethnic minorities but also the recruitment of minorities. Progress has been slow, particularly in small and mid-sized cities where many minority recruits ended up resigning, frustrated by the attitudes of the largely male, white, Canadian-born majority. The RCMP hired its first Black recruit in the late 1960s. One major disincentive for joining an organization such as the RCMP or OPP was the likelihood of being posted to small towns and rural areas that were almost entirely white. By the early 1990s roughly fifty of the force's nearly sixteen thousand members were Black and fewer than one hundred were of Asian origin. In 1989, only 4 percent of 5,500 uniformed Metropolitan Toronto Police officers were members of visible minorities, and all officers above the rank of staff sergeant were white. Less than 5 percent of the Peel Regional Police, which served a region where minorities were 12 percent of the population, were minorities. By the late 1990s there were few Black police officers in Canada outside of Ontario. Despite this, the Police Association of Ontario, which represented the rank and file of 120 departments, attacked affirmative action for lowering the standards of the profession, much like civilian review and restrictions on the use of firearms supposedly placed officers in danger and weakened crime control (Appleby 1989b).

Toronto in the 1980s and 1990s was a vivid example of how "blue power" or rank-and-file militancy and "common sense" could act as a counter to progressive policies suggested by both internal and external reformers. Toronto's limited police complaints procedures were studied by lawyer Arthur Maloney in 1975. Starting in 1978 an ad hoc approach developed whereby in certain municipalities police services and chiefs conducted initial investigations of public complaints; if not satisfied a complainant could request a hearing before the local board of commissioners of police. The final appeal was to the Ontario Police Commission. Starting in 1981 the Toronto department, on a trial basis, established a Public Complaints Investigation Bureau. A Public Complaints Commissioner was tasked with monitoring investigations, and subject to requests by the police commission, hearings could be conducted by a public complaints board (LeSage 2005). The Toronto system was made permanent in 1984 and extended to other municipalities several years later. The bureau was renamed the Public Complaints Commission (PCC). Under this system police chiefs and the commissioner of the OPP still wielded considerable power, and it did not solve the issue of police investigating police. Although empowered to conduct its own investigations, the PCC in the period up to the mid 1990s rarely did so (Hess 1996).

The *Police Services Act* of 1990 required Ontario police departments to set up public complaints investigation bureaus, and the PCC was assigned a mandate for the province. In 1992 a permanent board of inquiry was added to the complaints system. Citizens were able to make complaints directly to police services, to the commissioner or to the complaints board. The NDP government also instituted a requirement that officers who unholstered their guns had to file a mandatory report. The MTPA object to this "red tape" burden, suggesting that in certain divisions officers were deploying their weapons several times a week. Police chiefs still wielded considerable powers within the system; for example, they were able to order "no further action" in the investigation of complaints. In 1996, citizens filed 3,549 complaints with the police, but the PCC carried out only twenty-four investigations (LeSage 2005: 22). Following the 1995 election of the Harris Conservatives, who promoted a "Common Sense Revolution," the public complaints system was changed in order to remove community input. In 1997, the Ontario Police Commission was renamed the Ontario Civilian Commission on Police Services (OCCOPS) with a mandate to review police chiefs' responses to public complaints and to handle appeals in police disciplinary cases. OCCOPS also dealt with disputes between police services boards and municipal councils over budgets (LeSage 2005).

In 1988, following an investigation by the PCC, a Toronto constable was fired for assaulting a citizen. In response the MTPA, in a protest against civilian review, urged members to stop issuing parking tickets and summonses (Downey 1988). Although only 5 percent of all complaints before the PCC in 1987 had resulted in disciplinary action, in 1991 a journalist reported on growing unrest among the membership of the MTPA, who felt that they were "under siege" and were "fed up with all the criticism" (Appleby 1991a). Under pressure from reformist police commissioners appointed by the NDP government, the union admitted to no wrongdoing by the department or its members, and lashed out at the media, liberal judges and a public complaints office that was supposedly biased against the police (ibid.). Police and their political and media allies often fell back on the "police as heroes" defence and suggested that critics were jeopardizing the safety of both police and the public. The MTPA, experienced in fighting media and political campaigns against police reformers such as Toronto mayor John Sewell, remained hyper vigilant. One target was Susan Eng, a lawyer who became chair of the Police Services Board in 1991. In 2007 a media leak disclosed that in 1991 the Metro Toronto Police intelligence bureau, which was housed under detective services, had conducted surveillance, including telephone wiretaps, on Eng when she was chair and her friend, lawyer Peter Maloney. The documents disclosed in 2007 suggested that the police had investigated Maloney as a "security risk," but Eng believed that she had been monitored as she has been an outspoken critic of the police prior to her appointment. The chief of detectives in 1991 had been Julian Fantino, later chief of the force and, starting in 2007, commissioner of the OPP (Vincent 2007).

The main issue motivating rank-and-file protest in early 1990s Ontario was the institution of Canada's first civilian agency to investigate major wrongdoing by police. Following the shooting of a number of Black men by the Toronto police and mounting concerns about declining public confidence in the police, the provincial government appointed a task force in 1988. The Special Investigations Unit (SIU), a recommendation of the Task Force on Race Relations and Policing, was formed in 1990 with a mandate to investigate police-involved cases of sexual assault and serious injuries, deaths in custody, deaths from firearms and fatal collisions. The SIU had no jurisdiction over the RCMP or First Nations police. The SIU, an agency of the provincial Solicitor General, was operational starting in 1991, a period that coincided with the highly publicized Rodney King beating in California. Its job was not to handle "normal" complaints but investigate serious incidents. In 1992 Toronto experienced limiting rioting following the fatal shooting of Raymond Lawrence. The new agency was criticized from all sides. Police reformers and civil liberties advocates pointed to its limited resources, low-profile and non-aggressive approach, fuzzy mandate and reliance on former police officers as investigators. Yet many police services, the OPP Association and the MTPA were often hostile toward not only the SIU but also the very concept of civilian review of police misconduct. Compliance was uneven, and even the definition of serious incidents or injuries was in dispute (Jones 2012; MacAlister 2012).

The organized lower ranks appeared to oppose the very principal of civilian review. In 1993 Canadian police associations took part in a meeting of police associations in the United States that identified four major challenges to the rank and file: rising crime, budgetary pressures, tough contract negotiations over pay, benefits and complement and civilian review (Gammage 1993). In 1999 the Ontario *Police Services Act* was amended to require police chiefs to report any police-involved deaths or serious injuries to the SIU, yet the agency continued to learn of incidents from the media, not police services. André Marin, who served as SIU director and Ontario ombudsman, has described the agency as a "paper tiger." He also noted that despite resistance and criticism from police agencies and unions, SIU inquiries had exonerated all but 3 percent of officers investigated. Between 1993 and 2003, fewer than forty cases investigated by the SIU had resulted in charges (Marin 2012).

Despite localized and short-term controversies over the use of force, attitudes toward minorities or disputes over budgets, opinion polls continued to suggest that by the late twentieth century most Canadians supported the police as an institution (Tufts 1999) and viewed their primary mission as fighting crime, despite statistical evidence to the contrary (Expert Panel 2014: 28). Reports of violent crimes, organized crime and gangs, atmospheric journalistic accounts such as Stroud's *The Blue Wall* (1984) and the public relations of police associations conveyed to the public that policing was a dangerous occupation and that police deserved the support of the citizenry. Yet police services, as the example of community policing indicated, did not take this support for granted, particularly in the age of neo-liberalism when spending on public services was under attack. Increasingly the police voiced concerns that they were being forced to fill the gap when other public services had budgets frozen or slashed. Community policing, despite its ambiguous nature, was an attempt to regain public confidence and enhance legitimacy during an era of rapid social change. It was resisted by an occupational culture that rewarded solving major crimes and by hierarchical command and control structures. During the last three decades of the twentieth century the profession projected a dual face to the public: community policing and DARE officers on the one hand and a more militarized approach on the other.

The more aggressive look to policing included re-arming patrol officers with semi-automatic pistols, on the theory that police needed to match the firepower of criminals. Such was the recommendation of an Ontario Solicitor General's committee in 1990. Although Ontario police chiefs appeared to have mixed views on the need to relinquish the traditional .38 calibre revolver, the CPA argued that nine millimeter semi-automatic pistols were safer, more accurate and easier to use. Critics worried that arming police with the new weapons would give officers a more aggressive look and increase the chance of fatal shootings (Rogers 1990). Human rights and minority activists in Montreal feared that despite training and departmental and provincial rules governing the use of force, equipping officers with more powerful guns would lessen the likelihood of them using batons, pepper spray and other non-lethal types of force in threatening situations (*Montreal Gazette* 1993). In 1998, the Royal Newfoundland Constabulary (RNC) became the last police service in Canada to equip officers with pistols. Previously the RNC, which policed St. John's, Mount Pearl, the northeast Avalon Peninsula, Cornerbrook and Labrador West, had kept firearms locked in the trunks of their patrol cars and were required to seek permission of a senior officer before arming themselves. The RCMP in other parts of Newfoundland and Labrador were fully armed. The change in policy ended a century and a half of the unarmed constabulary in Canada.[7]

CONCLUSION

By the 1990s Canada's police services were facing more complex social and political environments. In addition to budgetary pressures driven in part by expectations of the rank and file for attractive wages, benefits and pensions, there were the challenges of increased oversight by the courts, criticism by organizations representing racial minorities and increased scrutiny by the news media, which was attracted to controversial issues. Police services made small to medium gains in attracting female and minority recruits, and recruits were both better educated and older than in the past. But police culture remained resistant to "lowering standards" for political reasons, which increased tensions with management. According to one recent study, diversification has had a "window dressing effect," an "appearance of positive action" that masked internal divisions over minority recruitment (Szeto 2014). And for the most part police chiefs and associations were successful in blocking or limiting civilian review of most citizen complaints, which prompted the Ontario Civilian Commissioner on Police in 1992 to decry a "culture of denial and insularity" (Martin 2007: 278).

Although technology was bringing many benefits to police services, it also represented a threat. In the interest of officer safety, but also to meet evidentiary rules and to curb citizen complaints and lawsuits, police services began to videotape interviews and interrogations of suspects by detectives and equip booking rooms, cell blocks and patrol cars with video cameras. Mass computer ownership, digital technology and the spread of low cost, handheld video cameras and personal cell phones allowed ordinary citizens to record and disseminate police interactions with the public. The potential of citizen journalism to publicize hitherto low-visibility police abuses of authority was dramatically proven by the Rodney King affair, where a citizen's video camera footage showed officers assaulting King. The advent of the Internet and social media by the end of the twentieth century also showed the potential of citizens to turn their own "vigilant eye" against the police. The Dziekanski incident of 2007 (discussed in the epilogue) became a national controversy as the result of a cellphone video (CBC 2014d). Surveillance technology in the hands of the police such as closed-circuit television (CCTV) troubled civil liberties advocates, but technology also had the potential to protect citizens from violent, illegal and uncivil treatment by the police. The Ontario Human Rights Commission (2003) for example, supported video cameras in police cruisers to help protect the rights of the province's two million visible minority residents. A decade later a number of police services such as the OPP had adopted dashboard cameras especially for traffic units, but their use was not uniform across Canada. In the second decade of the twenty-first century, police services began to experiment with body-worn cameras (BWCs). Governance bodies hope that BWCs will have a "moderating effect" on both the police and public and ensure that officers treat all citizens with respect. The proliferation of video cameras in police operations has raised privacy concerns among the police. Apparently not aware of the irony, the head of the MTPA worried about the impact of "Big Brother surveillance" on the rank and file (Tator and Henry 2006: 138; Gillis 2014).

Notes

1. Statistics Canada defines clearance rates as follows: "The clearance rate represents the proportion of criminal incidents solved by the police. Police can clear an incident by charge or by means other than the laying of a charge. For an incident to be cleared by charge, at least one accused must have been identified and either a charge has been laid, or recommended to be laid, against this individual in connection with the incident. For an incident to be cleared otherwise, an accused must be identified and there must be sufficient evidence to lay a charge in connection with the incident, but

the accused is processed by other means for one of many reasons" <statcan.gc.ca/pub/85-002-x/2012001/definitions-eng.htm#c47>.

2. Canadian Institute of Public Opinion, news release, April 12, 1970.
3. Canadian Institute of Public Opinion, news release, April 7, 1971.
4. Canadian Institute of Public Opinion, news release, February 2, 1972.
5. Canadian Institute of Public Opinion, news releases, September 19, 1970, and November 13, 1971.
6. Also Leslie Jeffrey, communication with author, February 23, 2015.
7. Newfoundland and Labrador Department of Justice, news release, November 28, 1997.

EPILOGUE

THE PRICE
OF BEING SAFE?

A 2013 Statistics Canada report indicated that Canada's most heavily-policed provinces, based on police officers relative to population, were Alberta and Newfoundland and Labrador. Almost two thirds of all public police were in two provinces, Ontario and Quebec, where the dominant models are provincial, regional and municipal constabularies. In Quebec the number of police services was reduced considerably between 2001 and 2014. During this same period the OPP also continued to expand its municipal contacts. Outside of central Canada, the RCMP was an important if not dominant presence, constituting 100 percent of officers in the Yukon and Northwest Territories and Nunavut. In British Columbia, RCMP under provincial and municipal contracts outnumbered municipal police by more than two to one. The Mounties, who "invaded" the Maritimes in the 1930s and Newfoundland after it joined Confederation, outnumbered municipal police in New Brunswick, PEI and Newfoundland and Labrador. Nationally, municipal governments, who rely primarily on property taxes for revenue, are responsible for 60 percent of total policing expenditures. Policing in the new century was still marked by a noticeable gender imbalance. As of 2009, roughly one in five constables was a women, and 12 percent of non-commissioned officers and 7 percent of officers were female (Statistics Canada 2013; Mahony 2011).

One significant change for both security and intelligence and policing in general was the passage in 2001 of Canada's first permanent anti-terrorism law. As noted in Chapter 5, the *Public Order Act* that followed the 1970 October Crisis had been a temporary measure. Passed in the wake of "9/11," the attacks on the New York

Trade Towers, Bill C-36, the *Anti-Terrorism Act* (ATA), defined terrorism and created new types of offences such as financing terrorist efforts. In part the law was enacted to reassure the United States, which in 2001, a dozen years after the end of the Cold War, created a Department of Homeland Security and launched a global "War on Terror." There was considerable support within Canadian political, policy and economic circles for the creation of a "North American security perimeter" (Whitaker, Kealey and Parnaby 2012: 433). One impact of the "war" was to make local and state police more active in gathering and sharing terrorism- related intelligence. Controversial with civil liberties advocates, the Canadian law centralized powers in the federal cabinet, allowed the federal government to ban organizations it deemed terrorist and included extreme penalties for various offences. The secretive Communications Security Establishment, a signals monitoring unit of the military, was permitted to share information with CSIS, the RCMP and Canadian Customs and Revenue (Palango 2008: 86). One power granted police, which as of the time of writing has yet to be used, was "preventive arrest" for up to seventy-two hours. Although few individuals were charged under the law (the first conviction was in 2008), the new security awareness benefited both the RCMP and CSIS and further blurred the boundaries between national security and law enforcement (Macleod 2015). As Whitaker, Kealey and Parnaby (2012: 437–8) explain, the ATA awarded few new powers to CSIS (although the government did expand the agency's budget) but expanded the role of the RCMP in the national security area.

The overall impact of the new geopolitical situation after 9/11 was a heightened sense of crisis, troubling to civil liberties and human rights advocates, that spilled over into security and intelligence, border security, airline travel and immigration and refugee policy (Borovoy 2007b). Civil liberties advocates feared not only increased threats to individual privacy and a chill against free speech but also anxieties over national security issues having an impact on criminal law, policing and corrections. Both border security and the treatment of refugees became more militarized and punitive. In 2003 the government of Canada, whose citizens for decades had taken solace in having low crime rates and no immediate enemies, organized a Department of Public Safety and Emergency Preparedness (now called Public Safety Canada), which was now responsible for the RCMP and CSIS. The Canadian Border Security Agency (CBSA), a merger of Canada Customs and enforcement personnel from Citizenship and Immigration Canada and the Canadian Food Inspection Agency, was formed that same year. Within a few years CBSA officers, formerly equipped with batons, handcuffs and pepper spray, were issued Beretta pistols, a dramatic symbol of Canada ceasing to be, in the eyes of politicians, a "peaceable kingdom."

As Murphy (2007) has noted, the higher profile of national security post 2001 resulted in policing in general becoming more "securitized." Examples included

Integrated National Security Teams (INSETs) and Integrated Border Enforcement Teams (IBETs). INSETs include the RCMP, CSIS, CBSA and other federal departments and agencies and provincial and municipal police services. IBETs included American federal and state agencies (Whitaker, Kealey and Parnaby 2012: 441). In a brief to a parliamentary committee in 2005, the British Columbia Civil Liberties Association expressed concern that the RCMP, in the name of national security, had targeted "animal, environmental and aboriginal activists and Muslim clerics" (British Columbia Civil Liberties Association 2005: 4). The association was also critical of the ATA's overly broad definition of terrorism, the abuse of security certificates to detain and deport non-citizens, a chill against legitimate dissent and "secret evidence" and "closed courtrooms" (ibid.: 31).

One the few publically-visible results of the *Anti-Terrorism Act* was the arrest of the so-called Toronto 18 in 2006. This investigation indicated that the newest threat to Canada (as defined by security agencies) — radical Islam — was being closely monitored and countered by methods that dated back to the 1920s. The suspects, three of them minors, were arrested for plotting to attack the Toronto Stock Exchange, the headquarters of the Canadian Broadcasting Corporation and of CSIS and the Parliament Buildings and to kidnap and murder the prime minister. In 2003 twenty-three Islamic men had been arrested in Toronto, but in the end terrorism-related charges were dropped and a number of the men were deported for violations of immigration regulations. The group arrested in 2006 had been under surveillance since 2004 and was infiltrated by two moles; one a paid confidential informant, who became an RCMP agent, arranged to supply the conspirators with fake bomb-making materials. Although sometimes portrayed as inept amateurs who knew nothing about firearms or explosives, the group had the potential to inflict real harm. In the end eleven of the men were charged, and by 2009 five had admitted guilt. Other convictions followed, and the courts rejected the defence argument of entrapment (Brodeur 2010: 237–8).

The degree to which the War on Terror subjected Canada's security, border control and law enforcement policies, and the privacy and other rights of its citizens, to American national security interests was highlighted by the Mahar Arar affair. Arar, a Canadian citizen born in Syria, was detained by the U.S. authorities in 2002 on the basis of information provided by the RCMP. The intelligence provided was undigested and contained errors and falsehoods and was not subjected to the normal high-level scrutiny before its transfer to the FBI. In 2001 the RCMP had been asked by an overburdened CSIS to take on a number of national security investigations of individuals with suspected ties to Al Qaeda. The effort had been partly prompted by requests by the FBI to investigate individuals who were deemed threats to the security of the United States, but it soon focused on preventing terrorist attacks in Canada. Project O Canada appeared to be uncritically concerned with convincing the American authorities that the RCMP was diligently fighting terrorism. With the involvement of the CIA the Canadian was subjected to "rendition," ending up in a Syrian prison where he was tortured into confessing that he had taken in part in Al Qaeda military training.

The American decision to deport Arar not to Canada, where he had been a citizen since 1995, but to Syria was likely based on the regime's practice of torturing political prisoners. The Syrian authorities, who at this time were cooperating with the Western War on Terror, eventually released Arar and he returned to Canada where his case was subject of a federal inquiry. Prior to this, Arar, like other Canadians jailed and tortured by the Syrian government, was subjected to a smear campaign by Canadian officials. In 2006 the O'Connor Inquiry, appointed by the government of Prime Minister Paul Martin, determined that Arar was not a terrorist but a wrongfully accused citizen and placed some blame for his mistreatment on the RCMP. The Canadian government and the RCMP apologized to Arar, and in 2007 he accepted a $10.7 million compensation package. The American authorities in contrast continued to view him as a security threat. Following the inquiry report, the commissioner of the RCMP resigned. The entire affair raised troubling questions about the accountability of Canada's security apparatus, particularly with the spread of collaboration among police and intelligence agencies, both within Canada and beyond its borders (Canada 2006; Pither 2008).

As criminologist Chris Murphy noted in 2007, the "securitization" of policing re-invigorated police services, especially the RCMP, after a decade or more of stagnant personnel growth and mounting doubts as to the actual effectiveness of policing. Between 2001 and 2006 national expenditures on policing rose between 5.3 and 7.7 percent yearly, and the number of uniformed and civilian employees grew. Police powers were expanded and "community safety" took on new meanings in the "insecurity discourse" of opportunistic politicians and police leaders. The increased emphasis on national security challenged "core policing," and community policing was in danger of being subverted into a mechanism for infiltrating "suspect communities." The other casualties of "securitized" policing, Murphy feared, would be transparency and public accountability, which were seriously compromised by the move toward integrated policing. The advent of an open-ended War on Terror added new intensity to a populist law-and-order agenda that identified crime as a top social problem, declared that it was caused by criminals, argued that victims, not offenders, deserved sympathy and assumed that enforcement and corrections strategies could actually make a difference (Reiner 2012).

The long-standing practice of the RCMP delivering rural and urban policing continued to create not only tensions within the policing world but also challenges for accountability and civilian oversight. In terms of discipline and public complaints, for example, the RCMP is not under provincial police acts; formal complaints against the Mounties are investigated by the Mounties. As Marin (2012) notes, Ontario's embattled SIU, although operating for a generation, has suffered from police mistrust and resistance and a lack of a clear legislative mandate. While police leaders believe that their oversight and complaints mechanisms are fairer and more effective than those of the United States, civilian critics are less convinced. Provincial governments have introduced SIUs and other accountability mechanisms, and in 2013 Parliament passed the *Enhancing RCMP Accountability Act*, which enhanced review procedures of serious incidents and modernized internal disciplinary mechanisms (Expert Panel 2014: 77). What protects police services from fuller accountability and civilian review is a combination of the tradition of operational autonomy on the one hand and public apathy on the other. The latter is reinforced by political and media voices that remind the public that trusting police services with a high degree of autonomy and authority is "the price of being safe."

The media, politicians and most of the public continue to mistakenly view the police primarily as crime fighters. The professional model has stressed this role since the early twentieth century, and in recent years police services have identified new threats to justify resources, such as cybercrime, child pornography and human trafficking. The contested nature of this claim, which for decades has been the cornerstone of police culture and resistance to civilian control and oversight, is suggested by 2009 statistics on crimes reported to the police. As noted elsewhere in this study, this set of statistics is not necessarily the best measure of criminal activity in Canada. Other studies estimate that at best 30 percent of crimes are reported to the police. The 2009 statistics (which excluded traffic-related offences) indicate that roughly 28 percent of reported offences involved violence, most of it interpersonal, such as assaults. Although technically "crimes," it would be difficult to argue that most of these offences were committed by "criminals." Similarly, 36 percent of reported offences were property crimes of a minor nature, more acts of desperation than part of a crime wave. Less than one third of 1 percent of reported offences were prostitution related, and drug violations constituted less than 1 percent of the total. More than 160,000 reported offences dealt with "criminal justice violations," violations of bail, probation, parole and various judicial undertakings. Almost absent from this list of offences are white-collar or corporate crimes. Even the traffic offence totals mask a large percentage of administrative offences such as failing to carry a driver's licence or proof of insurance. The reports of individual police services also suggest that serious crime is relatively rare. Without discounting the seriousness of offences such as sexual assault, robbery and extortion, it is difficult to reconcile the statistical evidence with dramatic claims about the police safeguarding Canada from a deluge of crime and disorder (Mahony 2011; Toronto Police Service 2011; Service de Police de la Ville de Montréal 2012; Ottawa Police Service 2013; Expert Panel 2014).

Then there is the issue of falling crime rates. On a national level the police-reported rate grew from 1961 to 1991 and then began a gradual decline. The rate of violent crime stabilized during the 1990s and early 2000s, but the rate of property offences dropped more dramatically (Statistics Canada 2013). *Criminal Code* offences per officer, on a national level, have been falling, although services such as the OPP report that traffic offences have remained stable. The situation is different with the policing of Aboriginal communities, especially remote reserves, whose rates of violence crime have increased. In recent years, law-and-order politicians, adopting more punitive victim's rights stances, have argued that official statistics do not reflect the actual extent of crime. In response to neo-liberal demands that their budgets be slashed in light of falling crime rates, police services have begun to publicize evidence that up to 80 percent of calls for service are "non-criminal," meaning that they rarely result in the laying of a *Criminal Code* charge. This pattern is a modern reminder of Weaver's observation on how the police became entangled into their communities. And in most jurisdictions, the "other" category, because of pressures on housing, social welfare and mental health budgets, has been growing. Within the police policy field, the growing and complex demands for police services have been situated with a "safety and security web," which consists of "private security, local health professionals, community and municipal groups — and other government organizations" (Expert Panel 2014: xi).

Most citizens in Canada have few contacts with the police other than seeing their vehicles on the street or highway, and most will never visit a police station, a courtroom or a jail. A 1996 Department of Justice study suggested that 20 percent of Americans had contact with police in the past year, mostly in traffic stops. One in every five hundred contacts had involved the threat or use of force. Visible minorities, specifically African Americans and Hispanics, were more likely to be stopped (Williams 2007: 13–4). By the late 1990s a majority of Americans and an overwhelming majority of African Americans believed that racial profiling was a reality (Gallagher et al. 2001). Recent operational studies indicate that a high volume of calls for service originate from specific individuals and neighbourhoods. Statistics Canada reported in 1999 that most Canadians were satisfied with the police but that persons who came into contact with them, either as victims or suspects, were less positive (Tufts 1999). Attitudes toward the police and the justice system are shaped by experience: "The law generally works for the dominant group, frequently to protect its interests and assets" (Manitoba 1999: chapter 16). The dominant group usually justifies controversial measures as necessary for the security of the public. In general, Canadians have experienced policing differentially based on a combination of race and/or culture plus socio-economic condition. The extreme example of this phenomenon, exemplified by First Nations individuals and communities, is a combination of over and under policing. Aboriginal victims, for example, feel that police do not take their complaints seriously. Tensions are higher in those urban centres with higher concentrations of First Nations population, such as Winnipeg, Regina, Saskatoon and Prince Albert, and of visible minorities, such as greater Vancouver and greater Toronto. The RCMP has attempted to hire more First Nations members, but few of the individuals recruited have been raised in reserve communities (Clairmont 2006: 16).

For Toronto's 300,000-strong African Canadian community, the police service's policy of carding (subsequently rebranded as "street checks") was especially problematic. In an era of falling crime rates, police services in large cities embarked on an aggressive approach, in the name of combatting gangs, drugs and street crime, by stopping people on the street and entering personal details such as name, gender, family status (even whether parents were married or divorced), names of associates and skin colour into a criminal intelligence databank. Few of the individuals were charged with offences as a result of the stops and almost none of them were engaging in suspicious activities. This data collection exercise was part of an intelligence-led policing strategy. Within three years the Toronto Police Service collected more than one million field information cards. As revealed in a series of investigative articles in the *Toronto Star* in 2002, carding appeared to have a strong racial slant, as Blacks, who were 8 percent of the population, constituted 27 percent of all persons stopped. In response to criticisms, the police service explained the patterns not in terms of race but socio-economic factors. The police chief, police union, police services board, the CACP and many politicians defended the practice in the name of both public and officer safety. The MTPA launched a lawsuit against the *Star* for defaming its members as racist (Rankin, Quinn, Shephard, Simmie and Duncanson 2002; Tator and Henry 2006: 128–9). The Law Union of Ontario (2014) deemed the program "a systematic violation of the rights of the people" and complained that officers often misrepresented why they were stopping individuals. In response to legal criticisms, supporters argued that carding was similar to random vehicle stops, which the courts have upheld, and was race neutral. In terms of minority resentment against the department, the deputy police chief explained that the institution was not responsible "for all the social ills that befall … a 24/7 service provider" (*Toronto Star* 2014). Following the media exposé, the volume of carding fell. The number of people carded in July 2013 was 75 percent less than during the previous July, possibly because officers were now required to provide persons stopped with a receipt (Rankin and Winsa 2014). The police service renamed the cards "community safety notes" but refused the request of the Toronto Police Accountability Coalition to end the practice and purge the data. Media reports have suggested that an officer's "card count" is part of his or her performance evaluation and affects promotion and pay (Rankin and Winsa 2012, 2013; Toronto Police Accountability Coalition 2015).

Since the turn of the twenty-first century the RCMP has experienced a series of scandals and controversies that constitutes the most serious threat to the force's legitimacy since the 1970s. Criticisms were especially visible in British Columbia, where more than half of the population was served by the force and where municipal leaders expressed dissatisfaction at levels of service (Palango 2008: 274–9). Both the RCMP and the Vancouver Police were criticized for failing to properly investigate the Robert Pickton serial murder case and protect sex workers from Vancouver's Downtown Eastside. Pickton was convicted of six counts of second-degree murder, but forensic teams found DNA from at least thirty-three women on his Port Coquitlam farm and he bragged of killing more. There were also allegations of harassment of female officers within the organization, resulting in a high turnover of female members and the failure of the force to meet its gender complement targets. In 2010 RCMP leadership announced that it planned to make the institution reflective of Canadian society. This would fight the tide of history, as it meant that white males would become a minority on the force. Employment equity goals to that date had been disappointing, with recent graduated classes of recruits comprising only 17 percent women, 7 percent visible minorities and 2 percent Aboriginal. The goal set in 2010 was for future classes of graduated recruits to be 30 percent female, 20 percent visible minorities and 10 percent Aboriginal. The RCMP was not the only police service failing to meet its diversity goals. The strategy supposedly caused some resentment from veteran officers who supported "merit" as the basis of recruitment (if not promotion) and continued to view policing as a physical occupation (Expert Panel 2014: 46–7; Freeze 2010).

Women did begin to make greater inroads into policing in the early twenty-first century, but as late as 2012 Status of Women Canada noted that no Canadian police agency had initiated specialized gender audits. By 2009, 20 percent of police officers in Canada were women, and individual forces, such as the Royal Newfoundland Constabulary, had made concerted efforts to attract female recruits. Research indicated that recruitment was only half of the equation; many women left policing before they were eligible for a pension, and many decided not to apply for promotion or specialized units because they believed that the process was based not on merit but traditional gender lines. This was a more subtle but still powerful disincentive to recruitment and retention than faced by the pioneer female officers of the 1970s and 1980s, who had faced inappropriate remarks, sexual advances, skepticism, patronizing attitudes and even hostility from male officers. Female officers also cited pressures relating to children and family. Status of Women Canada also reported that most police commissions and community advisory committees had made good progress with equal gender representation (Expert Panel 2014: 46–8).

Other recent controversies are related to the cost of policing. As crime rates

continued to fall after 2000, politicians began to question the wisdom of supporting large, well-funded police services with many specialized squads. In a parallel
to the end of the Cold War, potential savings for the taxpayer were viewed as a
"peace dividend." These did not materialize. Criminologists tend to explain the
drop in crime rates not in terms of more or more effective police but demographic
factors such as an aging population. With voters being told by neo-liberal politicians, think tanks and media that they are primarily taxpayers, policing became
another service under fiscal pressure. Even the tough-on-crime Harper government closed RCMP crime labs and in 2014 cut the budget of the RCMP. Although
Williams (2007) and other have argued that police unions, by employing the
rhetoric of crime fighting, have been more successful than other public sector
labour organizations in protecting wages and benefits, there are signs that times
are changing. "Common sense" arguments that large numbers of well-paid police
officers are necessary to fight crime wield less authority in an age of falling crime
rates. In 2013, for example, Statistics Canada reported that police-reported crime
rates had dropped to a forty-year low; this included a fall in the Crime Severity
Index. The exception was the continued high crime rate in First Nations communities (Statistics Canada 2013). Between 2000 and 2011, adjusting for inflation,
police expenditures increased by 50 percent, and most of the costs consisted of
salaries and benefits (Expert Panel 2014: 51–4).

Although the cost of policing and other branches of the criminal justice system
have risen in recent years, the increases are not out of line compared to other public services. A study of the cost-efficiency of policing Canada's top ten cities from
1991 to 2006 suggested that Montreal's "weighted clearance rates" were a problem.
Other municipal police departments were faulted for having too many officers or
maintaining pension plans that were overly generous and underfunded. The Service
de Police de la Ville de Montréal (SPVM) in 2010 promised to fight budget creep by
further commercializing services. As with the United States military in its foreign
wars, civilianization was another tactic for cutting costs. In Montreal this meant
that the police headquarters was guarded not by the police but a private security
firm (Aubin 2010). As in Great Britain, where the national government financially
assisted local policing, police services, which were traditionally well funded because
of the popularity of law-and-order politics, were targeted by neo-liberal politicians
who wanted to lower taxes and shrink government. In 2013 Canadian Public Safety
Minister Vic Toews, whose government was responsible for only 20 percent of the
nation's law enforcement budget, convened a summit on the economics of policing and proposed a research agenda to explore how to improve police efficiencies.
With the volume of crime decreasing, a Public Safety Canada document declared
that "police services must find more efficient and effective methods to sustain
current levels of policing services (Public Safety Canada 2013: 3). Coming from

a law-and-order government that also often rejected evidence-based public policy as "elitist," Toews's declaration was viewed by many police executives as an act of betrayal.

One sign that the fiscal austerity issue had become a genuine threat to police services was a resolution passed at the 2014 CACP convention that encouraged "governments, police governance bodies, academics and researchers, police agencies and all stakeholders" to stop using the expression "economics of policing" and substitute in its place "economics of community safety and wellbeing" (CACP 2014). The discussion was motivated by the argument that quality of life in a community depended on not simply police resources but also a host of public agencies and social actors, including private security. In an apparent nod to community policing, the CACP resolution suggested that too much was being expected of police services that were heavily involved with non-criminal issues, including mental illness and addictions (CACP 2014). The police were admitting what activists and academics had long known: most of what occupied the police was not related to serious crime. More specifically, neo-liberal policies that favoured market-based solutions, lower taxes, privatization and downsizing put pressure on public health, welfare and education programs, increased inequality and created more work for the police (Stern 2006). The 2014 resolution reflected both a current and historic reality of Canadian law enforcement: despite professional assertions to the contrary, the police officer is often the proverbial "social worker with a gun." And run-of-the-mill crime or disorder is caused not by selfish or evil "criminals" but by risk factors such as poverty, mental illness, addictions, sexual abuse, homelessness and low levels of education. Officers on patrol or responding to calls frequently encounter people in crisis, and alcohol and drug abuse continue to drive most petty crime. Recent statistics indicate that 80 percent of individuals admitted to federal corrections institutions report substance abuse problems (Mallea 2011: 141).

By the early twenty-first century a major controversy surrounding the police and people with substance abuse and mental health issues was centred on the use of non-lethal force. The most popular "stun gun," or conducted energy weapon (CEW), is manufactured by Taser International. With a range of five metres, the weapon consists of darts that send fifty thousand volts into the target's body. According to the company, the "Taser" incapacitates violent suspects without the use of firearms and batons, minimizes death and injury and also reduces the risk of litigation. A Victoria, B.C., police expert on the Taser interviewed in 1999, when Canadian police services were beginning to test the weapon, claimed that they were safer than fists or batons in subduing suspects. Civil liberties organizations were less convinced (Thomas 1999). Brodeur (2010: 287) describes the adoption of this weapon as an example of "market fuelled expansion." In 2000 Ottawa became the first Canadian city to adopt CEWs, but in contrast to other departments their use was confined to tactical units. As a result, the devices were deployed only 115 times in Ottawa between 2000 and 2008. In Edmonton, by contrast, they were used eighty-eight times in ten months of 2007 alone. Critics have argued that CEWs, rather than substitutes for firearms in serious incidents where officer or public safety was compromised, were being used for low-level situations, such as encounters with the mentally ill, simply for not complying with a verbal request (Cockburn 2008). Between 2003 and 2007 nearly twenty Canadians died after being shocked by CEWs; the devices became embroiled in controversy following the deaths of a number of citizens suffering from mental health or personality disorders.

The most famous incident was the death of Robert Dziekanski, a Polish immigrant subdued by RCMP officers at the Vancouver airport in 2007. Security camera and cell phone video footage depicted Dziekanski, who did not speak English and who had been stranded in the airport for eight hours, being shocked four times after he was handcuffed and pinned to the floor by four officers. The RCMP invested heavily in CEWs, whose use was endorsed by the CACP. The Dziekanski case was another black mark against the carefully crafted image of the RCMP. Although the Commission for Public Complaints Against the RCMP urged the force to limit the use of CEWs and to adopt better training and reporting procedures, the initial reaction of the force was to justify the actions at the Vancouver airport. The four officers were never charged with causing the death of the victim, although in later years one was convicted of perjury and sentenced to a term in penitentiary. After being criticized for attempting to manipulate media reporting of both the incident and reactions to it, the RCMP issued an apology to the victim's mother. In addition to a public inquiry (Braidwood 2010) the incident prompted British Columbia to establish the Independent Investigations Office to investigate police-related deaths and serious injuries (Braidwood 2009).

As the CEW controversy illustrates, Canadian police forces historically have adopted new trends, including equipment, from American law enforcement. One noticeable trend in the last decade is militarization (Murphy 2007). The American Civil Liberties Union (ACLU) in its 2014 report *The War Comes Home* warns of the consequences of an increasingly militarized style of policing. The report documents the use of heavily armed SWAT teams, not only in containing hostage or active shooter situations, which are scenarios suitable for SWAT, but also in enforcing search warrants, usually as part of the controversial War on Drugs. Critics explained this militarization, which they worried also involved a militarization of attitudes, on the War on Terror, but the trend had been evident since the late 1960s. Equipped with military-style uniforms and body armour, officers armed with automatic weapons, flash bang grenades, battering rams and in some cases armoured vehicles since the 1990s have been aggressively enforcing "no knock" warrants, usually in Black and Hispanic neighbourhoods. The report raised the concern that the "warrior cop" approach risks turning urban neighbourhoods into war zones and citizens into "enemies," a mentality that was escalated after the creation of the Department of Homeland Security in 2001. This type of mission creep, aided by the federal government, which has supplied law enforcement agencies with surplus military equipment such as armoured vehicles, helicopters, planes and machine guns from wars in the Middle East, has taken place with little public discussion or oversight (ACLU 2014).

Civil liberties advocates by the early twenty-first century had identified two other problematic police practices: "stop and frisk" tactics that suggested deliberate racial profiling and excessive violence and denial of due process in the policing of mass public protests. The former approach grew out of "broken windows" policing and has received much praise in American policing circles but has produced resentment in minority communities. Although controversies in Canada have been more muted than in the United States, academics and civil libertarians worry that these developments risk moving North America away from the civilian, minimal policing style envisioned by Peel toward an intrusive paramilitary model during an era when crime rates appear to be in decline. Critics of a more militarized approach to policing, and increased surveillance of persons and organizations deemed threats to national security, fear that democratic policing is being transformed into a more intimidating and authoritarian institution (Skolnick 1999). The paramilitary image has even been injected into the RCMP's famous musical ride, with heavily-armed ERT officers, clad in military-style uniforms, simulating a high-risk arrest using smoke grenades and an armoured vehicle (Egan 2015).

"Hot spot" or intelligence-led policing (ILP) is another imported American trend. The Saskatchewan RCMP report for 2012, for example, claims that ILP "works in harmony with community policing to ensure safer communities." Although many would be surprised to learn that Saskatchewan is a major centre of organized crime, the report further explains, in language apparently borrowed from the U.S. Pentagon, that ILP aims to "identify and disrupt" organized crime (RCMP 2012). Similarly in 2010 the RCMP J Division in New Brunswick claimed that the province's relatively low crime rate was in part the result of ILP (although its report also acknowledged social factors such as literacy, housing, substance abuse, employment, income and mental health). According to a study prepared for the Rand Corporation, ILP evolved from the order-maintenance approaches of the late twentieth century and focuses on maximizing the potential for "criminals being caught" (Treverton, Wollman, Wilke and Lai 2011: xv). ILP targets high crime areas, which tend to be neighbourhoods dominated by the poor and minorities. Popular with politicians and large sections of the public, when ILP is combined with stop-and-frisk tactics it draws criticism from minority and civil liberties organizations. Recently the Portland Police Bureau proposed to follow the lead of Milwaukee, Sacramento and other American cities by introducing hot-spot policing: the department's records indicate that 40 percent of reported crime takes place in less than 4 percent of the city's territory. The Bureau has assured the public that stop-and-frisk will not be part of the strategy, but the ACLU warns that racially-based stops will be "collateral consequences" (Damewood 2013).

The Toronto carding controversy discussed above reflects the approach of ILP or hot-spot policing and has echoes of New York's controversial stop-and-frisk tactics. A map of Toronto's thirteen "high priority" neighbourhoods indicates that they are characterized by low income, high levels of unemployment, single parent families, visible minorities and immigrants. Furthermore, carding was enforced not only in high-crime areas, which at least met the test of ILP, but in all of the city's more than seventy patrol zones, including largely white neighbourhoods (Rankin and Winsa 2012). The police service responded by explaining that carding was not racial profiling but intelligence-led policing. In most centres these practices are justified as part of a campaign against "gangs, guns and drugs." The newest promise arising out of ILP is that it not only can target offenders but also, through the use of "big data" and algorithms, predict the nature, intensity and location of crime. The New Brunswick RCMP (2010) for example explained that crime analysis suggests that 10 percent of "active criminals" (five hundred individuals) were responsible for nearly half of all reported crimes. Predictive policing, promoted by information technology contractors, is the newest fad in the United States where police services have been devastated by budget cuts, yet research has failed to prove its overall effectiveness. Canadian departments have been more cautious in moving to this technology, but their operational practices are very much in line with the theory. On the surface, terms and practices such as ILP, smart policing, hot-spot policing, crime mapping and analytics appear reasonable and efficient, but they do have implications for privacy, police-minority relations and the further militarization of policing (CBC 2015; Murphy 2007).

Following on developments in the late twentieth century, controversies have continued to surround the policing of demonstrations involving labour, anti-poverty, environmental and anti-globalization protests or disputes over foreign policy and visiting dignitaries (Wood 2014). Despite evidence of the "negotiated management approach" to strikes and large-scale protests, with its outward appearance of neutrality, the response to mass events suggested that police services were also fine-tuning established counter-intelligence methods (Williams 2007: 190). Security planning for mass protests aims to prevent a repeat of events in Seattle in 1999, where demonstrators forced the cancellation of a meeting of the World Trade Organization. In addition to the management of peaceful protest, increased coordination of security forces, greater use of intelligence, the policing of mass public events since the early twenty-first century has been associated with militarization. Protests against the Winter Olympics in Vancouver in 2010, which were muted compared to anti-G20 demonstrations that year in Toronto, brought out police armed with M4 carbines, the same weapon used by U.S. forces in Iraq and Afghanistan. In one media photograph an officer was portrayed as carrying a quick-firing shotgun and a bandoleer of shotgun shells, like an extra from a bad action movie. This operation involved several thousand police, 4,500 Armed Forces members and several thousand private security guards (Expert Panel 2014: 35).

That the police had learned lessons from the 1997 APEC fiasco and the 1999 Seattle protests was evident during the 2001 Summit of the Americas at Quebec City (Abbate 2001). The police, on the excuse that they feared anarchist violence, deployed six thousand officers and the military one thousand troops, with more on standby. The liaison approach was employed for labour demonstrators who promised to follow a planned parade route, arrive in buses and provide their own marshals. But the police response was also characterized by militarization and preemptive "diffusion" (De Lint and Hall 2009: 245–7). Civil liberties spokes-persons criticized a chain-link security fence that sealed off the representatives of thirty-four nations from anti-globalization protestors. Peaceful protest was per-mitted in a so-called Green Zone, and labour and non-profit organizations staged an alternative Peoples' Summit. Police plans for mass demonstrations revealed a counter-insurgency mentality, with a mass detention facility more suitable for prisoners of war than alleged violators of criminal law. Employing militarized lan-guage, the police spoke of defending "the perimeter." A minority of more aggressive protestors breached the security fence, and the police responded with water cannon, plastic bullets and thousands of canisters of tear gas. The use of lethal force was authorized if protestors were armed with sticks or clubs, fire or chemical substances. The summit area resembled a war zone, and there was liberal use of tear gas and preventive arrests. Nearly one hundred police officers and protestors were injured and more than three hundred people arrested. Amnesty International called for an investigation of police misconduct, but both the prime minister of Canada and the PQ minister of public safety praised the SQ for its security operation, which cost $100 million (Klein 2001; MacKinnon and McKenna 2001).

Building on tactics evident during the previous decade, the police and the military were a heavy presence at the 2002 Alberta meetings of G8 leaders, and there was special emphasis on intelligence. The expensive security operation at Calgary and rural Kananaskis involved tracking the movements of protestors and equipping the RCMP with expensive new communication technology. Protestors got no closer than seventeen kilometres to the main summit at Kananaskis, and demonstrations in Calgary were peaceful. The Calgary Police Service took credit for the uneventful demonstrations, explaining that it was necessary to infiltrate protest groups in order to facilitate "freedom of expression" (Maloney and Poole 2002).

Following the 2001 Summit of the Americas, Montreal continued to be a hotbed of public order challenges. In 2002, protestors gathered at Concordia University to oppose a speech by former Israeli prime minister, Benjamin Netanyahu. Police used gas, pepper spray and batons on pro-Palestinian demonstrators who broke a few windows and threw chairs. Five students were arrested. The following year, young music fans, angered that a show by the punk rock group The Exploited had been cancelled, smashed windows and set dozens of cars on fire. Only eight people were arrested, but street workers reported that the real causes of the violence was the presence of up to two thousand homeless youth, many involved with drugs, and their poor relationship with the police (McKinley 2003). That same year Montreal hosted a meeting for trade ministers from nations represented by the World Trade Organization. As in Quebec in 2001, the police were restrained in dealing with labour and other protest groups who followed the liaison approach. These took part in a large march in defence of immigrant and refugee rights that concluded without incident, but on the second day more militant anti-globalization protestors, many wearing gas masks, smashed store windows and clashed with police. More than two hundred were arrested and taken away on buses, suggesting a military operation. Some of the detained were released, but 140 spent the night in jail (CBC 2003).

In 2007 the SQ, the RCMP, Quebec City police and the Ste. Foy police were in charge of security surrounding the Security and Prosperity Partnership of North America meeting. This involved the presidents of the United States and Mexico and the Canadian prime minister. At one point more than one thousand labour, environmental and human rights protestors were on the scene at Montebello, Quebec, where a security perimeter was guarded by the RCMP and the SQ. Trade union protestors became convinced that three masked "protestors," who appeared to be attempting to provoke an attack on the police, were actually SQ *agents provocateurs*. Their police-issue boots supposedly had given them away. The SQ later admitted that it had planted plainclothes officers into protest ranks in order to root our acts of violence (CBC 2007).

This was not the last public order policing controversy in Quebec. In 2012, in what was dubbed the "Maple Spring," university students organized months of strikes and demonstrations against austerity measures promoted by the Liberal government, specifically a plan to raise post-secondary tuition. In the course of six months there were more than five hundred demonstrations in Montreal involving a total of tens of thousands of students and thousands of police. The anti-austerity protests, the largest student uprising in Canadian history, were strangely ignored by media outside of the province and condemned by conservative journalists within Quebec. More than 2,200 arrests were made and over two hundred complaints registered against the police. Most students were ticketed for minor infractions and avoided a criminal record. Both the SPVM and SQ racked up millions of dollars in overtime, and the former attempted to use mediators and social media to undercut tensions with the students. The SPVM report for 2012 refers to these as "public management efforts." The provincial police responded to more than four hundred demonstrations, including a serious incident at Victoriaville, where gas, chemical agents and plastic bullets were deployed against the students. One protestor lost an eye to a plastic bullet and another had her jaw and a number of teeth broken. In 2013 the provincial government appointed a commission to investigate methods for ensuring peaceful protests in the future (*Toronto Star* 2012; SPVM 2012; Nadeau-Dubois 2015).

In 2010 the "own the streets" mentality of increasingly militarized police services, together with rhetoric that protestors (who did include a small element of violent anarchists) were "terrorists" resulted in the largest mass arrest in Canadian history. The operation, which involved more than twenty thousand police, military and private security personnel, was later judged to have been poorly planned and executed (Morden 2012). In advance of the G20 Summit of world leaders, the Toronto City Council authorized a temporary detention facility consisting of holding cages in a commercial warehouse. A separate meeting of G8 leaders was planned for Huntsville, Ontario. It was later revealed that the Liberal provincial cabinet, avoiding a public debate in the Assembly, had secretly passed *Regulation 233/10*, giving the police extended powers by declaring the summit security perimeter a public work. Without the public being told in advance, it authorized police to search and arrest anyone who approached the zone and refused to state their name or explain why they were there. In the months leading up to the summit the RCMP, OPP and local police infiltrated and spied on various organizations in Ontario and made seventeen arrests. This Joint Intelligence Group, which involved up to five hundred officers, referred to some activists as "criminal extremists." Yet the charges laid consisted of "counselling mischief" and obstructing police, and in the end charges were dropped against eleven of the seventeen activists. The RCMP had adopted the same approach in British Columbia in 2008 and 2009 in advance of the 2010 Vancouver Olympics. The joint intelligence operations, carried out in the name of "protecting the public," continued after the events they were designed to protect (Groves and Dubinsky 2011).

The security operation in Toronto involved ten thousand police officers from all over Canada including an undisclosed number of plainclothes officers, wearing jeans, T-shirts and other informal garb, who in one video clip are threatening protestors and others with telescopic batons. The police, aided by nearly one hundred security cameras, engaged in extensive video surveillance. The authorities established a "free speech zone" at Queen's Park, but on the vague excuse that they had to prevent some type of undisclosed criminal activity, the police attacked the zone, intimidating and assaulting peaceful demonstrators with shields, clubs and pepper spray and "processing" (arresting) them. One of the more egregious violations of civil liberties was when seventy students sleeping in a university gymnasium were "processed" by heavily-armed tactical officers for "unlawful assembly," supposedly because pre-summit "intelligence" indicated that they had planned "mischief." To make matters worse, the students, probably as a form of intimidation to discourage official complaints, were charged with criminal conspiracy (CBC 2011; Wood 2014).

During the summit more than one thousand were arrested; many of these at first were "kettled" in sweltering heat without being given water or being permitted to use the washroom. First developed in Britain, kettling involves using phalanxes of riot police to box in demonstrators and limit their movements, often for hours at a time. It is a form of detention on the street, except that it exposes citizens to the elements. Video evidence indicated that from time to time officers would leave police lines and swoop in and assault or snatch various individuals within the box. Much to the consternation of the RCMP, which was in charge of overall operations, kettling was utilized several times during the G20 protests. In addition to protestors, it immobilized journalists and bystanders. In one incident, citizens were detained at an intersection during a thunderstorm. Some of the caged detainees were held for more than twenty-four hours under a form of preventive detention ("breach of the peace"). Young women were strip-searched and prisoners were denied water, food and medical attention. Citizens complained of that officers had used excessive force, had removed their name tags and denied access to legal counsel. Parts of downtown Toronto looked like they were under martial law, with large numbers of demonstrators having their wrists bound with plastic ties like prisoners of war and being handled by police whose faces were obscured by helmets and visors. For the first time in the history of the city, police fired AEPs at demonstrators. Given that many of the detained were not charged with criminal offences, the chief purpose of police tactics appeared to have been to intimidate and humiliate peaceful protestors (CBC 2011; Ombudsman Ontario 2010).

The G20 operation was criticized by the provincial ombudsman and resulted in several inquiries and lawsuits. Police Chief Bill Blair (who in 2015 was elected as a Liberal MP) consistently defended all police actions until shown video evidence of unprovoked aggressive behaviour by officers. The Office of the Independent Police Review ruled that kettling was unlawful. Ombudsman André Marin denounced *Regulation 233/10* as "an act of public entrapment." One result was that the Toronto police supposedly abandoned kettling. This was not the case in Montreal, where the SPVM used the tactic against student protestors. The Montreal police were aided by a controversial city bylaw, P-6, which forced protest organizers to file the route of their marches in advance and banned the wearing of masks. The Harper government also amended the *Criminal Code* effective 2013 to create a new offence, punishable by up to ten years in prison: wearing a mask during a riot or unlawful assembly. The private member who sponsored the bill described it as a sanction that had been requested by police. Another targeted use of criminal law was the Charest government's Bill 78, an attempt to nullify student protests. It banned demonstrations near colleges and universities and forced demonstrations of more than fifty people to clear their time, duration and route with police in advance. Bill 78 was condemned by the provincial human rights commission as a violation of Quebec's Charter of Rights and Freedoms (CBC 2012).

In 2011 the Occupy Movement protest against economic inequality, globalization and the power of corporations spread from the United States. This grassroots crusade to enlist the "99 percent" against the "1 percent" (the super wealthy) was idealistic and tolerated by local officials to an extent. Inspired by student movements of the Arab Spring, it attracted environmentalists, First Nations and anti-globalization activists and involved protest marches and demonstrations as well as "occupy camps" in big cities such as Vancouver and Toronto and smaller centres such as Fredericton. The police response in the United States included thousands of arrests with corresponding charges of police brutality and lawsuits against police services. Much vilified in the corporate press and by spokespersons for the status quo, this decentralized movement was accused of lacking a coherent philosophy and being unrealistic in their demands. In some cities the authorities responded with "peaceful co-existence," but in most the civic authorities used municipal fire safety and other bylaws and obtained injunctions to clear public parks and squares of Occupy tents before the end of the year (*Ottawa Citizen* 2011).

The Canadian public, whose views are shaped by the mainstream media, often ignores civil liberties or human rights issues, much like it embraces "common sense" understandings of law and order. Prominent in American political and media circles starting in the 1980s, this populist view blames activist judges, liberal politicians, various interest groups and academics for making the justice system too soft on crime. It often agrees with police unions that minority recruitment, civil liberties and civilian review undermine the police and make Canada less safe. Common sense views of crime also reject the evidence of official statistics and the opinions of criminologists that serious crime is in decline. Despite the populist assertion that the courts have granted too many protections to defendants and have ignored public safety and the rights of victims, there is evidence that judicial decisions have also strengthened police powers of search, seize and detention (Jochelson and Kramar 2014). Politicians, notably the Harris Conservatives in Ontario (1995–2002) and the Harper Conservatives who formed the government of Canada from 2006 to 2015, exploited fear of crime and enacted tougher penalties against offenders. Any criticism from criminologists or law professors was brushed aside as being elitist or "out of touch." In 2011 the Conservative campaign document *Here for Canadians* purported to reflect "the common-sense beliefs of law-abiding Canadians"

(Mallea 2011: 27). The Harper government's tough- on-crime agenda exerted a direct impact on the courts, prisons and parole, but aspects such as bail provision, wiretapping procedures and drug enforcement more directly affected the police. Police responses to the Harper agenda were relatively muted, but police chiefs in cities such as Toronto and Calgary have questioned the theory that crime can be countered simply by jailing more people for longer periods. Canadian police leaders and unions have been more restrained than their American counterparts with war-on-crime rhetoric. The fact that much of the country is policed by the RCMP under contract also minimizes provocative law and order statements, as RCMP commissioners, for various reasons, do not always speak their mind. On the other hand, the RCMP, despite the creation of the independent Commission for Public Complaints, remains largely protected from civilian oversight (Valiante 2014).

On the provincial and municipal levels police associations, reflecting an embattled "thin blue line" mentality, have lashed out at not only critics on the left but also neo-liberal politicians and mayors and city councils. In 1998, for example, the Vancouver Police Union took legal action against the city council for its use of public funds to support the hiring of security guards to patrol the streets under a program of a downtown business improvement association. The union argued that street patrol was the job of the public police and that more officers should be hired. In 2000 the Harris government, despite its tough-on-crime image, confronted the MTPA for its controversial "True Blue" telemarketing campaign, borrowed from the LAPD. The campaign aimed to raise funds from the public to lobby for pro-union and pro-police measures such as stricter penalties against young offenders and a national DNA bank for offenders (CBC 2000). Recently the Montreal Police Brotherhood has been in conflict with not only the municipal government but also the provincial labour relations board. In an ongoing dispute over pay, pensions and complement, the union members have engaged in tactics such as staging a rowdy protest at city hall, not wearing full uniforms and issuing fewer parking and other tickets. This echoed tactics adopted in 2008 when the union was without a contract (CBC 2014c). Prior to the 2014 provincial election, the OPP Association took the unprecedented step of paying for attack ads directed against the Conservative opposition, which was promising to freeze public sector salaries, interfere in labour relations and public pensions and fire 100,000 civil servants. Police associations have also identified stress, burnout and post-traumatic stress disorder as genuine issues for front line officers (Ivison 2014).

While recognizing new realities, such as the recruitment of women and minorities, the need to be more sensitive to public complaints and the challenges of policing under the Charter of Rights and Freedoms, police services in the early twenty-first century continue to reflect law-and-order concerns, and the rank and file tends to be less progressive than leaders. Because of its disciplinary framework and its lack of a union, the RCMP rank and file is not always able to voice concerns on policing-related issues. One recent example of this reality was the fatal shooting in 2014 of three RCMP officers and the wounding of two others in the force's Codiac (greater Moncton) detachment. The suspect was armed with an M305 semi-automatic rifle, and the officers who responded had nine millimeter pistols. The tragedy had echoes of the 2005 Mayerthope incident, where four Alberta Mounties were murdered by a suspect being investigated for auto theft and marijuana cultivation. Not for the first time in its history, the force protected its image by exploiting "fallen heroes" (Palango 2008: 331–7). Lashing out at critics and apparently absolving itself of any responsibility for the Moncton tragedy, the RCMP brass played up the heroic sacrifice of the officers and their families and sidestepped criticisms from ex-Mounties that the members had not been equipped with the proper body armour and assault rifles to deal with a heavily-armed hostile suspect. The Codiac detachment's limited number of C8 carbines, which the RCMP had acquired in the wake of the Mayerthorpe incident, were allocated for training and not available for officers on duty. Unlike the Alberta attack, which had not produced an official inquiry, the Moncton shootings resulted in an internal probe. One of its findings was that the officers who responded to reports of a possible active shooter were not even equipped with shotguns. In this case there was no union or rank-and-file organization to challenge management's interpretation of events (this situation was overturned several months later when the Supreme Court of Canada ruled that RCMP members had a right to organize and bargain collectively). In 2015 the events triggered an investigation under the federal labour code on the grounds that the RCMP had failed to properly train, equip and supervise its members. Despite public sympathy for the slain officers, calls for patrol officers in the RCMP and presumably other police services to be equipped with military-grade carbines represented a further escalation of militarization (CP 2015a, 2015b).

One of the realities of police in liberal democracies, because of the tradition of operational autonomy, is that both on the local and national levels they can diverge from their political masters. For the most part organizations such as the CACP and the CPA have promoted a relatively conservative crime control approach to the justice system in general and policing issues in particular. Yet starting in 2006 the advent of a neo-liberal federal government that reflected a mixture of social conservatism, libertarianism and common sense critiques of criminal law, the courts and various experts led to some interesting conflicts. This was compounded by the fact that most Canadians are policed by municipal, regional and provincial police services or municipal and provincial RCMP contract forces. The CACP, the RCMP and other police organizations, for example, opposed the Harper government's decision to scrap the national firearms registry. During the 1990s the Reform Party, which formed the base of the Conservative Party, had condemned the registry as wasteful and demeaning to law-abiding gun owners. The Conservatives in the 2006 and 2009 elections, who also promised to be tough on crime, pledged to side with "responsible" gun owners by scrapping the registry. A private member's bill in 2009 failed to pass, but once the Conservatives won a majority in 2011, despite being elected with less than 40 percent of the popular vote, the path was clear. In 2012 the registry was ended and the government ordered its databank to be erased. The CACP defended the program as a useful public safety measure and was backed up by organizations such as the Canadian Association of Police Boards and the Ontario Association of Chiefs of Police. The Saskatchewan Federation of Police Officers, on the other hand, reflected the "common sense" opinion that the registry was expensive and served no useful purpose. In recent years the National Firearms Association and its political supporters have been critical of the RCMP over the issue of classification of firearms (Brown 2012).

In addition to tensions over gun control, there are other policy areas where Canadian police found themselves on the wrong side of the federal government's "common sense" approach to the justice system, which involved an emphasis on victims' rights, "truth in sentencing," new mandatory minimum sentences and a resulting expanding prison population. One was the harm reduction approach to injection drug users and the other is a de-escalation of police actions against sex trade workers. In large cities such as Vancouver and smaller centres such as Saint John, New Brunswick, police leadership, working with public health agencies and community organizations devoted to assisting injection drug users and the homeless, have embraced aspects of harm reduction, realizing that drug abuse is a medical and social issue, not a criminal issue, and that drug addicts should be treated in a non-judgmental manner. The Vancouver police have supported aspects of harm reduction by referring high-risk drug users, particularly those involved with the sex trade, to Insite, the safe-injection facility. The project opened in 2002 and was granted exemption from federal drug laws as a research project. The municipal government and the Vancouver police supported Insite on those grounds, but that support was accompanied by crackdowns on public drug use and sales near the clinic. A former Vancouver police chief, writing in 2008, expressed the profound ambivalence of his officers toward Insite and advocated mandatory drug treatment for prison inmates (Graham 2008), and the RCMP were later found to have hired researchers to discredit the facility (Mason 2008).

Vancouver's Downtown Criminal Court, an innovative pilot project that attempts to minimize recidivism by connecting offenders with drug and mental health services, also has enjoyed some support from the police (Mallea 2011: 165–7). Although enforcement is one pillar in the City of Vancouver's Four Pillar Drug Policy, inspired by European practices, the police service supports supervised safe injection and the use of drug courts as an alternative to incarceration.

The federal government, in contrast, appeared to be more interested in a war on crime approach to drugs and attempted to close down the Insite program, which was saved only by a decision of the Supreme Court of Canada in 2011. In 2014 the Conservative government started to sponsor television advertisements — aimed at parents — denouncing marijuana smoking by youth, an offence that most police services no longer treat with much seriousness (City of Vancouver 2014).

In the final years of the Harper regime, federal government proposals to criminalize prostitution also threatened to disrupt innovative policies that had created alliances of police, drug treatment and counselling groups and organizations advocating on behalf of sex trade workers to lessen violence and substance abuse in the sex trade. In a number of Canadian cities police services have made considerable progress in helping public health and community organizations find compassionate and evidence-based solutions to the challenges of drug abuse, which is a problem for many who work as prostitutes. The Harper government in contrast had a record of ignoring expert evidence, starting with its scrapping of the long-form census, which makes it difficult for police services and other social agencies to study community issues. The government also dropped harm reduction as a goal of its national drug strategy. In 2013, the Supreme Court of Canada struck down the bawdy house, living on the avails and communicating provisions of the *Criminal Code.* The Conservative government responded in 2014 with a new law that banned, for the first time in Canadian history, the buying of sexual services. It also recriminalized aspects of communicating for the purpose of prostitution and banned third-party advertising and third parties receiving an economic benefit from the trade. The government explained that it was acting on behalf of vulnerable victims of the sex trade. The new direction appeared to be borrowed from the approach of Nordic countries where women are encouraged to exit the sex trade. Yet its apparent harm reduction roots may be shallow, given that the minister of justice denounced sex trade clients as "perverts," suggesting either an attempt to whip up a moral panic or a callous political strategy.

At the time of writing, the impact of the new law on both police and sex trade workers is unclear, and the issue of the sex trade does not appear high on the agenda of the new Trudeau government. Some police chiefs have spoken out in support of the *Protection of Communities and Exploited Persons Act* or at least parts of the law. Provincial authorities in Manitoba and Ontario have questioned the measure, including its constitutionality, and the Vancouver Police Department has reiterated its 2013 policy that enforcement will be "a last resort," with intervention limited to cases involving minors, violence, gangs and human trafficking (Pablo 2014; Flanagan 2014; Winter 2014).

CONCLUSION: COMMUNITY POLICING 2.0 OR POPULATION CONTROL?

At the March 2015 conference on the Economics and Future of Policing, organized by Public Safety Canada, both the history and future of policing were at stake. In media and political circles most attention was on the Harper government's controversial anti-terrorism legislation. For Canadian police services, the next stage in the War on Terror, which according to the defeated Harper government would be a war on "homegrown" Islamic extremists who "hate Canada," presents both opportunities and challenges. An immediate challenge for the RCMP was the redeployment of several hundred officers from criminal investigations to national security tasks in the wake of the murders of career soldier Patrice Vincent and army reservist Nathan Cirillo and an armed assault on the Parliament Building in late 2014. Yet aside from a partisan speech by the minister of public safety, terrorism was barely mentioned during the official proceedings of the three-day conference. For the most part, delegates were preoccupied with community policing, or in its new guise, police roles in the "safety and security web" (Expert Panel 2014: 110).

The new community-based model discussed at the summit, when combined with other trends such as crime mapping, big data, predictive policing and the blurring of criminal/public order and anti-terror policing, echoes aspects of classic military counter-insurgency. At an influential symposium on counter-insurgency hosted by the RAND Corporation in 1962, participants were advised that intelligence gathering (aided by undercover agents and informers), "search and sweep" operations, the use of force and "civic action" such as the provision of schools, jobs and public safety were all needed to defeat a guerilla force (Hosmer and Crane 1963: 28, 115, 119). More recently, the United States Department of the Army counter-insurgency manual of 2006 described "a safe and secure community" as the ultimate goal of the forces aiming to defeat insurgents, who were similar to organized crime groups in terms of organization, tactics and financing. Counter-insurgency above all is an "an intelligence war" that necessitates the use of human intelligence, signals intelligence, photography, CCTV and video surveillance and open sources. "Population control" also requires a detailed census of neighbourhoods and communities (Department of the Army 2006). Hot-spot policing, which on the surface appears to be a reasonable strategy for maximizing police resources, contains echoes of counter-insurgency and has the potential to increase tensions with poor and minority neighbourhoods. Exponents of hot-spot policing argue that most crime, particularly "stranger crime" such as robberies and auto thefts, take place in a limited and predictable number of specific locales in a given city and that targeted patrols would not displace crime to other neighbourhoods (Sherman 2010).

The current "insecurity" climate is a genuine barrier to meaningful reform in Canadian policing. In 2014, fatal "lone wolf" attacks in Ottawa and

Saint-Jean-sur-Richilieu, Quebec, raised concerns about radical Islamic terrorism within Canada, which politicians immediately exploited. With the support of the Liberal party, the Harper government responded with a new anti-terrorism bill that not only expanded the definition of terrorist threats but also gives CSIS police powers and seemed to open the door for disruptive tactics against suspected terrorists, all with little parliamentary oversight (CP 2015c). At the 2015 policing summit the minister of public safety repeated the government line that "radical jihadists" were seeking to destroy Canada's freedom and that the threat was "evolving." Much of the basis of the government's justification for enhancing security legislation and expenditures was the latest manifestation of radical Islam, ISIS, in Iraq and Syria. Even before the passage in 2015 of Bill C-51, there was evidence that the federal government and police and security agencies were associating and targeting legal, non-violent organizations and social movements as terrorist or quasi terrorist. The B.C. Civil Liberties Association, for example, has filed complaints against the RCMP and CSIS for spying on peaceful environmental groups and First Nations who oppose the proposed Enbridge Northern Gateway Pipeline from Alberta to British Columbia and sharing the intelligence gathered, such as reports on volunteers making protest signs in church basements, with the energy company (CBC 2014a). Equally disturbing is a leaked RCMP report that refers to "anti-Canada" environmental organizations and warns of "violent extremists" seeking to disrupt the Alberta oil sands and pipeline projects (McCarthy 2015).

In early 2016, more than at any other time in the recent past, Canadian policing appears to be at a crossroads. The vigilant eye is increasing both the power of its gaze and its secrecy. The implications of Bill C-51 for privacy, freedom of speech and assembly, due process and protection by the courts from illegal acts carried out in the name of national security are unknown. It is likely that part of the law, like much of the Harper government's tough-on-crime agenda, will be struck down by the Supreme Court of Canada or amended by the Liberal government that replaced the Conservatives in the fall of 2015. The Trudeau government appears commited to narrowing the definition of terrorism and instituting greater parliamentary oversight (McLeod 2015).

Yet critics still fear that the *Anti-terrorism Act*'s damage to the transparency and accountability of police and security agencies, and to democracy in general, will be considerable even if amended. In terms of the core mission of policing, an enhanced agenda of community policing, with police services cooperating with other government agencies, private security and community organizations, appears on the surface to be a detour away from the reinvigorated law-and-order approach of recent years. As Reiner (2012) notes, media and even popular culture have conditioned citizens to think in terms of risk, fear and insecurity, even without the added political and ideological pressures of the War on Terror.

Is the return to community policing, with its focus on partnerships, "hubs" and the safety and security web, a genuine movement or another set of buzz words and projects designed to mask a more intelligence-driven paramilitary approach to community pacification (Williams 2007: 221)? Past experience indicates that the rank and file opposes top-down, externally-driven initiatives such as community policing. The classic theory of police culture is that it is "resistant to outside political or community influence." The "traditional policing paradigm" also tends to "ignore, or mistrust forms of non-police knowledge, analysis and dialogue (Murphy and McKenna 2007: 9, 60). "Community policing 2.0" may simply be an updated strategy, influenced by continued budgetary pressures and falling crime rates, to further embed the vigilant eye within communities. The rhetoric at the 2015 Ottawa summit on the future of policing can be interpreted either way. Time will tell whether Canadian police agencies will be transformed into genuinely community-focused services with reasonable accountability mechanisms and a broader representation of Canadian society within their ranks. In the meantime it is imperative that academics, interest groups and ordinary citizens resist "common sense" and "police as hero" narratives and hold police organizations and their governance bodies accountable.

REFERENCES

Abbate, Gay. 2001. "Mounties Assailed for APEC Bungling." *Globe and Mail*, Aug. 7.

Abella, Irving. 1974. "Oshawa 1937." In Irving Abella (ed.), *On Strike: Six Key Labour Struggles in Canada, 1919–1949*. Toronto: James Lorimer.

Acheson, T.W. 1985. *Saint John: The Making of a Colonial Urban Community, 1815–60*. Toronto: University of Toronto Press.

ACLU (American Civil Liberties Union). 2014. *The War Comes Home: The Excessive Militarization of American Policing*. New York: American Civil Liberties Union.

Amaron, Douglas. 1947. "Drive on Abortionists Led by 2 Policewomen." *Globe and Mail*, April 11.

Appier, Janis. 1998. *Policing Women: The Sexual Politics of Law Enforcement and the LAPD*. Philadelphia: Temple University Press.

Appleby, Timothy. 1991a. "Anger Grows Among Police." *Globe and Mail*, May 25: A8.

____. 1991b. "New Role Awaits Police of the Future." *Globe and Mail*, September 20: A7.

____. 1989a. "Minorities Rejected by Police, Hearing Told." *Globe and Mail*, Feb. 4: A6.

____. 1989b. "Police Fear Affirmative Action Could Lower Standards." *Globe and Mail*, February 8: A14.

Atleo, Sawn. 2010. "Oka, 20 Years Later: The Issues Remain." *Globe and Mail*, September 20.

Aubin, Henri. 2010. "Montreal Police Come Up Short in Crime-Busting." *Montreal Gazette*, December 18.

Auger, M.F. 2008. "On the Brink of Civil War: The Canadian Government and the Suppression of the 1918 Quebec Easter Riots." *Canadian Hisorical Review* 89, 4 (December).

Austin, David. 2013. *Fear of a Black Nation: Race, Sex and Security in Sixties Montreal*. Toronto: Between the Lines.

Axelrod, Paul. 1989. "The Student Movement in the 1930s." In Paul Axelrod and John Reid (eds.), *Youth, University and Canadian Society: Essays in Higher Education*. Montreal: McGill-Queen's University Press.

Babcock, Robert. 1982. "The Saint John Street Railwaymen's Strike and Riot, 1914." *Acadiensis* XI (Spring).

Backhouse, Constance. 1985. "Nineteenth-Century Prostitution Laws: Reflections of a Discriminatory Society." *Histoire sociale/Social History* XVIII, 26 (November).

Baker, David. 2006. *Forms of Exclusion: Racism and Community Policing in Canada*. Oshawa: De Sitter.

Baker, J.H. 1977. "Criminal Courts and Procedure at Common Law 1550–1800." In J.S. Cockburn (ed.), *Crime in England, 1500–1800*. Princeton: Princeton University Press.

Baker, Melvin. 1982. "Policing St. John's, 1806–1870." In Melvin Baker, *Aspects of Nineteenth-Century St. John's Municipal History*. St. John's: Harry Cuff Publications.

Baker, William M. 1991. "The Miners and the Mounties: The Royal North West Mounted Police and the 1906 Lethbridge Strike." *Labour/ le Travail* 27 (Spring/Printemps).

Barlow, John Matthew. 1998. "Fear and Loathing in Saint-Sylvestre: The Corrigan Murder Case, 1855–1858." MA thesis, University of British Columbia.

Bayley, David H. 1985. *Patterns of Policing: A Comparative International Analysis*. New Brunswick, NJ: Rutgers University Press.

Beare, Margaret E. 2007. "Steeped in Politics: The Ongoing History of Politics in Policing." In Margaret E. Beare and Tonita Murray (eds.), *Police and Government Relations: Who's Calling the Shots?* Toronto: University of Toronto Press.

Beattie, John. 1995. "English Penal Ideas and the Origins of Imprisonment." In Wendy Barnes (ed.), *Taking Responsibility: Citizenship Involvement in the Criminal Justice System*. Toronto: Centre of Criminology, University of Toronto.

Beeby, Dean. 2000. "RCMP Had Plan to Intern 'Subversives.'" *Globe and Mail*, January 24.

Bercuson, David Jay. 1974. *Confrontation at Winnipeg*. Montreal: McGill-Queen's University Press.

Betke, Carl. 1980. "Pioneers and Police in the Canadian Prairies, 1885–1914." Canadian Historical Association, *Communications historiques/Historical Papers*.

____. 1972. "The Mounted Police and the Doukhobors in Saskatchewan, 1899–1909." *Saskatchewan History* 27, 1.

Bleasdale, Ruth. 1981. "Class Conflict on the Canals of Upper Canada in the 1840s." *Labour/ le Travail* 7 (Spring).

Bliss, Michael. 1991. *Plague: A Story of Smallpox in Montreal*. Toronto: Harper Collins.

Boritch, Helen. 1988. "Conflict, Compromise and Administrative Convenience: The Police Organization in Nineteenth-Century Toronto." *Canadian Journal of Law and Society* 3.

____. 1985. "The Making of Toronto the Good: The Organization of Policing and Production of Arrests, 1859 to 1955." PhD diss., University of Toronto.

Borovoy, Alan. 2007a. "Commentary." In Margaret E. Beare and Tonita Murray (eds.), *Police and Government Relations: Who's Calling the Shots?* Toronto: University of Toronto Press.

____. 2007b. *Categorically Incorrect: Ethical Fallacies in Canada's War on Terror*. Toronto: Dundurn.

Boswell, Randy. 2013. "Public Opinion of RCMP Down 'Significantly' in Past Five Years." *National Post*, January 1.

Boudreau, Michael. 2012a. *City of Order: Crime and Society in Halifax, 1918–35*. Vancouver: UBC Press.

____. 2012b. "'The Struggle for a Different World': The 1971 Gastown Riot in Vancouver." In L. Campbell, D. Clement and G.S. Kealey (eds.), *Debating Dissent: Canada and the Sixties*. Toronto: University of Toronto Press.

Braiden, Chris. 1993. "Community-Based Policing: A Process for Change." In James Chacko and Stephen E. Nancoo (eds.), *Community Policing in Canada*. Toronto: Canadian Scholars Press.

Braidwood, Thomas. 2010. *Why? The Robert Dziekanski Tragedy*. Victoria: The Braidwood Commission.

____. 2009. *Restoring Public Confidence in the Use of Conducted Energy Weapons in British Columbia*. Victoria: The Braidwood Commission.

Brewer, John. 1990. *The Royal Irish Constabulary: An Oral History*. Belfast: The Institute of Irish Studies.

Bridgeman, Ian. 1994. "The Constabulary and the Criminal Justice System in Nineteenth Century Ireland." In *Criminal Justice History* Vol. 15. Westport, CT: Greenwood Press.

British Columbia Civil Liberties Association. 2011. *Small Town Justice: A Report on the RCMP in Northern and Rural British Columbia*. Vancouver.

____ 2005. *National Security: Curbing the Excess to Protect Freedom and Security*. A Brief to the House of Commons Subcommittee on Public Safety and National Security and the Senate Committee on the Anti-Terrorism Act. Vancouver. <bccla.org/wp-content/uploads/2005/10/2005-BCCLA-Policy-National-Security-Curbing-Excess.pdf>.

Brodeur, Jean-Paul. 2010. *The Policing Web*. New York: Oxford University Press.

____. 1983. "High Policing and Low Policing: Remarks about the Policing of Political Activities," *Social Problems* 30, 5.

Brown, Lorne, and Caroline Brown. 1973. *An Unauthorized History of the RCMP*. Toronto: James Lewis and Samuel.

Brown, R. Blake. 2012. *Arming and Disarming: A History of Gun Control in Canada*. Toronto: University of Toronto Press.

Canada. 2010. *Air India Flight 182: A Canadian Tragedy*. Commission of Inquiry. Ottawa: Public Works and Government Services.

____. 2006. *Report of the Events Relating to Maher Arar: Factual Background Volume 1*. Commission of Inquiry. Ottawa: Minister of Public Works and Government Services.

____. 2000. *Annual Report 1999–2000*. Security and Intelligence Review Committee. <sirc-csars.gc.ca/anrran/1999-2000/sc01a-eng.html>.

____. 1990. *Police-Challenge 2000: A Vision of the Future of Policing in Canada*. Discussion Paper. October. Ottawa: Solicitor General Canada.

____. 1981. *Third Report: Certain R.C.M.P. Activities and the Question of Government Knowledge*. Commission of Inquiry. Ottawa: Supply and Services Canada.

____. 1970. *The Uncertain Mirror: Report of the Special Senate Committee on Mass Media*, Vol. 1. Ottawa: Queen's Printer.

____. 1846. "An Act for the Better Preservation of the Peace and the Prevention of Riots and Violent Outrages at and Near Public Works, While in the Progress of Construction." *The Provincial Statutes of Canada*. Montreal: Derbishire and Desbaret.

____. 1845. "An Act to Amend and Consolidate the Provisions of the Ordinance to Incorporate the City and Town of Montreal." *Statutes of Canada*. Montreal: Derbishire and Desbaret.

CAPC (Canadian Association of Chiefs of Police). 2014. *Resolutions Adopted at the 109th Conference, August, Victoria, British Columbia*. Ottawa: Canadian Association of Chiefs of Police.

Carrigan, D. Own. 1998. *Juvenile Delinquency in Canada: A History*. Irwin: Toronto.

Carstairs, Catherine. 2006. *Jailed for Possession: Illegal Drug Use, Regulation, and Power in Canada, 1920–1961*. Toronto: University of Toronto Press.

Cassell, Jay.1987. *The Secret Plague: Venereal Disease in Canada 1838–1939*. Toronto: University of Toronto Press.

CBC (Canadian Broadcasting Corporation). 2015. "Predictive Policing, Alibi Apps and More." *Spark*, June 29.

_____. 2014a. "Alleged CSIS, RCMP Spying on Northern Gateway Pipeline Protestors Prompts Complaints." CBC News British Columbia, February 6.

_____. 2014b. "First Nations Policing Slammed by Auditor General." CBC News, May 8.

_____. 2014c. "City, Police Union Battle Quota System Before Labour Board." CBC News, November 23.

_____. 2014d. "Vancouver Police Shooting Captured on Video by Teen." CBC News British Columbia, November 24.

_____. 2012. "Quebec Students Challenge Bill 78 in Court." CBC News, May 25.

_____. 2011. "You Should Have Stayed Home." *The Fifth Estate*, Febuary 25.

_____. 2007. "Undercover Cops Tried to Incite Violence in Montebello." CBC News, August 23.

_____. 2003. "Arrests in Montreal Anti-WTO Protest." CBC News, July 28.

_____. 2000. "Toronto Police Union Ends 'True Blue' Campaign." CBC News, February 4.

_____. 1988. *The Squamish Five*. Directed by Paul Donovan.

_____. 1969. "Montreal: A Night of Terror." Digital archives.

CBS. 2013. "Counter-Insurgency Cops: Military Tactics Fight Street Crime." *60 Minutes*, May 5.

Cernetig, Miro. 1997. "Judge Tough on Native Protestors." *Globe and Mail*, July 31.

Chacko, James, and Stephen E. Nancoo (eds.). 1993. *Community Policing in Canada*. Toronto: Canadian Scholars Press.

Chan, Janet, with Chris Devery and Sally Doran. 2009. *Fair Cop: Learning the Arts of Policing*. Toronto: University of Toronto Press.

Churchill, Peter. 1970. "91 Arrested at Anti-War Rally." *Globe and Mail*, May 11.

City of Vancouver. 2014. "Four Pillars Drug Strategy." <vancouver.ca/people-programsa/four-pillars-drug-strategy.aspx>.

Clairmont, Don. 2006. "Aboriginal Policing in Canada: An Overview of Developments in First Nations." <attorneygeneral.jus.gov.om.ca/inquiries/ipperwash/policy_part/research/pdf/Clairmont_Aboliginal_Policing.pdf>.

Clément, Dominque. 2008. *Canada's Rights Revolution: Social Movements and Social Change, 1937–82*. Vancouver: University of British Columbia Press.

_____. 2001. "Spies, Lies and a Commission: A Case Study in the Mobilization of the Canadian Civil Liberties Movement." *Left History* 7, 1.

Cleroux, Richard. 1992. "Minutes Link Cabinet, 'Dirty Tricks.'" *Globe and Mail*, May 27.

_____. 1991. *Official Secrets: The Inside Story of the Canadian Security Intelligence Service*. Toronto: McClelland and Stewart.

_____. 1989. "RCMP Security Team May Be Rival of CSIS." *Globe and Mail*, July 4.

_____. 1976. "His Men Broke Terrorist Ring, Olympics Security Chief Says." *Globe and Mail*, August 7.

____. 1975. "Quebec Police Are Taking Over Anti-Drug Work." *Globe and Mail*, April 29.

Cleroux, Richard, and Marina Strauss. 1977. "Quebec Police Say Bugging PQ Offices Resulted in Arrest of 4 Terrorists." *Globe and Mail*, December 2.

Cockburn, Neco. 2008. "How Ottawa Police Officers Use Tasers." *Ottawa Citizen*, July 14.

Comack, Elizabeth. 1990. "Law-and-Order Issues in the Canadian Context: The Case of Capital Punishment." *Social Justice* 17, 1 (Spring).

Conley, Carolyn. 1991. *The Unwritten Law: Criminal Justice in Victorian Kent*. New York: Oxford University Press.

Corporate Research Associates. 2014. "Majority of New Brunswickers Support the RCMP's Response to Rexton Protestors." January 9. <cra.ca/ majority-of-new-brunswickers-support-the-rcmp's-response-to-rexton-protestors>.

Couglan, D.W.F. 1988. "The History and Function of Probation." In R.C. Macleod (ed.), *Lawful Authority: Readings in the History of Criminal Justice in Canada*. Toronto: Copp Clark Pittman.

Cox, Kevin. 1990. "Clash of Innu, Court Halts Trial of Six Over CFB Protest." *Globe and Mail*, February 7.

____. 1983. "80,000 Rally Across Nation Against Cruise." *Globe and Mail*, April 25.

CP (Canadian Press). 2015a. "Moncton Shootings, Key Recommendations for RCMP." *Huffington Post*, January 16.

____. 2015b. "Amend Bill C-51 or Kill It." *National Post*, February 27: A8.

____. 2015c. "RCMP Hit with Labour Code Violations in Wake of Death." *National Post*, May 15.

____. 1994a. "RCMP Apologizes for Racist Comments." *Globe and Mail*, July 21.

____. 1994b. "Mohawks Threaten to Keep Quebec Police Out of Oka." *Globe and Mail*, November 19.

____. 1993. "Montreal Cops Need Riot Gear: Report." *Vancouver Province*, October 13.

____. 1992. "Quebec Police Won't Leave Kanesatake Area, Ryan Says." *Globe and Mail*, November 3.

____. 1991. "New Native Crisis Possible, Police Warn." *Globe and Mail*, May 3.

____. 1990a. "No Misconduct Found in CSIS Probe." *Globe and Mail*, February 6.

____. 1990b. "Army's Brinkmanship Was Effective." *Globe and Mail*, August 30.

____. 1989. "75 Innu Ejected from Base." *Globe and Mail*, April 20.

____. 1985a. "Three Charged After Siege to Enter Pleas of Not Guilty." *Globe and Mail*, March 21.

____. 1985b. "Armenian Threat to Bomb Subway Touches off Massive Police Search." *Globe and Mail*, March 30.

____. 1984. "RCMP Head Critical of Plans by Police for March on Noose." *Globe and Mail*, October 26.

____. 1981a. "Riot Squad Brutal, Report Charges." *Globe and Mail*, July 18.

____. 1981b. "Homosexuals Tracked for 20 Years: Panel." *Globe and Mail*, August 26.

____. 1980a. "Defiance at N.B. Park Simmered for 10 Years." *Globe and Mail*, April 7.

____. 1980b. "RCMP, SAVAK Spied on Iranians in Canada, Magazine Alleges." *Globe and Mail*, February 16.

____. 1979. "Montreal Hiring Policewomen for the First Time in 32 Years." *Globe and Mail*, July 3.

____. 1977. "Won't Be Arm of Government: Quebec Police." *Globe and Mail*, May 12.

____. 1976. "Forces Ready for Biggest Operation since Korea." *Globe and Mail*, February 24.

____. 1974a. "Indians Driven Off in Battle of Parliament Hill." *Globe and Mail*, October 1.

____. 1974b. "Buchanan Attacks Credibility of Indian Demonstration at Ottawa." *Globe and Mail*, October 2.

____. 1974c. "Allmand Snaps 'Horse Manure' to Charge of Police Brutality." *Globe and Mail*, October 3.

____. 1974d. "Indian Group Wants Inquiry into Violence." *Globe and Mail*, October 4.

____. 1971. "Police Issue Threat to Quebec Government." *Globe and Mail*, September 21.

____. 1969. "Campus Disturbances Linked to Agitators from U.S., RCMP Says." *Globe and Mail*, May 7.

____. 1968. "Bourgault Sent to Trial Over Riot." *Globe and Mail*, November 22.

____. 1966. "Investigation Planned after Stones Concert." *Globe and Mail*, July 24.

____. 1948. "Pamphlets, Books Seized in Montreal Raid." *Globe and Mail*, May 29.

____. 1944. "Montreal's Few Convictions Amaze Judge." *Globe and Mail*, July 11.

____. 1933a. "Strikers Passive as Radio Cabinets Leave Stratford." *Toronto Globe*, October 4.

____. 1933b. "Stratford Regains Her Leading Place in Industry Today." *Toronto Globe*, November 6.

____. 1930. "Red Parade Arrested by Hamilton Police." *Toronto Globe*. November 8.

____. 1925. "City of Montreal Profiteers in Vice, is Judge's Findings." *Toronto Globe*. May 14.

____. 1919. "Montreal Police Make Big Raid." *Toronto Globe*, July 2.

____. 1918. "Scathing Report on Montreal Vice." *Toronto Globe*, February 16.

Cross, Michael. 1971. "Stony Monday 1849: The Rebellion Losses Bill in Bytown." *Ontario History* LXIII.

Crouch, Cameron I. 2010. *Managing Terrorism and Insurgency: Regeneration, Recruitment and Attrition*. New York: Routledge.

Culbert, Lori. 2015. "More Police Officers Carry Guns in B.C. than in England and Wales Combined." *Vancouver Sun*, March 29.

Damewood, Andrea. 2013. "ACLU Wary that New Portland Police Tactics Could Increase Racial Profiling." *Williamette Week*, March 22.

Daschuk, James W. 2013. *Clearing the Plains: Disease, the Politics of Starvation and Loss of Aboriginal Life*. Regina: University of Regina Press.

Dauvergne, Mia. 2009. "Trends in Police-Reported Drug Offences in Canada." *Juristat* 29, 2.

Dawson, Michael. 1998. *The Mountie: From Dime Novel to Disney*. Toronto: Between the Lines.

De Lint, William, and Alan Hall. 2009. *Intelligent Control: Developments in Public Order Policing in Canada*. Toronto: University of Toronto Press.

Department of the Army (U.S.). 2006. *Counter-Insurgency*. Washington, DC: Department of the Army.

Doob, Anthony, and Carla Ceasoroni. 2004. *Responding to Youth Crime in Canada*. Toronto: University of Toronto Press.

Downey, Donn. 1988. "Public Held Hostage by Protesting Police, Commission Says." *Globe and Mail*, January 14.

Dowson, Ross. 1980. *Ross Dowson v. the RCMP*, foreword by Clayton Ruby. Toronto: Forward Publications.

Dubro, James, and Robin Rowland. 1992. *Undercover: Cases of the* RCMP's *Most Secret Operative*. Toronto: McClelland and Stewart.

Duchaine, Jean Francois. 1981. *Report on the Events of October, 1970*. Québec: Directeur genérale des publications gouvermentales.

Duchesne, Doreen. 1997. "Street Prostitution in Canada." *Juristat* 17, 2.

Dufresne, Martin. 2000. "La police, le droit pénale et le crime dans la premiere moitée su XIXe siècle. L'exemple de la ville de Québec." *Revue juridique Thémis* 34, 2.

Dunn, Sara. 2010. "Police Officers Murdered in the Line of Duty, 1961 to 2009." *Juristat* 30, 3.

Edmonton Journal. 1992. "Toronto Protest Erupts into a Riot." May 5.

Edwards, Frederick. 1942. "Big Rise in Toronto Juvenile Crime Seen as Result of War Conditions." *Globe and Mail*, October 6.

Edwards, Peter. 2003. *One Dead Indian: The Premier, the Police and the Ipperwash Crisis*. Toronto: McClelland and Stewart.

Egan, Kelly. 2015. "What the Hell Is This? RCMP Musical Ride Stuns with Guns, Military Might." *Ottawa Citizen*, June 30.

Emsley, Clive. 1991. *The English Police: A Political and Social History*. New York: St. Martin's Press.

____. 1987. *Crime and Society in England, 1750–1900*. New York: Longman.

____. 1983. *Policing and its Context 1750–1870*. London: MacMillan.

Eng, Susan. 2011. "A Dangerous Isolation: The Police are Moving Farther Away from the Public They Serve." *Literary Review of Canada*, April. <reviewcanada.ca/magazine/2011/04/>.

Ennett, S.T., C.L. Ringwall and R.L. Flewelling. 1994. "How Effective is Drug Education Resistance Awareness? A Meta-analysis of Project DARE Outcome Evaluations." *American Journal of Public Health* 84 (9) (September).

Ericson, Richard V., and Kevin D. Haggerty. 2008. *The New Politics of Policing*. Toronto: University of Toronto Press.

Expert Panel on the Future of Canadian Policing Models. 2014. *Policing Canada in the 21st Century: New Policing for New Challenges*. Ottawa: Council of Canadian Academies.

Fecteau, Jean-Marie. 1994. "Between the Old Order and Modern Times: Poverty, Criminality, and Power in Quebec, 1791–1840." In Susan Lewthwaite, Tina Loo and J. Phillips (eds.), *Essays in the History of Canadian Law, V: Crime and Criminal Justice*. Toronto: Osgoode Society.

Fine, Sean. 1998. "CSIS Forces Refugees to Inform, Activists Say." *Globe and Mail*, April 15.

Fingard, Judith. 1989. *The Dark Side of Life in Victorian Halifax*. Porter's Lake, NS: Pottersfield Press.

Firth, Edwin G. (ed.). 1966. *The Town of York, 1815–34*. Toronto: Champlian Society.

Flanagan, Tom. 2014. "The Prostitution Bill Is a Bizarre Work of Moral Panic." *Globe and Mail*, June 20.

Flink, James J. 1990. *The Automobile Age*. Cambridge, MA: MIT Press.

Frank, J.A. 1983. "The Ingredients in Violent Labour Conflict: Patterns in Four Case Studies." *Labour/Le Travailleur* 12 (Fall).

Freeze, Colin. 2010. "Mounties to Recruit for Women and Minorities." *Globe and Mail*, September 24.

French, Carey. 1989. "160 Protestors Charged at Arms Trade Show." *Globe and Mail*, May 24.

Friedman, Robert R. 1992. *Community Policing: Comparative Perspectives*. New York: St. Martin's Press.

Furlong, John, and J. Douglas Keefe. 2011. *The Night the City Became a Stadium: Independent Review of the 2011 Stanley Cup Riot*. Vancouver: Government of British Columbia.

Fyson, Donald. 2006. *Magistrates, Police and the People: Everyday Criminal Justice in Quebec and Lower Canada, 1764–1837*. Toronto: The Osgoode Society.

Gallagher, Catherine, et al. 2001. *The Public Image of the Police*. International Association of Chiefs of Police.

Gammage, Jeff. 1993. "Police Identify New Enemies." *Philly.com*. January 24.

Gatrell, V.A.C. 1990. "Crime, Authority and the Policeman-State." In F.M.L. Thompson (ed.), *The Cambridge Social History of Britain 1750–1950*. Cambridge: Cambridge University Press.

Gavigan, Shelley A.M. 2012. *Hunger, Horses and Government Men: Criminal Law on the Aboriginal Plains*. Vancouver: University of British Columbia Press.

Gellner, John. 1968. "The Gentle Art of Riot Control." *Globe and Mail*, May 4.

Giffen, P.J., Shirley Endicott and Sylvia Lambert. 1991. *Panic and Indifference: The Politics of Canada's Drug Laws: A Study in the Sociology of Law*. Ottawa: Canadian Centre on Substance Abuse.

Gilje, Paul A. 1987. *The Road to Mobocracy: Popular Disorder in New York City, 1763–1834*. Chapel Hill: University of North Carolina Press.

Gilkes, Margaret. 1989. *Ladies of the Night: Recollections of a Pioneer Policewoman*. Hanna, AB: Gorman & Gorman.

Gillis, Wendy. 2014. "Toronto Police to Wear Body Cameras in Test Project." *Toronto Star*, September 22.

Glasbeek, Amanda. 2009. *Feminized Justice: The Toronto Women's Court 1913–1934*. Vancouver: University of British Columbia Press.

Glazebrook, G.P De T. 1964. *A History of Transportation in Canada* Vol. I. Toronto: McClelland and Stewart.

Globe and Mail. 1985. "Police Board Reviews Washroom Sex Taping." March 5.

____. 1975. "Police Group Places Ad to Seek Public Support for the Death Penalty." June 5.

____. 1973. "Policemen Enticing Homosexuals, Spokesman Says." March 5.

____. 1970a. "Ban on Use of Mace, Tighter Gun Control for Ontario Police." April 11.

____. 1970b. "Adamson Says Minimum Force Applied." May 15.

____. 1966a. "Police Out in Force as 2,700 Demonstrators March on Hill to Protest War in Vietnam." March 28.

____. 1966b. "Many Who Scream for Civil Rights Irresponsible: Morality Chief." October 6.

____. 1958. "Women on the Police Force." August 15.

____. 1951. "Anti-Red Squad Grabs Pamphlets in North Raid." January 30.

Gordon, Todd. 2006. *Cops, Crime and Capitalism: The Law and Order Agenda in Canada*. Halifax: Fernwood Publishing.

Grace, Robert J. 2003. "Irish Immigration and Settlement in a Catholic City: Quebec, 1842–61." *Canadian Historical Review* 84, 2.

Graham, Jamie. 2008. "Supervised Injection Sites: A View from Law Enforcement." *British Columbia Media Journal* 50, 3 (April).

Grant, Donald. 1976. "Police Warned of Charges for Not Wearing Hats." *Globe and Mail*,

October 23.

Gray, John. 1980. "Trudeau Defends War Measures in Quebec Crisis." *Globe and Mail*, October 11.

Greer, Allan. 1992. "The Birth of the Police." In Allan Greer and Ian W. Radforth (eds.), *Colonial Leviathan: State Formation in Mid-Nineteenth Century Canada*. Toronto: University of Toronto Press.

Groves, Tim, and Zack Dubinsky. 2011. "G20 Case Reveals 'Largest Ever' Police Spy Operation." CBC News. <cbc.ca/news/Canada/g20-case-reveals-largest-ever-police-spy-operation>.

Ha, Tu Thanh. 1994. "CSIS Shorthanded, Ottawa Told." *Globe and Mail*, October 28.

Hagan, John, and Ruth D. Peterson. 1995. *Crime and Inequality*. Stanford: Stanford University Press.

Haggerty, Kevin D. 2001. *Making Crime Count*. Toronto: University of Toronto Press.

Hall, Anthony J. 2000. "Don't Bury the Tragedy at Gustafsen." *Vancouver Sun*, January 21.

Hamilton Spectator. 1849. September 19.

Hannant, Larry. 1995. *The Infernal Machine: Investigating the Loyalties of Canada's Citizens*. Toronto: University of Toronto Press.

Hansen, Ann. 2001. *Direct Action: Memoirs of an Urban Guerilla*. Toronto: Between the Lines.

Harring, Sidney. 1983. *Policing a Class Society: The Experience of American Cities, 1865–1915*. New Brunswick, NJ: Rutgers University Press.

Harvison, C.W. 1967. *The Horsemen*. Toronto: McClelland and Stewart.

Hay, Douglas. 1975. "Property, Authority and Criminal Law." In Douglas Hay et al. (eds.), *Albion's Fatal Tree: Crime and Society in Eighteenth-Century England*. New York: Pantheon.

Hermer, Joe, et al. 2005. "Policing in Canada in the Twenty-First Century: Directions for Law Reform." In Dennis Cooley (ed.), *Re-Imaging Policing in Canada*. Toronto: University of Toronto Press.

Hess, Henry. 1996. "Let Police Review Own Acts, Report Says." *Globe and Mail*, December 3.

Hewitt, Steve. 2010. *Snitch! A History of the Modern Intelligence Informer*. New York: The Continuum Publishing Group Incorporated.

____. 2006. *Riding to the Rescue: The Transformation of the RCMP in Alberta and Saskatchewan, 1914–1930*. Toronto: University of Toronto Press.

____. 2002. *Spying 101: The RCMP's Secret Activities at Canadian Universities, 1917–1997*. Toronto: University of Toronto Press.

____. 1997. "September 1931: A Re-interpretation of the Royal Canadian Mounted Police's Handling of the 1931 Estevan Riot." *Labour/le Travail* 39 (Spring).

Hickey, Harvey. 1959. "Newfoundland Seeks Damages in RCMP Case." *Globe and Mail*, April 12.

Higley, Dahn D. 1984. *OPP: The History of the Ontario Provincial Police Force*. Toronto: The Queen's Printer.

Horrall, S.W. 1998. "The (Royal) North-West Mounted Police and Prostitution on the Canadian Prairies." In William M. Baker (ed.), *The Mounted Police and Prairie Society 1873–1919*. Regina: Canadian Plains Research Centre, University of Regina.

____. 1980. "The Royal North-West Mounted Police and Labour Unrest in Western Canada, 1919." *Canadian Historical Review* LXI.

Horwood, Harold. 1986. *A History of the Newfoundland Ranger Force*. St. John's: Breakwater Books.

Hosmer, Stephen T., and Sybelle O. Crane. 1963. *Counter Insurgency: A Symposium, April 16–20, 1962*. Arlington: RAND Corporation.

Howard, Ross. 1997a. "Natives–Police Battle Extends to Trial." *Globe and Mail*, January 20.

____. 1997b. "Gustafsen Conspiracy Theories on Trial." *Globe and Mail*, May 5.

____. 1994. "Ban Uncurbed Crowds, Vancouver Told: Diversions Should Be Provided, Review of Stanley Cup Riot Says." *Globe and Mail*, November 8.

Howson, Gerald, 1987. *It Takes a Thief: The Life and Times of Jonathan Wild*. London: Cresset Library.

Hubner, Brian. 1995. "Horse Stealing and the Borderline: The NWMP and the Control of Indian Movement, 1874–1900." *Prairie Forum* 20, 2 (Fall).

Huey, Laura, Richard V. Ericson and Kevin Haggerty. 2005. "Policing in Fantasy City." In Dennis Cooley (ed.), *Re-imagining Policing*. Toronto: University of Toronto Press.

Huzel, James P. 1986. "The Incidence of Crime in Vancouver During the Great Depression." *BC Studies* 69–70.

Independent Commission on Policing for Northern Ireland. 1999. *A New Beginning: Policing in Northern Ireland: The Report of the Independent Commission on Policing for Northern Ireland*. Norwich: Copyright Unit.

Inwood, S. 1990. "Policing London's Morals: The Metropolitan Police and Popular Culture, 1829–1855." *London Journal* 15, 2.

Ivison, John. 2014. "Liberals 'Best Case' for OPP." *National Post*, June 5.

Jefferson, James. 1981. "Police Unions Called Too Powerful." *Globe and Mail*, May 29.

Jochelson, Richard, and Kirsten Kramar with Mark Doerksen. 2014. *The Disappearance of Criminal Law: Police Powers and the Supreme Court*. Halifax: Fernwood Publishing.

John Howard Society of Alberta. 1998. "Youth Crime in Canada: Perceptions vs. Statistical Information." <johnhoward.ab.ca/pub/C16.htm>.

Johnson, Marilyn S. 2003. *Street Justice: A History of Police Violence in New York City*. Boston: Beacon Press.

Johnson, William. 1980. "Cops-and-Robbers Antics Seem Senseless." *Globe and Mail*, February 8.

____. 1978. "Limit RCMP's Role Within Province, Quebec Advised." *Globe and Mail*, January 27.

____. 1971. "QPP Victory Humbles Choquette." *Globe and Mail*, October 2.

Jones, Gareth. 2012. "The Ten Top Things Not to Do When Setting Up a Police Oversight Agency." In David MacAlister et al. (eds.), *Police Involved Deaths: The Need for Reform*. Vancouver: BC Civil Liberties Association.

Kaplan, William. 1987. *Everything That Floats: Pat Sullivan, Hal Banks and the Seamen's Union of Canada*. Toronto: University of Toronto Press.

Kashmeri, Zuhair. 2000. "When CSIS Calls: Canadian Arabs, Racism and the Gulf War." In Gary Kinsman, Dieter Buse and Mercedes Steedman (eds.), *Whose National Security? Canadian State Surveillance and the Creation of Enemies*. Toronto: Between the Lines.

____. 1984. "Security Probe: Memos Trace Course of RCMP's Investigation of Career Civil Servant." *Globe and Mail*, August 17.

____. 1982. "'Crime Fighters' as Police Image Called Sales Pitch." *Globe and Mail*, November 5.

Kashmeri, Zuhair, and Brian McAndrew. 2005. *Soft Target: The Real Story Behind the Air*

India Disaster, 2nd ed. Toronto: Lorimer.

Kavanagh, Jack. 1914. *The 1913 Vancouver Island Miners Strike*. Vancouver: B.C. Miners' Liberation League.

Kealey, Gregory. 1992. "State Repression of Labour and the Left in Canada: The Impact of the First World War." *Canadian Historical Review* LXXIII, 3: 2.

_____. 1984. "The Orangemen and the Corporation: The Policing of Class During the Union of the Canadas." In Victor Russell (ed.), *Forging a Consensus: Historical Essays on Toronto*. Toronto: University of Toronto Press.

Kealey, Gregory S., and Reg Whitaker (eds.). 1994. RCMP *Security Bulletins: The Early Years, 1919–21*. Edmonton: Athabasca University Press.

Kelling, George L., and James Q. Wilson. 1982. "The Police and Neighbourhood Safety: Broken Windows." *The Atlantic* 249, 3 (March 1).

Kelly, William, and Nora Kelly. 1976. *Policing in Canada*. Toronto: MacMillan.

Kemp, Vernon. 1958. *Without Fear, Favour or Affection: Thirty-Five Years with the Royal Canadian Mounted Police*. Toronto: Longman's, Green and Company.

Kent, Joan. 1986. *The English Village Constable: A Social and Administrative Study*. Oxford: Oxford University Press.

Kern, Kathleen. 2009. *In Harm's Way: A History of Christian Peacekeeper Teams*. Cambridge, England: Lutterworth Press.

Keshen, Jeff. 2004. *Saints, Sinners and Soldiers: Canada's Second World War*. Vancouver: University of British Columbia Press.

Kinsman, Gary, and Patrizia Gentile. 2010. *The Canadian War on Queers: National Security as Sexual Regulation*. Vancouver: University of British Columbia Press.

Klein, Naomi. 2001. "The Bonding Properties of Tear Gas." *Globe and Mail*, April 25.

Klockars, Carl. 1985. *The Idea of Police*. Thousand Oaks, CA: Sage Publications.

Knafla, Louis A. N.D. "Law and Justice." *The Encyclopedia of Saskatchewan*. <esask.uregina.ca/entry/law_and_justice.html>.

Kozminski, Megan. 2009. "Empty Handed Constables and Notorious Offenders: Policing an Early Prairie City 'According to Order.'" In Esyllt W. Jones and Gerald Friesen (eds.), *Prairie Metropolis: New Essays on Winnipeg Social History*. Winnipeg: University of Manitoba Press.

Lambertson, Ross. 2004. *Repression and Resistance: Canadian Human Rights Activists, 1930–1960*. Toronto: University of Toronto Press.

Landau, Norma. 1984. *The Justices of the Peace, 1679–1760*. Berkeley: University of California Press.

Lavigne, Yves. 1984. "Gunning for Time." *Globe and Mail*, August 2.

Law Union of Ontario. 2014. Submissions to the Toronto Police Services Board. May 25. <lawunion.ca/2014/community-contacts/>.

Leahy, Gerald. 2004. *The Mounties: The First Fifty Years in Newfoundland and Labrador*. St. John's: Creative Publishers.

LeBeuf, Marcel-Eugène. 2012. *The Role of the Royal Canadian Mounted Police During the Indian Residential School System*. Ottawa: RCMP.

LeBeuf, Marcel-Eugène, and Julia McLean (eds.). 1997. *Women in Policing in Canada: The Year 2000 and Beyond — Its Challenges*. Workshop proceedings. Ottawa: Canadian Police College.

Leier, Mark. 1989. *Where the River Fraser Flows: The Industrial Workers of the World in British Columbia*. Vancouver: New Star Books.

LeSage, Patrick. 2005. *Report on the Police Complaints System in Ontario*. Toronto: Ontario Ministry of the Attorney General.

Lin, Zhiqiu. 2007. *Policing the Wild North-West: A Sociological Study of the Provincial Police in Alberta and Saskatchewan, 1905–32*. Calgary: University of Calgary Press.

Linden, Rick. 2005. "Policing First Nations and Métis People: Progress and Prospects. *Saskatchewan Law Review* 68, 2.

List, Wilfrid. 1980. "Anti-Union Police Bias Cited by OFL." *Globe and Mail*, November 28.

____. 1973. "Police vs Pickets in a Bitter Strike." *Globe and Mail*, September 22.

Luciw, Roma, and Colin Freeze. 2000. "Violence Explodes at Legislature Protest." *Globe and Mail*, June 16.

MacAlister, David. 2012. "Policing the Police in Canada: Alternative Approaches to the Investigation of Serious Police Wrongdoing." In David MacAlister et al. (eds.), *Police Involved Deaths: The Need for Reform*. Vancouver: BC Civil Liberties Association.

MacFarlane, Bruce. 2001. "Mounties Tell St. Simon Residents They're Sorry for Actions in Protests." *Saint John Telegraph Journal*, May 24.

Macgillivray, Don. 1974. "Military Aid to the Civil Power: The Cape Breton Experience in the 1920s." *Acadiensis* III, 2 (Spring).

MacIsaac, Ron. 1995. *Clayoquot Mass Trials: Defending the Rainforest*. East York, ON: Hushian House Publishing.

MacKenzie, David. 2001. *Canada's Red Scare, 1945–1957*. Ottawa: Canadian Historical Association.

MacKinnon, Mark, and Barrie MacKenna. 2001. "Use of Lethal Force was an Option." *Globe and Mail*, April 23.

Macleod, Ian. 2015. "Canada's Post 9/11 Anti-Terror Laws." *Ottawa Citizen*, January 16.

Macleod. R.C. 1998. "Crime and Criminals in the North-West Territories, 1873–1905." In William M. Baker (ed.), *The Mounted Police and Prairie Society 1873–1919*. Regina: Canadian Plains Research Centre, University of Regina.

____. 1976. *The North-West Mounted Police and Law Enforcement, 1873–1805*. Toronto: University of Toronto Press.

Macleod, Rod, and Bob Beale. 1984. *Prairie Fire: The 1885 North-West Rebellion*. Edmonton: Hurtig Publishers.

Mahony, Tina Hotton. 2011. *Women and the Criminal Justice System*. Ottawa: Statistics Canada.

Makin, Kirt. 1985. "Mounties' 'Dirty Tricks' Destroyed Trotskyite Organization, Court Told." *Globe and Mail*, October 10.

Mallea, Paula. 2011. *Fear Monger: Stephen Harper's Tough-on-Crime Agenda*. Toronto: James Lorimer.

Malleck. Dan. 2012. *Try to Control Yourself: The Regulation of Public Drinking in Post-Prohibition Ontario, 1927–44*. Vancouver: University of British Columbia Press.

Maloney, Tom, and Emma Poole. 2002. "Police Played Role in Quiet Protest." *Calgary Herald*, June 29.

Manikis, Marie. 2012. "Criminal Justice and the Canadian Charter of Right and Freedoms." In Michelle G. Grossman and Julian Roberts (eds.), *Criminal Justice in Canada: A Reader*.

Toronto: Nelson Education.

Manitoba. 1999. *Report of the Aboriginal Justice Inquiry of Manitoba*, Vol. 1. Winnipeg: Aboriginal Justice Inquiry Commission.

Manley, John. 1992. "Preaching the Red Stuff: J.B. McLachlan, Communism and the Cape Breton Miners, 1922–1935." *Labour/le Travail* 30 (Fall).

Mann, Edward, and John Alan Lee. 1979. RCMP vs. *The People*. Don Mills: General Publishing Co.

Marin, André. 2012. "The Ontario Special Investigations Unit: Seeking Independence and Impartiality." In David MacAlister et al. (eds.), *Police Involved Deaths: The Need for Reform*. Vancouver: BC Civil Liberties Association.

Marquis, Greg. 2012. "'Incriminating Conditions of the Body': The Breathalyzer and the Reframing of Alcohol and Deviance in Late 20th Century Canada." *Social History of Alcohol and Drugs* 26, 1 (Winter).

_____. 2005a. "Policing Two Imperial Frontiers: The Royal Irish Constabulary and the Northwest Mounted Police, 1867–1914." In J. Swainger and L. Knafla (eds.), *Laws and Societies in the Canadian Prairie West, 1670–1940*. Vancouver: University of British Columbia Press.

_____. 2005b. "Regeneration Rejected: Policing Canada's War on Liquor, 1890–1930." In Chris McCormick and Len Green (eds.), *Crime and Deviance in Canadian Historical Perspectives*. Toronto: Canadian Scholars Press.

_____. 2003. "State, Community and Petty Justice in Halifax, Nova Scotia, 1815–67." In Louis Knafla (ed.), *Violent Crime in North America*. Westport: Praeger.

_____. 2000a. "Social Contract/Private Contract: The Evolution of Policing and Private Security." In *Police and Private Security: What the Future Holds*. Ottawa: Police Futures Group Study Series No. 1.

_____. 2000b. "The Evolution of Information Technology in Private Security: Recent History." In M.-E. LeBeuf (ed.), *Conference Proceedings: Police and Information Technology: Understanding, Sharing and Succeeding*. CD-ROM. Ottawa: Canadian Police College.

_____. 1997. "The 'Irish Model' and Nineteenth-Century Canadian Policing." *Journal of Imperial and Commonwealth History* XXV.

_____. 1996. "Policing in Nineteenth-Century Montreal and Quebec City." Unpublished paper.

_____. 1995a. "Towards a Canadian Police Historiography." In L.A. Knafla and Susan Binnie (eds.), *Law, State and Society: Essays in Legal History*. Toronto: Law Society of Upper Canada.

_____. 1995b. "Vancouver Vice: The Police and the Negotiation of Morality, 1904–35." In J. McLaren and H. Foster (eds.), *Essays in the History of Canadian Law v: British Columbia and the Yukon*. Toronto: Osgoode Society.

_____. 1994. "The Technology of Professionalism: The Identification of Criminals in Early Twentieth-Century Canada." *Criminal Justice History* XV.

_____. 1993. *Policing Canada's Century: A History of the Canadian Association of Chiefs of Police*. Toronto: University of Toronto Press.

_____. 1992. "The Police as a Social Service in Early Twentieth-Century Toronto." *Histoire sociale/Social History* XXV.

_____. 1991. "Canadian Police Chiefs and Law Reform: The Historical Perspective." *Canadian*

Journal of Criminology XIV.

____. 1990. "The History of Policing in the Maritime Provinces: Themes and Prospects." *Urban History Review* XIX.

____. 1989. "Police Unionism in Early Twentieth-Century Toronto." *Ontario History* LXXXI, 2.

____. 1988. "Enforcing the Law: The Charlottetown Police Force." In Douglas Baldwin and Thomas Spira (eds.), *Gaslights, Epidemics and Vagabond Cows: Charlottetown in the Victorian Era*. Charlottetown: Ragweed Press.

____. 1986a. "'A Machine of Oppression under the Guise of the Law': The Saint John Police Establishment, 1860–90." *Acadiensis* XVI.

____. 1986b. "The Early Twentieth-Century Toronto Police Institution." PhD diss., Queen's University.

____. 1982. "The Police Force in Saint John, New Brunswick, 1860–90." MA thesis, University of New Brunswick.

____. 1980. "Crime and Law Enforcement in Halifax." Honours thesis, St. Francis Xavier University.

Martel, Marcel. 2014. *Canada the Good: A Short History of Vice Since 1500*. Waterloo, ON: Wilfrid Laurier University Press.

____. 2012. "'Riot' at Sir George Williams: Giving Meaning to Student Dissent." In L. Campbell, D. Clement and G.S. Kealey (eds.), *Debating Dissent: Canada and the Sixties*. Toronto: University of Toronto Press.

____. 2006. *Not This Time: Canadians, Public Policy, and the Marijuana Question, 1961–1975*. Toronto: University of Toronto Press.

Martin, Diane. 2007. "Accountability Mechanisms: Legal Sites of Executive-Police Relations – Core Principles in a Canadian Context." In Margaret E. Beare and Tonita Murray (eds.), *Police and Government Relations: Who's Calling the Shots?* Toronto: University of Toronto Press.

Martin, Lawrence. 1977a. "Gay Group Claims RCMP is Unfair to Homosexuals." *Globe and Mail*, August 23.

____. 1977b. "Party Strategy, Fund Data Unearthed when RCMP probed NDP Members." *Globe and Mail*, November 3.

____. 1977c. "RCMP Distributed Private OHIP Data to Disrupt Extremists." *Globe and Mail*, November 14.

____. 1977d. "Over 60 Groups Communist Controlled in '70s, Secret Files Say." *Globe and Mail*, December 17.

____. 1976. "Potential Terrorists Watched for 3 Years to Safeguard Games." *Globe and Mail*, March 24.

Martin, Robert. 1986. "Maritime Police Back Nova Scotia Stand Against Gays." *Globe and Mail*, July 11.

Mason, Gary. 2008. "Insite Revelations Prove RCMP Need Watching." *Globe and Mail*, October 11.

Matas, Robert. 2010. "The Complicated Legacy of Gustafsen Lake." *Globe and Mail*, September 18.

McAuliffe, Gerald. 1974. "Police Violence? Nine Toronto Cases Say Yes." *Globe and Mail*, October 15.

McCandless, Richard. 1974. "Vancouver's Red Menace of 1935: The Waterfront." *B.C. Studies* 22.

McCarthy, Shawn. 2015. "'Anti-Petroleum' Movement a Threat to Canada, RCMP Says." *Globe and Mail*, February 17.

McCullouch, Michael. 1990. "'Most Assuredly Perpetual Motion': Police and Policing in Quebec City, 1838–58." *Urban History Review* 19, 2.

McDougall, David. 1995. "The Origins and Growth of the Canadian Customs Preventive Service Fleet in the Maritime Provinces and Eastern Quebec, 1872–1932." *The Northern Mariner* V, 4 (October).

McInnis, Peter. 2012. "'Hothead Troubles' Sixties-Era Wildcat Strikes in Canada." In L. Campbell, D. Clement and G.S. Kealey (eds.), *Debating Dissent: Canada and the Sixties*. Toronto: University of Toronto Press.

McKenna, Katherine. 2003. "Lower Class Women's Agency in Upper Canada: The Prescott Board of Police Records, 1834–50." *Histoire sociale/Social History* 36.

McKinley, Jesse. 2003. "Divining the Wellspring of Rage that Incited the Montreal Punk Riot." *New York Times*, October 23.

McLaren, John. 1986. "The Fraser Committee: The Politics and Process of a Special Committee." In J. Lowman et al. (eds.), *Regulating Sex: An Anthology of Commentaries on the Badgley and Fraser Reports*. School of Criminology, Simon Fraser University.

McLaren, John, and John Lowman. 1990. "Enforcing Canada's Prostituton Laws 1892–1920: Rhetoric and Practice." In Martin Friedland (ed.), *Securing Compliance: Seven Case Studies*. Toronto: University of Toronto Press.

McLeod, Ian. 2015. "Liberals Plan Swift Overhaul of Controversial Anti-Terrorism Act, or Bill C-51." *National Post*, October 22.

McLynn, Frank. 1989. *Crime and Punishment in Eighteenth-Century England*. London: Routledge.

McMullan, John L. 1995. "The Political Economy of Thief-Taking." *Crime, Law and Social Change* 23, 2.

_____. 1987. "Crime, Law and Order in Early Modern England." *British Journal of Criminology* 27.

Melançon, Benoît. 2009. *The Rocket: A Cultural History of Maurice Richard*. Vancouver: Greystone Books.

Missing Women Commission of Inquiry. 2012. *Forsaken: The Report of the Missing Women's Commission of Inquiry*, Vol. 1. British Columbia.

Mofina, Rick. 2002a. "'Aggressive Criminals' Behind Recent Shootings, Police Say." *Vancouver Sun*, March 12.

_____. 2002b. "RCMP Kept Secret 'Red Power' File on Dissident Natives." *Vancouver Sun*, March 18.

Monkkonen, Eric. 1981. *Police in Urban America, 1869–1920*. New York: Cambridge University Press.

Montgomery, Charlotte. 1985. "CSIS Knew of Terror Threat, MP Says." *Globe and Mail*, March 19.

Montreal Gazette. 1993. "Excellent Ideas on Police Weapons: MUV Should Stress Non-Lethal Alternatives to Guns." March 9.

Moon. Peter. 1988. "Praxis, Ottawa Make Deal in Suit over Stolen Papers." *Globe and Mail*,

May 4.

____. 1979. "Mounties Used Dirty Tricks Against Indians: Affidavits." *Globe and Mail*, March 7.

Mopas, Michael. 2005. "Policing in Vancouver's Downtown East Side: A Case Study." In Dennis Cooley (ed.), *Re-Imagining Policing in Canada*. Toronto: University of Toronto Press.

Morden, J. 2012. *Independent Civilian Review into Matters Relating to the G20 Summit*. <http://www.tpsb.ca/g20/ICRG20Mordenreport.pdf>.

Morris, Chris. 1997. "Acadians to Keep Their Schools." *Globe and Mail*, July 25.

____. 1987. "Riot Squad Clears Way for Trucks at NB Mill." *Globe and Mail*, June 10.

Morrison, William R. 1985. *Showing the Flag: The Mounted Police and Canadian Sovereignty in the North, 1894–1925*. Vancouver: University of British Columbia Press.

Morton, Desmond. 1974. "Aid to the Civil Power: The Stratford Strike of 1933." In Irving Abella (ed.), *On Strike: Six Key Labour Struggles in Canada, 1919–1949*. Toronto: James Lorimer.

Morton, Suzanne. 2003. *At Odds: Gambling and Canadians 1919–1969*. Toronto: University of Toronto Press.

Mosher, Clayton. 1998. *Discrimination and Denial: Systematic Discrimination in Ontario's Legal and Criminal Justice Systems, 1892–1961*. Toronto: University of Toronto Press.

Moulton, David. 1974. "Ford Windsor 1945." In Irving Abella (ed.), *On Strike: Six Key Labour Struggles in Canada, 1919–1949*. Toronto: James Lorimer.

____. 1996. "Minorities and Misdemeanours: The Treatment of Black Public Order Offenders in Ontario's Criminal Justice System, 1892–1930." *Canadian Journal of Criminology* 33 (October).

Mulgrew, Ian, and Lorne Slotnick. 1983. "Police Plan to Arrest Others Over Litton Bombings." *Globe and Mail*, January 22.

Murphy, Christopher. 2007. "'Securitizing' Canadian Policing: A New Paradigm for the Post 9/11 Security State?" *The Canadian Journal of Sociology* 32, 4 (Fall).

Murphy, Christopher, and Curtis Clarke. 2005. "Policing Communities and Communities of Policing: A Comparative Study of Policing and Security." In Dennis Cooley (ed.), *Re-Imagining Policing in Canada*. Toronto: University of Toronto Press.

Murphy, Chris, and Paul McKenna. 2007. *Rethinking Police Governance, Culture & Management: A Summary Review of the Literature*. Prepared for the Task Force on Governance and Cultural Change in the RCMP. Ottawa: Public Safety Canada.

Murray, John Wilson. 1904. *Memoirs of a Great Detective: Incidents in the Life of John Wilson Murray*. London: William Heineman.

Myers, Tamara. 2006. *Caught: Montreal's Modern Girls and the Law, 1869–1945*. Toronto: University of Toronto Press.

Nadeau-Dubois, Gabriel. 2015. *In Defiance*. Toronto: Between the Lines.

New York Times. 1992. "Riot Erupts at Concert Starring Guns n' Roses." August 11.

Nierobisz, Annette, Mark Searl and Charles Théroux. 2008. *Human Rights Commissions and Public Policy: The Role of the Canadian Human Rights Commission in Advancing Sexual Orientation Equality Rights in Canada*. Ottawa: Canadian Human Rights Commission.

Normandeau, André, and Barry Leighton. 1993. "A Growing Canadian Consensus: Community Policing." In James Chacko and Stephen E. Nancoo (eds.), *Community*

Policing in Canada. Toronto: Canadian Scholars Press.

NWMP (North-West Mounted Police). 1886–87. *Reports of the Commissioner of the North-West Mounted Police.* Ottawa: Maclean, Roger and Company.

O'Leary, Dillon, 1946. "Hamilton Vets Parade with Steel Strikers." *Globe and Mail,* August 29.

O'Neil, Peter. 2012. "Canadians' Faith in Police has Plunged, Poll Finds." Canada.com. <Canada.com/news/Canadians+faith+police+plunged+polls+finds/6518673/story.html>.

O'Reilly, Thomas. 1978. "The Montreal Police Strike of 1969: A Case Study of Group Defiance of the Law." MA thesis, Brunel University.

Obomsawin, Alanis. 2002. *Is the Crown at War with Us?* National Film Board of Canada. Documentary.

Ombudsman Ontario. 2010. *Investigation Into the Ministry of Community Safety and Correctional Services' Conduct in Relation to Ontario Regulation 233/10 Under the Public Works Protection Act: Caught in the Act.* Toronto: Ombudsman Ontario.

Ontario. 1974. *Task Force on Police in Ontario.* Toronto: Ministry of the Solicitor General. Toronto.

Ontario Human Rights Commission. 2003. *Paying the Price: The Human Cost of Racial Profiling Inquiry Report.* Toronto: Ontario Human Rights Commission.

Ottawa Citizen. 2011. "Cities Across Canada Take Action to Move Occupy Protestors: Edmonton Group Latest to Be Told to Go." November 20.

Ottawa Police Service. 2013. *Annual Report.* <ottawapolice.ca/en/annual-report/>.

Pablo, Carlito. 2014. "Canada's New Prostitution Law Won't Change Policing Priorities in Vancouver." *Georgia Strait,* November 26.

Palango, Paul. 2008. *Dispersing the Fog: Inside the Secret World of Ottawa and the RCMP.* Toronto. Key Porter Books.

_____. 1998. *The Last Guardians: The Crisis in the RCMP … and in Canada.* Toronto: McClelland and Stewart.

Palmer, Stanley. 1988. *Police and Protest in England and Ireland, 1780–1850.* New York: Cambridge University Press.

Parnaby, Patrick. 2003. "Disorder Through Dirty Windshields: Law, Order and Squeegee Kids." *Canadian Journal of Society* 28, 2 (Summer).

Pearlston, Karen, 2000. "APEC Days at UBC: Student Protests and National Security in the Era of Trade Liberalization." In Gary Kinsman, Dieter Buse and Mercedes Steedman (eds.), *Whose National Security? Canadian State Surveillance and the Creation of Enemies.* Toronto: Between the Lines.

Phillips, Jim, and Joel Fortune. N.D. "Murray, John Wilson (1840–1906)." *Dictionary of Canadian Biography.*

Picard, André. 1995. "Quebec Faces Mass Police Protest." *Globe and Mail,* August 5.

_____. 1990."Quebec Police Threaten Boycott of St-Jean Bapitste Celebrations." *Globe and Mail,* May 1.

Pieterson, Beth. 2004. *Canada's Drug Strategy: An Update on the Program.* Ottawa: Health Canada.

Pither, Kerry. 2008. *Dark Days: The Story of Four Canadians Tortured in the Name of Fighting Terrorism.* Toronto: Viking Canada.

Plaitel, Rudy. 1984. "Radical Results: Canadian Native Leaders Ponder Outcome of Militancy of 1970s." *Globe and Mail*, October 1.

____. 1974a. "Maoists Were Known and Accepted Part of Indian Caravan, Party Spokesman Says." *Globe and Mail*, October 9.

____. 1974b. "Chiefs Considered Further Militant Action, Frustrated Kenora Indians Tell Buchanan." *Globe and Mail*, November 9.

____. 1968. "Chiefs Oppose Change in Homosexual Law." *Globe and Mail*, September 7.

Platt, Anthony, and Lynn Cooper (eds.). 1974. *Policing in America*. Engelwood Cliffs, NJ: Prentice Hall.

Poirier, Patricia. 1991. "Unhappy Public Put Forces Under Scrutiny." *Globe and Mail*, July 16.

____. 1990. "Quebec to Modify Police Revolvers." *Globe and Mail*, July 6.

Postmedia Network Inc. 2007. "New Details Revealed about Mounties' 'Dirty Tricks.'" Canada.com., December 6.

Potter, Claire Bond. 1998. *War on Crime: Bandits, G-Men and the Politics of Mass Culture*. New Brunswick, NJ: Rutgers University Press.

Price, Janet. 1990. "Raised in Rockhead, Died in the Poorhouse: Female Petty Criminals in Halifax, 1864–1890." In Phillip Girard and Jim Phillips (eds.), *Essays in the History of Canadian Law III: Nova Scotia*. Toronto: Osgoode Society.

Prince, William S. 1868. "Statistics of Crime from 1867." *Toronto Globe*, February 4.

Public Safety Canada. 2013. *Summit of the Economics of Policing: Strengthening Canada's Police Advantage, Summit Report, Ottawa June 16–17, 2013*. Ottawa: Public Safety Canada.

Pue, W. Wesley (ed.). 2000. *Pepper in Our Eyes: The APEC Affair*. Vancouver: University of British Columbia Press.

Pugliese, David, and Jim Bronskill. 2001a. "Keeping the Public in Check: Special Mountie Team, Police Tactics Threaten Right to Free Speech, Critics Say." *Ottawa Citizen*, August 18.

____. 2001b. "Spying on the Protest Movement." *Ottawa Citizen*, August 19.

____. 2001c. "Secret Files Chill Foes of Government: State Dossiers List Peaceful Critics as Security Threats." *Ottawa Citizen*, August 20.

____. 2001d. "How Police Deter Dissent: Government Critics Decry Intimidation." *Ottawa Citizen*, August 21.

____. 2001e. "Mounties in Masks: A Spy Story." *Ottawa Citizen*, August 22.

____. 2001f. "Police Spying Shocks Ex Minister." *Ottawa Citizen*, August 23.

Quebec Chronicle-Telegraph. 1964. "1964 Saw Slight Rise in Crime in the City." December 31.

Rankin, Jim, Jennifer Quinn, Michelle Shephard, Scott Simmie, John Duncanson. 2002. "Singled Out." *Toronto Star*, October 19.

Rankin, Jim, and Pat Winsa. 2014. "Carding Drops but Proportion of Blacks Stopped by Toronto Police Rises." *Toronto Star*, July 26.

____. 2013. "Toronto Police Sued by Black Action Defence Committee for $65M over Racial Profiling." *Toronto Star*, November 17.

____. 2012. "Police Services Board Decision on 'Carding' Stuns Activists." *Toronto Star*, April 14.

RCMP (Royal Canadian Mounted Police). 2014. *Missing and Murdered Aboriginal Women: A National Operational Overview*. Ottawa: Royal Canadian Mounted Police.

____. 2010. *Becoming Canada's Safest Province: Intelligence-Led Policing*. RCMP New Brunswick. <rcmp-grc.gc.ca/nb/publications/annualreport-rapportannuel/2010/safest-sure-eng.

htm>.

Read, Colin. 1982. *The Rising in Western Upper Canada, 1837–38: The Duncombe Revolt and After*. Toronto: University of Toronto Press.

Reaney, James C. (ed.). 2004. *The Donnelly Documents: An Ontario Vendetta*. Toronto: The Champlain Society.

Reilly Schmidt, Bonnie. 2013a. "Contesting a Canadian Icon: Police Bodies and the Challenge to the Masculine Foundations of the Royal Canadian Mounted Police in the 1970s." In Patrizia Gentile and Jane Nicholas (eds.), *Contesting Bodies and Nation in Canadian History*. Toronto: University of Toronto Press.

____. 2013b. "Women in Red Serge: Female Bodies and the Disruption to the Image of the Royal Canadian Mounted Police." PhD diss., Simon Fraser University.

Reiner, Robert. 2012. "Policing and Social Democracy: Resuscitating a Lost Perspective." *Journal of Police Studies* 4, 25.

____. 1998. "Policing, Protest and Disorder in Britain." In Donatella della Porta and Herbert Reiter (eds.), *Policing Protest: The Control of Mass Demonstrations in Western Societies*. Minneapolis: University of Minneapolis Press.

____. 1984. *The Politics of the Police*. Oxford: Oxford University Press.

Repetto, Thomas. 2012. *American Police: A History, 1945–2012: The Blue Parade*, Vol. II. New York: Enigma Books.

Report of the State Trials Before a General Court Martial Held at Montreal in 1838–39, Exhibiting a Complete History of the Late Rebellion. 1839. Montreal: Armour and Ramsay.

Roach, Kent. 2007. "Four Models of Police-Government Relationships." In Margaret Beare and Tonita Murray (eds.), *Police Government Relations: Who's Calling the Shots?* Toronto: University of Toronto Press.

Rogers, Dave. 1990. "Not All Area Police Forces Want Increased Firepower." *Ottawa Citizen*, December 20.

Rogers, Nicholas. 1984. "Serving Toronto the Good: The Development of the City Police Force, 1834–1884." In Victor Russell (ed.), *Forging a Consensus: Historical Essays on Toronto*. Toronto: University of Toronto Press.

Roy, Patricia E. 1989. *A White Man's Province: British Columbia Politicians and Chinese and Japanese Immigrants 1858–1914*. Vancouver: University of British Columbia Press.

Royal Commission on Aboriginal Peoples. 1993. *Aboriginal Peoples and the Justice System: Report of a National Round Table on Aboriginal Justice Issues*. Ottawa: Royal Commission on Aboriginal Issues.

Russwurm, Lani. 2007. "Constituting Authority: Policing Workers and the Consolidation of Police Power in Vancouver, 1918–1939." MA thesis, Simon Fraser University.

Sacco, Vincent. 2005. *When Crime Waves*. Thousand Oaks, CA: Sage.

Sallot, Jeff. 2002. "Chretien's Ignorance of JTF2's Operations Under Fire." *Globe and Mail*, Febuary 20.

____. 1984. "Mounties Filed Phony Tax Returns to Harass 'Subversive.'" *Globe and Mail*, January 31.

Sanders, Trevor. 2000. "Sentencing of Young Offenders in Canada, 1998/99." *Juristat* 20, 7.

Sangster, Joan. 2001. *Regulating Girls and Women: Sexuality, Family and the Law in Ontario, 1920–1960*. Toronto: Oxford University Press.

____. 1999. "Criminalizing the Colonized: Ontario Native Women Confront the Criminal

Justice System, 1920–1960," *Canadian Historical Review* 80 (March).

Sawatsky, John. 1980. *Men in the Shadows: The Shocking Truth About the* RCMP *Security Service.* Toronto: Totem Books.

Scher, Len. 1996. *The Un-Canadians.* Ottawa: National Film Board.

Schneider, John. 1980. *Detroit and the Problem of Order, 1830–1880: A Geography of Crime, Riot, and Policing.* Lincoln: University of Nebraska Press.

See, Scott. 1993. *Riots in New Brunswick: Orange Nativism and Social Violence in the 1840s.* Toronto: University of Toronto Press.

Séguin, Rhéal. 1990. "Cabinet Knew of Risk at Oka." *Globe and Mail*, September 8.

Senior, Elinor Kyte. 1988. "The Influence of the British Garrison on the Development of Montreal Police, 1832 to 1853." In R.C. Macleod (ed.), *Lawful Authority: Readings on the History of Criminal Justice in Canada.* Toronto: Copp, Clark Pittman.

_____. 1981. *British Regulars in Montreal: An Imperial Garrison, 1832–1854.* Montreal: McGill-Queen's University Press.

Sethna, Christabelle. 2000. "High School Confidential: RCMP Surveillance of Secondary School Student Activists." In Gary Kinsman, Dieter Buse, and Mercedes Steedman (eds.), *Whose National Security? Canadian State Surveillance and the Creation of Enemies.* Toronto: Between the Lines.

Sethna, Christabelle, and Steve Hewitt. 2009. "Clandestine Operations: The Vancouver Women's Caucus, the Abortion Caravan and the RCMP." *Canadian Historical Review* 90, 2 (September).

Sewell, John. 2010. *Police in Canada: The Real Story.* Toronto: James Lorimer.

_____. 1985. *Police: Urban Policing in Canada.* Toronto: James Lorimer.

Sharpe, J.A. 1984. *Crime in Early Modern England, 1550–1750.* New York: Longmans.

Sharpe, Robert J. 2011. *The Lazier Murder: Prince Edward County, 1884.* Toronto: Osgoode Society for Legal History.

Sheppard, Robert. 1981. "Police Should Be Charged, Keable Says." *Globe and Mail*, March 7.

_____. 1980. "RCMP Breaks Silence, Admits Employing Hart as Informer on Blacks." *Globe and Mail*, January 18.

Sherman, Lawrence. 2010. "Crime Hot Spots Chat." Evening News, Manchester, UK. <youtube.com/watch?v=6krdMnHnqvo>.

_____. 1998. "Policing for Crime Prevention." In Lawrence W. Sherman, Denise Gottfredson, Doris MacKenzie, John Eck, Peter Reuter, and Shawn Bushway (eds.), *Preventing Crime: What Works, What Doesn't, What's Promising: A Report to the United States Congress Prepared for the National Institute of Justice.* Washington: U.S. Department of Justice.

Simpson, James. 1961. "Mayor Reads Riot Act, 9 SIU Pickets Arrested." *Globe and Mail*, July 15.

Singh, Gurmukh. 2010. "History Maker: Sikh Officer says RCMP Has Made Strides, But Not Enough." *Globe and Mail*, April 17.

Skogan, Wesley G. 1992. *Disorder: Crime and the Spiral of Decay in Urban Neighbourhoods.* Los Angeles: University of California Press.

Skolnick, Jerome. 1999. "On Democratic Policing." Police Foundation, *Ideas in American Policing*, August. <policefoundation.org/sites/g/files/g798246/f/Skolnick%20%281999%29%20-%20On%20Democratic%20Policing.pdf>.

Slotnick, Lorne. 1983. "Cruise Foes Notice of Public Scrutiny by Police." *Globe and Mail*,

April 13.

Smith, Keith D. 2009. *Liberalism, Surveillance and Resistance: Indigenous Communities in Western Canada*. Edmonton: Athabasca University Press.

SPVM (Service de police de la ville de Montréal). 2012. *Protecting the Safety of Montrealers. Annual Review 2012*. Montreal: SPVM.

Starnes, John. 1998. *Closely Guarded: A Life in Canadian Security and Intelligence*. Toronto: University of Toronto Press.

Statistics Canada. 2013. "Police-Reported Crime Statistics 2013." *The Daily*, July 23.

Steedman, Carolyn. 1984. *Policing the Victorian Community: The Formation of English Provincial Police Forces, 1856–1880*. London: Routledge and K. Paul.

Steele, Sir Samuel Bentfield. 1915. *Forty Years in Canada: Reminiscences of the Great North-West with Some Account of His Service in South Africa*. Toronto: McClelland, Goodchild and Stewart.

Stern, Vivien. 2006. *Creating Criminals: Prisons and People in a Market Society*. Halifax: Fernwood Publishing.

Stonier-Newman, Lynn. 1991. *Policing a Pioneer Province: The BC Provincial Police, 1858–1950*. Madeira Park: Harbour Publishing.

Storch, Robert. 1989. "Policing Rural Southern England before the Police: Opinion and Practice, 1830–1856." In D. Hay and F. Snyder (eds.), *Policing and Prosecution in Britain, 1750–1850*. Oxford: Clarendon Press.

____. 1976. "The Policeman as Domestic Missionary: Urban Discipline and Popular Culture in Northern England, 1850–1880." *Journal of Social History* 9, 4.

____. 1975. "The Plague of Blue Locusts: Police Reform and Popular Resistance in Northern England, 1840–1857." *International Journal of Social History* 20, 1 (April).

Strange, Carolyn. 1995. *Toronto's Girl Problem: The Perils and Pleasures of the City, 1880–1930*. Toronto: University of Toronto Press.

Stroud, Carsten. 1984. *The Blue Wall: Street Cops in Canada*. Toronto: McClelland and Stewart.

Sunhara, Ann Gomer. 1981. *The Politics of Racism: The Uprooting of the Japanese Canadians During the Second World War*. Toronto: James Lorimer and Company.

Szeto, Justin K. 2014. "Policing Diversity with Diversity: Exploring Organizational Rhetoric, Myth and Minority Police Officers' Perceptions and Experiences." MA thesis, Simon Fraser University.

Tanovich, David M. 2006. *The Colour of Justice: Policing Race in Canada*. Toronto: Irwin.

Task Force on Race Relations and Policing. 1989. *Report on Race Relations and Policing*. Toronto: Task Force on Race Relations and Policing.

Tator, Carol, and Francis Henry, with Charles Smith and Maureen Brown. 2006. *Racial Profiling in Canada: Challenging the Myth of 'A Few Bad Apples.'* Toronto: University of Toronto Press.

Taylor, Conynghan Crawford. 1892. *Toronto, Called Back From 1892 to 1848*. Toronto: William Brigg Publishers.

Taylor, Ian. 1987. "Theorizing the Crisis in Canada." In R.S. Ratner and John L. McMullan (eds.), *State Control: Criminal Justice Politics in Canada*. Vancouver: University of British Columbia Press.

Taylor-Butts, Andrea. 2004. "Private Security and Public Policing in Canada, 2001." *Juristat*

24, 7.

Tetley, William. 2006. *The October Crisis, 1970: An Insider's View*. Montreal: McGill-Queen's University Press.

Thomas, Don. 1999. "Taser Trial Program has Rights' Group Worried." *Edmonton Journal*, September 17.

Thompson, Scott, and Gary Genosko. 2009. *Punched Drunk: Alcohol, Surveilance and the LCBO 1927–1975*. Halifax: Fernwood Publishing.

Tobias, J.J. 1979. *Crime and Police in England 1700–1900*. Dublin: Gill and MacMillan.

Toronto Globe. 1898. "Toronto's Police Report." February 4.

____. 1887a. "In the Police Cells." August 16.

____. 1887b. "Reform in the Police Cells." August 18.

____. 1887c. "A Week in Gaol." August 30.

____. 1886. "The Police Department." May 18.

____. 1883. "Hamilton Police to Be Furnished with Firearms." December 28.

____. 1881. "Our Police Forces." May 11.

____. 1873. "Crime Statistics of the City of Toronto." February 5.

____. 1855a. "Statistics of Crime in Montreal." February 10.

____. 1855b. "Our Police." December 16.

____. 1844. "Orange Proceedings on the Twelfth July." July 16.

Toronto Police Accountability Coalition. 2015. <tpac.ca/index.cfm>.

Toronto Police Service. 2011. *2011 Statistical Report, Toronto*. Toronto Police Service.

Toronto Star. 2014. "Carding Drops but Proportion of Blacks Stopped by Toronto Police Rises." December 7.

____. 2012. "Hearings Begin into Quebec's 2012 Student Protests." September 23.

Torrance, Judy. 1986. *Public Violence in Canada, 1867–1982*. Montreal: McGill-Queen's University Press.

Tremblay, Sylvan. 1999. "Illicit Drugs and Crime in Canada." *Juristat* 19, 1.

Treverton, Gregory F., Matt Wollman, Elizabeth Wilke and Deborah Lai. 2011. *Moving Towards the Future of Policing*. Santa Monica, CA: Rand Corporation.

Trudeau, Pierre Elliot. 1974. *The Asbestos Strike*, trans. James Boake. Toronto: James Lewis and Samuel.

Tufts, Jennifer. 1999. "Public Attitudes towards the Criminal Justice System." *Juristat* 20, 12.

Vair, George. N.D. "The 1948 Canadian Seamen's Union Strike." <wfhathewaylabourexhibitcentre.ca/labour-history/the-1949-canadian-seamen-s-union-strike/>.

Valiante, Guisepe. 2014. "RCMP Rejects 90% of Formal Complaints." *Toronto Sun*, October 27.

Valpy, Michael. 2002. "RCMP Infiltrated Agency that Spawned Future Political Stars." *Globe and Mail*, March 18.

____. 1990. "Toronto Police Show Outdated Mentality." *Globe and Mail*, December 13.

Vincent, Donovan. 2007. "Eng Furious about Being Spied Upon." *Toronto Star*, May 17.

Vogler, Richard. 1991. *Reading the Riot Act: The Magistracy, the Police and the Army in Civil Disorder*. Baltimore: Open University Press.

Waiser, W.A. 2003. *All Hell Can't Stop Us: The On to Ottawa Trek and Regina Riot*. Calgary: Fifth House.

Waite, P.B. 2012. *In Search of R.B. Bennett*. Montreal: McGill-Queen's University Press.

Walden, Keith. 1982. *Visions of Order: The Canadian Mounties in Symbol and Myth*. Toronto: Butterworth and Company.

Wallace, Gerald F., William Higgins and Peter McGahan. 1994. *The Saint John Police Story. Volume 4. The McLeese Years 1941–1947*. Fredericton: New Ireland Press.

Warson, Albert. 1964. "'Meddling' Police Unions Annoy Convening Chiefs." *Globe and Mail*, September 10.

____. 1963. "Blames Lack of Public Disgust for Growth of Homosexuality." *Globe and Mail*, November 14.

Weaver, John. 1995. *Crimes, Constables and Courts: Order and Transgression in a Canadian City, 1816–1970*. Montreal: McGill-Queen's University Press.

____. 1990. "Social Control, Martial Conformity, and Community Entanglement: The Varied Beat of the Hamilton Police, 1895–1920." *Urban History Review* XIX, 2.

____. 1988. "Crime, Public Order and Repression: The Gore District in Upheaval, 1832–1851." *Ontario History* 78, 3.

Weinberg, Paul. 2015. "The Praxis Affair: There's a Reason We Put Limits on Spying in Canada." Canadian Centre for Policy Alternatives. *Connexions*, March 1. <connexions.org/CxLibrary/CX17294.htm>.

Wente, Margaret. 2003. "Gangs, Guns and Race." *Globe and Mail*, August 12.

Westall, Stanley. 1959. "Metropolitan Toronto: Youth Bureau's Task." *Globe and Mail*, April 13.

Whitaker, Reg. 1993. "Apprehended Insurrection? RCMP Intelligence and the October Crisis." *Queen's Quarterly* 100, 2 (Summer).

Whitaker, Reg, Gregory Kealey and Andrew Parnaby. 2012. *Secret Service*. Toronto: University of Toronto Press.

Williams, David Ricardo. 1998. *Call in Pinkerton's: American Detectives at Work for Canada*. Toronto: Dundurn Press.

Williams, Kristian. 2007. *Our Enemies in Blue: Police and Power in America*. Cambridge: South End Press.

Wilson, James Q. 2011. "Crime and the Great Recession." *City Journal*, March 23. <city-journal.org/2011/21_3_crime-decline.html>.

Winnipeg Police Service. 2014. "History of the Winnipeg Police." <winnipeg.ca/police/History/>.

Winsor, Hugh. 1974. "Officer Says Riot Squad Used After Police Hit by Spikes." *Globe and Mail*, October 2.

Winter, Jesse. 2014. "Police, Sex-Trade Workers Confused." *Winnipeg Free Press*, December 13.

Wolfe, Alan. 1974. "Political Repression and the Liberal Democratic State." In Anthony M. Platt and Lynn Cooper (eds.), *Policing America*. Englewood Cliffs, NJ: Prentice Hall.

Wood, Lesley J. 2014. *Crisis and Control: The Militarization of Political Policing*. Toronto: Between the Lines.

Woodsworth, J.S. 1909. *Strangers within Our Gates or Coming Canadians*. Edited by Marilyn Barber. Toronto: University of Toronto Press, 1972.

Yaffe, Barbara. 1980. "Squatters Pledge to Continue Fight as Tension Mounts at Troubled Park." *Globe and Mail*, April 26.

Zirker, Malvin (ed.). 1988. *An Inquiry into the Causes of the Late Increase in Robbers, and Related Writings* by Henry Fielding. Oxford: Clarendon Press.

INDEX